DOUBLING
WITH DE

Surrey's Twin Triumphs 2000

*With very best wishes
from Trevor Jones*

TREVOR JONES

Foreword by
The Rt Hon John Major, CH MP

Sporting Declarations Books

www.sportingdeclarations.co.uk

First published in 2001 by Sporting Declarations Books

© Trevor Jones 2001

All rights reserved. No part of this publication may be reproduced, stored in a retrieval system, or transmitted, in any form or by any means, electronic, mechanical, photocopying, recording or otherwise, without the prior written permission of the publishers

ISBN 0 9535307 3 6

Cover Photographs

FRONT TOP:
The players celebrate their County Championship triumph on the top balcony of the pavilion at Old Trafford.
Photo by John Dawson - Cricket Images

FRONT BOTTOM:
Celebration time at The Oval after the presentation of the NCL Division Two champions trophy at the end of the match versus Durham.
Photo by Richard Spiller

BACK:
Adam Hollioake cradles the County Championship and NCL Division Two champions trophies.
Photo by Phil Booker

Design by Trevor Jones

Printed and bound in Great Britain by MPG Books, Bodmin, Cornwall
Colour work by APG, Unit 9, Mitcham Industrial Estate, Mitcham, Surrey

Contents

Foreword by The Rt Hon John Major, CH MP 5

Introduction 6

1 **Everyone Starts Equal?** 7

2 **Wet Wet Wet** *11*
County Championship Match One: Somerset at Taunton
National Cricket League Match One: Glamorgan Dragons at Cardiff

3 **A Shock to The System** *24*
County Championship Match Two: Durham at Chester-le-Street
National Cricket League Match Two: Durham Dynamos at Chester-le-Street

4 **Rain, Rain, Go Away** *38*
County Championship Match Three: Kent at The Oval
National Cricket League Match Three: Middlesex Crusaders at The Oval
County Championship Match Four: Kent at Canterbury
National Cricket League Match Four: Essex Eagles at The Oval

5 **Back From The Brink** *58*
National Cricket League Match Five: Hampshire Hawks at The Oval
County Championship Match Five: Hampshire at The Oval

6 **The Darkest Hour** *76*
County Championship Match Six: Derbyshire at Derby
National Cricket League Match Six: Derbyshire Scorpions at Derby

7 **A New Dawn?** *94*
County Championship Match Seven: Somerset at The Oval
National Cricket League Match Seven: Warwickshire Bears at Edgbaston

8 **Onwards And Upwards** *112*
County Championship Match Eight: Hampshire at Southampton
National Cricket League Match Eight: Hampshire Hawks at Southampton

9 **Ali Brown's Glorious Schooldays** *127*
County Championship Match Nine: Leicestershire at Oakham School

10 Tykes Trumped And Dragons Slain *142*
County Championship Match Ten: Yorkshire at The Oval
National Cricket League Match Nine: Glamorgan Dragons at The Oval

11 Bickers' Finest Hours *161*
County Championship Match Eleven: Leicestershire at Guildford
National Cricket League Match Ten: Nottinghamshire Outlaws at Guildford

12 Red Rose Revenge *181*
County Championship Match Twelve: Lancashire at The Oval

13 Homing In On Glory *195*
National Cricket League Match Eleven: Middlesex Crusaders at Lord's
National Cricket League Match Twelve: Warwickshire Bears at Whitgift School
County Championship Match Thirteen: Derbyshire at The Oval
National Cricket League Match Thirteen: Derbyshire Scorpions at The Oval

14 Decisive Days And Dastardly Deeds *217*
National Cricket League Match Fourteen: Essex Eagles at Colchester
County Championship Match Fourteen: Yorkshire at Scarborough
National Cricket League Match Fifteen: Nottinghamshire Outlaws at Trent Bridge

15 So Near Yet So Far *239*
County Championship Match Fifteen: Durham at The Oval
National Cricket League Match Sixteen: Durham Dynamos at The Oval

16 Doubling Up With Delight *257*
County Championship Match Sixteen: Lancashire at Old Trafford

17 Leading Questions, Leading Answers *269*

18 Looking Back, Looking Forward *274*

19 Appendix - Averages And Statistics *278*

Acknowledgements *284*

Foreword

I grew up watching the great Surrey team of the 1950s win seven successive championships. Since then - with the exception of 1971 - it has been a lean period until Adam Hollioake's team became County Champions in 1999. In Millennium year, as Surrey closed in on their second successive Championship, it seemed hardly possible to recall the wet start to the season with the dismal draw at Somerset followed by the shocking defeat by Durham. It seemed to me that the team was too talented to fizzle away from the previous year's champagne performance... but there were doubts. Mine persisted only until early June when an Alex Tudor caught and bowled gave Surrey victory over Hampshire by the slender margin of two runs. A game was won that had very nearly been lost. The Gods were with us - and they needed to be - for if that game had slipped away, the Championship might have gone with it. But winning is a habit and Surrey has acquired it.

In 1999 the team did not lose a Championship match all season. In 2000 they lost twice but were still comfortably the best team in the County Championship. Their strength was in the way they played as a team but the season contained some remarkable individual performances. Martin Bicknell at Guildford proved unplayable on what had seemed like a good wicket; Alistair Brown at Oakham notched one of the highest scores in Surrey's long history; and Gary Butcher took four wickets in four balls to send Derbyshire to defeat. Around the Oval there was an air of anticipation that we would retain the Championship - and we did. But if Surrey's Championship performance repeated the success of the previous year, the team's record in the One Day game was completely transformed. Where they had crumbled in 1999 they triumphed in 2000.

As the season neared its climax, the smiles on the faces of the Surrey faithful grew ever broader. The team looked extremely well balanced with the most formidable bowling attack in the country - an echo of their famous seven-in-a-row predecessors. Once is good, twice is better but a hat-trick is special in cricket and a maturing Surrey now have that ambition in their sights.

'Doubling Up With Delight' records the flavour of cricket in the Millennium and a famous season for Surrey.

John Major
President, Surrey County Cricket Club

March 2001

Introduction

This is becoming something of a habit! After my first book, *'Pursuing The Dream'*, I said that I would only repeat the exercise if Surrey won a trophy, preferably the County Championship, in 1999. They did ... and I did! I was subsequently delighted with the response to *'The Dream Fulfilled'* and quite amazed by the number of people who came up to me at The Oval, and places beyond, to tell me how much they had enjoyed reading it. I should like to record here my grateful thanks to everyone who passed on kind comments to me.

As the 2000 season drew towards a close I was back in a familiar position, with Surrey homing in on a double triumph and people asking me if there would be another book. I had kept very detailed notes about every day's play throughout the season but, since a book about a single county cricket team is never likely to prove financially successful, I had to give the matter serious consideration. It was quite clear to me that I could only go ahead with the project if I could find sponsors to help offset a large part of the production costs of the book. Unfortunately, the sponsors of the two competitions won by Surrey showed no inclination to become involved in terms of either advertising or sponsorship and a few other companies I approached because they had a track record of supporting Surrey cricket were even greater disappointments, failing to acknowledge my letter or return my phone calls. The corporate world had given me no encouragement whatsoever and things were not looking good.

Fortunately, however, I had much greater luck with a Sponsor-Subscriber scheme that targeted mail-order purchasers of my previous books and members of the Supporters' Club. Suddenly, with sponsorship coming in from this scheme and a generous contribution towards my costs being granted to me by Surrey County Cricket Club, I was back on track and increasingly confident of recording the 2000 season for posterity.

I therefore decided to take the plunge, come what may, and began to throw myself into the not inconsiderable task of converting a mountain of notes, press cuttings and photos into *'Doubling Up With Delight'*.

I hope you will find my efforts worthwhile and will enjoy reliving another quite magnificent season for Surrey County Cricket Club. Success in sport is often fleeting, so I am a strong believer in enjoying the good times while you can and also in ensuring that the triumphs are properly documented for future generations of fans. This is what I set out to do with this book and I hope you will feel that I have succeeded.

Trevor Jones

March 2001

1 Everyone Starts Equal?

It's a well-worn cliché in sport that at the start of a new season everyone starts equal. That was hardly the case with the 2000 county cricket season, however, since the County Championship was, for the first time, going to be a two-division affair. Thus, nine counties were considered to be of a higher standing than the other nine before a ball had even been bowled and the probability of winning county cricket's greatest prize had already been slashed from a one-in-eighteen chance to a one-in-nine shot. Additionally, amongst those nine counties in the first division of the new set-up there were clearly a few who would not be serious contenders for the title at the end of the five-month campaign that lay ahead. For example, I doubt that there were many followers of Derbyshire or Durham who expected their team to end the season in possession of the 2000 County Champions pennant. Fans of Somerset, Kent and Hampshire would also have needed to be reasonably optimistic to see glory ahead for their team, although the latter county's hopes would have been boosted by the close season arrival of two match-winning bowlers in the shape of Alan Mullally and Shane Warne. To many eyes it looked as if the principal contenders for the Championship title were going to be the sides who filled the leading four positions in the final 1999 table, namely Surrey, Leicestershire, Lancashire and Yorkshire. In the early days of April, I penned a pre-season preview item for a cricket website on the Internet - this is how I rated the prospects of the nine County Championship Division One teams:-

DERBYSHIRE

At the start of the 1999 season I predicted that Derbyshire would finish bottom of the County Championship. I was proved to be well wide of the mark as Dominic Cork's men made it into Division One by securing ninth place in the table during their final game of the season against Hampshire, amidst claims of collusion and skullduggery. Despite this, I am again, with even greater conviction, expecting to see the county languishing at the foot of the table come the end of the season. After yet another winter of discontent, the squad has lost half-a-dozen decent cricketers and replaced them with a smaller band of players who are, for the most part, past their best or yet to make an impression in the county game. It doesn't augur well for a successful season. Although the county's battery of seamers - Cork, Munton, Aldred, Dean and Smith - looks pretty impressive, their batting resources appear desperately thin and the only spinner with any first-class experience at all would seem to be the 25-year-old off-spinner, Simon Lacey. I don't wish to be unkind but... if Corky can keep this squad in Division One then it will be a miracle and he should be offered the England captaincy forthwith!

DURHAM

There has been very little player movement at the Riverside during the close season and it seems that Durham are continuing to look to young home-grown talent in an effort to improve their fortunes. This is a highly creditable approach which deserves to be rewarded with a measure of success. Given a few more years, their policy may well bring results but, at this moment in time, I can only foresee a difficult season looming ahead of them. I have no doubt that they will miss the leadership of David Boon as well as his presence in the middle-order alongside the also-departed John Morris. The latter was very much a 'mood' player but, at his best, provided some real quality and if I were a Durham member I would be looking at the batting line-up with some trepidation. Although, in Jon Lewis and Michael Gough, they look to have a decent pair of openers, the squad appears to lack quality players to fill positions three to six and a huge amount will rest on the shoulders of the highly-rated young Australian, Simon Katich. That burden may well prove too great for a young man with little experience of English conditions. The spin bowling department is also short of the necessary skill and experience, relying on the former Sussex off-spinner, Nicky Phillips, and the promising young Graeme Bridge. A degree of hope is offered by the pace bowling quintet of Harmison, Brown, Killeen, Betts and Wood - but if Durham are to maintain a place in Division One then these guys will need to stay fit and come up with a very significant haul of wickets.

HAMPSHIRE

The County Championship often throws up a surprise package and this season it could be Hampshire. Although I don't believe they have sufficient overall strength to actually win the title, they could well give some of the bigger counties a run for their money. The county has been boosted by the arrival of Messrs Warne and Mullally, and if these two, plus Alex Morris, can stay fit and available for the whole summer then they should be more than capable of bowling the opposition out. Their occasionally suspect batting made good progress in 1999 and if this upward trend can be maintained by the core batsmen - Laney, Kenway, Smith, Kendall and Aymes - then a top four finish is quite possible. Injuries to any of their key men could quickly put a spanner in the works, however, as the squad could be found wanting in terms of depth.

KENT

The biggest worry for coach John Wright ahead of the season must be how his side is going to pick up the twenty wickets required to win a match on a decent pitch. With Dean Headley contracted to England and only one spinner with any degree of experience in Min Patel, the attack looks bereft of penetration or guile and I can see the season becoming something of a struggle unless Martin McCague and Ben Phillips suddenly hit form again or a young tyro bursts through to make an instant impression. The recruitment of Rahul Dravid and Paul Nixon will undoubtedly add solidity to a previously unstable batting line-up, but it won't be possible to retain a place in Division One place through weight of runs alone. An interesting season lies ahead... but probably at the 'wrong' end of the table.

LANCASHIRE

Had Muttiah Muralitharan been in Lancashire's ranks for the 2000 season then they would have been title contenders. Without him, they look short of the bowling penetration required to win county cricket's major competition. Can one man make such a difference? Of course he can - remember how the red rose county was struggling before the Sri Lankan's arrival last term. The other thing that has damaged Lancashire hopes is the award of central England contracts to three key players - their best opening batsman, their premier all-rounder and their only truly dangerous spin bowler. Saurav Ganguly should prove a fine overseas registration but, in choosing a batsman ahead of a cutting-edge bowler, the powers that be at Old Trafford appear to have signalled once again that success in one-day cricket is more important to them than the capture of a first outright County Championship title since 1934. Even with an experienced new coach at the helm in Bobby Simpson, I think they will struggle to make a major impact on the division.

LEICESTERSHIRE

It has been a busy close season at Grace Road, with plenty of movement in and out of the club. Time alone will tell if this major upheaval/rebuild will affect the Foxes spirit and competitiveness but I would never underestimate a side moulded by the wily Jack Birkenshaw. Some of his new signings, most notably the Indian leg-spinner Anil Kumble, whose arrival will surely create plenty of interest from the local community, could prove to be very shrewd. It remains difficult to predict Leicestershire's fortunes for 2000, though. If the new faces blend well with the established core of Wells, Maddy, Smith, Habib, Lewis and Brimson, and if some of the younger players, such as Jon Dakin and James Ormond, can make progress then I expect Birkenshaw's men to once again be contenders for the title - if, on the other hand, things don't work out so well then the Foxes could find themselves finishing in a comfortable mid-table position.

SOMERSET

The most significant impact of an England contract will probably be felt at Taunton this season. Although the Somerset batting looks strong and has depth I feel that a Caddick-less bowling line-up will almost certainly struggle to dismiss the opposition twice in a match. Because they will prove hard to beat, especially on their own patch at Taunton, I don't see Dermot Reeve's side struggling at the wrong end of the table but it's equally difficult to imagine a very average-looking attack propelling them into the top three. The return to fitness of Graham Rose and Mark Lathwell, who both suffered badly with knee injuries last year, will clearly be a big plus point for the team and the signing of Ian Blackwell will bolster their spin options, but it looks like they could be the draw specialists of the division - too good to lose many games, yet not strong enough in bowling to win a great number either. Mid-table.

SURREY

It hasn't been a bad winter for the reigning County Champions, Surrey, with their chances of retaining their title enhanced by recent events. First, the announcement of central England contracts left the county with just one player, Alec Stewart, tied to England for the season. With other recent England players, Graham Thorpe, Mark Butcher and Alex Tudor, all ignored and probably free to play for Surrey for at least half of the season, if not all of it, the champions will be a very tough side to beat. Further good news for the men from The Oval came when the Pakistan Cricket Board decided to release the brilliant Saqlain Mushtaq from his country's mid-summer tour of Sri Lanka. 'Saqi' will therefore be available for as many as twelve of the county's sixteen Championship matches, having captured an incredible 58 wickets in just seven matches last term. There have been few changes to the playing staff during the close season, with only Darren Bicknell's departure to Nottinghamshire of any real concern. Even this loss should, however, be more than covered by the increased availability of Thorpe and Butcher plus the return to fitness of Nadeem Shahid, who missed almost all of the 1999 campaign with a broken arm which then became infected. Certain to challenge strongly for the title again.

YORKSHIRE

The pace bowling looks awesome and the middle-order batting appears to be up there with the best in county cricket. The opening batting positions, on the other hand, seem to be a real problem area. In 1999 the opening berths were usually filled by various combinations of Michael Vaughan, Greg Blewett and Matthew Wood, with only very limited success. With Blewett now replaced by Darren Lehmann, the jewel in the middle-order, Michael Vaughan quite possibly required by England throughout the summer and Wood having looked uncomfortable in the role and unable to reproduce the form of his excellent first season, who will fill the void in 2000? Anthony McGrath could move up from the middle-order, but his career seems to have been disrupted by constant changes of batting position and he looked to have found his niche last year at number five in any case. It looks to be a real problem for David Byas - but it still fades into insignificance, however, when set alongside the dearth of quality spin bowling in the squad. I foresee very little joy for the white rose county if they have to play any matches on turning wickets, which must be a strong possibility in a division which will boast a good number of top-quality slow bowlers. With major difficulties in these two areas, it is hard to see Yorkshire being able to make a realistic challenge for the title, especially if the balance of their side is then further disrupted by international calls for the surprisingly England-contracted Craig White. Their wealth of resources in the fast bowling department suggests that Darren Gough won't be too badly missed and that they will not be in danger of relegation come September but the long wait for a first Championship triumph since 1968 looks set to be extended by yet another year.

SUMMARY

It is notoriously difficult to predict the outcome of the County Championship, owing to the ever-present possibility of injuries and Test calls to leading players. In recent times, 'rogue' pitches have made life even more difficult for anyone trying to gaze into their crystal ball at the start of a new season, but, with pitches now under greater scrutiny, this may be less of a problem in 2000. If we do, indeed, see an improvement in pitches - and I fully expect to see decent surfaces at Leicester, Taunton, Southampton, The Oval, Canterbury and Derby at least - then the teams which possess a quality bowling attack should rightly be to the fore by the end of the season. That said, there appears to be little to choose between many of the counties this term, with some looking strong in pace but weak in spin and others blessed with better spin than seam. Since Surrey's attack is the best-balanced of all and is backed up by a strong hand of batting talent I feel that they have an outstanding chance of retaining their title - I wouldn't be at all surprised, in fact, if the battle at the bottom of the table turns out to be more exciting than the fight for the title in the closing weeks of the campaign. I know it's a risky and foolish thing to attempt but I'll stick my neck out and predict this final order of teams for Division One - with the rider that I expect very few points to separate the teams finishing between third and seventh place.

1st SURREY; *2nd* LEICESTERSHIRE; *3rd* HAMPSHIRE; *4th* SOMERSET; *5th* YORKSHIRE; *6th* LANCASHIRE; *7th* KENT; *8th* DURHAM; *9th* DERBYSHIRE

I had most definitely put my belief in my county on the line! But, encouragingly enough, I wasn't alone. Whereas in the run-up to the 1999 season the vast majority of my Surrey friends were not expecting Championship glory for the team, this term it was different, with most people believing that Surrey would start the new century in the same way they had ended the last - as County Champions.

What we thought counted for little, however - it was down to the players and how they performed out on the field. Would they be complacent after 1999's triumph? Would the weight of expectation prove to be a problem? Would the pressure of *defending* as opposed to winning a title prove too much? We were about to find out.

2 Wet Wet Wet

The opening weeks of the season were little short of a disaster as far as the weather was concerned. Although the north of England appeared to be relatively unaffected, the rest of the nation suffered from constant rain and, as a result, saw very little cricket. Surrey's week of pre-season friendlies against Glamorgan and Kent was a complete wash-out and then the qualifying phase of the reinstated Benson And Hedges Cup competition was reduced to a farce as games in both the South and the Midlands/West/Wales groups were abandoned one after another. Surrey's first two matches, against Essex at Chelmsford on 15th April and versus Kent at The Oval the following day, were both casualties of the vast amount of rain that had fallen, the latter frustratingly so, since the day of the match itself was bright and sunny. The enduring image of these first few days of the season was that of Adam Hollioake walking from the pitch upon the abandonment of the Kent game frustratedly kicking a spray of surface water into the air as he went. It was that wet.

Two days later the team was scheduled to play at Hove and I made the trip down to the south coast with major doubts as to whether I would see my first cricket of the season. Amazingly enough I did and, even more surprisingly, we got off to a prompt start too! Put into bat by Adam Hollioake, a Sussex line-up lacking Michael Bevan - who had only just arrived in England from a one-day tournament in South Africa - was completely outclassed by Surrey's seam and swing attack of Bicknell (2-15), Tudor (2-28), Bishop (2-22) and Ratcliffe (3-15). From a promising start of 30-0 the home side crumbled to 72-9 before a last wicket stand of 25 almost succeeded in pushing the total up to three figures.

Although drizzle was a feature of the later stages of Sussex's innings and conditions worsened during Surrey's reply the umpires sensibly allowed play to continue and, once ten overs of the second innings had been completed, victory was assured for the visitors, despite the loss of Ali Brown with the score on 28. Persistently heavy rain finally forced the players off for the day with the score at 61-1 after 20 overs and Surrey ran out comfortable 35-run victors under the Duckworth-Lewis system, thanks to steadfast efforts from both Mark Butcher (23 not out) and Alec Stewart. This efficient and thoroughly professional performance had made for an encouraging first outing of the season.

SCOREBOARD - BENSON AND HEDGES CUP (SOUTH GROUP)

Sussex 97 from 44 overs   (J.D. Ratcliffe 3-15)
Surrey 61-1 from 20 overs
Surrey won by 35 runs (Duckworth-Lewis method)

Umpires: D.J. Constant and J.H. Harris

Gold Award Winner - I.E. Bishop (Surrey)

The late Easter weekend staged the two rounds of matches which would decide the fate of the teams in the South group. Our next opponents, Middlesex, had not managed to get on to the field of play as yet and were therefore boasting an unbeaten record of played three, abandoned three! The match between the London-based rivals was due to take place on Good Friday at Lord's but such was the state of the outfield at the home of cricket that the match was hurriedly switched to Southgate at less than 24 hours notice. The change of ground was so poorly publicised, however, that Middlesex apparently employed staff to stand outside the ground at Lord's handing out maps and details of how to get to the new venue! It turned out to be a futile exercise, however, since the Walker ground was almost as sodden as cricket's headquarters and play was called off after a noon inspection. Communication between Middlesex C.C.C. and Ceefax seemed a little suspect during this whole affair - at the same instant as I was hearing from a Middlesex official at Southgate that the game had just been abandoned, the caption on Ceefax was changing to tell me that there was another inspection at 1pm!

Having secured that early victory over Sussex, and generated a very impressive Net Run Rate in the process, we were sitting pretty at the top of the group. Things were, however, very tight after all the abandoned matches and everyone was aware that defeat in the final game versus Hampshire, coupled with other results going against us elsewhere, could yet see us being dumped out of the competition.

The all-important match was at The Oval on Easter Monday and, with the weather set fair for a change, spectators turning up at the ground expected a prompt start. We were in for a shock. A heavy and prolonged thunderstorm had hit south-east London at around 5.30pm on the previous afternoon and, consequently, the outfield had been thoroughly soaked once again. Several inspections followed with Hampshire much the keener to play for the simple reason that an abandonment put them out of the competition, while a single point from the no result would see Surrey safely into the quarter-finals. Finally, at around 5pm, the umpires decided that there could be some action, with the contest reduced to 10-overs-per-side, and Hampshire, put in by Adam Hollioake, recovered well from a poor start of 14-3 through a fifty-run stand in four overs by Kenway and Laney. Kenway was hugely impressive in scoring 47 from 29 balls, taking heavy toll of three truly dreadful overs from Ian Bishop and the Surrey skipper. The other four bowlers all emerged with great credit though as the visitors totalled 87-7.

With the Surrey line-up containing eight front-line batsmen, plus exceptional lower-order men in Bicknell and Tudor, they still looked favourites to take the spoils and, at 60-3 after just six overs, few doubted the probability of a home victory. Two magical overs from Shane Warne changed the picture, however. As well as picking up the wickets of Graham Thorpe and Adam Hollioake, both for sixteen, and having Mark Butcher dropped behind the wicket, he conceded just six runs from his allotted two overs to leave ten runs required from the final over. It was now even-stevens, but Alan Mullally, having bowled a very poor first over at the start of the innings, came back to bowl a magnificent final six balls to take his side through to the quarter-finals with a two-run victory. But what did this result mean for Surrey? With Sussex having beaten Essex at Chelmsford the picture was looking bleak since we were now sure to finish third in the group - though there was still hope that we might qualify as one of the two best third-placed counties. This was a job for teletext! Downstairs in the Sandham Room supporters checked the results from the other groups and feared the worst. We had fewer points than the third team in the North group and, with Warwickshire having only just edged out Worcestershire in another ten-overs-a-side match, it appeared that the men from New Road would retain their third position in the Midlands/West/Wales group and pip us on net run rate. This was a huge disappointment - it looked like we had already missed out on one of the season's four possible trophies before even reaching the end of April.

Fortunately, however, there was one aspect of the competition rules that we had all been unaware of and didn't discover until a couple of hours later. When teams were tied on points in the group table, positions were not calculated solely by net run rate as we had assumed - instead they were decided, initially, by the results of the matches between the tying teams. In this case, where three teams were level on five points, Warwickshire had enjoyed the best of the results (most of which were, admittedly, abandonments!) in the series of games with Worcestershire and Northamptonshire and were therefore adjudged to have finished third. Since Surrey had the same number of points as Warwickshire, but a vastly superior net run rate, +1.10 as opposed to -1.79, it was they who progressed into the quarter-finals. That was the very good news. The slightly disappointing news was that we had been drawn away to Yorkshire, probably the toughest of the available tasks in the last eight. But at least we were still in with a chance of four trophies!

SCOREBOARD - BENSON AND HEDGES CUP (SOUTH GROUP)

Hampshire 87-7 from 10 overs (D.A. Kenway 47, J.D. Ratcliffe 2-5, A.J. Tudor 2-12)
Surrey 85-5 from 10 overs (S.K. Warne 2-6, P.J. Hartley 2-22)
Hampshire won by 2 runs

Umpires: R.A. White and A.G.T. Whitehead

Gold Award Winner - S.K. Warne (Hampshire)

FINAL BENSON AND HEDGES CUP QUALIFYING GROUP TABLES

SOUTH GROUP	P	Pts	W	L	T	N/R	Net Run Rate
Sussex	5	6	2	1	0	2	0.28
Hampshire	5	6	2	1	0	2	0.06
SURREY	5	5	2	1	0	2	1.10
Kent	5	5	1	1	0	3	0.84
Essex	5	4	1	2	0	2	-0.52
Middlesex	5	4	0	1	0	4	-1.54

NORTH GROUP	P	Pts	W	L	T	N/R	Net Run Rate
Yorkshire	5	7	3	1	0	1	0.31
Lancashire	5	6	3	2	0	0	0.06
Durham	5	6	3	2	0	0	0.64
Derbyshire	5	6	2	1	0	2	0.11
Leicestershire	5	4	1	2	0	2	-0.04
Nottinghamshire	5	1	0	4	0	1	-1.47

MIDS/WEST/WALES GRP	P	Pts	W	L	T	N/R	Net Run Rate
Glamorgan	5	6	2	1	0	2	-1.43
Gloucestershire	5	6	2	1	0	2	1.03
Warwickshire	5	5	1	1	0	3	-1.79
Northamptonshire	5	5	1	1	0	3	0.35
Worcestershire	5	5	1	1	0	3	2.04
Somerset	5	3	0	2	0	3	-0.23

THE CHAMPIONS' CAMPAIGN HITS THE ROAD

Thanks to the ECB's fixture list, Surrey's defence of their County Championship title had been given the toughest possible start in terms of travelling. Four days in Taunton were to be followed by five days at Chester-le-Street, with one of the two days in between the two Championship matches being spent in Cardiff fulfilling the season's opening National Cricket League fixture. The team therefore faced ten days of cricket in eleven days with the maximum possible south-west to north-east travel involved. It was enough to give me the impression that someone at the ECB didn't like Surrey!

To be honest, I wasn't too upset that we were playing at Taunton in late April since the ground had not been a lucky one for us in recent times and I figured that if any game was to be disrupted by April showers then it might as well be this one. As things turned out, I ended up with more rain than I had bargained for!

COUNTY CHAMPIONSHIP - MATCH ONE

SOMERSET versus SURREY
at The County Ground, Taunton

First Day - Wednesday 26th April

No play - rain

A saturated county ground, drenched by pre-match rain, never offers any hope of play on a day of further showers, some of which are quite heavy. To nobody's surprise, play is abandoned for the day after a post-lunch inspection at 1.55pm.

No cricket proves possible in any of the other five County Championship games which were due to start today at Derby, Nottingham, Bristol, Canterbury and Worcester, making this the first opening day washout of an entire Championship programme since 1966. This was not a very auspicious start to the season!

VIEW FROM THE DRESSING ROOM - ADAM HOLLIOAKE

Did the players find any new ways to keep themselves amused at a very wet Taunton?
AH - We had already had more than enough indoor nets, so we didn't tend to hang around at the ground. Instead, we spent almost every day of this match at the local gym, doing a lot of work on our fitness, which was a sign to me of the guys maturing. In the old days we would probably have sat around playing cards so it was encouraging to see everyone now taking advantage of the time to work on their fitness. I think it was a good omen for the season ahead.

Second Day - Thursday 27th April

Surrey 185; Somerset 4-0

After a reasonably dry night, followed by a bright morning, the umpires inspect the ground at noon and then again at 2pm before the announcement comes over the public address system that the captains want to play and that the umpires have agreed to a 3pm start, with a minimum of 51 overs to be bowled. From the information given it appears that the umpires aren't as keen as the two skippers to get the Championship season underway.

The Teams And The Toss - *Apart from Saqlain Mushtaq, absent with Pakistan until the end of May, Surrey are able to select, arguably, their strongest side. Somerset, likewise, appear to have what they would consider to be their best possible eleven available. In seemingly good bowling conditions, Surrey are invited to bat when Adam Hollioake calls incorrectly at the toss.*

The Surrey skipper is soon ruing his erroneous call of the coin as his side is quickly reduced to a rather perilous 11 for 3 by the dangerous new-ball pairing of Andy Caddick and Matt Bulbeck. Ian Ward goes first, taken bat-pad at short leg off Caddick in the third over, Graham Thorpe edges a good delivery and is well caught by Rob Turner low to his left in the England bowler's next over and then Mark Butcher pads up to a lifting Bulbeck delivery and is adjudged lbw. With the ball moving about quite dramatically at times and often beating the bat, the Surrey fourth-wicket pairing of Stewart and Brown is grateful to receive the occasional loose delivery from the young left-arm swing bowler as they attempt to get the innings back on a sound footing. The recovery partnership is building nicely until, with the score advanced to 38, Bulbeck gains a measure of revenge by winning a second leg-before decision, this time against Stewart. Despite this shaky start to the new campaign, Ali Brown, having earlier driven his first ball of the season through wide mid-on for four, looks in good touch and, courtesy of a pull, a steer, a drive and a push, picks up eleven runs from Caddick's last over of the match's first session.

Tea:- Surrey 61-4 (Brown 31*, A. J. Hollioake 7*) from 19 overs

Surrey's momentum continues to build after tea with Adam Hollioake taking nineteen runs, including four boundaries, from Caddick's first two overs of the session. With both batsmen looking in good form, the fifty partnership comes up at a run a minute and the England opening bowler is replaced at the old pavilion end of the ground by Steffan Jones. The Somerset paceman's first over is not one he will wish to remember, however, as Hollioake, driving with power and authority, crashes two further boundaries and a three in an over which costs twelve runs. This over sees Surrey passing the hundred mark and, with fifty runs having rattled up inside ten overs since tea, the match situation appears to be levelling up. Disaster strikes for Ali Brown with the last ball of Jones's second over, however, when an edged drive finds the safe hands of Marcus Trescothick at second slip to terminate Brown's fine knock three runs short of a half-century. Fortunately for Surrey, Adam Hollioake, now joined at the wicket by brother Ben, appears unpertubed by the loss of his partner and in the very next over reaches a 73-minute fifty when he crashes Graham Rose to the extra cover boundary. At the other end, the strapping Jones, now into his rhythm and generating a good head of steam, is beginning to cause the batsmen an increasing number of problems and, having beaten Ben several times outside the off stump in his third over, he strikes a huge blow for the home side in his fourth when he gets a delivery to lift and jag back more than Adam expects. Hollioake senior tries desperately to raise his bat out of the way but to no avail as the ball brushes a glove on the way through to Rob Turner. As the Surrey captain departs for a very well played 59 his team is back in trouble at 129-6.

Despite the skipper's demise the pace of the innings doesn't slacken, with the returning Bulbeck again proving a little expensive. Jones is still quite a handful, though, and he picks up his third wicket of the innings when Martin Bicknell, having just taken the total past 150 with a square driven boundary, plays a lifting ball down onto his leg stump and goes for 18.

After a quiet start, Ben Hollioake now moves up a gear, clipping Bulbeck to the midwicket fence for four and then cutting Jones to the square cover boundary in successive overs. Having conceded nineteen runs in three unimpressive overs, Bulbeck is predictably replaced by Caddick at the river end and this change brings the desired result for the Somerset skipper, Jamie Cox. One has to wonder whether it is over-confidence which gets the better of Hollioake as a glorious drive to the extra cover boundary is followed by a hook stroke which, though middled, flies straight to that man Jones at long leg - 167-8.

There is still hope in the Surrey camp that Ian Salisbury and Alex Tudor might at least conjure up a batting point but Jones is quickly in the action again, removing the Surrey leg-spinner with a fine outswinger which takes the edge and is well caught again by Turner. With Championship-best bowling figures already guaranteed, the former Bristol rugby union player is now on an unstoppable roll and, despite a late flurry of strokes from Tudor, he completes a five-wicket haul and ends the Surrey innings when he beats last man Ian Bishop for pace with a quick, straight delivery.

A total of 185 represents a disappointing start to the campaign by the defending champions, even allowing for the fact that the conditions have favoured the bowlers, and as Jones leads the Somerset team from the field with a return of 5-41 to celebrate it's clear that Surrey will have to bowl well to get back into the match.

With four overs left for play, the visitors harbour hopes of snatching an early wicket but apart from one anxious moment, when Cox edges Bicknell just short of Brown at third slip, the Somerset openers survive comfortably.

Close:- Somerset 4-0 (Cox 2*, Trescothick 0*) from 4 overs

VIEW FROM THE DRESSING ROOM - ADAM HOLLIOAKE

You looked to be in great form in your first innings of the season - had you been working on any specific aspects of your game during the winter in Australia?
AH - I worked on my whole game, especially on hitting the ball straighter, and throughout the 2000 season I think I got back to playing a little more like the way I used to play. Having been somewhat out in the wilderness for a couple of years, you almost forget how to bat for a long period of time and that's something that I still have to work harder on. But, overall, I was really happy with my technique, the way I was hitting the ball and the way I was lining up to hit it - and that's something that I couldn't have said about the way I played in the previous couple of seasons.

We appeared to bat with a lot of freedom. Were we trying to make up for the time that had been lost to rain?
AH - Not really. When the ball swings around as it did here the fast bowlers tend to pitch the ball up a lot more in order to get wickets. We hit a lot of boundaries but they were really just a by-product of the full length they bowled. This was like net practice for us as I think the guys were not in the best of form until about June. We really had to work hard to rein ourselves in as the year progressed because we were batting too positively in the early weeks of the season.

Third Day - Friday 28th April

Surrey 185; Somerset 15-2

Play starts on time in reasonably bright conditions and with the second ball of the morning Martin Bicknell strikes an early blow for Surrey by trapping Jamie Cox lbw on the front foot. The visitors are clearly jubilant at the dismissal of the potentially dangerous Tasmanian and they are further boosted just four balls later when the left-handed Piran Holloway flicks at a legside delivery and is well picked up by Alec Stewart diving to his right behind the stumps. One over completed and it's a double-wicket maiden! Sadly, however, only four further overs are completed by Bicknell and Tudor before increasingly heavy drizzle drives the umpires and players from the field. Worse still, it continues to fall, albeit quite lightly, for the next three hours, giving little hope of any possible resumption. Finally, at 3.30pm there comes a more serious downpour which results in play being abandoned for the day at 4.15pm.

Thus far, this game has closely followed the pattern of Surrey's 1999 match at Worcester and it now looks certain that the final day tomorrow will become nothing more than a battle for bonus points.

Close:- Somerset 15-2 (Trescothick 0*, Bowler 6*) from 9 overs

Fourth Day - Saturday 29th April

Surrey 185; Somerset 302-8dec

Match Drawn - Somerset 10pts, Surrey 6

Although the weather has taken a turn for the better, with bright sunshine the order of the day, the start of play is delayed until 11.30am as the ground is still wet following overnight rain. A potentially interesting contest has been reduced to a day of bonus point-collecting, which is pretty disappointing - but then who knows how valuable any points gained today could turn out to be at the end of the season?

Opening the day's proceedings from the old pavilion end of the ground, Alex Tudor starts poorly, conceding boundaries to Peter Bowler from his first two deliveries and generally straying to leg too often in a spell which also sees him overstepping the crease on several occasions. He also allows Marcus Trescothick to get his innings under way after fifty minutes - spread over three periods of play - stuck on nought. Rather surprisingly, Martin Bicknell is also a little inconsistent from the river end and the overnight pairing experiences only occasional difficulties as they push the score past fifty.

With his opening bowlers making little impression, Adam Hollioake eventually turns to brother Ben, who gets off to a mixed start in his first over - having conceded a no-ball and a legside three to Bowler, he produces a much better delivery which finds Trescothick's edge and speeds away to the third man boundary. Ian Bishop meanwhile takes over from Bicknell and in the third over of an accurate first spell he provides his team with the much sought-after breakthrough which brings their first County Championship point of the season. Although Bowler had looked the more secure of the Somerset duo, it is he who departs, beaten on the front foot and trapped lbw for 37 just five minutes before lunch.

Lunch:- Somerset 96-3 (Trescothick 34*, Burns 0*) from 30 overs

Hollioake and Bishop continue their spells after the restart, but with contrasting results. The former, looking rather ragged and rusty, yields four boundaries in his first four overs while the latter looks the pick of the bowlers used to date and has the misfortune to see Burns, on nine, missed by Graham Thorpe at first slip. Meanwhile, Trescothick, with his trademark drives now to the fore, is beginning to look more commanding and he brings up his personal half-century (176 minutes) and the fifty partnership for the fourth wicket by punching a rare Bishop half-volley to the mid-off boundary.

With clear skies overhead, the ball seems to be doing very little for the bowlers although a new spell from Bicknell, taking over from Hollioake at the old pavilion end, does at least seem to unsettle Burns, who looks a little ill-at-ease in trying to pull and hook a few shorter deliveries. He also appears less comfortable when confronted for the first time in the innings by spin. Ian Salisbury's entrance after forty-eight overs looks to have been delayed rather too long, however, as the Somerset pair now look pretty well established. The partnership in fact reaches three figures when Trescothick drives the returning Tudor to the cover fence and Burns then completes a 112-minute fifty by slog-sweeping Salisbury to the deep midwicket boundary. Although Trescothick has a lucky escape shortly afterwards when he edges the leg-spinner just past his leg stump, this is a rare moment of anxiety for the batsmen on what appears to be a typically good Taunton pitch. The hosts pass 200 just before the arrival of the tea interval and Surrey draw their first blank of the season by failing to take a single wicket in the session.

Tea:- Somerset 208-3 (Trescothick 84*, Burns 56*) from 60 overs

Having failed to gain a batting bonus point, Surrey are looking at a meagre return of just one bowling point as the final session of the match begins. With three more wickets required to notch a second point, it surely has to be all-out attack for Surrey and, consequently, Adam Hollioake puts his trust in pace and leg-spin by pairing Tudor and Salisbury.

It appears that Alec Stewart must be either ill or injured, since he is nowhere to be seen and Mark Butcher is keeping wicket. This seems a strange choice since Ali Brown, the stand-in hero of last season's Glamorgan match, is on the field and Butcher is, by all accounts, being prevented from bowling because of a knee problem. Surely, in that case, the last thing you would want to do is crouch down and keep wicket for a couple of hours?!

The wisdom of this decision is further called into question when Burns immediately edges Tudor just short of Thorpe at first slip. The end result is four runs but there is a definite feeling that a more skilled 'keeper would have dived in front of Thorpe to complete a catch.

Surrey do finally strike a blow in the next over from Salisbury, though, when Trescothick miscues a drive straight to Ali Brown at wide mid-on and departs for a well-constructed 85. There is an element of irony in this dismissal for the Surrey leg-spinner - having failed to claim a single Championship wicket through an 'outfield' catch in the whole of the summer of 1999, his first victim of 2000 has been picked up in exactly that manner!

Salisbury's second wicket of the campaign comes in similar fashion, too, when the new batsman, Rob Turner, quickly falls to a breathtaking catch at short fine leg. The Somerset keeper's top-edged sweep initially looks to be sailing over Alex Tudor's head but the big fast bowler leaps, stretches and clings on to an amazing left-handed catch as he falls backwards and crashes to the ground. Turner makes his way disconsolately back to the pavilion with a duck to his name as Tudor's team-mates rush over to congratulate him on a stunning effort.

Surrey's second bowling point is now just one wicket away and it arrives just five overs later when Tudor gets due reward for both that magnificent catch and also his best spell of bowling in the match as Ian Blackwell edges a fine lifting delivery to Thorpe at first slip. Somerset's previously strong position has rather crumbled with 218-3 having become 225-6 and their chances of picking up more than another two batting points have all but evaporated. They move closer to their second point with a mixture of edges and genuine strokes before Butcher has another bad moment behind the stumps, missing a fairly routine chance offered by Burns off Salisbury. Fortunately, however, the stand-in keeper's blushes are spared when the leg-spinner traps the same batsman lbw on the back foot with just one run added to his personal score and two to the total.

Surrey have fought well in pegging their hosts back to 249-7 but from here on in it's nearly all Somerset as Graham Rose and Andy Caddick defy Salisbury and the returning Ben Hollioake during a stubborn partnership for the eighth wicket.

Salisbury has had a very good day on a wicket not best suited to leg-spin bowling, yet he attracts some criticism from one rather ignorant Somerset fan when he produces a couple of rare loose deliveries. Provoked by the injustice of his comments, the travelling Surrey supporters, as one, tell him that they wouldn't swap Salisbury for any other England-qualified spin bowler. Predictably enough, he promptly scoffs at this view so, unable to let the matter rest there, I ask him which English spinner he would rather have in his team. He thinks for a few seconds and then offers "Richard Illingworth". The man's credibility is instantly destroyed and the Surrey faithful break into fits of involuntary laughter. This magical moment has suddenly become the highlight of the day for all of us!

A final bowling point would now put the icing on the cake but it doesn't materialise. Although Adam Hollioake takes the ball and eventually parts the eighth-wicket pair by slipping a ball through Caddick's defences with the total at 294, Somerset declare upon securing their third batting point at 300 in order to deny us the chance of completing our full hand for bowling.

While the draw has been on the cards since day three, a return of just six points represents a disappointing start to the campaign for the defending champions.

Surrey 185; Somerset 302-8dec
Match Drawn. Somerset 10pts, Surrey 6

SOMERSET v SURREY at TAUNTON. Played from 26th - 29th April

Somerset won the toss
Umpires:- J.W. Lloyds & A.G.T. Whitehead

SURREY - First Innings   **SOMERSET bowling**

Fall of wkt	Batsman		How Out	Score	Balls	4s	6s		O	M	R	W
3- 11	M.A. Butcher		lbw b Bulbeck	4	18	1	0	Caddick	16	2	71	3
1- 3	I.J. Ward	c Burns	b Caddick	1	8	0	0	Bulbeck	12	3	44	2
2- 3	G.P. Thorpe	c Turner	b Caddick	0	5	0	0	Rose	7	1	29	0
4- 38	A.J. Stewart +		lbw b Bulbeck	16	22	2	0	Jones	10	2	41	5
5- 112	A.D. Brown	c Trescothick	b Jones	47	61	4	0					
6- 129	A.J. Hollioake *	c Turner	b Jones	59	76	9	0					
8- 167	B.C. Hollioake	c Jones	b Caddick	20	28	3	0					
7- 151	M.P. Bicknell		b Jones	18	17	1	0					
9- 173	I.D.K. Salisbury	c Turner	b Jones	2	15	0	0					
	A.J. Tudor		Not Out	16	13	3	0					
10- 185	I.E. Bishop		b Jones	0	7	0	0					
	Extras (2w)			2								
	TOTAL		(45 overs)	185								

SOMERSET - First Innings   **SURREY bowling**

Fall of wkt	Batsman		How Out	Score	Balls	4s	6s		O	M	R	W
1- 4	J. Cox *		lbw b Bicknell	2	14	0	0	Bicknell	19	5	48	2
4- 218	M.E. Trescothick	c Brown	b Salisbury	85	191	14	0	Tudor	21	5	81	1
2- 4	P.C.L. Holloway	c Stewart	b Bicknell	0	4	0	0	B.C. Hollioake	15	3	66	0
3- 90	P.D. Bowler		lbw b Bishop	37	75	5	0	Bishop	12	5	24	1
7- 249	M. Burns		lbw b Salisbury	81	151	9	0	Salisbury	24	6	56	3
5- 222	R.J. Turner +	c Tudor	b Salisbury	0	9	0	0	A.J. Hollioake	4.2	1	23	1
6- 225	I.D. Blackwell	c Thorpe	b Tudor	2	16	0	0					
	G.D. Rose		Not Out	37	76	5	0					
8- 294	A.R. Caddick		b A.J. Hollioake	19	40	3	0					
	M.P.L. Bulbeck		Not Out	3	7	0	0					
	P.S. Jones	did not bat										
	Extras (1b, 3lb, 10w, 22nb)			36								
	TOTAL		(95.2 overs)	302 - 8 dec								

VIEW FROM THE DRESSING ROOM - IAN SALISBURY

It was a very frustrating four days with bucketloads of rain - how did the guys pass the time?
IS - I think we were fairly stir crazy by this stage! What with all the build-up, the expectations and being defending champions we were desperate to get started, but we were being thwarted by the weather all the time, which was very frustrating. Quite a few of us went to the gym and we worked on one or two things in the nets, though there's only so much you can do in there. We also talked a lot about our one-day cricket - how we were going to bowl, how the lower-order was going to bat and so on. So we used our time quite constructively.

You got off to a great start with a very impressive spell of bowling - does wintering in Australia help you to get out of the blocks quickly in April?
IS - Conditions are obviously very different over here so you have to adjust in that respect, but it does help with regard to the actual 'mechanics' of my bowling - having been bowling for the previous few months it's much easier to get back into the groove, as it were.

During the Australian summer you had won the O'Reilly medal for your performances in Grade cricket. Can you tell me a bit more about the award and how you won it?
IS - It's awarded to the person who accumulates the most points over the course of the season. The points are awarded by the umpires at the end of each match, with the best player on each side being given three points, the second best player getting two and the third best player receiving one. For each game there's always a report in which the umpires have to give the reasons for their choices. They also publish a table of the leading players so you can see how well you are doing as the season progresses. I missed a few games at the start, then had a good run of points before missing another three games as a result of picking up a couple of injuries. I thought that would put me out of the running for the award so I didn't look at the points table again until the last few games. To my surprise I was still up there and I then got enough points in the last two games to win the medal. I was delighted to come out on top as very few English players have ever won the award - so far as I know, only Geoff Boycott, Tony Greig and Mike Gatting had won the medal before me.

While you were in Australia did you work on any particular aspects of your game?
IS - There was nothing specific, I'm just always trying to improve in every way - batting, bowling and fielding. I even managed to improve my back - which had been giving me some problems and hindering my mobility for a couple of years - by seeing a specialist out there! Sorting that out has been a great help to me.

I read somewhere that you could have been selected to play as an overseas registration for New South Wales had Stuart MacGill not been available. Is there any truth in that?
IS - Yes, that's true. They are allowed to have an overseas player, but they don't encourage it. New South Wales were in a bad way, so if they hadn't had MacGill available then I think they would probably have asked me to play.

VIEW FROM THE DRESSING ROOM - ADAM HOLLIOAKE

What is it about Surrey and Taunton? We seem to have struggled there in recent times.
AH - It's hard to say. I hadn't actually noticed it until a few of the guys pointed it out when we left there after this match. Everything points to the fact that we should do well there because they have a very good wicket, so I think it might just be the opposition that we struggle with rather than the ground - I'm not sure why it should be but Somerset have been difficult opponents for us throughout my career at least.

KEITH MEDLYCOTT'S ASSESSMENT

It was disappointing to lose the toss and get put in when the wicket was giving assistance to the seam bowlers after a couple of days under the covers. I think if we had batted second, when the wicket was just a little bit easier, then we might have had a better couple of days' cricket at Taunton.

Other Division One Matches

26-28 April
Canterbury:- **Lancashire drew with Kent.** Lancashire 186 (Flintoff 77); Kent 29-1. **Kent 7pts, Lancashire 4**

Derby:- **Derbyshire drew with Leicestershire.** Derbyshire 359 (Bailey 118, Di Venuto 70) and 2-0dec; Leicestershire 309 (DeFreitas 79, Stevens 78). **Derbyshire 10pts, Leicestershire 9**

NATIONAL CRICKET LEAGUE CAMPAIGN OFF TO A GOOD START

The National Cricket League Division Two season started with a trip to Cardiff for a potentially awkward opener against Glamorgan, one of the more fancied teams in the league. After two years of hugely disappointing underachievement in the short-course limited-overs competition, the general feeling was that a run of early victories was important if the possibility of a repeat performance was to be avoided. History shows that if you lose your first few games in this competition then you can be left struggling to make up the ground on the early leaders. And so to Cardiff...

NCL DIVISION TWO - MATCH ONE

GLAMORGAN DRAGONS versus SURREY LIONS
at Sophia Gardens, Cardiff on Sunday 30th April

Surrey Lions (185-9) beat Glamorgan Dragons (175) by 10 runs

On a difficult Sophia Gardens pitch, a stand of 91 in 23 overs by Mark Butcher and Graham Thorpe for the second wicket laid the foundations for a decent Surrey total after Adam Hollioake had won the toss and decided to bat. Shrugging aside the loss of Ali Brown for a quick-fire sixteen in the sixth over, the two England left-handers picked up runs quite comfortably, with a series of elegant off-side boundaries studding the first fifteen overs when the fielding restrictions were in force.

Having reached 70-1 at this point, a large total looked possible but tight spells in the middle third of the innings by Croft and Wharf dragged the run rate down and eventually earned the wicket of a frustrated-looking Butcher, who perished when swinging across the line of a straight ball from the Glamorgan seamer. Although good running between the wickets and sensible accumulation of runs had given the visitors a fine platform from which to press onwards, the desired acceleration failed to materialise. Thwarted by the regular loss of wickets, brought about by disciplined bowling and a slow pitch on which the ball often seemed to stop or pop, the Lions managed only seven boundaries in their entire innings and, almost unbelievably, none at all after a Thorpe on-drive off Thomas in the eighteenth over. The Surrey left-hander's 61 was a classy effort which showed the value of expert placement and aggressive running when confronted by accurate bowling, notably from Croft, and keen fielding. A final total of 185-9 certainly looked competitive in the conditions, especially since the home side had been dealt a blow before the start of play when their Australian Test star, Matt Elliott, was forced to pull out after his son was involved in what turned out to be, thankfully, a minor accident.

The left-handed opener's withdrawal turned out to be a crucial factor in the match since the Dragons, despite having Steve James in their line-up, surprisingly chose to open with two pinch hitters in Croft and Wharf. In the prevailing conditions this looked to be a bad move and so it proved as both were outwitted by the wily Bicknell - Wharf deceived by a slower, full-length delivery and Croft popping up a simple catch to a deep-set mid-off - inside the first five overs.

The initial bursts from the Lions' opening bowlers left Glamorgan struggling at 31-2 after eleven overs, but a wayward spell by the inexperienced Bishop, who followed Tudor into the attack at the Cathedral Road end, suddenly changed the face of the game. With the third-wicket pair of Maynard and Powell both scoring heavily on the legside and bringing up a fifty partnership in eleven overs, Surrey's total began to look rather vulnerable until Adam Hollioake replaced Bishop and almost immediately induced a mistimed stroke from Powell to deep midwicket where Butcher picked up a good low catch.

Although this breakthrough was crucial, it was obvious that the Lions still needed to pick up regular wickets if they were to win the match, with the free-flowing Maynard's scalp the major prize. After a good opening effort by Ben Hollioake the most vital period of the match seemed to have arrived with the introduction of Ian Salisbury at the river end and there was immediate evidence of significant turn for the leg-spinner.

Fortunately for Surrey, the key duel of the innings was won by Salisbury who, having been cut square for four from the previous ball, had Maynard caught by Jon Batty when attempting to repeat the stroke to the next delivery. This left Glamorgan on 106-4 in the 25th over and facing a target of eighty runs from twenty overs - a fairly straightforward target in good batting conditions, but not here.

A tense period of play followed as the experienced Dale and James attempted to wrest control from Salisbury and the Hollioake brothers, but with little success. Ben Hollioake, in a particularly impressive second spell of 5-0-7-0, simply strangled the scoring rate while Salisbury attacked and eventually snared Dale, who edged a drive to slip with 56 required from ten overs.

The life was simply being squeezed out of the Dragons as the required run rate began to climb rapidly towards seven, and then eight, runs per over. Eventually, with 42 needed from thirty-one balls, the game took a decisive shift towards Surrey when Newell and James departed in the space of five balls to Bicknell and Adam Hollioake respectively.

Although Darren Thomas bravely attempted to resurrect his team's hopes with three late boundaries, the Lions were not going to be denied now and when Tudor defeated the Glamorgan left-hander's attempted steer to third man the last-wicket pair of Watkin and Parkin were left with a target of eleven runs from Adam Hollioake's final over. The partisan home crowd still harboured hopes of a Welsh win but the Surrey skipper needed just one ball to decide the match in the visitors' favour, bowling Parkin behind his legs as the batsman shuffled across his stumps. A close and exciting curtain-raiser for the National League season had resulted in a winning start for the Lions.

Surrey Lions (185-9) beat Glamorgan Dragons (175) by 10 runs

Surrey Lions 4pts

GLAMORGAN DRAGONS v SURREY LIONS at CARDIFF. Played on 30th April

Surrey Lions won the toss Umpires:- A.A. Jones & R. Julian

SURREY LIONS

Fall of wkt	Batsman	How Out	Score	Balls	4s	6s
2- 116	M.A. Butcher	b Wharf	47	91	3	0
1- 25	A.D. Brown	c & b Parkin	16	12	1	0
4- 144	G.P. Thorpe	b Parkin	61	87	3	0
3- 135	J.N. Batty + c Powell	b Croft	8	13	0	0
6- 167	A.J. Hollioake *	c & b Watkin	16	22	0	0
5- 147	B.C. Hollioake	b Croft	1	5	0	0
7- 177	I.J. Ward c Maynard	b Parkin	10	21	0	0
9- 185	M.P. Bicknell	run out	12	14	0	0
8- 185	I.D.K. Salisbury	b Thomas	2	4	0	0
	A.J. Tudor	Not out	0	1	0	0
	I.E. Bishop	did not bat				
	Extras (1b, 5lb, 6w)		12			
	TOTAL	(45 overs)	185-9			

GLAMORGAN bowling

	O	M	R	W
Watkin	9	0	38	1
Parkin	9	0	39	3
Thomas	9	0	38	1
Wharf	9	0	36	1
Croft	9	0	28	2

GLAMORGAN DRAGONS

Fall of wkt	Batsman	How Out	Score	Balls	4s	6s
2- 13	R.D.B. Croft c Salisbury	b Bicknell	3	13	0	0
1- 8	A.G. Wharf	b Bicknell	4	7	1	0
3- 72	M.J. Powell c Butcher	b A.J. Hollioake	30	50	5	0
4- 103	M.P. Maynard * c Batty	b Salisbury	46	56	4	0
5- 130	A. Dale c A.J. Hollioake	b Salisbury	19	49	1	0
7- 149	S.P. James	b A.J. Hollioake	22	55	1	0
6- 145	K. Newell c Thorpe	b Bicknell	6	15	0	0
9- 175	S.D. Thomas	b Tudor	20	12	3	0
8- 167	A.D. Shaw +	lbw b A.J. Hollioake	3	5	0	0
10- 175	O.T. Parkin	b A.J. Hollioake	1	3	0	0
	S.L. Watkin	Not Out	0	1	0	0
	Extras (1b, 5lb, 12w, 3nb)		21			
	TOTAL	(44.1 overs)	175			

SURREY LIONS bowling

	O	M	R	W
Bicknell	9	2	28	3
Tudor	6	0	25	1
Bishop	3	0	26	0
B.C. Hollioake	9	0	19	0
A.J. Hollioake	8.1	0	39	4
Salisbury	9	0	32	2

Other NCL Division Two Matches

April 30
Chelmsford:- **Essex Eagles beat Middlesex Crusaders by 60 runs.** Essex 143 in 22.4 overs (Hussain 60); Middlesex 83-9 in 23 overs (Irani 3-10). **Essex Eagles 4pts**

Trent Bridge:- **Nottinghamshire Outlaws beat Durham Dynamos by four wickets.** Durham 208-6 (Daley 53); Nottinghamshire 209-6 in 44.5 overs (Gallian 74, Morris 50). **Nottinghamshire Outlaws 4pts**

May 1
Derby:- **Middlesex Crusaders beat Derbyshire Scorpions by 71 runs.** Middlesex 185-6; Derbyshire 114 in 36.5 overs (Weekes 4-26). **Middlesex Crusaders 4pts**

Southampton:- **Warwickshire Bears beat Hampshire Hawks by 97 runs.** Warwickshire 215-8 (Penney 51); Hampshire 118 in 35.5 overs. **Warwickshire Bears 4pts**

3 A Shock To The System

On paper, two things looked racing certainties as Surrey's team and supporters headed north to Chester-le-Street. Firstly, a visit to the Riverside in early May didn't promise too much in terms of an improvement in the weather conditions experienced to date and, second, a win for the visitors looked equally predictable since Durham had lost every match of every type against Surrey since their elevation to the first-class ranks in 1992. The scheduling of this fixture so early in the campaign was, therefore, a disappointment as there seemed to be a good chance that the inclement north-eastern weather could deprive us of an expected victory. Both sport and the weather are, however, famed for being unpredictable... with good reason.

COUNTY CHAMPIONSHIP - MATCH TWO

DURHAM versus SURREY
at The Riverside, Chester-le-Street

First Day - Tuesday 2nd May

Durham 234; Surrey 47-2

The Teams And The Toss - *The Surrey team sheet shows just one change from the opening Championship match at Taunton, with the injured Alec Stewart being replaced by Jon Batty. Opener Michael Gough (back problem) misses out for Durham as does John Wood (side strain), although it's questionable whether the latter would have made it into a starting eleven which contains no specialist spinner but a strong hand of seam bowlers in Brown, Harmison, Betts and Killeen. Seventeen-year-old batsman Nicky Peng profits from Gough's injury, making his County Championship debut. On a fine, sunny and surprisingly warm morning, Adam Hollioake wins the toss and asks Durham to bat.*

Surrey, opening with the expected combination of Bicknell (Finchale end) and Tudor (Lumley end), make an early breakthrough in the fifth over of the morning when Jimmy Daley is defeated and bowled through an airy drive at Bicknell with the score on five. With both bowlers quickly into their stride and offering up very few loose deliveries, Jon Lewis and the Australian, Simon Katich, struggle to make any impression and runs prove very hard to come by. Eventually, in Tudor's sixth over, Lewis appears to lose patience, dragging an intended off-drive into his stumps, and Durham's position then declines further when Katich also falls on the drive, edging Bicknell to Thorpe at first slip just three overs later. The home side is now struggling at 25-3 and Surrey are clearly on top, but Paul Collingwood launches something of a counter-attack, pulling Tudor to the midwicket fence and then greeting Ben Hollioake's entrance into the attack with a repeat performance. The Surrey all-rounder hits back in his second over, however, picking up his first wicket of the season, courtesy of Nick Speak's edged drive to Jon Batty.

The Durham skipper's departure for three brings the young debutant, Nicky Peng, to the crease and, with just the unpredictable Martin Speight and a rather fragile-looking tail to come, Surrey are already hoping to move in for the kill. Given the match situation, the Durham teenager looks to be easy prey but he shows great composure, opening his account with a sweetly timed square-driven boundary after fifteen scoreless deliveries and appearing more secure than Collingwood who edges Ian Bishop through gaps in the slip cordon on no fewer than four occasions in the run-up to lunch.

Lunch:- Durham 72-4 (Collingwood 41*, Peng 5*) from 33 overs

After a few good opening overs from Bicknell and Tudor, Peng shows early glimpses of quality with glanced and driven boundaries before Collingwood reaches an 87-ball half-century with a straight drive for four off Bicknell. Although both batsmen enjoy a few moments of good fortune, the Durham debutant continues to look very correct and impressive while his partner finds the boundary three times in Ian Salisbury's second over, the leg-spinner having taken over from Bicknell at the Finchale end. At this point the fifth-wicket partnership has produced a very valuable 71 runs, but it goes no further as Tudor makes the breakthrough for Surrey with the first ball of his next over, having Collingwood taken by Batty down the legside from a short delivery which appears to flick the glove. Durham are 119-5 and the visitors look to have the edge again.

Recovering quickly from Collingwood's early assault on him, Salisbury is soon on the mark, beating the outside edge regularly and causing both Peng and the newly-arrived Speight plenty of problems. Runs prove pretty hard to come by during this period and, with Bicknell back into the attack at the Lumley end, the young debutant begins to look really vulnerable for the first time. He manages to outlast his more experienced colleague, however, as Speight departs for nine, trapped lbw on the back foot by the deserving Bicknell with the score advanced to 143. The Surrey swing bowler really appears to have the measure of Peng at this stage but fortune isn't smiling on him as successive edged boundaries to third man see the 17-year-old to an otherwise very impressive fifty after 104 balls and 141 minutes at the crease. Having come through testing spells by the visitors' two senior bowlers, he then takes an instant liking to the bowling of the recalled Bishop, forcing him through extra cover and driving him wide of mid-on for two classy fours in his first over. His partner, Neil Killeen, never looks comfortable, however, and another bowling change, Ben Hollioake for Bicknell, brings about the burly seamer's downfall as Ali Brown dives to his right at third slip and clings on to a brilliant one-handed catch. With Killeen gone for seven, Durham are now 175-7 and that soon becomes 176-8 when Melvyn Betts goes for a duck in the very next over, clean bowled by Bishop as he drives at an outswinger.

This double strike appears to have a very positive effect on Peng as, with very little batting support left, the pressure is off him and he is now free to really open out. His initial efforts to cut loose result in a difficult catching chance to Salisbury at mid-off from the bowling of Bishop but he survives and promptly cuts the disappointed bowler to the point boundary. Meanwhile, at the other end, Harmison gets away with a nick to Brown at third slip off Hollioake and then emulates his partner by crashing the next ball to the fence. Luckily for Surrey, the lanky Durham quickie doesn't profit hugely from his escape, falling leg-before to the same bowler as he hits across the line, but by this stage Peng has advanced to 89 with two further boundaries taken from the inconsistent Bishop.

There's real tension in the air as the last man, Simon Brown, comes to the wicket. Can the young Durham Academy player register a century on debut? Confronted again by the shrewdly-recalled Salisbury, he sweeps his way into the nineties and, with the level of excitement growing, straight drives Hollioake to the boundary to move within two runs of the cherished landmark. Nerves become evident when he then inside edges a ball onto his pad and the ball trickles past his leg stump but the debutant is unable to capitalise on this moment of good fortune as he slashes rather recklessly at the next delivery, a short ball wide of the off stump, and presents Jon Batty with a straightforward catch.

Although he has fallen short of his century, the young lad's marvellously mature innings of 98, including seventeen boundaries, has been largely responsible for pushing Durham's total up to 234 and he leaves the field to a fine ovation as the new holder of the record for the highest score by a Durham player on Championship debut. The Surrey team joins in the applause and it's nice to see Adam Hollioake offering a congratulatory pat on the back for a very promising young talent.

Tea:- Between innings

As Surrey commence their reply, the consensus of opinion is that the Durham total is something like par for the course, as there has clearly been help for the seam bowlers. Simon Brown and Melvyn Betts certainly make an accurate start for Durham, with the first run of the innings not coming until Ian Ward pushes a legside single in the sixth over and the first ten overs yielding a mere three runs. Ward does eventually loosen the shackles slightly with a square-cut boundary in Brown's sixth over but it's more of a struggle for Mark Butcher who is unable to get off the mark until over number thirteen. Although runs aren't a great concern at this stage, since the priority for the visitors is not to lose wickets in the final session, it always looks to be a tough task for the openers to survive until the close with the ball quite often beating the bat. It isn't a huge surprise then that Butcher and Ward are eventually parted before stumps but the manner of the dismissal is almost farcical, and certainly avoidable, as Ward fails to cash in on a huge stroke of luck. Having edged Neil Killeen straight to Betts at third slip and seen the straightforward chance spilled, he is called through for a tight single by Butcher but fails to beat a brilliant direct-hit shy at the non-striker's stumps by Katich from second slip. Much credit must go to the quick-thinking Australian but, from a Surrey point of view, it's a terrible waste of a valuable wicket. It also puts extra pressure on Graham Thorpe, who comes in at number three and rarely looks completely at ease, twice edging Harmison over the slips to the third man boundary and then being dropped off the same bowler at backward square leg. The tall paceman is not to be denied, however, and he eventually gets his man, courtesy of a top-edged cut to Speight behind the stumps in the penultimate over of the day. An interesting contest looks in store tomorrow as Surrey, with eight wickets in hand, reach stumps still 187 runs in arrears.

Close:- Surrey 47-2 (Butcher 10*, Tudor 0*) from 28 overs

VIEW FROM THE DRESSING ROOM - ADAM HOLLIOAKE

You were quoted as saying that you could see Nicky Peng had talent from a very early stage of his innings. What was it that you saw in him?
AH - It was just the way he hit the ball and the way he lined it up very straight. We probably didn't bowl quite as well against him as we might have done and it's also true to say that he did play and miss quite a bit but, overall, he played really well and I think that he could go on to become a very fine player in a few years time.

Second Day - Wednesday 3rd May

Durham 234 and 121-7; Surrey 104

Play starts in indifferent light on a gloomy and chilly morning with Melvyn Betts passing the edge of Alex Tudor's swishing blade no fewer than four times in his first over. This is an early indication that there is going to be plenty of sideways movement available to the Durham pace attack. With conditions so much in the bowlers' favour, the overnight batsmen are parted inside seven overs when Mark Butcher edges a Simon Brown outswinger low to Simon Katich at first slip - 57-3.
Much worse is to follow, however, as Surrey lose two more wickets in the next two overs. Tudor is the first of these departures, miscuing a pull at Betts high towards deep mid-on where Brown takes a good running catch over his shoulder, and then Ben Hollioake falls to a stunning effort by Martin Speight behind the stumps, his inside-edged drive pouched by the 'keeper low down as he manages to change direction at the last moment.
At 62 for 5, things are looking bleak, especially in conditions which are unlikely to ease as the day progresses. Surrey supporters are left hoping that the sixth-wicket pairing of Ali Brown and

Adam Hollioake might be able to launch a stirring counter-attack but it's not to be as Neil Killeen, replacing Betts at the Finchale end, strikes a devastating blow in his second over. Inducing Brown to edge a catch low to Speight's right, the burly seamer sparks off further Durham celebrations as he reduces the county champions to a miserable 68-6. An already desperate situation for the visitors then further deteriorates when Killeen beats Jon Batty with the final ball of his next over and wins an lbw verdict from umpire Burgess.

The innings is now collapsing like a house of cards in the face of some very testing seam and swing bowling and even the normally reliable Martin Bicknell is unable to turn the tide as he gets a leading edge to a drive in the next over from Brown and sends a catch spiralling to Betts in the gully.

With the score standing at 73-8, Surrey are 161 runs behind their hosts and still require a further dozen runs to avoid the follow-on. This target is quickly reduced by four runs as Adam Hollioake cuts Killeen to the boundary at backward point but, after a couple of leg byes and an inside-edged single which gets Ian Salisbury off the mark in unconvincing fashion, the visiting skipper perishes in a disappointing, yet unlucky, fashion. Despite the fact that two fielders are posted on the boundary for the hook shot, Hollioake willingly takes up the challenge when Killeen drops the ball in short but miscues the ball high into the open space at backward square leg. It looks, initially, as if the ball is going to drop safely and even earn a precious run for the batsman but Paul Collingwood has other ideas as he races in from the boundary and dives forward to pick up a truly astounding catch at full stretch. This further example of electrifying Durham fielding condemns a rueful Hollioake to a mournful walk back to the pavilion and leaves Surrey's last-wicket pair to find another four runs to avoid the possibility of being forced to bat again.

A tense period of play is now envisaged but it fails to materialise as Ian Bishop, with precisely zero first-class runs to his name, immediately drives Simon Brown handsomely through mid-off for two and then Salisbury strikes Killeen rustically wide of mid-on for another brace of runs in the next over. Although the follow-on has been avoided escape from defeat is looking a lot more unlikely, even at this stage. The last-wicket pair actually manages to add a useful twenty-three runs with Bishop producing several pleasant drives and Salisbury repeatedly running the ball skilfully to third man before another marvellous catch, taken at full stretch above his head by Betts on the cover boundary, appropriately ends the innings.

The Durham bowling and fielding has been exemplary and, at times, quite brilliant as they have established a very strong position for themselves by gaining a first innings lead of 130. The new captain, Nick Speak, looks to have made all the right moves, too, and can be very pleased with his efforts.

On the other side of the coin, it has, quite literally, been a shocking morning for Surrey players and supporters alike. We are now left hoping that Durham might 'freeze' as they have done in the past when confronted with the realisation that they are now the favourites to win a game. One thing is certain - Surrey's opening bowlers simply must make early inroads into the Durham second-innings if their team is to retain any hope of launching a comeback.

Although Lewis and Daley manage to survive two overs before the interval, with one heart-stopping moment when Bicknell appeals loudly for lbw against Lewis, the feeling is that the next session could prove critical in deciding the course the match will eventually take.

Lunch:- Durham 1-0 (Lewis 1*, Daley 0*) from 2 overs

After a boundary apiece from the Durham openers, a Surrey fightback begins in earnest after the break as magnificent bowling from Bicknell and Tudor produces a return of four wickets in the space of just seven overs.

Daley goes first, in the seventh over, when he unwisely offers no stroke to a Bicknell inswinger and departs lbw with the score on eleven then, just eight balls later, with the score unchanged, Tudor claims the wicket of Lewis when he finds the outside edge of a defensive bat. Although Simon Katich then gets off the mark with a sliced drive for two past a diving Ian Ward at point, Tudor is soon back in the act with another wicket in his fifth over. His victim this time is Paul Collingwood, brilliantly held low and one-handed by Mark Butcher at second slip.

The feeling is now growing that we might yet have a game on our hands and this is amplified three overs later when Speak edges Bicknell to Batty to leave Durham struggling at 14-4. The home side already leads by 144, however - a significant advantage in these early season conditions - and the consensus of opinion amongst the Surrey faithful is that we won't want to be chasing more than 250 in the final innings. Wickets therefore have to be captured at regular intervals if the comeback is to be maintained. The crucial question is whether the back-up seamers can keep the pressure on the batsmen once Bicknell and Tudor conclude their opening spells. This is one problem for Adam Hollioake. The other is the increasing assurance being shown by Katich, who gathers runs quietly but steadily as Durham's first innings hero, Nicky Peng, makes a very edgy start after opening his account with a well-timed legside boundary.

In order to maximise the number of overs delivered by his trusted opening bowlers, Tudor is kept going from the Lumley end for ten overs before being replaced by Bicknell, who had given way to Ben Hollioake at the Finchale end after an initial eight-over burst. Bicknell's first over of his new spell costs ten and it is then followed by an eight-run Hollioake over as the batsmen start to take control. With Bishop and Salisbury being held back, the Surrey skipper's high-risk policy looks to be failing until his senior paceman suddenly finds sufficient strength and inspiration to remove Peng, courtesy of an outside edge to Jon Batty.

A score of 61 for 5 then very nearly becomes 64 for 6 when the new batsman, Martin Speight, drives Hollioake uppishly into the covers and sees Ian Ward just fail to cling on to a brilliant left-handed attempt at the catch. Since the opening bowlers are now pretty much a spent force, it seems possible that this could be a crucial moment and the feeling is underlined when Ian Bishop is battered out of the attack after starting promisingly with two maiden overs. Although enjoying some moments of good fortune along the way, Speight is particularly severe on any loose deliveries served up by Surrey's back-up bowlers and as the tea interval approaches it is clear that he has won the initiative back for his team.

Tea:- Durham 104-5 (Katich 37*, Speight 28*) from 42 overs

Under darkening skies it's inevitable that Adam Hollioake turns to his opening bowlers to start the final session. It is also no surprise to see Speight continuing to play his shots as he immediately despatches Bicknell to the boundary twice to complete a very important fifty partnership with the composed Katich. Fortunately for Surrey, Alex Tudor brings the dangerous former Sussex player to book in the next over before he can do any more damage, first striking him a painful blow on the knee and then having him taken down the legside by Batty.

The light is already pretty poor at this stage but Katich unexpectedly turns down the umpires' offer to leave the field and is soon made to regret his decision as Killeen is beaten through the gate and bowled in the following over from Bicknell. The home side is now effectively 248-7, giving Surrey another glimmer of hope, but the visitors are unable to make further inroads into the Durham tail as the umpires are soon conferring again about the light. This time, Katich doesn't need to be asked for his opinion - he is off the field like a shot, without even consulting his new batting partner.

Close:- Durham 121-7 (Katich 43*, Betts 2*) from 48 overs

Third Day - Thursday 4th May

Durham 234 and 186; Surrey 104 and 85

Durham beat Surrey by 231 runs
Durham 16pts, Surrey 3

Surrey need three very quick wickets to stay in contention as the third day's play gets underway with Martin Bicknell operating from the Finchale end and Alex Tudor from the Lumley end.
　Much to the disappointment of the visiting team and their supporters the early overs fail to produce a wicket, although Betts leads a charmed life, twice snicking to third man and then inside-edging past his leg stump on two further occasions. Katich, meanwhile, remains steadfastly in control and the sixth boundary of his innings, cut airily past a diving gully off Bicknell, takes him through to a highly accomplished 140-ball half-century. The young Australian's excellent effort has kept his side firmly on top in a match which begins to slip further away from the visitors when Betts starts to locate the middle of his bat with two fine square-driven fours, the second of which takes the eighth-wicket partnership up to fifty. It goes no further, however, as Bicknell wins a front foot lbw verdict against the Durham seamer to terminate a valuable innings of twenty-three. Steve Harmison then follows quickly, his off stump sent cartwheeling by the final ball of the next over, delivered by Ben Hollioake, but the Durham lead has, by now, passed 300 and the damage has already been done. Although Hollioake soon takes his sixth wicket of the match and ends the innings by beating Katich as he plays forward, Surrey clearly have a huge fight on their hands to make 317 to win on this seamer-friendly pitch. Durham's young Australian leaves the field to a warm ovation for a very impressive innings of 65, while the Surrey players are left to contemplate the size of the task that lies ahead.
　Mark Butcher and Ian Ward are soon back in the middle to get Surrey's run chase under way and they make a confident start against Melvyn Betts and Steve Harmison, who is surprisingly handed the new ball ahead of Simon Brown. The tall speedster is only allowed three overs before he gives way to Brown, however, as runs rattle up with surprising ease. Both batsmen produce some high quality strokes and there have been few alarms as lunch is reached at 39-0. It's been a very satisfactory start for the visitors but, despite the fact that I am an optimist by nature, I give us only a five percent chance of winning when pressed for an opinion by a fellow Surrey supporter.

Lunch:- Surrey 39-0 (Butcher 20*, Ward 15*) from 12 overs

Nick Speak hands the ball to Neil Killeen and Simon Brown after lunch and stalemate reigns supreme until Ian Ward breaks a run of four maidens by edging Killeen to third man for two runs.
　As things turn out, Surrey, at 41-0, have now reached the zenith of their second innings since Ward's defensive bat can only deflect Killeen's very next ball to Paul Collingwood at second slip. This loss of a wicket so early in the session is a big setback for the visitors' victory hopes but worse is to follow as, within the space of three deliveries in the next over from Brown, they are almost completely extinguished. Having clipped the third ball of the over sweetly through midwicket for four, Butcher then plays the following delivery onto his stumps and just two balls later Ben Hollioake pushes forward and is adjudged lbw when defeated by inswing. It's now 45-3 and batting is suddenly looking almost impossible, even though the sun has broken through to provide the best weather of the match.
　For a very brief period Graham Thorpe and Ali Brown battle to refloat the sinking ship, the latter bringing up his team's fifty with a rasping pulled boundary off Killeen, before a two-in-two blast by Durham sees the reigning champions almost down and out. Brown goes first, to the final ball of the twenty-third over, trapped leg-before by Killeen, then Harmison, having replaced

Simon Brown at the Lumley end, removes Thorpe with his first delivery, the England left-hander cutting a short, wide delivery low to Daley at deep backward point. It's a feather in the lively Harmison's cap that he has thus dismissed Thorpe in both innings and, perhaps fired-up by this knowledge, he has Jon Batty dropped second ball by Betts at third slip and then strikes the Surrey stumper on the helmet with a short delivery two balls later. The champions are clearly reeling and the contest is certainly over when Adam Hollioake receives an unplayable shooter from Killeen and is palpably lbw to the final ball of the twenty-seventh over of the innings, leaving the visitors in a hopeless mess at 50-6.

Despite having seen their pace bowlers decimate the Surrey batting with six wickets for nine runs in the space of just sixty-five deliveries, many of the Durham members around me are far from convinced that their team has the game won. It's true that they have lost many games from promising positions, including some against Surrey, but their lack of confidence still astounds me. With the weather set fair and another day's play available tomorrow it should be obvious to anyone that there is no escape route for the visitors and the home pessimists gradually come round to this way of thinking as Batty's brief resistance ends with an edged drive at the returning Betts which finds the safe hands of Katich at first slip. A dismal 57-7 then becomes 58-8 three deliveries later when Ian Salisbury falls second ball, clean bowled as he drives at a ball of full-length from Harmison.

For Surrey's players and supporters this is truly distressing stuff and the end is, fortunately, in the circumstances, not delayed for too long. Martin Bicknell eventually loses his off stump to Melvyn Betts as another flawed drive is punished then, after a brief flourish by Alex Tudor, Ian Bishop perishes in almost identical fashion, the bowler this time being Simon Brown.

Having set the unenviable record of the lowest recorded County Championship score against Durham when dismissed for 104 in their first innings, Surrey have now been routed for just eighty-five in their second knock and Durham win the match, against all expectations, by the crushing margin of 231 runs. After their deceptively promising start, the visitors have lost all ten wickets for just forty-four runs in 25.3 overs and a contest that was very much alive at lunch is over by 4.03pm. The Durham players and supporters deservedly celebrate a well-merited victory and the team has to be congratulated on a marvellous performance. For Surrey, on the other hand, this is an unexpected setback and a shock to the system. The scenes of cricketing carnage that we have witnessed are almost unbelievable, with the county's proud one-hundred percent record against Durham now well and truly consigned to the history books.

Still rather dazed by it all, I find it hard to tear myself away from the ground as I contemplate an unexpected and unwanted free day tomorrow and I wander around the Riverside, looking across to the pavilion for signs of activity in the area of the Surrey dressing room. There is no sign of life at all. Are the players now discussing where they have gone wrong in this match? Are they feeling as numb about this annihilation as I do at this moment in time? These are, I guess, the type of questions that flash through the mind of any supporter after his or her side has received a hammering such as this one. Fortunately, with the season having only just started, there is plenty of time to put this disaster behind us and recover from the unexpectedly poor return of just nine points from our first two Championship outings of the campaign.

As I stroll around in the pleasant late afternoon sunshine I start to come to terms with what has happened until I stumble across the Durham bowlers enjoying a dip in the temporary whirlpool bath which has been set up as part of the family entertainment for Saturday's NCL match. Understandably, they are in very high spirits, toasting their triumph with a well-deserved drink. This sight is sufficient to bring all the very worst moments of the past few days flooding back to me - I decide that this is a good time to leave the ground.

Durham 234 and 186; Surrey 104 and 85
Durham won by 231 runs. Durham 16pts, Surrey 3

DURHAM v SURREY at CHESTER-LE-STREET. Played from 2nd - 4th May

Surrey won the toss   Umpires:- G.I. Burgess & T.E. Jesty

DURHAM - First Innings

SURREY bowling

Fall of wkt	Batsman		How Out	Score	Balls	4s	6s		O	M	R	W
2- 21	J.J.B. Lewis		b Tudor	10	33	1	0	Bicknell	20	5	52	3
1- 5	J.A. Daley		b Bicknell	1	18	0	0	Tudor	17	5	39	2
3- 25	S.M. Katich	c Thorpe	b Bicknell	8	30	0	0	Bishop	13	1	54	1
5- 119	P.D. Collingwood	c Batty	b Tudor	66	104	7	0	B.C. Hollioake	13.4	3	41	4
4- 48	N.J. Speak *	c Batty	b B.C. Hollioake	3	26	0	0	Salisbury	12	2	39	0
10- 234	N. Peng	c Batty	b B.C. Hollioake	98	145	17	0					
6- 143	M.P. Speight +		lbw b Hollioake	9	33	1	0					
7- 175	N. Killeen	c Brown	b B.C. Hollioake	7	29	1	0					
8- 176	M.M. Betts		b Bishop	0	7	0	0					
9- 219	S.J. Harmison		lbw b B.C. Hollioake	15	19	2	0					
	S.J.E. Brown		Not Out	4	12	0	0					
	Extras (3b, 6lb, 4nb)			13								
	TOTAL		(75.4 overs)	234								

SURREY - First Innings

DURHAM bowling

Fall of wkt	Batsman		How Out	Score	Balls	4s	6s		O	M	R	W
3- 57	M.A. Butcher	c Katich	b Brown	15	98	1	0	Brown	18	7	29	3
1- 13	I.J. Ward		run out	12	44	1	0	Betts	15	7	19	1
2- 46	G.P. Thorpe	c Speight	b Harmison	18	38	3	0	Killeen	13	4	19	3
4- 57	A.J. Tudor	c Brown	b Betts	5	28	1	0	Collingwood	2.5	1	3	1
5- 62	B.C. Hollioake	c Speight	b Brown	2	11	0	0	Harmison	7	0	24	1
6- 68	A.D. Brown	c Speight	b Killeen	9	20	1	0					
9- 81	A.J. Hollioake *	c Collingwood	b Killeen	7	27	1	0					
7- 70	J.N. Batty +		lbw b Killeen	0	7	0	0					
8- 73	M.P. Bicknell	c Betts	b Brown	1	3	0	0					
	I.D.K. Salisbury		Not Out	11	33	0	0					
10- 104	I.E. Bishop	c Betts	b Collingwood	12	26	0	0					
	Extras (10lb, 2w)			12								
	TOTAL		(55.5 overs)	104								

DURHAM - Second Innings

SURREY bowling

Fall of wkt	Batsman		How Out	Score	Balls	4s	6s		O	M	R	W
2- 11	J.J.B. Lewis	c Batty	b Tudor	5	27	1	0	Bicknell	27	6	85	5
1- 11	J.A. Daley		lbw b Bicknell	4	20	1	0	Tudor	19	4	45	3
10- 186	S.M. Katich		lbw b B.C. Hollioake	65	157	7	0	B.C. Hollioake	13.1	6	27	2
3- 13	P.D. Collingwood	c Butcher	b Tudor	0	3	0	0	Bishop	4	2	20	0
4- 14	N.J. Speak *	c Batty	b Bicknell	1	12	0	0	A.J. Hollioake	2	1	1	0
5- 61	N. Peng	c Batty	b Bicknell	23	37	3	0					
6- 113	M.P. Speight +	c Batty	b Tudor	36	53	7	0					
7- 118	N. Killeen		b Bicknell	0	9	0	0					
8- 168	M.M. Betts		lbw b Bicknell	23	66	2	0					
9- 173	S.J. Harmison		b B.C. Hollioake	0	2	0	0					
	S.J.E. Brown		Not Out	4	13	1	0					
	Extras (8lb, 17nb)			25								
	TOTAL		(65.1 overs)	186								

SURREY - Second Innings

DURHAM bowling

Fall of wkt	Batsman		How Out	Score	Balls	4s	6s		O	M	R	W
2- 45	M.A. Butcher		b Brown	24	61	3	0	Betts	10	1	36	2
1- 41	I.J. Ward	c Collingwood	b Killeen	17	41	1	0	Harmison	12	4	19	2
5- 50	G.P. Thorpe	c Daley	b Harmison	1	19	0	0	Brown	8.4	6	8	3
3- 45	B.C. Hollioake		lbw b Brown	0	2	0	0	Collingwood	1	0	6	0
4- 50	A.D. Brown		lbw b Killeen	4	16	1	0	Killeen	10	5	14	3
6- 50	A.J. Hollioake *		lbw b Killeen	0	12	0	0					
7- 57	J.N. Batty +	c Katich	b Betts	7	29	1	0					
9- 66	M.P. Bicknell		b Betts	7	26	0	0					
8- 58	I.D.K. Salisbury		b Harmison	0	2	0	0					
	A.J. Tudor		Not Out	17	31	3	0					
10- 85	I.E. Bishop		b Brown	2	12	0	0					
	Extras (2b, 2w, 2nb)			6								
	TOTAL		(41.4 overs)	85								

VIEW FROM THE DRESSING ROOM - ADAM HOLLIOAKE

We struggled badly with the bat throughout - can you put your finger on why?
AH - I think our lack of time in the middle was a huge factor, but it must be said that they bowled very well and used the conditions better than we did. Although our bowling was perhaps a little below par our batting fell way short of what we expect and when you put the two things together it makes for a very poor performance.

We certainly had the worst of the overhead conditions during the game. With hindsight, should we perhaps have batted first or maybe played another seamer in place of Ian Salisbury, who hardly bowled?
AH - I don't think either of those things would have made any difference. I think you've always got to go into a game with a spinner in your side and Sals is so useful to have on any surface - he can always nip a couple of batsmen out and he allows the seamers to take a rest. Had the overhead conditions been reversed then it might have been a slightly closer game but there's no getting away from the fact that we were outplayed and they deserved to win.

Was this defeat a blessing in disguise, since it showed us there was no room for complacency?
AH - Yes, it was a huge wake-up call as they outbatted and outbowled us throughout the match. There was a lot of hard work ahead of us because we had let ourselves down badly.

VIEW FROM THE DRESSING ROOM - MARTIN BICKNELL

Did blame for this defeat lie solely with the batsmen or do you feel we could also have bowled a little better?
MB - I think one of the problems we had was the make-up of our side. Tudes and I had to bowl a lot of overs and got very tired, whereas they were able to rotate their four seamers and keep them all fresh. With the bat, I think we struggled, largely, through lack of practice - we'd had virtually no outdoor practice and all the pre-season friendlies had been washed out.

Surrey fans were left shell-shocked by this defeat. What was the dressing room reaction?
MB - We gave full credit to Durham - they fully deserved to win and it made us think long and hard about what we needed to do to retain the Championship. Losing this game set us off on the wrong foot and it made the point to us that the season wasn't going to be easy and we were going to have to work really hard.

KEITH MEDLYCOTT'S ASSESSMENT

We were absolutely slaughtered - no excuses. Even though the ball moved around a great deal, their seamers bowled brilliantly and even if we had batted four times I don't think we would have got their scores. We were outplayed and it was a huge wake-up call for us, something which was maybe beneficial to us in the long run. It was not what we expected, of course, but they played very well and we didn't. It also showed us that if you played below par in Division One then you were going to get whacked.

Other Division One Matches

May 3-5
Southampton:- **Somerset beat Hampshire by nine wickets.** Hampshire 232 (Kenway 93 not out, Caddick 5-62) and 126 (White 78 not out, Caddick 7-64); Somerset 319 (Cox 153, Bowler 56, Turner 56) and 40-1. **Somerset 18pts, Hampshire 4**

Headingley:- **Yorkshire beat Derbyshire by an innings and 79 runs.** Derbyshire 239 (Di Venuto 70) and 190 (Bailey 54 not out); Yorkshire 508-5dec (Vaughan 155, Wood 100 not out, Lehmann 95, Aldred 4-97). **Yorkshire 20pts, Derbyshire 2**

May 3-6
Old Trafford:- **Lancashire beat Leicestershire by an innings and 25 runs.** Leicestershire 265 (Wells 56, Martin 7-67) and 198 (Schofield 4-82); Lancashire 488 (Fairbrother 138, Flintoff 119, Schofield 66, Ormond 4-122). **Lancashire 20pts, Leicestershire 4**

COUNTY CHAMPIONSHIP DIVISION ONE AT 6TH MAY

Pos	Prev		P	Pts	W	D	L	Bat	Bowl	Last	Three	Res
1	n/a	Somerset	2	28	1	1	0	6	6	W18	D10	N/A
2	n/a	Lancashire	2	24	1	1	0	5	3	W20	D4	N/A
3	n/a	Yorkshire	1	20	1	0	0	5	3	W20	N/A	N/A
4	n/a	Durham	1	16	1	0	0	1	3	W16	N/A	N/A
5	n/a	Leicestershire	2	13	0	1	1	5	4	L4	D9	N/A
6	n/a	Derbyshire	2	12	0	1	1	4	4	L2	D10	N/A
7	n/a	Surrey	2	9	0	1	1	0	5	L3	D6	N/A
8	n/a	Kent	1	7	0	1	0	0	3	D7	N/A	N/A
9	n/a	Hampshire	1	4	0	0	1	1	3	L4	N/A	N/A

SPEEDY REVIVAL NEEDED FOR NCL ENCOUNTER

Surrey needed to regroup rapidly for the NCL Division Two match between the two counties two days later. Since Durham had now recorded their first four-day victory over the men from the Oval could they do the double and notch their first limited-overs win?

NCL DIVISION TWO - MATCH TWO

DURHAM DYNAMOS versus SURREY LIONS
at The Riverside, Chester-le-Street on Saturday 6th May

Surrey Lions (230-7) beat Durham Dynamos (164) by 66 runs

Despite being put in to bat in cold and bleak conditions likely to favour the seam bowlers, Surrey got away to a reasonable start through the opening pairing of Butcher and Brown, who notched thirty-six runs in the first eight overs. At this point Brown edged Neil Killeen to slip but Alec Stewart then entered the fray to play the innings around which the visitors were able to build an impressive total. Unfazed by the loss of Butcher (27) and Thorpe (0) to Nicky Phillips in quick succession, Stewart maintained concentration and kept the scoreboard ticking over as he made his way to 41 from 80 balls before slashing Harmison high to deep point with the score at 120.

This was the one bright moment of a poor afternoon for the Durham fast bowler who failed to find any consistency and then received a late hammering from Stewart's replacement in the middle, Ben Hollioake.

Following a fairly slow start, the young all-rounder, partnered by Jason Ratcliffe, turned the heat up on the home attack with a blistering assault in the last five overs of the innings. Fifty-five runs accrued as Harmison was taken for sixteen runs from three balls in the forty-first over, Hollioake pulling a four and a six before launching an incredible drive over the extra cover boundary with a stroke of tremendous power and timing. Ratcliffe was no less impressive, scoring from almost every ball he received and then adding to the hapless Harmison's woes with three successive boundaries in the gangling paceman's final over.

Although three Durham bowlers - Betts, Killeen and Phillips - emerged with credit for some accurate and intelligent bowling, Paul Collingwood was almost as loose as Harmison, conceding no fewer than thirteen runs in wides, as the home side gifted their visitors an appalling fifty-one runs in extras.

In order to challenge Surrey's total the home side needed a confident start but their key batsman, Simon Katich, could make no impression against high-quality opening bowling and fell lbw to a Bicknell off-cutter for just six in the ninth over.

When Daley, lbw as he hit across the line, and Speight, top-edging a legside flick to long leg, fell soon afterwards to Alex Tudor, Durham were really struggling on 42-3 and desperately needed two batsmen to produce a steadying stand. This duly materialised as Collingwood and Speak added fifty-seven for the fourth wicket but, with Surrey's first change pairing of Greenidge and Ben Hollioake keeping good control, the required run rate was always rising.

Eventually, Collingwood, backing up too far at the non-striker's end and unable to regain his ground when sent back, was run out by Thorpe's direct hit from midwicket and a sustained spell of good, straight bowling from Ratcliffe and Adam Hollioake ensured that the necessary acceleration could not be achieved. Aiming to hit an off stump delivery to leg, Speak became the Surrey skipper's first victim in the thirty-second over with 117 runs still required and, apart from a few bold hits from Lewis and Phillips, the lower order subsided meekly thereafter as Durham slipped away from 129-5 to 164 all out.

It was greatly encouraging from the visitors' viewpoint that Hollioake appeared to be back to something close to his limited-overs best in claiming five wickets, his deadly slower ball accounting for three of his victims, and, with the margin of victory a comfortable sixty-six runs, Keith Medlycott's team had bounced back with a very efficient and professional performance which augured well for the National League promotion campaign. The county's week in Chester-le-Street had, in the end, offered a degree of encouragement for the season ahead, but a far harder test lay ahead with the Benson And Hedges Cup quarter-final against Yorkshire at Headingley just three days away.

Surrey Lions (230-7) beat Durham Dynamos (164) by 66 runs

Surrey Lions 4pts

DURHAM DYNAMOS v SURREY LIONS at CHESTER-LE-STREET. Played on 6th May
Durham Dynamos won the toss   Umpires:- G.I. Burgess & T.E. Jesty. Third Umpire:- R.A. White

SURREY LIONS

Fall of wkt	Batsman	How	Out	Score	Balls	4s	6s
2- 71	M.A. Butcher		b Phillips	27	47	4	0
1- 36	A.D. Brown	c Katich	b Killeen	19	23	4	0
4- 120	A.J. Stewart +	c Lewis	b Harmison	41	80	6	0
3- 85	G.P. Thorpe		b Phillips	0	7	0	0
5- 149	A.J. Hollioake *		b Killeen	17	30	2	0
7- 219	B.C. Hollioake	st Speight	b Collingwood	42	50	2	2
6- 157	I.J. Ward		lbw b Killeen	3	7	0	0
	J.D. Ratcliffe		Not Out	25	24	3	0
	A.J. Tudor		Not Out	5	5	0	0
	M.P. Bicknell	did not bat					
	C.G. Greenidge	did not bat					
	Extras (5b, 14lb, 26w, 6nb)			51			
	TOTAL		(45 overs)	230-7			

DURHAM DYNAMOS bowling

	O	M	R	W
Betts	9	0	31	0
Killeen	9	2	37	3
Harmison	9	0	66	1
Phillips	9	0	31	2
Collingwood	9	0	46	1

DURHAM DYNAMOS

Fall of wkt	Batsman	How	Out	Score	Balls	4s	6s
1- 30	S.M. Katich		lbw b Bicknell	6	19	1	0
3- 42	M.P. Speight +	c Bicknell	b Tudor	21	40	3	0
2- 38	J.A. Daley		lbw b Tudor	5	15	1	0
4- 99	P.D. Collingwood		run out	28	41	1	0
5- 114	N.J. Speak *		b A.J. Hollioake	24	57	1	0
6- 129	R. Robinson		b Ratcliffe	7	25	0	0
7- 140	J.J.B. Lewis		b A.J. Hollioake	16	20	1	0
9- 159	N.C. Phillips		b A.J. Hollioake	17	16	2	0
8- 156	M.M. Betts	c B.C. Hollioake	b A.J. Hollioake	4	6	0	0
10- 164	N. Killeen	c Stewart	b A.J. Hollioake	4	10	0	0
	S.J. Harmison		Not Out	1	2	0	0
	Extras (11lb, 16w, 4nb)			31			
	TOTAL		(41.3 overs)	164			

SURREY LIONS bowling

	O	M	R	W
Bicknell	7	2	15	1
Tudor	7	0	26	2
Greenidge	8	1	29	0
B.C. Hollioake	6	0	27	0
A.J. Hollioake	7.3	0	29	5
Ratcliffe	6	0	27	1

Other NCL Division Two Matches

May 7
Chelmsford:- **Nottinghamshire Outlaws beat Essex Eagles by 3 runs.** Nottinghamshire 190-7 in 42 overs (Grayson 3-23); Essex 187-9 in 42 overs (Hussain 55). **Nottinghamshire Outlaws 4pts**

Lord's:- **Middlesex Crusaders beat Hampshire Hawks by four wickets.** Hampshire 147 in 44.5 overs (Smith 71, Johnson 3-37); Middlesex 148-6 in 43.2 overs (Warne 3-33). **Middlesex Crusaders 4pts**

Edgbaston:- **Warwickshire Bears beat Glamorgan Dragons by nine wickets.** Glamorgan 125 in 39.2 overs (Brown 3-23); Warwickshire 127-1 in 26.5 overs (Knight 68 not out). **Warwickshire Bears 4pts**

NCL DIVISION TWO AT 7TH MAY

Pos	Prev		P	Pts	W	T	L	N/R	Last	Three	Res
1	n/a	Nottinghamshire Outlaws	2	8	2	0	0	0	W	W	N/A
=	n/a	Surrey Lions	2	8	2	0	0	0	W	W	N/A
=	n/a	Warwickshire Bears	2	8	2	0	0	0	W	W	N/A
4	n/a	Middlesex Crusaders	3	8	2	0	1	0	W	W	L
5	n/a	Essex Eagles	2	4	1	0	1	0	L	W	N/A
6	n/a	Derbyshire Scorpions	1	0	0	0	1	0	L	N/A	N/A
7	n/a	Durham Dynamos	2	0	0	0	2	0	L	L	N/A
=	n/a	Glamorgan Dragons	2	0	0	0	2	0	L	L	N/A
=	n/a	Hampshire Hawks	2	0	0	0	2	0	L	L	N/A

SUPERB STEWART STEERS SURREY TO SEMIS

Surrey's advance to the semi-finals of the Benson And Hedges Cup with an exciting and largely unexpected seven-run victory owed much to a marvellous innings by Alec Stewart, some rather fortunate umpiring decisions and a continuation of the team's impressive limited-overs bowling and fielding.

Put in to bat in very testing conditions, Surrey were almost blown away during a fine spell by Matthew Hoggard, who removed Mark Butcher, Ali Brown, Graham Thorpe and Adam Holloake as the visitors subsided to 39-4. During this opening Yorkshire assault, Stewart appeared fortunate to survive a confident lbw appeal by his England colleague, Darren Gough, and also had a reprieve when David Byas missed a very hard chance, diving to his right at second slip, off Hoggard. The Yorkshire skipper's decision not to have a third slip despite having the opposition reeling on the ropes proved a very costly one.

Stewart battled gamely through the difficult early overs, however, and, after losing another partner when Ian Ward edged a wide Hamilton delivery to slip with the score on 71, became the dominant partner in a pivotal sixth-wicket stand with Ben Hollioake.

Like Stewart before him, Hollioake benefited greatly from an early stroke of luck when his outside edge to the 'keeper off Hamilton went undetected by umpire Harris. That could have reduced Surrey to a desperate 79-6 but, with Surrey's senior pro playing outstandingly well at the other end, the young all-rounder settled in to play a fine supporting role as the foundations for a workable total were established.

Although Yorkshire were fielding a very strong attack, the run rate was steadily increased and a more violent assault was then launched in the closing overs. Hollioake (44) eventually skied White to deep cover in the forty-seventh over with the stand worth ninety-six but his replacement, Jason Ratcliffe, then provided further late impetus with fifteen unbeaten runs from eleven balls. Although Stewart was left three runs short of what would have been a very well-deserved century when the overs ran out, his high quality innings had given his team a definite chance of success.

Early wickets were now required to keep the pendulum swinging towards Surrey and, with Bicknell on the button and Tudor generating good pace, the visitors did indeed strike early blows in the second, third and eighth overs of the innings. While Byas (0) was defeated by Bicknell's swing, the other two wickets - White (4) and Blakey (5) - came courtesy of a brace of excellent catches in the gully by Ben Hollioake off Tudor as Yorkshire slipped to 15 for 3.

With the inexperienced Craven and Fellows at seven and eight in the order and a fragile tail to follow, Adam Hollioake kept his opening bowlers going for seven overs apiece in an attempt to remove the dangerous Lehmann and break the back of the batting.

Fortunately for Yorkshire, though, the burly Australian took most of the strike in seeing off Bicknell and Tudor and, well supported by Matthew Wood, began to increase the tempo against some poorly-directed bowling from Greenidge, Ratcliffe and Ben Hollioake.

The home side's hundred eventually came up, without any further loss of wickets, in the twenty-ninth over, and even the sensible reintroduction of Tudor failed to produce the vital breakthrough for Surrey. A Yorkshire victory was now looking quite likely but the balance of the game was altered just in the nick of time when the Surrey skipper snared Lehmann, rather fortunately, just two balls after the batsman had completed an excellent 71-ball half-century. Although the umpire adjudged that the sturdy Aussie had fatally flicked a legside delivery to Stewart behind the stumps, television replays clearly showed that the ball had only made contact with the batsman's pad. Buoyed by this further stroke of good luck and now very much back in the match, Hollioake struck again in his next over as Craven clipped the ball straight to square leg to reduce the home side to 130-5.

Bearing in mind the paucity of the batting to come, Surrey now looked marginal favourites but Wood and Fellows eased their side back into the driving seat with a partnership which produced thirty-six valuable runs in nine overs.

The crucial wicket of Wood, excellently caught by Stewart from an inside-edged drive at a slower off-cutter from Ben Hollioake, was to turn the game once again, however. As the home side's lower order began to panic under pressure, Fellows, Gough and Hamilton all fell in quick succession to direct-hit run outs by Greenidge, Brown and the younger Hollioake, leaving the last-wicket pair of Sidebottom and Hoggard to gather sixteen runs for victory from the final two overs. Having bowled exceptionally well from the rugby stand end during an unbroken spell that had only started in the thirty-first over, Adam Hollioake was not about to give anything away now to two players with no great batting skill and his penultimate over yielded just two singles and two leg-byes.

After some deliberation, the last over was then entrusted to Jason Ratcliffe and, having conceded just four runs from the first four deliveries, the experienced former Warwickshire man deceived and bowled a charging Sidebottom with a fine slower delivery to seal victory and spark some serious Surrey celebrations.

This rare win at Headingley was a marvellous achievement, brought about by the exceptional batting of Alec Stewart, a good all-round display by Ben Hollioake, and some superb bowling (Bicknell 1-22, Tudor 2-39, Adam Hollioake 2-30) backed up by very fine outfielding. A semi-final against Glamorgan at Cardiff now beckoned and the prospect of a first Lord's final since the Benson And Hedges Cup victory of 1997 looked a real possibility.

SCOREBOARD - BENSON AND HEDGES CUP QUARTER-FINAL

Surrey 198-6 from 50 overs (A.J. Stewart 97 not out, M.J. Hoggard 4-39)
Yorkshire 191 from 49.5 overs (M.J. Wood 59, D.S. Lehmann 50)
Surrey won by 7 runs

Umpires: A. Clarkson and J.H. Harris

Gold Award Winner - A.J. Stewart (Surrey)

4 Rain, Rain, Go Away!

The Benson And Hedges Cup victory over Yorkshire, coupled with a winning start in the National League, had offered some degree of compensation for the county's unexpectedly poor start to the Championship campaign and the next two weeks appeared to give further cause for optimism since a National Cricket League game against a still ring-rusty Middlesex was sandwiched between the season's two Championship clashes with Kent. Although no-one could see any good reason for this peculiar back-to-back scheduling of the matches against our home counties rivals, no-one was complaining much since Matthew Fleming's team was struggling with injuries in the seam bowling department. The absence of the experienced trio of Dean Headley, Julian Thompson and Martin McCague would surely be a major handicap for Kent in these encounters and give Surrey an added advantage over a side that looked to be somewhat lacking in depth of talent and quality. Given a spell of good, dry weather, our Championship campaign would surely soon be back on track.

COUNTY CHAMPIONSHIP - MATCH THREE

SURREY versus KENT
at The Oval

First Day - Thursday 11th May

No Play - Rain

Another wretchedly wet and frustrating day means that a quarter of the match is instantly lopped off, decreasing, at a stroke, the prospects of the morale-boosting win that everyone connected with Surrey is craving. To make matters worse, more poor weather is forecast for later in the week.

Second Day - Friday 12th May

Surrey 278-6

The Teams And The Toss - *Surrey are able to field their strongest available side, with the only changes from the defeat at Chester-le-Street being the inclusion of a fit-again Alec Stewart for Jon Batty and Rupesh Amin for Ian Bishop. Kent meanwhile prefer Ed Smith and James Hockley to David Fulton and Matthew Walker in their batting line-up and, as a result of the injuries which have depleted their seam bowling resources, are forced to include two relatively inexperienced pacemen, Martin Saggers and David Masters, in their eleven. When play gets under way twenty-four hours late, Matthew Fleming calls correctly and, quite predictably, asks Surrey to bat.*

In helpful conditions for the seamers, Kent's early bowling is inconsistent. While Mark Ealham induces an outside edge from Ian Ward which flies just wide of third slip's left hand in the opening over and then sees the same batsman inside-edge a delivery to the fine leg boundary six overs later, the two other front-line pacemen in the visitors' attack struggle badly. Martin Saggers strays constantly to leg during an initial three-over burst from the Vauxhall end and his replacement, David Masters, suffers, to a lesser degree, from the same problem. It is only when the veteran Kent skipper takes the ball that the Surrey openers receive a proper test, both men being beaten outside the off stump on a number of occasions as Fleming produces a fine first spell of six consecutive maidens. The captain lacks support, however, as Saggers continues to concede easy runs on the legside, despite a switch to the pavilion end.

Since his seamers are proving largely unreliable, Fleming is forced into using Min Patel as early as the nineteenth over but the former England left-arm spinner poses few problems as Butcher and Ward complete their first fifty partnership of the season just five overs later. The Kent skipper continues to switch his bowlers regularly and eventually finds some encouragement when Masters, in a new spell from the Vauxhall end, finds Ward's outside edge only for Rahul Dravid to spill a fairly easy chance at second slip. This miss caps a poor morning in the field by the visitors, who have been guilty of numerous misfields and poor throws, and it looks as if they will go to lunch wicketless until Ward, failing to capitalise on his escape, clips Masters straight to Ed Smith at square leg and departs for thirty-eight with the total on seventy-eight. Graham Thorpe then makes a confident start by driving the successful bowler through extra cover for a boundary in the final over of a session which has undoubtedly been won by Surrey.

Lunch:- Surrey 82-1 (Butcher 33*, Thorpe 4*) from 36 overs

An improved performance in the opening overs after lunch sees Kent coming close to, and then achieving, a second breakthrough, with Mark Butcher the man in the thick of the action. After edging Saggers just wide of second slip for four runs and then surviving a loud lbw appeal when hit on the foot by a ball of yorker length from the same bowler, he raises the Surrey hundred with boundaries from successive deliveries before losing his wicket to the persevering Matthew Fleming. Having conceded his first runs of the innings when being edged to the third man boundary by Graham Thorpe in his eighth over, it is, ironically, one of the Kent skipper's poorest deliveries which claims the second Surrey wicket - Butcher slices a drive at a wide delivery and is brilliantly held low to his left by a diving Min Patel at backward point. The visitors are seemingly showing greater fight in these early stages of the afternoon and this impression is given greater credence just three overs later when Thorpe is adjudged lbw to Saggers - Surrey 105 for 3.

Alec Stewart appears unconcerned by this sudden shift in fortunes, however, clipping successive deliveries from the previously frugal Fleming to the rope at backward square leg and then driving Saggers on the up through point to add four further runs to his score. Ali Brown makes a less certain start, however, and, in bizarre style, manages to present the opposition with two opportunities of a wicket from the same ball. Still on nought, he survives a low caught-and-bowled chance to Fleming and then watches in horror as the ball deflects from the bowler's hands onto the non-striker's stumps. Fortunately, Stewart survives the inevitable appeal and promptly thrashes the recalled Ealham through the covers for two fours in the next over. Surrey's honorary club captain is looking set to continue his magnificent recent form at this stage but an uncharacteristically less-than-fluent Brown then monopolises the strike for a considerable period of time. Although the partnership continues to thrive and reaches fifty when Brown forces Masters to the cover fence, Stewart's frustration is almost tangible and, as tea approaches, he falls in unfortunate fashion to an unlikley bowler, tickling a legside delivery from Rahul Dravid to Nixon behind the stumps. Although the dismissal owes much to luck, the Kent skipper deserves credit for having the courage to give the occasional off-spinner a spell just before the break.

Tea:- Surrey 187-4 (Brown 46*, A.J. Hollioake 0*) from 73 overs

The day's final session gets off to a slow start as Saggers, again firing too many balls down the legside, and Patel, continuing a lengthy stint from the pavilion end, keep the run rate in check while rarely looking threatening. Just eleven runs, four of them byes, accrue in seven overs before Adam Hollioake breaks the spell with successive lofted off-driven boundaries off Patel, the first of which brings Surrey to two-hundred and a first batting point of the season. A single to Ali Brown in the following over then finally takes the Surrey fans' favourite to one of his slower half-centuries in 131 minutes. He has faced 121 balls and struck only four boundaries, yet it has been a valuable effort for the team and further demonstrated to any remaining doubters that he is not a one-dimensional batsman.

Although Masters, having taken over from Saggers at the Vauxhall end, and Patel continue to work diligently, the scoring rate picks up a little and by the time the fifth-wicket partnership reaches fifty, courtesy of Brown's midwicket drive off Masters, it has been achieved at three runs per over. At 234-4, Surrey are now looking to be in complete command but they are suddenly rocked back on their heels when the tall, willowy Masters strikes with a quick one-two for Kent. First he traps Brown lbw as the batsman misses a rather ambitious-looking pull stroke, then, four overs later, Ben Hollioake, having clipped the previous ball to the square leg boundary, chips the gentlest of catches to Smith at midwicket.

These two rapid blows leave the home side on 244-6 and another period of stalemate develops as Adam Hollioake and Martin Bicknell seem unable to raise the tempo. It's clear that an unusual situation is developing out in the middle, however, as the umpires hold a lengthy discussion which seems to involve both batsmen and the Kent captain, with the ball the centre of attention. It all seems rather strange since a new 'cherry' is soon to become available anyway. Has the ball been tampered with in some way, perhaps? Spectators are left none the wiser, though, as the new ball is not taken and a further conference subsequently follows out on the square. Eventually, Fleming, apparently with some reluctance, gives up the old ball and the day ends much as it began with Ealham finding both the inside and outside edges of the bat - this time Adam Hollioake's - without gaining any reward.

Close:- Surrey 278-6 (A.J. Hollioake 46*, Bicknell 10*) from 107 overs

VIEW FROM THE DRESSING ROOM - MARTIN BICKNELL

There was an unusual incident towards the end of the day. The umpires insisted on a change of ball because it had gone unreasonably soft when we were batting, I believe?

MB - Yes, we had a lot of problems during the season with balls going soft and out of shape very quickly. On this occasion the ball had become like a hacky-sack and you could hardly hit it off the square. Kent used it to their advantage - they didn't have the attack to bowl us out so they wanted to keep bowling with it in an attempt to 'strangle' us. Eventually we asked the umpires to intervene and sort it out.

Third Day - Saturday 13th May

Surrey 417; Kent 115-2

Adam Hollioake completes his half-century in the second over of the day, steering a Mark Ealham delivery to third man to reach the milestone in 135 minutes from 113 balls. Sadly for Surrey, Hollioake's innings goes no further, though, as Ealham bowls him through a crooked-looking stroke with a delivery which nips back a little from just outside off stump.

With the score now 288-7, Kent are probably feeling that they are back on level terms in the match but the Surrey lower-order proves hard to dislodge. Bicknell and Salisbury bat with typical good sense, utilising all their experience in seeing off the opening spells of Ealham and Masters on the way to a fifty-run partnership inside thirteen overs.

The first-change bowlers, Min Patel and Martin Saggers, look no more likely to separate the eighth-wicket pair, however, with Bicknell being especially severe on the left-arm spinner, driving him to the cover fence and then lofting him twice over mid-off for further boundaries en route to an excellent 108-ball fifty. Although he maintains a better line than on day two, Saggers looks far from dangerous and, with Patel conceding five fours in an unimpressive six-over spell, Matthew

Fleming takes the ball himself at the Vauxhall end and tries Dravid again at the pavilion end. These changes fail to produce an instant result for Kent, though, with Salisbury's dab to third man bringing up the hundred partnership and Bicknell then picking Fleming up over square leg for another boundary and lofting him over mid-off for three to take Surrey past 400.

Dravid's newly-discovered 'golden arm' does provide his team with the breakthrough in the following over, however, as Bicknell's fine innings of seventy-three ends with a skimming drive to deep mid-off which is well held by Masters down by his ankles. The eighth-wicket partnership is therefore terminated after adding a very valuable 113 runs, with Salisbury's share of the stand being forty-four.

In the remaining four overs up to the lunch break the Surrey leg-spinner advances to his half-century, having taken only 117 minutes and 73 balls to reach the mark.

Lunch:- Surrey 409-8 (Salisbury 50*, Tudor 2*) from 141 overs

The Surrey innings is terminated in eleven deliveries after the restart. Ian Salisbury's fine knock ends with the first ball of the final session when he is adjudged lbw to Saggers and then Rupesh Amin, seeking an impossible-looking single, is sent back by Alex Tudor and fails to beat an accurate throw to the non-striker's end. Although the final total of 417 represents a very good effort in the circumstances, the rather sluggish tempo of the innings means that only four of the maximum five batting points have been secured. Kent require a daunting 268 to avoid the follow-on but with less than five sessions of play remaining it's obvious that it will take an incredible bowling and fielding display by Surrey to force a victory.

There's a good-sized crowd in the ground as Ed Smith ensures that the visitors get off to a confident start with an impressive array of front-foot strokes that take his personal score into the twenties by the end of the tenth over. At this point, Martin Bicknell complains to the umpires about the state of the ball and, after some discussion, it is replaced. Bicknell then immediately tests the hardness of the replacement ball by banging it in short to Smith, who pulls a catch straight to a deliberately positioned deep backward square leg and departs looking extremely angry. Good thinking by the bowler? Unwise shot selection by the batsman against the first delivery with the 'new' ball? Either way, the dismissal raises a question for regular Surrey watchers which no-one can immediately answer - when was the last time 'Bickers' took a wicket with a bouncer?

The loss of this opening wicket results in a short period of stalemate as Robert Key and the new batsman, Rahul Dravid, drop anchor to see off the remainder of the opening bursts from Bicknell and Tudor. The Indian Test star is soon showing his class, however, by driving and pulling Ben Hollioake for boundaries in the twenty-first over to bring up the Kent fifty.

Before too long, spin makes an appearance in the form of Rupesh Amin at the Vauxhall end and he is quickly joined in the attack by Ian Salisbury. This bowling combination brings a wicket for the home side within two balls when Key, after a rather laboured innings of nineteen, nicks a leg-break low to slip, where Ben Hollioake hangs on to a good catch - 63-2. Spin is immediately looking a better option than seam on this particular pitch but Allan Wells, despite one or two early scares, plays very positively from the start and Dravid, displaying the type of nimble footwork that one always associates with players from the sub-continent, is soon skipping down the track to drive Salisbury to the pavilion fence. With no further wicket forthcoming before tea only a dramatic final session can now save the match from drifting towards the inevitable draw.

Tea:- Kent 92-2 (Dravid 29*, Wells 16*) from 34 overs

Sadly, only eleven overs are bowled after the resumption before rain and bad light bring an early close at 5.20pm. The batsmen are rarely troubled during this short period of play as Dravid continues his spin masterclass and the third-wicket partnership moves past fifty when Wells pulls a Salisbury long-hop to the midwicket boundary.

Close:- Kent 115-2 (Dravid 44*, Wells 22*) from 45 overs

Fourth Day - Sunday 14th May

Surrey 417 and 17-0 declared; Kent 115-2 declared and 255-8

Match Drawn - Surrey 8pts, Kent 6

Much to everyone's surprise, a dying match is brought to life on the final morning when a deal is struck between the two captains. Instead of seeing the overnight pair of Dravid and Wells resuming Kent's first innings we witness Mark Butcher and Ian Ward striding out to the middle for an extremely short Surrey second innings. It last precisely four balls as Robert Key lobs up 'junk' deliveries which Butcher crashes for 4-6-6-1. Adam Hollioake then declares to set Kent a target of 320 from a minimum of ninety-three overs and the consensus of opinion in the pavilion is that Surrey have got much the better of the deal.

The punters' view is then strengthened almost immediately as Ed Smith steers a low catch to Ali Brown, the finer of two gullies, in Alex Tudor's second over and departs for five with the score on just seven. This brings Dravid to the crease against the new ball - exactly what Surrey would have wanted, given the Indian's mastery of spin bowling. He starts pretty well against the pace of Tudor, nevertheless, clipping his second ball through square leg for four as he carries on from where he had left off on day three.

At this point there is a fairly lengthy delay in play as umpire Harris retires from the fray due to illness, with the two coaches appearing to agree to share square leg umpiring duties for the rest of the day. Keith Medlycott opts for the first shift and, therefore, has a close view of Dravid continuing his confident start by glancing Bicknell and on-driving Tudor for further boundaries. In this form it seems possible that he could give Kent a sniff of victory if he can bat for enough overs but, luckily for the hosts, his position is soon made much more difficult by the loss of three wickets at the other end in the space of just six overs. With both Surrey opening bowlers producing fine spells, Key edges a Bicknell outswinger to Alec Stewart in the eleventh over (31-2), Wells gets a touch to a fine, lifting Tudor delivery three overs later (40-3) and Hockley is beaten on the crease by a ball from Bicknell which nips back to trap him lbw (45-4) in the seventeenth over. Surrey now hold a clear advantage, despite the continued presence of Dravid, and one would imagine that Matthew Fleming must be regretting his decision to keep the game alive.

Lunch arrives with Kent struggling desperately and the reigning county champions, seeking six further wickets in a minimum of seventy overs, starting to fancy their chances of recording their opening win of the 2000 campaign.

Lunch:- Kent 63-4 (Dravid 37*, Ealham 10*) from 23 overs

As the afternoon session gets under way it's clear that a couple of early wickets would make a Surrey victory almost a formality but, despite the best efforts of Martin Bicknell and Ian Salisbury, the Kent fifth-wicket pair resists stoutly. Ealham is consistently troubled by the Surrey leg-spinner, who beats the bat on numerous occasions without managing to find the edge, while Dravid continues to look a class act, eventually moving through to a 137-minute half-century with an off-driven boundary from Alex Tudor as soon as the big fast bowler replaces Bicknell at the pavilion end. Although Ealham's gutsy effort keeps Kent afloat, his innings continues to be something of a patchy affair as he mixes fortuitous edges with nicely-middled strokes, the best of which is a pulled six over midwicket from a Salisbury long-hop.

Shortly after the midpoint of the session, with Tudor's four-over blast having yielded no breakthrough, the spinners are back in tandem. Amin gives nothing away in a steady spell while Salisbury continues to look the man most likely to split the Kent pair, again finding Ealham's edge only for the ball to elude the grasping hands of Brown at slip. Meanwhile, Dravid, though more circumspect against the spinners, looks head and shoulders above his team-mates in everything he does and finally breaks loose, driving successive deliveries from the leg-spinner wide of mid-on and then mid-off as the hundred partnership clicks up and Surrey's hopes of victory start to fade.

It seems that the home side will go through the whole afternoon wicketless, in fact, when the Surrey skipper suddenly opts to give Martin Bicknell the final over of the session from the Vauxhall end as part of a plan to switch Salisbury to the pavilion end. His decision proves inspired as the tall swing bowler's fifth delivery induces Dravid to play his first real false stroke of the match. To everyone's immense surprise it's the Bicknell bumper which yields fruit for the second time in two days as the Indian Test star appears to get caught in two minds and consequently miscues the ball high in the air towards cover, where Adam Hollioake takes a straightforward catch. As Dravid departs for a beautifully-crafted seventy-one it appears that we might, after all, have an interesting finale to the match.

Tea:- Kent 147-5 (Ealham 48*, Nixon 0*) from 57 overs

The final session gets off to an uneventful start with almost six overs completed before Mark Ealham moves from his tea score to a very valuable fifty by cutting Salisbury to the cover point boundary. His determined innings has spanned almost three hours and gone some way towards rescuing his side from a potentially embarrassing defeat.

Although to onlookers there seems to be no real prospect of a Kent victory, Ealham still appears hopeful as he suddenly launches into a three-over assault which yields twenty-four runs. This brief blitz includes nine runs from an over in which Bicknell drops too short, a off-driven six into the pavilion off Salisbury and two successive boundaries in the first over of a new spell by Rupesh Amin. As Kent hopes rise slightly, Paul Nixon manages to maintain this increased tempo by driving the left-arm spinner to the long-off boundary to complete a brisk fifty partnership but the balance of the game then tips back towards Surrey when the first ball of the following over from Salisbury brings the crucial wicket of Ealham. Having had the better of a good battle with the England all-rounder, it's not totally unexpected when a well flighted googly sneaks through the gate as Ealham assays another flamboyant drive. With the mainstay of their innings now departed for eighty-three and the score standing at 199-6 it appears that Kent's slim victory chance has now gone.

Sure enough, the next five overs produce just two runs before, in the final two overs before the game enters its last hour, Amin is despatched for three fours and Salisbury is pulled for six by Nixon. At this stage it's hard to tell whether or not Kent still harbour a genuine belief in their ability to reach the 320 target but when Matthew Fleming falls in the next over everyone quickly realises that the limit of their ambition is now a draw. It's another winning bowling change by Adam Hollioake which ends the visitors' dream as Alex Tudor, replacing Amin at the Vauxhall end, induces a checked drive from the Kent skipper which provides mid-off with a simple catch.

With fifteen overs remaining, Surrey now have a strong scent of victory but no further wicket is immediately forthcoming. Despite the fact that a Kent win is now out of the question, Nixon and Patel attempt, probably quite sensibly, to play as naturally as possible, the former even managing to launch Salisbury for six over long-on during an over in which he is also beaten three times. Hollioake wisely continues to rotate his three most penetrative bowlers and eventually, in the ninth of the last sixteen overs, Salisbury comes up with the wicket his side needs so badly by trapping Patel on the crease with a googly.

Forty-six balls remain in which to claim the final two wickets but, even with fielders clustered around the bat, the slow pitch always looks likely to frustrate Surrey. Salisbury continues to wheel away from the Vauxhall end while Tudor replaces Bicknell for the last two overs from the pavilion end but the young Masters and the highly competitive Nixon hang on with great determination, the Kent wicket-keeper completing his half-century with a square-driven boundary in the penultimate over bowled by Salisbury. Finally, it boils down to Tudor versus Masters for the final over - surely Surrey's ideal scenario - but, despite the big fast bowler's best efforts, the visitors' young seamer survives to claim four draw points for his side.

Surrey 417 and 17-0 dec; Kent 115-2 dec and 255-8
Match Drawn. Surrey 8pts, Kent 6

SURREY v KENT at THE OVAL. Played from 11th - 14th May

Kent won the toss   Umpires:- M.J. Harris & A.A. Jones

SURREY - First Innings   **KENT bowling**

Fall of wkt	Batsman		How Out	Score	Balls	4s	6s		O	M	R	W
2- 101	M.A. Butcher	c Patel	b Fleming	47	121	6	0	Ealham	25	5	76	1
1- 78	I.J. Ward	c Smith	b Masters	38	107	3	0	Saggers	23	6	66	2
3- 105	G.P. Thorpe		lbw b Saggers	11	25	2	0	Masters	28	8	75	3
4- 181	A.J. Stewart +	c Nixon	b Dravid	36	86	5	0	Fleming	23	8	59	1
5- 234	A.D. Brown		lbw b Masters	60	139	6	0	Patel	36	7	98	0
7- 288	A.J. Hollioake *		b Ealham	51	117	7	0	Dravid	7.5	3	16	2
6- 244	B.C. Hollioake	c Smith	b Masters	6	11	1	0					
8- 401	M.P. Bicknell	c Masters	b Dravid	73	149	8	0					
9- 409	I.D.K. Salisbury		lbw b Saggers	50	74	5	0					
	A.J. Tudor		Not Out	7	25	1	0					
10- 417	R.M. Amin		run out	3	3	0	0					
	Extras (10b, 17lb, 8w)			35								
	TOTAL		(142.5 overs)	417								

KENT - First Innings   **SURREY bowling**

Fall of wkt	Batsman		How Out	Score	Balls	4s	6s		O	M	R	W
1- 34	E.T. Smith	c Salisbury	b Bicknell	24	35	2	0	Bicknell	9	3	19	1
2- 63	R.W.T. Key	c B.C. Hollioake	b Salisbury	19	76	3	0	Tudor	8	4	18	0
	R. Dravid		Not Out	44	102	6	0	B.C. Hollioake	6	2	14	0
	A.P. Wells		Not Out	22	59	3	0	A.J. Hollioake	3	2	4	0
								Amin	9	2	27	0
	Extras (2w, 4nb)			6				Salisbury	10	3	33	1
	TOTAL		(45 overs)	115 - 2 dec								

SURREY - Second Innings   **KENT bowling**

Fall of wkt	Batsman		How Out	Score	Balls	4s	6s		O	M	R	W
	M.A. Butcher		Not Out	17	4	1	2	Key	0.4	0	17	0
	I.J. Ward		Not Out	0	0	0	0					
	TOTAL		(0.4 overs)	17 - 0 dec								

KENT - Second Innings   **SURREY bowling**

Fall of wkt	Batsman		How Out	Score	Balls	4s	6s		O	M	R	W
1- 7	E.T. Smith	c Brown	b Tudor	5	7	1	0	Bicknell	25	7	53	3
2- 31	R.W.T. Key	c Stewart	b Bicknell	7	33	0	0	Tudor	18.5	2	67	3
5- 147	R. Dravid	c A.J. Hollioake	b Bicknell	71	137	6	0	B.C. Hollioake	2	0	9	0
3- 40	A.P. Wells	c Stewart	b Tudor	0	11	0	0	Salisbury	35	10	81	0
4- 45	J.B. Hockley		lbw b Bicknell	2	7	0	0	Amin	12	2	40	0
6- 199	M.A. Ealham		b Salisbury	83	194	8	2					
	P.A. Nixon +		Not Out	50	104	6	2					
7- 224	M.V. Fleming *	c Amin	b Tudor	7	23	1	0					
8- 244	M.M. Patel		lbw b Salisbury	7	24	1	0					
	D.D. Masters		Not Out	0	24	0	0					
	M.J. Saggers	did not bat										
	Extras (5lb, 4w, 14nb)			23								
	TOTAL		(92.5 overs)	255 - 8								

VIEW FROM THE DRESSING ROOM - MARTIN BICKNELL

The final day collusion between the captains came as a surprise to the spectators, since this was still early days in the season. Were you expecting this deal to be done?
MB - I have to say that I was a bit surprised because I felt we were gambling quite a lot to try and force a win on what was a very flat pitch. I would have been happy for us to add some bowling points to the four draw points and those we had gained for batting.

I did feel that the captains' deal of 320 runs in 93 overs was loaded in our favour, though - would you agree with that?
MB - Yes, I think their only real chance was if Rahul Dravid had scored 150 - but he's the sort of player who could have been capable of doing that.

I was certainly very impressed with Dravid every time I saw him play during the 2000 season. It sounds like you rate him highly, too.
MB - Very much so. I think he's one of the best players I've ever bowled to - he had so much time and ability that he made the game look ridiculously easy. And technically he's as good as anyone I've seen.

How confident were we of victory when they slipped to 45-4?
MB - It was the kind of situation where if Saqi had been in the side then I think we would have won. Without him, we were just a little bit short.

There was something of a collector's item in this game in that you picked up TWO wickets with bouncers - Smith in the first innings and Dravid in the second - the first of which looked very clearly planned. What was the thinking behind these two wickets and were you as surprised as we were in the pavilion?!
MB - Nothing was happening and the pitch was pretty dead, so sometimes you have to try something a bit different to see if the batsman is concentrating. The Smith dismissal was certainly planned but in Dravid's case it was just a short ball that he pulled up in the air, so I won't claim any credit for that one!

Paul Nixon proved impossible to dislodge and, not for the first time, was a real thorn in our side as Kent secured the draw. What makes him such a tough competitor and do you think he has deserved his England call-up for the winter?
MB - He a gutsy player who doesn't give his wicket away and he has plenty of technical ability. I've always rated him as the second best wicketkeeper-batsman in the country, behind Alec, so I definitely think his selection was justified - he was unlucky not to have gone on the previous winter's tour to South Africa, in my book.

With hindsight, did we regret sacrificing the possibility of obtaining three bowling points or had it been a worthwhile exercise to get some really competitive action under our belts at this stage of the season?
MB - I think we would have played just as competitively if we'd only been playing for the bowling points, as opposed to chasing a win. It was disappointing to come out of this game with very little to show for our efforts and it put us even further behind the early leaders.

We had now completed three matches and had picked up just seventeen points - how concerned were we about this stuttering, rain-blighted start to our Championship defence?
MB - It's true that some teams had got well ahead of us but there were still so many games to go

that we weren't overly concerned. Since we were now going to be playing every team twice we knew there would be plenty of chances for us to catch up.

KEITH MEDLYCOTT'S ASSESSMENT

We batted extremely well, while Kent were very defensive in the field, as they tended to be throughout the season. If the game had not been ruined by the rain then I think we could have got into a position to win it - we certainly weren't going to lose once we got four-hundred on the board.

Other Division One Matches

Surrey's disappointing start to the Championship campaign was compounded by the fact that their three expected challengers for the title all recorded victories in this round of matches. While Yorkshire made it two wins out of two by humbling Hampshire, and Lancashire, after a few scares, came through to easily defeat Durham, Leicestershire's victory over Somerset looked to be the most impressive of the three results. Although the season had only just begun it was, nevertheless, a little worrying that these three rivals had started so strongly.

May 11-13
Chester-le-Street:- **Lancashire beat Durham by 141 runs.** Lancashire 263 (Ganguly 73, Schofield 50, Harmison 4-74) and 134 (Brown 7-51); Durham 164 (Chapple 6-42) and 92 (Smethurst 7-50). **Lancashire 17pts, Durham 3**

May 11-14
Leicester:- **Leicestershire beat Somerset by six wickets.** Somerset 262 (Trescothick 105, Blackwell 58) and 246 (Kumble 5-61); Leicestershire 387 (Habib 172 not out, Dakin 135, Rose 5-74, Grove 5-90) and 124-4. **Leicestershire 19pts, Somerset 4**

May 12-14
Headingley:- **Yorkshire beat Hampshire by an innings and 100 runs.** Hampshire 101 (Gough 4-23) and 198 (Kendall 78 not out); Yorkshire 399 (Hamilton 125, Lehmann 85). **Yorkshire 19pts, Hampshire 3**

COUNTY CHAMPIONSHIP DIVISION ONE AT 14TH MAY

Pos	Prev		P	Pts	W	D	L	Bat	Bowl	Last Three		Res
1	2	Lancashire	3	41	2	1	0	7	6	W17	W20	D4
2	3	Yorkshire	2	39	2	0	0	9	6	W19	W20	N/A
3	5	Leicestershire	3	32	1	1	1	9	7	W19	L4	D9
=	1	Somerset	3	32	1	1	1	8	8	L4	W18	D10
5	4	Durham	2	19	1	0	1	1	6	L3	W16	N/A
6	7	Surrey	3	17	0	2	1	4	5	D8	L3	D6
7	8	Kent	2	13	0	2	0	0	5	D6	D7	N/A
8	6	Derbyshire	2	12	0	1	1	4	4	L2	D10	N/A
9	9	Hampshire	2	7	0	0	2	1	6	L3	L4	N/A

46

THE SURREY-YORKSHIRE DIVIDE GROWS

Surrey sat out the next round of Championship matches, which consisted of just two games - Derbyshire v Yorkshire and Leicestershire v Hampshire. The weather interfered with both matches and draws resulted, though Yorkshire's ten-point haul from a rather unconvincing display at Derby was sufficient to take them to the top of the table ahead of Lancashire. After three matches Surrey were already thirty-two points off the pace in seventh place and a win in the forthcoming return match against Kent, currently propping up the table, albeit with a game in hand, was looking more important than ever.

May 17-20
Derby:- **Derbyshire drew with Yorkshire.** Derbyshire 303 and 209-1 (Stubbings 84 not out, Di Venuto 81 not out); Yorkshire 349 (Lehmann 133, Craven 58, Cassar 6-76). **Derbyshire 10pts, Yorkshire 10**

Leicester:- **Leicestershire drew with Hampshire.** Hampshire 229 (Aymes 74 not out) and 123-8 (DeFreitas 4-41); Leicestershire 289 (Burns 67 not out, Habib 66, Warne 5-86). **Leicestershire 9pts, Hampshire 8**

COUNTY CHAMPIONSHIP DIVISION ONE AT 20TH MAY

Pos	Prev		P	Pts	W	D	L	Bat	Bowl	Last	Three	Res
1	2	Yorkshire	3	49	2	1	0	12	9	D10	*W19*	*W20*
2	1	Lancashire	3	41	2	1	0	7	6	*W17*	*W20*	D4
3	3	Leicestershire	4	41	1	2	1	11	10	D9	*W19*	L4
4	3	Somerset	3	32	1	1	1	8	8	L4	*W18*	D10
5	8	Derbyshire	3	22	0	2	1	7	7	D10	L2	D10
6	5	Durham	2	19	1	0	1	1	6	L3	*W16*	N/A
7	6	Surrey	3	17	0	2	1	4	5	D8	L3	D6
8	9	Hampshire	3	15	0	1	2	2	9	D8	L3	L4
9	7	Kent	2	13	0	2	0	0	5	D6	D7	N/A

NCL DIVISION TWO - MATCH THREE

SURREY LIONS versus MIDDLESEX CRUSADERS
at The Oval on Sunday 21st May

Match Abandoned

Surrey lost their chance to maintain their one-hundred percent National Cricket League record when the keenly-anticipated London derby against Middlesex was abandoned without a ball being bowled. In truth there was never any hope of play at a saturated Oval and the game was called off well before the scheduled starting time.

Surrey Lions 2pts, Middlesex Crusaders 2

Other NCL Division Two Matches

With the Nottinghamshire Outlaws and the Warwickshire Bears both unaffected by rain and able to complete comfortable victories, Surrey dropped to third place in the NCL Division Two table.

May 21
Chester-le-Street:- **Glamorgan Dragons beat Durham Dynamos by 15 runs (Duckworth-Lewis method).** Durham 91-3 in 28 overs; Glamorgan 70-2 in 18 overs. **Glamorgan Dragons 4pts**

Trent Bridge:- **Nottinghamshire Outlaws beat Derbyshire Scorpions by four wickets.** Derbyshire 186 in 44.3 overs (Stubbings 59, Lucas 3-55); Nottinghamshire 189-6 in 41.2 overs (Morris 54, Bicknell 51, Smith 3-45). **Nottinghamshire Outlaws 4pts**

Edgbaston:- **Warwickshire Bears beat Hampshire Hawks by five wickets.** Hampshire 154 in 44.4 overs (Laney 69); Warwickshire 158-5 in 39.3 overs (Brown 45 not out). **Warwickshire Bears 4pts**

NCL DIVISION TWO AT 21ST MAY

Pos	Prev		P	Pts	W	T	L	N/R	Last	Three	Res
1	1	Nottinghamshire Outlaws	3	12	3	0	0	0	W	W	W
=	1	Warwickshire Bears	3	12	3	0	0	0	W	W	W
3	1	Surrey Lions	3	10	2	0	0	1	N/R	W	W
4	4	Middlesex Crusaders	4	10	2	0	1	1	N/R	W	W
5	5	Essex Eagles	2	4	1	0	1	0	L	W	N/A
6	7	Glamorgan Dragons	3	4	1	0	2	0	W	L	L
7	6	Derbyshire Scorpions	2	0	0	0	2	0	L	L	N/A
8	7	Durham Dynamos	3	0	0	0	3	0	L	L	L
=	7	Hampshire Hawks	3	0	0	0	3	0	L	L	L

SURREY AND KENT TO TRY AGAIN AT CANTERBURY

The second of the back-to-back Championship encounters with Kent was brought forward one day to Tuesday 23rd May because of Surrey's participation in the Benson And Hedges Cup semi-final against Glamorgan at Cardiff on the following Saturday. Unfortunately, this rearrangement still left Keith Medlycott's men with a potentially arduous trip from the south-east of England to south Wales on the Friday evening - hardly ideal preparation for a showpiece semi-final. The perfect solution in the ideal world would, of course, be for Surrey to win the Championship game at Canterbury in two or three days to allow themselves a little breathing space before taking on Glamorgan. That was always a very unlikely scenario, however. Not only were Kent very unlikely to just roll over and die, as demonstrated in the match at The Oval, but the weather around the country remained very unsettled. The long-term forecast was so bad, in fact, that there seemed little prospect of a rain-free match, let alone an early finish, at the St. Lawrence ground.

COUNTY CHAMPIONSHIP - MATCH FOUR

KENT versus SURREY
at The St. Lawrence Ground, Canterbury

First Day - Tuesday 23rd May

Surrey 135-2

The Teams And The Toss - *Both counties show changes from the first encounter just two weeks previously. Surrey replace Alec Stewart (rested by England) with Jon Batty and opt for an additional seam bowler, Carl Greenidge, instead of Rupesh Amin, while Kent drop Ed Smith, James Hockley and Martin Saggers in favour of David Fulton, Matthew Walker and Kristian Adams. Adams, a left-arm pace bowler, is making his first-class debut as a result of Kent's seam bowling injury crisis and a good performance in the National League against Leicestershire at Grace Road. Adam Hollioake wins the toss for Surrey and chooses to bat on an overcast morning.*

    Kent open up with Mark Ealham and Kristian Adams in conditions which look likely to prove testing for the Surrey openers but there are few early alarms apart from the sight of one ball keeping very low in Adams' third over. Although Ealham is guilty of straying too often to leg, it is his inexperienced new-ball partner who is on the receiving end of the harshest punishment, being struck three times to the off-side rope in his first spell.
    After five overs apiece, with little sign of an initial breakthrough, the opening bowlers give way to Masters and Fleming, who offer their side a little more encouragement by inducing one or two false strokes from both batsmen. The ball fails to go to hand for the home side, however, and with the ground fielding also proving less than reliable the Surrey fifty eventually comes up during an expensive over from Masters. This prompts the Kent captain to recall Ealham at the Nackington Road end and, after a shaky start to the first over of his new spell when Butcher twice drives him through the covers, the move pays dividends as the former England left-hander gets a faint outside edge to a ball angled across him. Butcher is out for 32 and Surrey are 66 for 1.
    With one successful bowling change already under his belt, Matthew Fleming then hits the jackpot again when he brings Kristian Adams back at the pavilion end five overs later. Having survived a confident lbw appeal in the final over of Fleming's stint two overs previously, Graham Thorpe is less fortunate when Adams goes up for a catch behind the wicket from the fifth ball of his new spell. Umpire Clarkson's finger rises, Thorpe looks very disappointed as he drags himself from the crease and Surrey have lost two wickets in adding just three runs.
    Although the visitors get through to lunch without further loss, there is one more scare along the way when Ward hooks at Ealham and the ball loops to first slip. Kent appeal, Ward stays put and umpire Steele agrees with the batsman's view that the ball has ricocheted into the air off his helmet and nothing else.

Lunch:- Surrey 81-2 (Ward 39*, B.C. Hollioake 5*) from 32 overs

    Both batsmen make a confident start to the afternoon session, Ward pulling Ealham to the midwicket boundary with the help of yet another Kent misfield and Ben Hollioake cutting Masters to the rope backward of point. Within fours overs of the restart Surrey's dependable left-handed opener is through to a 155-minute, 112-ball half-century as he drives Masters wide of mid-on for the seventh four of his innings and the visitors' hundred follows soon afterwards when he notches his eighth boundary with a leg glance off Ealham.

Both players are looking in good touch at this stage and the introduction of spin, in the shape of Min Patel at the pavilion end, does nothing to stem an increasing flow of runs as Hollioake advances and drives him delightfully through extra cover for another four. Surrey are very much on top now as the third-wicket partnership passes fifty and this is underlined when their former England all-rounder takes ten runs from the first over of a new Fleming spell from the Nackington Road end.

Salvation is at hand for Kent, though, as just one further over from Patel is possible before a heavy downpour hits the ground at 2.55pm. Umpires, players and spectators scurry for cover and, frustratingly for everyone, no further play proves possible.

Tea and Close:- Surrey 135-2 (Ward 73*, B.C. Hollioake 24*) from 47.1 overs

Second Day - Wednesday 24th May

Surrey 283-7

There's a dramatic start to day two when Ben Hollioake edges the first ball of the morning from Matthew Fleming to Robert Key at first slip. It's a very acceptable chance, low to the fielder's right hand side, but the Kent opener fails to hang on and Hollioake escapes. The home captain doesn't have long to wait before he does snare his man, however, as the Surrey all-rounder fences at a lifting delivery in his next over and directs the ball to second slip where Rahul Dravid makes no mistake.

With the ball swinging for both Fleming and Mark Ealham the early overs of the day prove quite testing but Ian Ward, though scoring from only one delivery in the day's first nine overs, continues to bat in characteristically composed fashion. At the other end, Ali Brown looks less secure but keeps the scoreboard ticking over and soon starts to strike the ball nicely, taking nine runs from Ealham's sixth over of the morning. This minor assault brings about a change of bowling, however, and the new man from the pavilion end, David Masters, brings Brown's innings to a rather disappointing end in his second over. Having miscued the previous delivery over mid-off and seen the ball fall just out of the fielder's reach as he chased back, Brown middles a pull shot straight to Patel at midwicket and departs for twenty-eight.

This wicket visibly lifts Kent's spirits and the new batsman, Adam Hollioake, gives them further encouragement by making a rather sticky start. Min Patel is soon operating from the pavilion end, replacing Masters after a spell of just three overs, and hard though Hollioake tries to dominate the left-arm spinner he fails to time the ball or find the gaps in the field. Ward meanwhile continues serenely on his way, moving comfortably into the nineties as Adams fails to make any impression in his opening spell and gives way to Masters at the Nackington Road end.

The new bowler's contest with Hollioake turns out to be a good one, with a brace of well-timed boundaries by the batsman being counter-balanced by two moments of good fortune. Hollioake's first stroke of luck sees Key at first slip putting down an almost identical catch to the one he missed at the start of the day and he then has another escape when a mis-hit pull stroke sends the ball spiralling into a large gap in the field backward of square leg. As Surrey pass two-hundred and Ward moves closer to a century with an all-run four from a forcing stroke through the covers, Fleming calls up 'golden arm' Dravid... and once again he produces a breakthrough for his captain. It's almost a complete replica of Alec Stewart's dismissal in the game at The Oval, too, as the Surrey captain gets a faint touch to a legside delivery and Nixon completes the 'strangle'. The players promptly leave the field for lunch with Ian Ward, as at Derby in 1999 when he made his maiden first-class century, left to stew on ninety-eight not out.

Lunch:- Surrey 211-5 (Ward 98*) from 79.4 overs

Luckily, Ward doesn't have to wait long to reach three figures after the resumption as a cut at Patel in the second over results in a thick edge to the third man boundary. Although there is a hint of good fortune about the stroke that takes him to his second first-class century, it is well deserved since he has batted in a most controlled manner throughout a five-and-a-half hour innings, spanning 243 balls, which has included a dozen fours. Ward's effort has been all the more creditable for the fact that no other member of his team has looked as comfortable or been able to go on after making a start.

His post-tea partner, Jon Batty, is no exception to this rule, looking confident while scoring ten runs inside five overs before falling lbw to a good inswinger from the left-arm rookie, Adams. The visitors' innings has now declined somewhat to 225-6 but, with considerable batting talent in the lower-order and Ward still in occupation, Surrey's hopes of raising a good total and securing further batting points remain very much alive.

Martin Bicknell does indeed keep his colleague good company and the total rises above 250 by dint of sensible accumulation of runs as the best efforts of Min Patel and Matthew Fleming are repelled. With the second new ball drawing ever closer, Masters replaces Fleming at the Nackington Road end and Dravid is once again tried for an over, this time without success.

To be fair to the Kent bowlers they do at least maintain decent control even though they don't look especially dangerous and it's a telling statistic that the fifty partnership between Ward and Bicknell, which arrives during the second over with the new ball, takes almost eighteen overs and contains just three fours. The stand ends, however, later in the same over when Bicknell edges a fine lifter from Masters to Nixon behind the wicket and departs for a typically well-played twenty-seven. As the new batsman, Ian Salisbury, arrives at the crease there is, unfortunately, increasingly heavy drizzle in the air and it isn't long before everyone is leaving the field for an early tea.

Sadly, conditions don't improve - in fact, they deteriorate - and, having lost fifty-seven overs on day one, we lose a further forty-eight today. It seems impossible to get through a day's play without rain interference at this stage of the season and any hopes Surrey harboured of getting to Cardiff early for the Benson And Hedges Cup semi-final have already been washed away.

This is clearly something of a disappointment but as I trudge back to my accommodation in driving rain I am even more concerned about the fact that another potentially winnable match against a below-strength Kent side is heading for a damp draw.

Tea and Close:- Surrey 283-7 (Ward 127*, I.D.K. Salisbury 4*) from 103 overs

Third Day - Thursday 25th May

Surrey 283-7 (No Play - Rain)

Further overnight rain has left the ground absolutely saturated and as I walk around the edge of the outfield taking some photos every step creates an audible splash. Even though it is only 10.30 in the morning I can't see any hope of play today - and this turns out to be the verdict of the umpires, too, when they carry out their inspection. It is all very depressing for the players and supporters of both counties and the fear is beginning to grow that Surrey's Championship defence could be undermined by these frustrating losses of playing time. Apart from the obvious irritation of missing out on the chance to win matches and gain points, it is also worrying that the players are being left desperately short of time out in the middle as the season nears the end of its sixth week. How damaging could this prove to be when the chips are down in forthcoming matches, I wonder?

Fourth Day - Friday 26th May

Surrey 348-8

Match Drawn - Surrey 7pts, Kent 6

Any slim chance of the two captains agreeing to set up a run chase is ruled out when an early inspection of the ground makes it obvious that the start of play is going to be delayed. The weather forecast is also very poor for later in the day so the few hardy souls who have turned up know immediately that another battle for the odd bonus point is the limit of what they will witness... if, indeed, they see any cricket at all. In the hope of eking something out of the wreckage of this match, the umpires sensibly decide to take an early lunch.

With the weather remaining fine throughout the morning it would appear that some action will be possible, but the visitors must have mixed emotions about this. Naturally enough, they would like the opportunity to add to the two batting points that they have already earned, especially in view of the advantage that the leading teams in the table are already building. On the other hand, an important cup semi-final lies ahead tomorrow on the other side of Britain.

As it happens, following their post-lunch inspection the umpires decide on a 1.30pm start, with a minimum of sixty-seven overs to be bowled if the weather remains fine. This certainly doesn't look likely as the players take the field, though, since cloud is once again building up all around the ground.

With the ball only three overs old, Matthew Fleming inevitably opens up with Ealham and Adams and the former soon has another wicket to his name when Ian Salisbury slices a drive to David Fulton in the gully. Kent's third bowling point looks almost a formality now, while Surrey's chances of adding further batting points have receded considerably.

Fortunately for the visitors, however, Alex Tudor immediately smashes the ball through backward point for a boundary which seems to set the tone for his innings. With the dependable Ward also taking fours off both bowlers the score rattles past three-hundred in unexpectedly quick time, aided by some more poor ground fielding. Adams soon gives way to Fleming at the Nackington Road end but this does nothing to slow the scoring rate as Ward posts his first-ever first-class 150 after 464 minutes at the crease. He has struck seventeen boundaries in a monumental 343-ball demonstration of concentration which has, in effect, spanned four days.

Although, at this point, play has only been underway for some forty minutes, dark, threatening clouds are already closing in on us, as forecast, and by the time Tudor drives Fleming handsomely through point to register the fifty partnership in just 9.1 overs everyone knows that the end of the game is nigh. Before long, rain is falling and, as it becomes increasingly heavy, both sides make a late bid to grab an extra bonus point - for Surrey, Tudor drives two more superb fours off the newly introduced Masters and Ward glances Fleming fine for another boundary, while the Kent skipper runs back to his mark throughout what turns out to be the final over in a desperate attempt to clinch the ninth wicket that will bring his side's final bowling point. Although the players appear quite happy to continue despite the rapidly deteriorating conditions, the umpires are having none of it and they lead the players from the field with both teams still just short of achieving their objectives.

A very wet and frustrating game is then put out of its misery by a heavy downpour which ensures that no further play will be possible. With the grassy areas which act as car parks around the ground quickly becoming quagmires a request is made over the P.A. system for people to move their cars before they become stuck fast in the mud. This announcement nicely sums up Surrey's wretched rain-ruined four days at Canterbury!

Surrey 348-8
Match Drawn. Surrey 7pts, Kent 6

KENT v SURREY at CANTERBURY. Played from 23rd - 26th May

Surrey won the toss   Umpires:- A. Clarkson & J.F. Steele

SURREY - First Innings

Fall of wkt	Batsman	How Out	Score	Balls	4s	6s
1- 66	M.A. Butcher	c Nixon b Ealham	32	57	4	0
	I.J. Ward	Not Out	158	365	18	0
2- 69	G.P. Thorpe	c Nixon b Adams	3	15	0	0
3- 143	B.C. Hollioake	c Dravid b Fleming	29	73	5	0
4- 176	A.D. Brown	c Patel b Masters	28	37	1	0
5- 211	A.J. Hollioake *	c Nixon b Dravid	17	55	2	0
6- 225	J.N. Batty +	lbw b Adams	10	16	1	0
7- 275	M.P. Bicknell	c Nixon b Masters	27	52	2	0
8- 284	I.D.K. Salisbury	c Fulton b Ealham	5	6	1	0
	A.J. Tudor	Not Out	33	32	5	0
	C.G. Greenidge	did not bat				
	Extras (1b, 5lb)		6			
	TOTAL	(118 overs)	348 - 8			

KENT bowling

	O	M	R	W
Ealham	29	8	91	2
Adams	22	4	58	2
Masters	23	8	74	2
Fleming	22	5	60	1
Patel	20	4	49	0
Dravid	2	0	10	1

KENT did not bat
Team:- D.P. Fulton, R.W.T. Key, R. Dravid, A.P. Wells, M.A. Ealham, M.J. Walker, + P.A. Nixon, * M.V. Fleming, M.M. Patel, D.D. Masters, K. Adams

VIEW FROM THE DRESSING ROOM - IAN WARD

Since you were always, for four days, one of the 'not out' batsmen I assume that you couldn't often totally switch off in case you had to go out and bat again. Was that a good test of your powers of concentration and therefore a good experience?
IW - It's certainly fair to say that I could never totally 'switch off' until the close of play, but it's something that you have to get used to when you play cricket, especially in this country and especially during the early part of the season.

Until Alex Tudor came in towards the end of the match, no-one seemed to find batting as easy as you did. Any ideas why this might have been?
IW - I can't say that I found batting particularly easy myself because the ball moved about a bit throughout the innings but Tudes certainly made it look pretty straightforward when he came in. He was extremely positive and perhaps, with hindsight, that was the best way to play on that wicket. He certainly got the impetus going again when we were chasing batting points towards the end.

Had the weather and the forecast been good at the start of the final day do you think that the captains might have looked to set up a run chase or was that always a non-starter?
IW - I wouldn't know what Adam and Matthew Fleming had in mind but if it had been down to me I'd have been happy to take the batting points and wait for the change to better weather. Thankfully, since the introduction of four-day cricket we have got rid of all that nonsense of joke bowling and setting targets.

After four days of almost constant rain I personally couldn't wait to get away from Canterbury - was that how the players felt too?
IW - It was a difficult situation because we had the Benson and Hedges Cup semi-final ahead of us. Once the rain had pretty much ruined the first two days a positive result was always going to be unlikely so we were keen to get away from Canterbury as soon as possible, with as many points as possible, to start preparing for the semi-final. But, yes, it was a very frustrating four days for everyone.

We had now played four games and had no wins and only twenty-four points to show for our efforts. Since Yorkshire and Lancashire had both got off to a good start, having had more joy with the weather than us, were we starting to become a little concerned about our position in the Championship table?

IW - It was very early days but you've obviously got to keep an eye on Yorkshire and the other possible title contenders. They were making the early running but that was always likely with the battery of seam bowlers they have, given the amount of movement that is available to them early in an English season. Obviously there was a bit of frustration on our part but you can only control the controllables, as they say, and there was nothing we could do about the weather or what our rivals were doing. We just had to keep trying to win games whenever we were able to get out on the field.

KEITH MEDLYCOTT'S ASSESSMENT

As in the game at The Oval we batted well - with Ian Ward outstanding here - against some tight, defensive bowling. With the rain destroying any chance of a result, we had now played four matches with barely a sniff of a victory. This was partly down to the weather, which we could do nothing about, and partly because when the weather had been fine in Durham we'd had a few bad days at the office. We knew we could pick things up, though, especially since we had all the key opponents still to play home and away. We were also confident that we would soon get on a roll and that, once we did, we would have the capability to make it last.

Other Division One Matches

Although Yorkshire were displaced at the top of the table by Leicestershire, they must have been delighted to be the only team in the division not involved in a round of matches which was very badly affected by widespread rain across the country. Surrey's meagre seven-point return from their visit to Canterbury meant that Yorkshire now held an advantage of twenty-five points with a game in hand. With a quarter of our matches now completed, the situation was starting to give some cause for concern.

May 23-26
Southampton:- **Hampshire drew with Lancashire.** Lancashire 215 (Mascarenhas 4-52); Hampshire 175-4 (Smith 61). **Hampshire 7pts, Lancashire 6**

May 24-27
Chester-le-Street:- **Durham drew with Leicestershire.** Leicestershire 336 (Dakin 89, DeFreitas 81 not out); Durham 302-8dec (Katich 137 not out, Hunter 63). **Durham 10pts, Leicestershire 9**

Taunton:- **Somerset drew with Derbyshire.** Somerset 240 (Bowler 57); Derbyshire 101-0. **Somerset 5pts, Derbyshire 7**

Pos	Prev		P	Pts	W	D	L	Bat	Bowl	Last	Three	Res
1	3	Leicestershire	5	50	1	3	1	14	12	D9	D9	W19
2	1	Yorkshire	3	49	2	1	0	12	9	D10	W19	W20
3	2	Lancashire	4	47	2	2	0	8	7	D6	W17	W20
4	4	Somerset	4	37	1	2	1	9	8	D5	L4	W18
5	6	Durham	3	29	1	1	1	4	9	D10	L3	W16
6	5	Derbyshire	4	29	0	3	1	7	10	D7	D10	L2
7	7	Surrey	4	24	0	3	1	7	5	D7	D8	L3
8	8	Hampshire	4	22	0	2	2	2	12	D7	D8	L3
9	9	Kent	3	19	0	3	0	0	7	D6	D6	D7

COUNTY CHAMPIONSHIP DIVISION ONE AT 27TH MAY

DISMAL DAYS IN CARDIFF AS SURREY CRASH OUT IN B&H SEMI

Surrey's rather disappointing start to the season continued when they missed out on a place in the Benson And Hedges Cup final following a below-par performance spread over two days at a rain-drenched Sophia Gardens.

Had this not been a cup semi-final with Sky TV cameras present, it's fair to assume that there would have been no action on day one but, given the circumstances, play was able to get under way at 4pm after heroic efforts by the ground staff.

Glamorgan, having elected to bat after winning the toss, got off on the wrong foot in their bid to reach their first Lord's final since 1977, losing both openers within the first nine overs, before the match's decisive stand between Michael Powell and Matthew Maynard steadied the ship. With too many deliveries straying to leg and both Alex Tudor (three fours to Powell) and Ben Hollioake (fifteen runs, including a magnificent straight six by Maynard) yielding expensive overs, the home side soon gained the upper hand. Despite Martin Bicknell's excellent spell of 8-0-21-1, the Welsh county reached 99-2 from 24.1 overs before bad light and then rain ended the first day's play a little prematurely. It looked like the advantage was with Glamorgan, especially as the pitch appeared better suited to bowling than batting.

The match resumed on the reserve day at 11.30am after more overnight rain had necessitated another mopping-up operation and, after briefly playing themselves in again, both overnight batsmen continued to take advantage of some ragged and ill-disciplined bowling. With the exception of the under-used Jason Ratcliffe, all the Surrey bowlers were guilty of failing to maintain a consistent line as Powell and Maynard took their stand to 133 before the junior partner played a well-disguised slower ball from Tudor (2-46) onto his stumps. Maynard was not to be deflected from his task by the loss of his partner, however, and, helped on his way by a dreadful legside over from Ben Hollioake, raced to a fine century from just 109 balls. Although the Glamorgan skipper holed out to long-on soon after reaching this landmark and the tail then surrendered with startling rapidity to some intelligent bowling from Adam Hollioake, a final total of 251 looked rather daunting in the circumstances. If Surrey were to fail in their task then the finger would have to be pointed at a poor display with the ball and, with the exception of some late run outs, an indifferent fielding display.

A solid start and a lengthy knock from Ali Brown were clearly going to be vital ingredients for a successful run chase but, unfortunately, neither was forthcoming as Surrey's master blaster was dismissed in the third over, well held low down at short midwicket, and Alex Tudor, promoted to number three, fell lbw to the next delivery. Tudor's elevation was a mystery to all bar those of us who had witnessed his outstanding run-a-ball innings at Canterbury just two days previously. It was something of a gamble, nevertheless, and, having failed, it gave Glamorgan a huge lift to see a scoreboard reading 11-2.

Responding well to these early setbacks, Mark Butcher and Alec Stewart partially pulled things around, the latter driving a straight six in Owen Parkin's loose sixth over, but the third wicket then fell in rather controversial circumstances with the score at 65. Having dragged his back foot forward as Robert Croft beat him outside the off stump, Butcher (32) was adjudged out by the television replay umpire, whose comment on Sky TV as he lit the fatal red light suggested that he wasn't one-hundred percent certain about the decision.

Although Graham Thorpe helped Stewart take the total past 100 without further loss, neither batsman was really able to take control against some very good straight bowling by Croft and Dale and, as the required run rate climbed, Alex Wharf produced a deadly second spell which brought the wickets of Thorpe (21) and both Hollioakes in the space of five overs. When Croft then removed the in-form Ian Ward - wasted at number eight in the order - in the very next over, Surrey's hopes were in tatters at 125-7.

Two rain interruptions in quick succession then led to a Duckworth-Lewis revised target of 245 in 46 overs and when the batsmen came out again they blasted the ball to all parts of the ground. Jason Ratcliffe played a valiant hand in scoring twenty-four from eighteen balls before perishing to a fine overhead catch on the long-on boundary and then Martin Bicknell upped the tempo still further, scoring sixteen out of the seventeen runs taken from Owen Parkin's comeback over.

This burst had given the visitors a faint glimmer of hope but in Parkin's next over Steve James plucked a skimming drive out of the air to remove Bicknell with 44 runs needed from 23 balls and the writing was on the wall again. Stewart bravely lofted his next two deliveries for four and six to maintain Surrey's late charge but then found that man James again, this time at wide mid-on, as Glamorgan sealed their place in the final. While justifiably joyous celebrations broke out amongst the Welsh county's players and supporters, everybody with Surrey loyalties was left to reflect on a very wet and miserable couple of weeks.

SCOREBOARD - BENSON AND HEDGES CUP SEMI-FINAL

Glamorgan 251 from 49.1 overs (M.P. Maynard 109, M.J. Powell 67, A.J. Hollioake 3-36)
Surrey 212 from 43 overs
(A.J. Stewart 85, O.T. Parkin 4-60, A.G. Wharf 3-37, R.D.B. Croft 3-42)

Glamorgan won by 32 runs (Duckworth-Lewis Method)

Umpires:- D.J. Constant and J.W. Holder   Third Umpire:- V.A. Holder

Gold Award Winner - M.P. Maynard (Glamorgan)

NCL DIVISION TWO - MATCH FOUR

SURREY LIONS versus ESSEX EAGLES
at The Oval on Monday 29th May

Match Abandoned

The NCL Division Two match against Essex Eagles had been moved back to the Bank Holiday Monday, 29th May as a result of Surrey's Benson And Hedges Cup semi-final. In view of the Sunday finish to that match and the deeply deflating result, I would imagine that there weren't too many members of the team and management who were disappointed when this game was abandoned early in the afternoon after a prolonged period of rain. The events of the past week had certainly emphasised how overcrowded the fixture list can be at times. It had been a tough start to the season in terms of travelling, too, for Surrey's players and supporters, so everyone was now looking forward to a week at home against Hampshire.

Surrey Lions 2pts, Essex Eagles 2

Other NCL Division Two Matches

Nottinghamshire Outlaws again took advantage of Surrey's forced inactivity to open up a four point gap at the top of the table by maintaining their one-hundred percent record with a narrow three-run victory over Durham Dynamos.

May 28
Chester-le-Street:- **Nottinghamshire Outlaws beat Durham Dynamos by 3 runs (Duckworth-Lewis method).** Nottinghamshire 199-6 (Morris 73); Durham 190-8 in 43 overs (Franks 6-27). **Nottinghamshire Outlaws 4pts**

May 29
Cardiff:- **Glamorgan Dragons beat Derbyshire Scorpions by six wickets.** Derbyshire 185-7; Glamorgan 186-4 in 43 overs (Elliott 88 not out). **Glamorgan Dragons 4pts**

Pos	Prev		P	Pts	W	T	L	N/R	Last	Three	Res
1	1	Nottinghamshire Outlaws	4	16	4	0	0	0	W	W	W
2	1	Warwickshire Bears	3	12	3	0	0	0	W	W	W
3	3	Surrey Lions	4	12	2	0	0	2	N/R	N/R	W
4	4	Middlesex Crusaders	4	10	2	0	1	1	N/R	W	W
5	6	Glamorgan Dragons	4	8	2	0	2	0	W	W	L
6	5	Essex Eagles	3	6	1	0	1	1	N/R	L	W
7	7	Derbyshire Scorpions	3	0	0	0	3	0	L	L	L
=	8	Hampshire Hawks	3	0	0	0	3	0	L	L	L
9	8	Durham Dynamos	4	0	0	0	4	0	L	L	L

NCL DIVISION TWO AT 29TH MAY

5 Back From The Brink

Surrey's next opponents, Hampshire, had made a pretty disastrous start to the season, with seven defeats and only two wins to their credit in the three major competitions. One of those victories had, of course, come in the farcical ten-overs-a-side Benson And Hedges Cup group match at The Oval, so 'revenge' could be added to the list of reasons why Surrey needed to win the upcoming NCL and Championship matches. Top of the list, of course, was the requirement to kick-start the team's spluttering attempt to retain the County Championship title. At this early stage of the campaign, the Surrey team could be likened to a very fast and powerful car that had not yet got close to moving into top gear. This was, admittedly, partly due to an excess of rain getting into the engine! Hopes were still high, however, because, to continue the analogy, the Surrey engine was about to receive a delivery of four-star fuel in the form of the return of Saqlain Mushtaq from Pakistan's tour of the West Indies. Thankfully, he had emerged from the series unscathed although, to most people's surprise, he hadn't taken a great number of wickets. Despite this, everyone at The Oval was confident that he would soon be bamboozling county batsmen again and leading a Surrey surge up the Championship table. With the Hampshire batting having looked extremely brittle thus far, the reappearance of the spin genius looked well timed.

NCL DIVISION TWO - MATCH FIVE

SURREY LIONS versus HAMPSHIRE HAWKS
at The Oval on Tuesday 30th May

Surrey Lions (95-3) beat Hampshire Hawks (94) by seven wickets

The temporary floodlights erected at The Oval for this day-night encounter had barely come into play when the Surrey Lions completed an emphatic victory by seven wickets with almost twenty-four overs to spare. The Hampshire Hawks were simply blown out of the sky by Martin Bicknell and Alex Tudor, both of whom proved far too good for the visiting batsmen on a pitch which offered pace, bounce and a degree of sideways movement.

Having won the toss and elected to bat, the top-order Hawks batsmen proved easy prey for Bicknell and Tudor as the visitors slumped to 15-4 by the end of the seventh over. After Derek Kenway fell to the fifth ball of the match, bowled by a ball from Bicknell which nipped back and took a thin inside edge, Adie Aymes then nicked a fine delivery from Tudor to first slip, Jason Laney edged a drive at the same bowler to the 'keeper and Giles White snicked an excellent Bicknell delivery to give Thorpe a second catch at first slip. Bicknell then struck a fifth blow in his sixth over by having John Stephenson taken behind the wicket by Jon Batty and Tudor ensured there would be no recovery three overs later when he had Dimitri Mascarenhas well caught by Ben Hollioake low to his left at third slip. This wicket rewarded Adam Hollioake's typically attacking and intelligent captaincy, since he had placed four slips, something almost unheard of in limited-overs cricket.

Although the Lions hadn't removed Robin Smith at this stage, anything other than a home win already looked out of the question. The Hampshire skipper struggled badly, in any case, paradoxically looking in increasingly poor touch the longer he batted, before falling lbw for twenty to Jason Ratcliffe, Tudor's replacement at the Vauxhall end. Thirty-two runs had been added for the seventh wicket during Smith's desperate battle but most of these had come from the bat of Shane Warne, who produced his best batting form of the season after starting his county career by recording a 'pair' in each of his first two Championship matches.

Already in dire straits at 74-7, Hampshire's last remaining hope of respectability disappeared rapidly as Udal presented Thorpe with another slip catch off the bowling of the accurate Ratcliffe

(2-19) and then Mullally fell in the next over when hitting across the line of a Tudor delivery. Despite a valiant attempt by the last pair of Warne and Francis to raise three figures, it was not to be as Ian Salisbury pulled off an outstanding catch, knocking a skimming drive up in the air and then twisting to take the ball one-handed as it fell behind him, to terminate his fellow leg-spinner's bright knock of thirty-four. The Hawks were therefore all out for a paltry 94 - a total that they would surely be unable to defend unless they could strike several early blows.

Hampshire did, in fact, get off to the ideal start when Mark Butcher cut Alan Mullally hard and low to backward point without a run on the board but no further wickets were to fall until the game was all but over. Ian Ward, rightly promoted to number three after being so shamefully wasted in Cardiff, played the leading role in a second-wicket partnership of sixty-three with Ali Brown which completely extinguished any flickering Hampshire hopes. Scoring all around the wicket, Ward made light of the loss of his partner to Mascarenhas with just thirty-two runs required and saw the Lions to within sight of their victory target before being bowled by a Warne delivery which penetrated his attempted drive. Graham Thorpe and Adam Hollioake then quickly saw their side through to a crushing victory just as the natural light was about to give way to the floodlighting.

It was, of course, disappointing for the crowd that they had been denied the anticipated floodlit spectacle but compensation came with the knowledge that Surrey were now level with the Nottinghamshire Outlaws on sixteen points.

Surrey Lions (95-3) beat Hampshire Hawks (94) by seven wickets

Surrey Lions 4pts

SURREY LIONS v HAMPSHIRE HAWKS at THE OVAL. Played on 30th May
Hampshire Hawks won the toss   Umpires:- J.W. Holder & R. Palmer. Third Umpire:- K. Shuttleworth

HAMPSHIRE HAWKS

Fall of wkt	Batsman	How Out	Score	Balls	4s	6s
3- 6	J.S. Laney	c Batty b Tudor	2	11	0	0
1- 2	D.A. Kenway	b Bicknell	0	3	0	0
2- 5	A.N. Aymes +	c Thorpe b Tudor	0	3	0	0
7- 74	R.A. Smith *	lbw b Ratcliffe	20	57	2	0
4- 15	G.W. White	c Thorpe b Bicknell	2	14	0	0
5- 38	J.P. Stephenson	c Batty b Bicknell	3	10	0	0
6- 42	A.D. Mascarenhas	c B.C. Hollioake b Tudor	1	8	0	0
10- 94	S.K. Warne	c Salisbury b B.C. Hollioake	34	52	2	0
8- 80	S.D. Udal	c Thorpe b Ratcliffe	1	7	0	0
9- 81	A.D. Mullally	lbw b Tudor	0	5	0	0
	S.R.G Francis	Not Out	8	14	0	0
	Extras (11lb, 8w, 4nb)		23			
	TOTAL	(30.2 overs)	94			

SURREY LIONS bowling

O	M	R	W
Bicknell	9	2	18	3
Tudor	9	1	26	4
Ratcliffe	8	1	19	2
B.C. Hollioake	4.2	0	20	1

SURREY LIONS

Fall of wkt	Batsman	How Out	Score	Balls	4s	6s
1- 0	M.A. Butcher	c Udal b Mullally	0	3	0	0
2- 63	A.D. Brown	c Francis b Mascarenhas	23	48	4	0
3- 81	I.J. Ward	b Warne	44	51	4	0
	G.P. Thorpe	Not Out	14	17	2	0
	A.J. Hollioake *	Not Out	6	9	1	0
	B.C. Hollioake	did not bat				
	J.D. Ratcliffe	did not bat				
	J.N. Batty +	did not bat				
	A.J. Tudor	did not bat				
	M.P. Bicknell	did not bat				
	I.D.K. Salisbury	did not bat				
	Extras (1lb, 5w, 2nb)		8			
	TOTAL	(21.1 overs)	95 -3			

HAMPSHIRE HAWKS bowling

O	M	R	W
Mullally	5	2	23	1
Francis	3	0	17	0
Warne	7.1	1	26	1
Mascarenhas	6	1	28	1

Other NCL Division Two Match

The evening after Surrey Lions' crushing victory over Hampshire Hawks, the division's two other early pacesetters clashed in a floodlit showdown at Edgbaston, where the Warwickshire Bears recorded a comfortable 38-run win over the Nottinghamshire Outlaws to preserve their own one-hundred percent record and end that of the visitors. As a result, the Bears moved to the top of the table, courtesy of the fact that they had played one match fewer than the Lions and the Outlaws. At the other end of the table, Derbyshire Scorpions, Durham Dynamos and Hampshire Hawks had yet to register a point between them in eleven starts.

May 31
Edgbaston:- **Warwickshire Bears beat Nottinghamshire Outlaws by 38 runs.** Warwickshire 222-7 (Welch 55, Ostler 55); Nottinghamshire 184-8. **Warwickshire Bears 4pts**

NCL DIVISION TWO AT 31ST MAY

Pos	Prev		P	Pts	W	T	L	N/R	Last	Three	Res
1	2	Warwickshire Bears	4	16	4	0	0	0	W	W	W
2	1	Nottinghamshire Outlaws	5	16	4	0	1	0	L	W	W
3	3	Surrey Lions	5	16	3	0	0	2	W	N/R	N/R
4	4	Middlesex Crusaders	4	10	2	0	1	1	N/R	W	W
5	5	Glamorgan Dragons	4	8	2	0	2	0	W	W	L
6	6	Essex Eagles	3	6	1	0	1	1	N/R	L	W
7	7	Derbyshire Scorpions	3	0	0	0	3	0	L	L	L
8	7	Hampshire Hawks	4	0	0	0	4	0	L	L	L
=	9	Durham Dynamos	4	0	0	0	4	0	L	L	L

COUNTY CHAMPIONSHIP - MATCH FIVE

<u>SURREY versus HAMPSHIRE</u>
at The Oval

First Day - Thursday 1st June

Surrey 268-8

The Teams And The Toss - The Surrey team shows two changes from the match at Canterbury, with Saqlain Mushtaq and Jason Ratcliffe replacing Carl Greenidge and Ben Hollioake. The unfortunate Greenidge, who had failed to take any part at all in the previous match because of the abysmal weather, is omitted because of the home side's desire to play two spinners at The Oval, while Hollioake is ruled out with a calf strain picked up in the floodlit NCL game. Peter Hartley misses out for Hampshire with a similar problem and Simon Francis deputises. Rather surprisingly, the visitors choose to field an extra batsman ahead of their second spinner, Shaun Udal. Surrey win the toss and elect to bat.

In keeping with the recent depressing weather, the game starts in chilly, grey conditions and Ian Ward lasts just six overs before edging a rising delivery from Francis to Warne at second slip. Adding to this disappointment, a sprinkling of rain then results in a suspension of play fifteen minutes later.

Fortunately, only four overs are lost and the bowlers, rather than the batsmen, seem to be the ones most affected by the short break as Butcher and Thorpe help themselves to four boundaries in four overs. This prompts a change, with Mullally and Francis giving way, briefly, to the medium-paced duo of Mascarenhas and Stephenson. The latter's spell lasts only three overs, however, before Hampshire's expensive Aussie import is handed the ball for over number twenty-two. Although he immediately poses some problems for Mark Butcher and turns one delivery sharply past both the batsman and Adie Aymes, the former England opener responds well by driving the leg-spinner handsomely through extra cover for three. This turns out to be the last shot of any note in the session since the flow of runs dries up in the final half-hour before lunch when Mullally joins forces with Warne. Given the circumstances, a substantial drop in the run rate is a fair trade-off against the fact that Butcher and Thorpe are still together at the interval.

Lunch:- Surrey 52-1 (Butcher 20*, Thorpe 21*) from 31 overs

The fifty partnership for the second wicket arrives in the first over of the afternoon when Butcher drives Francis to the cover boundary. After a lively start, the young pace bowler is now looking less threatening and it's his partner at the pavilion end, Dimitri Mascarenhas, who appears more likely to provide a breakthrough for his side, inducing a couple of false strokes from Butcher and appealing loudly for a catch behind the wicket against Thorpe. Mascarenhas goes unrewarded, however, and the second Surrey wicket falls to a run out when Thorpe, having set off for a short single, sees Butcher collide with the bowler and sends him back too late to beat a throw to the non-striker's end. It's a sad waste of Butcher's wicket and it puts the game back in the balance at 79-2 but it doesn't deter the experienced England middle-order man from continuing to steal quick singles with his new partner, Adam Hollioake. With Warne having replaced Francis and boundaries at a premium, this tactic appears to be the only way to keep the scoreboard moving until, suddenly, Thorpe pulls a full-toss from the Australian leg-spinner to the midwicket fence and then sweeps him for a second boundary in the same over to reach fifty in 162 minutes from 120 balls. This also raises the Surrey hundred in the forty-eighth over, a statistic which bears testimony to some accurate Hampshire bowling.

By now the early cloud cover has dispersed and, with the sun shining through brightly for the first time in what seems like weeks, the fascinating contest between bat and ball continues with another surprisingly short pairing of the Mullally-Warne combination. The England left-armer contributes just four overs before John Stephenson returns to momentarily unsettle Hollioake with a brace of lbw appeals. Although the Surrey skipper quickly hits back with a pair of elegant cover drives, the former Essex player eventually succeeds with a third leg-before shout, this time against Thorpe on fifty-eight, to peg Surrey back to 124-3.

Clearly unaffected by the loss of his partner, Hollioake nonchalantly lofts the very next delivery, bowled by Shane Warne, into the pavilion for six and then follows up by sweeping a full-toss for four. Although the newly-arrived Ali Brown then takes a leaf out of his captain's book by plundering fourteen runs from Stephenson's badly directed next over, any hopes that this burst of scoring has damaged Hampshire morale are rapidly dispelled by a double break which restores the equilibrium of the contest as tea approaches. Hollioake is the first to go, adjudged lbw to Stephenson with the score on 153, then Jason Ratcliffe attempts to sweep Warne and is bowled behind his legs with just three runs added.

Tea:- Surrey 159-5 (Brown 21*, Batty 0*) from 68 overs

After a loose opening over from Warne, Surrey are plunged into trouble at 166-6 when Ali Brown pulls Mullally's fourth delivery of the afternoon straight to midwicket. It seems that we have arrived at the first crunch period of the match so it therefore comes as something of a surprise when Mullally is again withdrawn after just four overs and replaced at the Vauxhall end by Simon Francis. There appears to be no obvious reason for this move and Surrey prosper, initially, as Martin Bicknell and Jon Batty make confident starts to their innings.

When John Stephenson then takes over from Warne just a few overs later with the score past 200, it looks as if Robin Smith has rather lost the plot - but Francis is about to justify his captain's faith with two wickets in two overs. The young seamer first removes Batty, who cuts low to the finer of two gullies with the score at 207, and then, eight runs later, accounts for Ian Salisbury, who departs in similar fashion, slashing a catch to Kenway at backward point. From a Surrey viewpoint, the most disappointing feature of the team's slide from 153-3 to 215-8 has been the fact that the last four wickets have all fallen to fairly wanton strokes. A significant repair job is now needed by Messrs Bicknell, Tudor and Mushtaq if the home side is to gather more than one batting point and post a challenging total.

Given Surrey's rather precarious position, Warne's rapid return at the pavilion end is entirely understandable, though Bicknell seems unconcerned as he immediately late cuts the Aussie spin king to the third man boundary to advance his score into the thirties. While Alex Tudor appears less than happy against this quality of spin bowling, he does, however, enjoy a brief high-octane battle with the slippery young Francis who is still charging in from the Vauxhall end - in one exhilarating over costing eighteen runs a straight-driven three and a hooked six over fine leg sandwich two streaky boundaries to fine leg, picked up via an inside edge and a glove. Bicknell meanwhile continues to look as comfortable against Warne as any of the top-order batsmen and by cover-driving and slog-sweeping the Australian for further fours he moves through to an excellent fifty, containing eight boundaries, from 85 balls in 104 minutes. The half-century partnership for the ninth wicket arrives in the next over when Tudor cuts Stephenson to the cover fence and by the close Surrey appear to have edged in front again after an absorbing day's cricket.

Close:- Surrey 268-8 (Bicknell 53*, Tudor 29*) from 100 overs

VIEW FROM THE DRESSING ROOM - ALEX TUDOR

We had Saqi back for this game. I guess that must have given the side a real boost?
AT - Whenever he walks into the changing room it really lifts the players. Even though we are already a very good side, it does make a difference having a world-class spinner like Saqi as our overseas player because his presence gives everyone even greater confidence. And it's great for Bickers and myself because we know that he will take some of the workload off us.

How did you enjoy the challenge of facing Shane Warne?
AT - It was very tough, of course, but I think everyone was really excited when they first heard he was coming over to play county cricket because we knew it was going to be a great challenge to face the best leg-spinner in world cricket.

Second Day - Friday 2nd June

Surrey 333; Hampshire 207-8

Surrey's pursuit of a third batting point receives an early blow when Martin Bicknell becomes Simon Francis' fourth victim of the innings in the young paceman's second over of the morning. Playing across the line of a ball which maybe keeps a little low, the Surrey man is bowled and departs with fifty-nine excellent runs to his name and the score advanced to 278. Any thoughts of a nervous crawl to another point are quickly dispelled, however, when Saqlain Mushtaq launches his second ball from Francis high over cover for four runs and then takes two further boundaries, one glanced to fine leg and the other picked up over square leg, from the next over bowled by Alan Mullally. With his team-mate having set the mark, Alex Tudor sees his side past three-hundred in the following over from Francis with three high-quality strokes - a huge hooked six, a glorious off-drive and then a violent square slash. This blistering assault on the Hampshire bowling, which provides stunning early morning entertainment for the crowd, then continues in Francis' next over. This time Tudor forces the youngster through extra cover for three to complete a quick-fire fifty from 59 balls in 85 minutes (2 sixes, 5 fours) before Saqlain blasts successive deliveries over extra cover for one-bounce fours. Needless to say, Francis is immediately withdrawn from the attack at the Vauxhall end and replaced by John Stephenson. The former Essex and England man is no more able to escape punishment, however, as Tudor drives his first ball to the extra cover boundary off the back foot and pulls his second over midwicket for another four. The first of these boundaries raises the fifty partnership in an astonishing 33 balls while the second sees the big Surrey fast bowler through to his highest score in the County Championship, erasing his 56 against Leicestershire at Leicester in 1995 from the record books.

With the score now advanced to 333, a once highly-improbable fourth batting point is coming into view but the introduction of Shane Warne in place of Mullally ends the fun instantly as Saqlain misses a sweep at the leg-spinner's first delivery and is adjudged lbw. In just 10.1 overs this morning, Surrey have added sixty-five thrilling runs to build a total which seems sure to put pressure on Hampshire's struggling batting.

The visitors certainly face a testing time in the period up until lunch and they lose their first wicket in only the third over. Having fallen lbw to Martin Bicknell in both innings of the 1999 match between these counties at Guildford, Jason Laney does at least get a bat on the ball this time but only succeeds in edging low to Ali Brown at third slip. Laney has failed to trouble the scorers and Hampshire are immediately on the back foot at 9-1. Nor do their prospects look bright as the new batsman, Will Kendall, immediately looks ill-at-ease when confronted by Tudor's pace and is frequently beaten outside the off stump by both opening bowlers. Luckily for Hampshire, Giles White is looking a little more convincing and, despite a couple of loud appeals for lbw and a catch at short leg, manages to produce some handsome strokes off the front foot. Kendall's good fortune cannot last, though, and his uncomfortable stay at the crease ends when he falls to the ever dangerous Bicknell just three overs before lunch. His mode of dismissal is entirely predictable, too, as he flirts outside the off stump once too often and edges a routine catch to Graham Thorpe at first slip - 33 for 2.

Surrey have now got their opponents under the cosh as the interval looms and the pressure tells when Robin Smith goes for a second-ball duck in Bicknell's next over. Although it's a fine delivery which takes the former England batsman's outside edge and is well caught, high to his right, by Jon Batty, there is a definite feeling that Smith could have allowed the ball to pass outside the off stump. This doesn't worry the Surrey team, however, as they head off contentedly to lunch with Bicknell boasting the very impressive figures of 9-3-12-3. Hampshire are 299 runs behind and know that they have it all to do if they are to stay in the match.

Lunch:- Hampshire 34-3 (White 23*, Kenway 0*) from 18 overs

White and Kenway find fortune smiling upon them as they both edge fours over the slip cordon in the opening three overs after lunch. Although White follows his streaky boundary with two successive meaty pulls for four off Tudor to raise the Hampshire fifty, Kenway continues to struggle, nicking the young Surrey quickie first through, and then just over, the hands of Mark Butcher at second slip in quick succession. When White then survives a very confident lbw shout in the next over from Bicknell it starts to look like the bowlers are in for a frustrating afternoon but the picture changes just a few overs later when the deserving Tudor puts Kenway out of his misery, courtesy of a good low catch at third slip by Ali Brown. The promising young Hampshire batsman departs with few fond memories of a ten-over struggle during which he has scored twelve runs by way of three edged boundaries.

At 73-4 the visitors are now very much up against it and they almost lose Adrian Aymes immediately when Ian Salisbury at short leg just fails to cling on to a low bat-pad chance offered off Bicknell. While his colleagues continue to struggle at the other end, White is making batting look comparatively easy, however, as he on-drives Bicknell for three to post an impressive 90-ball half-century after 134 minutes at the crease.

Since Adam Hollioake's willing opening bowlers have, by now, delivered all but four of the first thirty-three overs of the innings it's no surprise when the captain changes his mode of attack by turning to spin at both ends. Although Ian Salisbury takes a while to settle into a consistent line and length, at one point being cut and driven for successive fours by White, Saqlain is soon probing away and causing problems for the fifth-wicket pair. The final half-hour before tea sees the flow of runs reduced to a trickle and both bowlers finding the outside edge of the Hampshire wicketkeeper's bat but no breakthrough is forthcoming as the White-Aymes alliance continues to prosper. The game is nicely poised as the interval arrives.

Tea:- Hampshire 143-4 (White 88*, Aymes 25*) from 59 overs

Giles White continues confidently after the break, lofting Saqlain straight for four to move into the nineties, and bringing up the visitors' 150 three overs later as he moves his personal contribution on to ninety-five. He has added just a single, though, when he finds Saqlain taking rapid revenge for that early boundary. Drawn forward by the Pakistani spin wizard, a combination of bat and pad sends the ball flying up into the air directly in front of the batsman, who can do nothing but look on helplessly as Ian Ward dives forward from short leg to take a splendid catch.

With White's excellent innings now terminated and a much-needed breakthrough achieved Surrey soon find themselves back on top when John Stephenson falls in Saqlain's next over to reduce Hampshire to 161-6. The veteran all-rounder departs with just six runs to his name after a bizarre death-or-glory effort - having survived a big appeal for a bat-pad catch, he edges for two runs, drives over mid-on for four and then skies the next ball almost vertically to slip from a leading edge in attempting to repeat the stroke. It follows the pattern of his previous desperate efforts against the Surrey off-spinner and it leaves his colleagues with some work to do in order to avoid the follow-on. With only twenty-three runs needed, the threat isn't too serious, however, and it rapidly recedes as the new batsman, Shane Warne, finds the boundary twice in quick succession. There is one slight scare for the visitors when Aymes offers a difficult chance to Ali Brown at third slip off Martin Bicknell with five runs still required but the Hampshire 'keeper survives to sweep Saqlain for the boundary which leaves Surrey with no option but to bat again. Aymes doesn't prosper for much longer though, falling victim to Alex Tudor as soon as the big fast bowler replaces Bicknell at the pavilion end. His painstakingly determined effort is ended with the score on 193 by a fine low catch at gully by Adam Hollioake from a very thick defensive edge.

The prospect of a decisive first innings lead for the home side is now growing and it is further enhanced when Tudor strikes again in his next over, clean bowling Warne with a good delivery of full length. As Alan Mullally walks to the wicket the vultures are gathering but, unfortunately for Surrey, so are the grey clouds overhead and only four further overs are possible before the umpires offer the light to the batsmen. To nobody's surprise they accept the invitation to leave the field.

Despite White's fine knock, Surrey have taken today's honours, thanks largely to the all-round efforts of Tudor and Saqlain and an outstanding bowling display from Bicknell.

Close:- Hampshire 207-8 (Mascarenhas 2*, Mullally 8*) from 82 overs

VIEW FROM THE DRESSING ROOM - ALEX TUDOR

After a few early escapes on day one you played some tremendous shots in your innings of 64 not out - would it rank as your best innings for Surrey so far?
AT - It would definitely be up there as one of my best, especially because of the state of the game - it wasn't as if I went to the wicket with four-hundred already on the board, so they were important runs and I certainly felt very comfortable at the wicket. It's always nice as a batsman, especially a lower-order batsman, to start the day with thirty runs already to your name as I did on this occasion - it does give you added confidence.

Having been 124-2 at one point, we rather lost our way in our first innings, didn't we?
AT - Yes, it was disappointing after we had got a good start but the lower-order came to the rescue, as we have a habit of doing. I thought Bickers batted tremendously well, with help from me and Saqi, to get us up to a respectable total.

Third Day - Saturday 3rd June

Surrey 333 and 142; Hampshire 210 and 58-2

With Martin Bicknell and Saqlain Mushtaq giving nothing away, the Hampshire first innings is polished off very efficiently with a mere three runs being added in ten overs for the loss of the last two wickets. Dimitri Mascarenhas goes in the third over of the morning, offering a limp defensive bat and edging low to Ali Brown at second slip, while Simon Francis prods a catch to silly point after seven further overs of strokeless resistance from the last-wicket pair. Having bowled sixty-three overs between them, and taken a wicket apiece to end the innings, Bicknell (4-52) and Saqlain (3-65) finish with impressive figures as the Surrey team leaves the field. The home side has gained a very healthy first innings lead of 123 runs and it would take a brave man to bet against the county champions now, especially as we are only just over halfway through the match in terms of elapsed time.

Hampshire clearly have to make early inroads into Surrey's second innings to stay alive in the match and they make a good start towards this goal when Mullally removes Mark Butcher in the third over, the batsman top-edging a cut high to Warne at second slip. With Francis then dislodging Ian Ward just four balls later, courtesy of an outside edge which is very well picked up low to his left by Adrian Aymes, Surrey are momentarily on the back foot at 4 for 2.

The visitors now sense that there might be a way back into the game and their hopes rise further when Graham Thorpe goes in Mullally's fifth over with the score advanced only as far as twenty-four. Having made a promising start by driving and cutting his England colleague to the cover boundary, Thorpe gets his come-uppance when he is pinned on the crease by an inswinger and adjudged lbw.

The nerves of Surrey fans are then further tested by a shaky start from Ali Brown who mishits his first delivery fractionally over mid-on's head for a single and then picks up two runs through extra cover off a leading edge. Mullally is causing no end of problems at this stage and Brown's luck doesn't hold as the England left-armer extracts his leg stump with a fine swinging yorker, delivered from around the wicket, in his next over. It's now 45-4 but, with Adam Hollioake looking reasonably secure and Jason Ratcliffe making a confident start, Surrey manage to stay in control of the match by reaching lunch without losing any further wickets.

Lunch:- Surrey 61-4 (Hollioake 22*, Ratcliffe 10*) from 19 overs

Having gone to lunch with figures of 10-3-18-3, everyone is expecting another assault from Alan Mullally, in partnership with Shane Warne, immediately upon the resumption in an attempt to break the back of Surrey's batting. It doesn't happen, however, as Robin Smith rather surprisingly opts for the inexperienced Francis at the pavilion end. Never one to look a gift horse in the mouth, Smith's opposite number takes full advantage of this rather puzzling move, crashing the young seamer's first two deliveries through the covers for four in an over which eventually costs fifteen runs. While Warne probes away at the Vauxhall end, Francis concedes another eight runs from two further overs before Smith finally comes to his senses and reverts to Mullally at the pavilion end. The lead has moved well past two-hundred by this time, however, and, although Warne induces Hollioake to chop onto his stumps in his next over, Surrey are breathing a little easier. The captain's aggressive knock of forty-one appears to have saved his side from potential disaster and has been largely responsible for the score's advance to ninety.

Further nerve-wracking moments lie ahead, though, as Warne poses problems aplenty by pitching into the rough outside the right-handers' leg stump from around the wicket. John Stephenson, replacing Mullally after a wicketless five-over burst from the England seamer, meanwhile keeps things tight from the pavilion end. Consequently, the cricket becomes increasingly tense as the batsmen, apparently unable to fathom how to counter Warne's line of attack, first become overly passive and then eventually get themselves out. Jon Batty tries to break the shackles by using his feet to get down the pitch but only succeeds in edging a leg-break to slip, while Ratcliffe is bowled, after a handy innings of twenty-six, when his drive is defeated by an equally impressive delivery.

Suddenly it's 109-7, the lead is a far from unassailable 232 and we once again appear to be in a 'game on' situation. The crowd, quite often a good barometer of the match position, offers confirmation of this as singles begin to earn applause and a couple of well-struck boundaries from Bicknell receive an exaggeratedly rapturous response. There is even a ripple of excitement when umpire John Holder decides to interpret a legside delivery from Warne as 'negative bowling' and signals a wide. It seems a strange call since the Australian leg-spinner has, only minutes earlier, picked up two wickets but, given the situation, the two-run contribution is gratefully accepted by Surrey. Umpire Holder's gift then appears even more welcome when Warne snares Alex Tudor at silly point in his next over to leave the hosts leading by 244 with just two wickets left to fall.

Surrey are now in a far from comfortable position and, in an effort to increase the pressure, Robin Smith recalls Mullally to replace the flagging Stephenson. The move yields almost immediate results, too, as Bicknell succumbs to an lbw decision from the left-armer's fourth delivery - the batsman does appear to be unlucky, however, since the ball, delivered from round the wicket, looks to be rising over the top of the stumps.

The Surrey lead has at least extended beyond 250 and it is then increased by six when, to everyone's amazement, Saqlain suddenly pulls Mullally high over the midwicket boundary. His fun is ended with the first ball of the next over, though, when Warne completes a well-deserved return of 5 for 31 by having him caught at the wicket from an outside edge. The Aussie spin wizard's outstanding effort has finished the job which Mullally (4-31) started and it has given the visitors an outside chance of victory. As the players head off for tea the equation is simple - Hampshire need 266 runs to win, Surrey require ten wickets to triumph and there are four sessions, equating to a minimum of 130 overs, left for play. Given fair weather, the draw looks to be out of the question, so there is all to play for.

Tea:- Between Innings

After Giles White drives the first delivery of the innings from Martin Bicknell through mid-off for four, the Surrey opening bowlers dominate the early exchanges. Alex Tudor, running in well from the Vauxhall end, produces a marvellous first over to Jason Laney and then removes the hapless Hampshire opener with the second ball of his second over. As the red-headed right-hander edges a good delivery low to Adam Hollioake in the gully and departs for a duck he extends a truly miserable sequence against Surrey in Championship cricket. His record over the past three seasons now reads 2, 0, 0, 7, 0, 0 - nine runs at an average of 1.50 - and his only minor consolation is that he has not fallen to his nemesis, Martin Bicknell, on this occasion... though the fact of the matter is that all eight deliveries he faced were from Alex Tudor!

Following this early setback White and his new partner, Will Kendall, attempt to dig in and, apart from one Tudor over where eleven runs accrue through off-side drives and forces, the bowlers remain largely on top without making another breakthrough. Saqlain eventually replaces Tudor for the fourteenth over of the innings and Ian Salisbury soon joins him in the attack when Bicknell retires to the outfield after a dangerous but wicketless new-ball spell.

Ominously for Hampshire, the spinners are quickly into their rhythm and, supported by some fine ground fielding, they begin to apply real pressure. Predictably enough, with the ball turning more generously, White looks less comfortable against the spinners second time around and falls victim to a good piece of bowling at the start of Salisbury's fourth over. Having almost played on to a well-disguised googly, the former Somerset batsman advances down the wicket to his next delivery and is left hopelessly stranded as a leg-break fizzes past his outside edge. Batty completes a routine stumping and Hampshire's first innings hero is on his way back to the pavilion for twenty-three, with the scoreboard now reading 40-2. Surrey's spin twins are now very much in control, causing several nervous moments for Robin Smith before he eventually gets off the mark after twenty-five minutes at the crease, and, despite a couple of well-timed boundaries by Kendall off Salisbury in the closing overs, the home side clearly holds all the aces at the end of day three.

Close:- Hampshire 58-2 (Kendall 23*, Smith 3*) from 34 overs

VIEW FROM THE DRESSING ROOM - ALEX TUDOR

We found things rather difficult in our second innings, with Alan Mullally bowling really well and Shane Warne causing us a lot of problems bowling from around the wicket. We looked uncertain as to how to play that angle of attack. Is that a fair comment?
AT - Yes, it's a fair point. After Alan Mullally had bowled a very good spell, as he has often done in the past for Leicestershire against us, Shane Warne bowling around the wicket to us was never going to be easy and he bowled tremendously well. From that angle of attack you are in two minds - whether to kick the ball away or play at it with the bat - and more often than not he managed to pitch in the rough, so the ball was always doing something. We did have a game plan but putting it into action effectively against a world-class bowler like Shane Warne is a completely different ball game. From our point of view, as a team, I would hope that if we come up against that situation again then we will cope better than we did on this occasion.

When bowling to you, Warne was called for a legside wide, with the umpire interpreting it as negative bowling. Did the umpire's decision surprise you? As we now know, the two runs we picked up as a result of that judgement turned out to be crucial.
AT - I think it was John Holder who called the wide and the ball, apparently, only missed my leg stump by inches, but bowlers know that umpires can call them for wides down the legside if they interpret the bowling as being negative. I think Warne's comment to the umpire was 'Come on, John, am I a negative bowler?' which everyone knows he's not... but at the end of the day the decision was made and those runs certainly proved vital.

Fourth Day - Sunday 4th June

Surrey 333 and 142; Hampshire 210 and 263

Surrey beat Hampshire by 2 runs
Surrey 18pts, Hampshire 4

With all the other games in this round of Championship matches completed, the final day's play starts with the stakes for this contest having been raised by Kent's victory over Durham. Everyone now knows that the losers of this game will drop to the bottom of the first division table while the victors will move up to fourth place. Considering the fragile state of the visitors' out-of-sorts batting, it is, however, hard to imagine anything other than a Surrey win sending Hampshire to the foot of the table by the end of the day.

The visitors desperately need the overnight pair of Kendall and Smith to build a solid foundation for the innings but any hope of this happening is extinguished in the seventh over of the morning when the former England batsman edges a lifting Bicknell delivery to third slip where Mark Butcher holds on to a sharp catch.

With Saqlain wheeling away cannily at the Vauxhall end and making run-scoring extremely difficult, most of the runs that do accrue in the early stages are as a result of edges to third man off Bicknell. The Surrey swing maestro certainly doesn't enjoy the best of luck and he is very unfortunate to end his initial spell of the day with just Smith's wicket to show for seven overs of hard labour.

By way of contrast, his replacement at the pavilion end, Alex Tudor, enjoys an almost instant double success, picking up wickets with his second and ninth balls during a four-over spell of play which appears to decide the destiny of the match. Tudor's first victim is Derek Kenway, whose miserable match is complete when Adam Hollioake picks up an outstanding catch, low and left-handed, in the gully from a flashing sliced drive, and then Adie Aymes departs in the big paceman's next over to a thin edge from a ball which holds its line.

As if this double-break isn't bad enough for the visitors, they then lose John Stephenson in the following over from Saqlain to another very sharp catch from the Surrey skipper, this time at silly point. In little more than fifteen minutes a reasonably competitive score of 84-3 has declined to a hopeless 87-6 and the game looks all over bar the shouting.

Shane Warne is clearly in no mood to surrender meekly after his fine bowling, however, and, after only the briefest reconnaissance, pulls and drives Tudor to the boundary before slog-sweeping Saqlain for a mighty six. This counter-attack seems to unsettle Surrey briefly before Tudor gets his team back on track for victory with the wicket of Kendall, whose battling innings of forty-one is ended by a smart low catch at first slip by Graham Thorpe.

A daunting 138 runs are still required with just three wickets to fall and, as in the first innings, the new batsman, Dimitri Mascarenhas, emerges with a runner as a result of a hamstring injury picked up early in the match. Even though the odds are heavily stacked against his side, Warne continues to counter-attack fiercely, flaying four more boundaries in the final four overs of the session to move within eight runs of what would be a breathtaking half-century.

Lunch:- Hampshire 148-7 (Warne 42*, Mascarenhas 4*) from 64 overs

With the field now set a little deeper for Warne, runs come largely in singles during the early overs from the trusted Surrey bowling pairing of Bicknell and Saqlain. One such single, from a push into the covers off Bicknell, finally takes the Aussie leg-spinner through to a very well-played half-century (74 minutes, 65 balls) in the fifth over after the break and his fighting effort to keep the game alive is rewarded with a generous ovation.

The applause has barely died away, however, when he tries to turn the first ball of the next over from Saqlain to leg, only to be undone by the Pakistani's "wrong 'un" which takes the leading edge and loops a straightforward return catch to the bowler. Surrey players and supporters celebrate the vital breakthrough - with just Mullally and Francis to accompany the hobbling Mascarenhas, Hampshire look to have no chance of scoring a further 105 runs to win the match. This belief is then underlined just four overs later when Mullally miscues a drive at Saqlain into the space behind the bowler and Jason Ratcliffe runs round from mid-on to complete the catch. With the visitors now desperately gasping for breath at 173-9, a most welcome three-place rise up the Championship table beckons for the reigning county champions.

It seems just a matter of time before victory is clinched as Francis makes a very uncomfortable and unconvincing start, inside-edging a drive at Saqlain narrowly past his leg stump for four runs. Mascarenhas continues to battle gamely at the other end, though, taking boundaries off both the Surrey spin-king and the returning Alex Tudor to raise the visitors' two-hundred.

At this stage the last-wicket stand is merely irritating but Adam Hollioake opts for a change anyway, giving Ian Salisbury his first bowl of the day in place of Tudor at the pavilion end. With the spinners now operating in tandem, the flow of runs slows considerably and the ball beats the bat on numerous occasions without either Hampshire batsman getting the vital edge that will end the match. Eventually, Francis, having most definitely looked a more accomplished batsman than Mullally, breaks out of his shell by cutting Salisbury to the point boundary and then, later in the same over, three byes bring forth a totally unexpected and improbable fifty partnership.

Some Surrey supporters are, by now, starting to feel uneasy and many are puzzled by field placings which allow Mascarenhas to take an easy single not only at the **start** of overs but at the **end**, too. One spectator attempts to allay home fans' fears by asking if anyone knows what the record last-wicket stand is for Hampshire versus Surrey. We consult our statistics sheets and discover that the 63-year-old record is seventy-three. 'There you go then, they'd need to beat that mark by twenty runs to win the game - it's not going to happen,' he sagely decrees... as he puffs away nervously on a cigarette. His sound logic does make everyone feel just a little happier, though.

Cricket matches don't always follow a logical path, however, and the total continues to edge upwards, largely through singles and extras. With the stand past sixty and some members getting very frustrated - one seemingly 'well-oiled' gentleman appears twice on the restaurant balcony to loudly implore Adam Hollioake to 'change the bowlers' - the possibility is growing that it could be Surrey, and not Hampshire, who will be bottom of the league at the conclusion of the match.

The home skipper, though keeping faith with a somewhat weary-looking Saqlain at the Vauxhall end, does eventually make a change at the pavilion end by recalling Martin Bicknell. The move is not successful, however, as Mascarenhas pulls two boundaries in the Surrey seamer's second over to reach a brave 143-minute half-century and then forces the ball to the extra cover fence later in the over to ensure that the names of Mascarenhas and Francis replace those of Budd and Heath in the Hampshire record book. Now we are getting seriously worried. History has just been made in one way and a truly memorable victory for Hampshire is suddenly no longer out of the question.

Encouragingly for the home side, the ball is still beating the bat occasionally and everyone knows that one moment of Saqlain magic could end all this torture in a trice... but the number of runs required by the visitors is shrinking slowly by the over. The main hope for Surrey is that Mascarenhas and Francis who have been battling away as hopeless underdogs with no significant expectation of success will soon feel the pressure of becoming favourites to win the match. A new ball is also looming as the tea interval, already delayed because Hampshire were nine wickets down at the scheduled time, draws closer. That said, it remains a mystery as to how we have arrived at this desperate stage in the first place!

Finally, with the last-wicket pair just ten runs shy of victory and only two overs to be bowled before tea, the new ball is taken and Tudor rejoins Bicknell in the attack, ending Saqlain's all-day marathon at the Vauxhall end. Strangely, even though they have a new 'cherry' in their hands, both bowlers operate with just one slip fielder. Although runs are obviously extremely precious, a wicket is required to win the match, so why would you want to bowl without a second and third slip? There are more puzzled frowns in evidence in the pavilion as the tension grows still greater.

As if to emphasise Surrey's field-placing folly, Francis then edges Bicknell to third man in the final over before the interval. It's possible that his snick might not have resulted in a catch, even with three slips in place, but it certainly yields four runs for Hampshire to reduce their target to just five in what will be a high-pressure period after the break. For Surrey, tea might just have come along at the right time.

Tea:- Hampshire 261-9 (Mascarenhas 57*, Francis 30*) from 103 overs

It may be a cliché to talk about 'almost unbearable tension' but there are no better words to describe the atmosphere on the pavilion balcony during the tea-break. Having put themselves in a position where the game was as good as won, Surrey are now facing the worrying possibility of dropping to the bottom of the Championship. It's a bleak thought and I can't help but wonder what damage will be done to the team's morale if they let this match slip through their fingers. Adam Hollioake's captaincy during the afternoon session has been called into question by a few people but, while it is true to say that some of his decisions have been rather puzzling, it must also be said that he gets far more decisions right than wrong - and that is all you can expect from the captain of any cricket team, since it is impossible to make the right move *every* time.

As the players re-emerge onto the field one thing is for sure - with only five runs or one wicket required to finish the game off, we won't be stuck on the edge of our seats for very much longer!

What should be the shortest session of the season starts with Tudor bowling to Mascarenhas. The young all-rounder pulls a shortish delivery to long-on and picks up an easy single from the opening delivery. It's understandable that we want Francis on strike but can we really afford to give these singles away when only five runs from defeat? With only four now needed it's a terrifying thought that a streaky edge from Francis can now win the match. The young seamer successfully plays out the rest of the over, though the final ball turns out to be a fine yorker which he does well to dig out.

Now it's Bicknell to Mascarenhas. The first ball is pushed to long-off - one run scored, just three required. Surrey's swing king now has five balls to pit his vast experience against the callow youth of Francis. After a fairly wide opening ball, Bicknell is right on the mark, forcing three successive forward defensive strokes and then beating the batsman comprehensively outside off stump with a fine delivery. Maybe it isn't meant to be for Surrey. Maybe we are going to find ourselves at the bottom of the table with almost a third of the season completed.

This disturbing thought is still on my mind as Tudor runs in to Mascarenhas again. The first ball is short and wide outside the off stump. The batsman cuts at it... and misses. There's an almost audible sigh of relief from the Surrey faithful as if to say 'we got away with that one' and it's obvious, even from the distance of the pavilion, that Mascarenhas fully appreciates the opportunity he has just missed.

The second ball sees him driving towards mid-on without timing. Both batsmen and the runner clearly think about taking a single but then eventually stay put. With clear signs of Hampshire nerves showing out in the middle I find myself pondering what might be going through Mascarenhas's mind at this precise moment in time. Is he still thinking about the missed chance from the first delivery? Or maybe about the run he has just turned down?

I guess the truth will never be known but something clearly causes him to lose his concentration as Tudor bangs the next ball in short. The batsman attempts a pull, the ball hits the bat and, from my viewing angle on the pavilion balcony, I am momentarily uncertain as to where the ball is going. Then I realise... it's lobbing straight back towards the bowler for a simple catch. Tudor steadies himself slightly in his follow-through and grabs the ball with his big hands. We've won!

The Surrey paceman throws the ball high in the air and immediately races away to the Vauxhall end of the ground, with his joyous team-mates in hot pursuit. Eventually, when he can run no further, he throws himself to the ground and is rapidly submerged by his colleagues. The celebration is more football than cricket, but it's entirely understandable.

There's a feeling of huge relief in the pavilion and the cheer that had gone up as the catch was taken is repeated as the players finally make their way back from the other end of the ground. Tudor, with 5-57, is the hero of the hour and leads the team off, but great credit must also go the hard-working Bicknell (1-60 from 26 overs) and Saqlain (3-89 from 44 overs), since their figures don't really do them justice. A word in defeat, too, for Hampshire's brave last-wicket pair, whose efforts deserve better than a two-run defeat and bottom place in the table.

With the players all back in the pavilion there are two major talking points. The first is the controversial legside wide given against Shane Warne for negative bowling on day three which has proved more important than anyone could have imagined at the time. The second is that there is a clear comparison to be drawn between this game and the Somerset match at The Oval in 1999. On that occasion everyone felt that the nail-biting finish was a sign that it was going to be Surrey's year. This victory at the death leaves everyone with a distinct sense of deja vu. Maybe we are now on an upward curve and ready to take the Championship by storm once again.

Surrey 333 and 142; Hampshire 210 and 263
Surrey beat Hampshire by 2 runs. Surrey 18pts, Hampshire 4

SURREY v HAMPSHIRE at THE OVAL. Played from 1st - 4th June
Surrey won the toss   Umpires:- J.W. Holder & K.E. Palmer

SURREY - First Innings								**HAMPSHIRE bowling**			
Fall of wkt	Batsman		How Out	Score	Balls	4s	6s		O	M	R	W
2- 79	M.A. Butcher		run out	32	134	5	0	Mullally	23	8	43	1
1- 6	I.J. Ward	c Warne	b Francis	5	17	0	0	Francis	23	5	95	4
3- 124	G.P. Thorpe		lbw b Stephenson	58	149	9	0	Mascarenhas	14	6	30	0
4- 153	A.J. Hollioake *		lbw b Stephenson	37	72	3	1	Stephenson	20	4	74	2
6- 166	A.D. Brown	c sub	b Mullally	24	27	2	0	Warne	30.1	9	81	2
5- 156	J.D. Ratcliffe		b Warne	0	3	0	0					
7- 207	J.N. Batty +	c Kendall	b Francis	16	56	1	0					
9- 278	M.P. Bicknell		b Francis	59	109	9	0					
8- 215	I.D.K. Salisbury	c Kenway	b Francis	1	9	0	0					
	A.J. Tudor		Not Out	64	68	8	2					
10- 333	Saqlain Mushtaq		lbw b Warne	21	18	5	0					
	Extras (1b, 9lb, 4w, 2nb)			16								
	TOTAL		(110.1 overs)	333								

HAMPSHIRE - First Innings								**SURREY bowling**			
Fall of wkt	Batsman		How Out	Score	Balls	4s	6s		O	M	R	W
5- 151	G.W. White	c Ward	b Saqlain	96	196	11	0	Bicknell	29	12	52	4
1- 9	J.S. Laney	c Brown	b Bicknell	0	6	0	0	Tudor	16	5	52	3
2- 33	W.S. Kendall	c Thorpe	b Bicknell	7	40	0	0	Saqlain	34	10	65	3
3- 33	R.A. Smith *	c Batty	b Bicknell	0	2	0	0	Salisbury	13	4	33	0
4- 73	D.A. Kenway	c Brown	b Tudor	12	33	3	0					
7- 193	A.N. Aymes +	c Hollioake	b Tudor	44	149	4	0					
6- 161	J.P. Stephenson	c Thorpe	b Saqlain	6	7	1	0					
8- 198	S.K. Warne		b Tudor	19	40	3	0					
9- 207	A.D. Mascarenhas	c Brown	b Bicknell	2	17	0	0					
	A.D. Mullally		Not Out	8	37	0	0					
10- 210	S.R.G. Francis	c Hollioake	b Saqlain	2	27	0	0					
	Extras (6b, 2lb, 2w, 4nb)			14								
	TOTAL		(92 overs)	210								

71

SURREY - Second Innings | | | | | | | *HAMPSHIRE bowling* | | | |
---|---|---|---|---|---|---|---|---|---|---|---
Fall of wkt | Batsman | | How Out | Score | Balls | 4s | 6s | O | M | R | W
1- 4 | M.A. Butcher | c Warne | b Mullally | 2 | 15 | 0 | 0 | Mullally | 17 | 5 | 31 | 4
2- 4 | I.J. Ward | c Aymes | b Francis | 0 | 4 | 0 | 0 | Francis | 10 | 0 | 58 | 1
3- 24 | G.P. Thorpe | | lbw b Mullally | 13 | 16 | 2 | 0 | Warne | 21.1 | 7 | 31 | 5
5- 90 | A.J. Hollioake * | | b Warne | 41 | 74 | 6 | 0 | Stephenson | 9 | 4 | 16 | 0
4- 44 | A.D. Brown | | b Mullally | 7 | 6 | 0 | 0 | | | | |
7- 109 | J.D. Ratcliffe | | b Warne | 26 | 89 | 2 | 0 | | | | |
6- 106 | J.N. Batty + | c Stephenson | b Warne | 9 | 39 | 1 | 0 | | | | |
9- 131 | M.P. Bicknell | | lbw b Mullally | 14 | 43 | 2 | 0 | | | | |
8- 121 | A.J. Tudor | c Laney | b Warne | 0 | 24 | 0 | 0 | | | | |
| I.D.K. Salisbury | | Not Out | 8 | 23 | 1 | 0 | | | | |
10- 142 | Saqlain Mushtaq | c Aymes | b Warne | 10 | 11 | 0 | 1 | | | | |
| Extras (2b, 4lb, 4w, 2nb) | | | 12 | | | | | | | |
| TOTAL | | (57.1 overs) | 142 | | | | | | | |

HAMPSHIRE - Second Innings | | | | | | | *SURREY bowling* | | | |
---|---|---|---|---|---|---|---|---|---|---|---
Fall of wkt | Batsman | | How Out | Score | Balls | 4s | 6s | O | M | R | W
2- 40 | G.W. White | st Batty | b Salisbury | 23 | 71 | 2 | 0 | Bicknell | 26 | 8 | 60 | 1
1- 4 | J.S. Laney | c Hollioake | b Tudor | 0 | 8 | 0 | 0 | Tudor | 19.3 | 8 | 57 | 5
7- 125 | W.S. Kendall | c Thorpe | b Tudor | 41 | 169 | 6 | 0 | Saqlain | 44 | 15 | 89 | 3
3- 74 | R.A. Smith * | c Butcher | b Bicknell | 12 | 61 | 1 | 0 | Salisbury | 16 | 7 | 31 | 1
4- 84 | D.A. Kenway | c Hollioake | b Tudor | 1 | 12 | 0 | 0 | | | | |
5- 86 | A.N. Aymes + | c Batty | b Tudor | 2 | 7 | 0 | 0 | | | | |
6- 87 | J.P. Stephenson | c Hollioake | b Saqlain | 1 | 7 | 0 | 0 | | | | |
8- 161 | S.K. Warne | | c & b Saqlain | 50 | 60 | 7 | 1 | | | | |
10- 263 | A.D. Mascarenhas | | c & b Tudor | 59 | 119 | 7 | 0 | | | | |
9- 173 | A.D. Mullally | c Ratcliffe | b Saqlain | 4 | 11 | 0 | 0 | | | | |
| S.R.G. Francis | | Not Out | 30 | 115 | 3 | 0 | | | | |
| Extras (7b, 19lb, 14nb) | | | 40 | | | | | | | |
| TOTAL | | (105.3 overs) | 263 | | | | | | | |

VIEW FROM THE DRESSING ROOM - ALEX TUDOR

You looked to be in good form as you picked up four of the first seven wickets in Hampshire's second innings. How did you feel you were bowling at this relatively early stage of the season?
AT - I felt things were going very well. I was in good rhythm coming into this match and, going into the second innings, everything seemed to be clicking, which is important for me because I am a rhythm bowler. Once I've picked up one or two wickets I do tend to be the type of bowler who goes on to pick up a few more.

At 125-7 and 173-9 the game looked won. What went wrong during the last wicket stand? Were we guilty of taking our foot off the gas and assuming that the game was over?
AT - We got the ninth wicket quite early in the afternoon session and I think we thought the game would be over by about three o'clock, but cricket's a funny game, as they say, and it drifted on with them picking up ones and twos here and there. It became very frustrating after a while and I think, with hindsight, we maybe needed to change the bowlers a little bit earlier because Saqi was getting tired after a very, very long spell and Sals wasn't getting through either. Having said that, when the opposition is nine down and those two are bowling then they finish things off very quickly nine times out of ten. We should also give credit to the batsmen, who both played really well - Mascarenhas got a very good fifty and Francis hung on well with him.

Hand on heart, would we have lost but for the intervention of the tea interval?
AT - That's a very good question. I can honestly say, though, that I always felt we would win the

game even if it ended up being by just one run. But tea did come at a good time for us and you could see how nervous they were getting as they got closer to winning - some of the shots Dimi was playing after tea showed that. It was really like a cup final out there and, though it was very nerve-wracking for the coach and the Surrey supporters, it was a great spectacle for everyone who was there and that sort of exciting finish is good for the game.

Are you able to tell me what was said in the dressing room at tea time?
AT - The Surrey dressing room is always a very positive place and, even though it was a little quieter than usual because we were disappointed not to have wrapped the game up, there was no feeling of doom and gloom because we hadn't lost the game - it was still there to be won. We had a new ball to help us and Adam, Keith and one or two of the senior guys emphasised that just one wicket, one good ball, was all we needed to win the game.

There was huge pressure on you and Bickers as you tried to pick up the all-important last wicket with the new ball - was that the most tense situation you have ever faced when bowling in a first-class match? And did you have any particular plan of attack in that final period of play?
AT - It was definitely the most nervous I have ever felt in any county game, including my debut - we were yet to win a Championship match so this was a big game that we needed to win to kick-start our season. Bickers and I always tend to pick up early wickets with the new ball, so there seemed no reason why we shouldn't do it on this occasion and the main aim was to give Mascarenhas a single and bowl to Francis as much as possible. When I got to bowl at Dimi, though, I thought it would be worth digging one in - the new ball was a bit harder and I had a man back on the hook anyway... and luckily, with him being tense, the ball went straight up in the air.

Was it, in some ways, a risky tactic to dig that final ball in short at Mascarenhas? If he had got hold of it then it could have been game, set and match to Hampshire.
AT - I've bowled at Dimi a few times over the years and he's never really taken me on so I didn't think it was too risky, especially as I had the man back on the boundary - he would have needed to hit the ball extremely well to beat him. The way he was playing I felt he was just as likely to drive me back down the ground if I pitched it up to him, anyway.

There were amazing celebrations when you took the final wicket. What was the story behind that and can you describe your feelings as you ran away to the Vauxhall end?
AT - During the tea interval I had told the guys to watch me if I got the final wicket, so I think they were worried that I was going to do something really stupid! The crowd had been getting very restless during the afternoon and one or two Surrey supporters had been shouting abuse at the captain, which wasn't on as we hadn't lost the game at that stage, so I thought I'd just run down to the Vauxhall end and throw myself onto the ground. It could have been very embarrassing if the other lads had just walked off and left me there by myself but everyone was feeling very emotional, having just clinched a critical victory, so they all followed me and piled on top! I was just so happy to have got the final wicket and completed another five-wicket haul in front of my home crowd. To be fair, we got a good reception from the Surrey fans when we eventually came off the field at the end.

If we had lost this game we would have been bottom of the table. Had that happened, do you believe that we could still have bounced back to retain the Championship title?
AT - It would have been difficult for us, for sure. Even though it was still quite early we would have lost three matches and probably would have deserved to be bottom. We are always capable of getting on a roll and winning several games in a row, though - as we did, in fact - so I think it

would still have been possible to get back to the top. Looking back, I think this win was probably the turning point of the season.

VIEW FROM THE DRESSING ROOM - ADAM HOLLIOAKE

In the final innings we looked to have the game sewn up at 173-9. Was it complacency on our part that resulted in them almost snatching victory from us?
AH - Not particularly - I think it was more a case of the last pair playing very well. We needed a kick up the backside at this stage of the season, though, because we were kidding ourselves that we were just going to rock up and win the Championship. The dressing room attitude was that we could still win games at half-power and our attention to detail was shoddy. We certainly weren't batting well enough - in this match, for example, Hampshire should have been chasing at least 300 to win but we had collapsed in our second innings.

How critical, in terms of the final result, was the intervention of the tea interval?
AH - I don't think the break had any effect on the way that we played but it might have built up some tension for them. Maybe they had too much time during tea to think about things because I don't think Mascarenhas would have played that fatal shot <u>before</u> tea.

How did you go about rallying the troops at tea time?
AH - I said to the guys that we couldn't worry about what had gone before - we just had to face the fact that after tea they needed five runs while we had a new ball in our hands and we needed one wicket. We could either look at the situation and say "we've thrown this away" or we could look at it and say "what a great opportunity for someone to be a hero". Who was going to take the wicket? Who was going to take a diving catch? Everyone on that field had a chance to be the hero. And Tudes was the man - he was fired up, he came roaring in and, with the new ball, he found a bit of extra pace and bounce to force the miscue from Mascarenhas. Then he went off on his run and I think I was the only one who didn't have the energy left to chase him. I was so drained after such a tense afternoon that I just needed to go and sit down!

Had we lost then we would have dropped to the bottom of the table. If that had happened do you think we could still have come back to retain the Championship?
AH - The final Championship table suggests that we would still have gone on to win the title but, who knows? Thankfully, since we won the game, we didn't need to find out whether or not we could do it!

KEITH MEDLYCOTT'S ASSESSMENT

This was a huge win and, overall, I thought we played very good cricket throughout the game, especially when you consider that we were up against the man who has been the number one spinner in world cricket over the past decade. It was a tense finish and I think the pressure got to just about everyone but, even though it looked like the game could slip away late in the day, we hung on in there and got the result we deserved.

Other Division One Matches

Surrey profited from the fact that the other three Division One matches were all badly rain-affected by taking closer order towards the top of the table. Kent's win over Durham moved them up two places to seventh while Hampshire slipped to the bottom of the division. What a difference three runs can make!

May 31-June 3
Tunbridge Wells:- **Kent beat Durham by 190 runs.** Kent 177 (Wood 5-36) and 237-9dec (Ealham 72 not out); Durham 81 (Masters 6-27) and 143. **Kent 15pts, Durham 3**

Old Trafford:- **Derbyshire drew with Lancashire.** Derbyshire 170 (Martin 5-44) and 24-2; Lancashire 213. **Lancashire 8pts, Derbyshire 7**

Headingley:- **Leicestershire drew with Yorkshire.** Yorkshire 296 (DeFreitas 70, Maddy 63); Leicestershire 146-4. **Yorkshire 7pts, Leicestershire 7**

COUNTY CHAMPIONSHIP DIVISION ONE AT 4TH JUNE

Pos	Prev		P	Pts	W	D	L	Bat	Bowl	Last	Three	Res
1	1	Leicestershire	6	57	1	4	1	16	13	D7	D9	D9
2	2	Yorkshire	4	56	2	2	0	12	12	D7	D10	W19
3	3	Lancashire	5	55	2	3	0	9	10	D8	D6	W17
4	7	Surrey	5	42	1	3	1	10	8	W18	D7	D8
5	4	Somerset	4	37	1	2	1	9	8	D5	L4	W18
6	6	Derbyshire	5	36	0	4	1	7	13	D7	D7	D10
7	9	Kent	4	34	1	3	0	0	10	W15	D6	D6
8	5	Durham	4	32	1	1	2	4	12	L3	D10	L3
9	8	Hampshire	5	26	0	2	3	3	15	L4	D7	D8

CRUSADERS v DRAGONS TIE CHEERS LEADERS

Two NCL Division Two matches took place on the 4th June but had no effect on the leading positions in the table. The tie between Middlesex Crusaders and Glamorgan Dragons at Lord's appeared to be a particularly good result for the leading three teams, while the Essex Eagles' slow start to the campaign continued with a surprising defeat at the hands of the Durham Dynamos.

June 4
Ilford:- **Durham Dynamos beat Essex Eagles by 7 runs.** Durham 182-7 (Katich 61, Lewis 60); Essex 175 in 44.5 overs (S.G. Law 63, Hunter 4-29). **Durham Dynamos 4pts**

Lord's:- **Middlesex Crusaders tied with Glamorgan Dragons.** Middlesex 185-9; Glamorgan 185-9 in 44 overs (James 54 not out). **Middlesex Crusaders 2pts, Glamorgan Dragons 2**

NCL DIVISION TWO AT 4TH JUNE

Pos	Prev		P	Pts	W	T	L	N/R	Last	Three	Res
1	1	Warwickshire Bears	4	16	4	0	0	0	W	W	W
2	2	Nottinghamshire Outlaws	5	16	4	0	1	0	L	W	W
3	3	Surrey Lions	5	16	3	0	0	2	W	N/R	N/R
4	4	Middlesex Crusaders	5	12	2	1	1	1	T	N/R	W
5	5	Glamorgan Dragons	5	10	2	1	2	0	T	W	W
6	6	Essex Eagles	4	6	1	0	2	1	L	N/R	L
7	8	Durham Dynamos	5	4	1	0	4	0	W	L	L
8	7	Derbyshire Scorpions	3	0	0	0	3	0	L	L	L
9	8	Hampshire Hawks	4	0	0	0	4	0	L	L	L

6 The Darkest Hour

Although the Hampshire victory had saved Surrey from an embarrassing and potentially disastrous slump to the bottom of the County Championship table, it was worrying that the last-wicket pair had been able to survive for so long and take the south coast county within three runs of a stupendous triumph. One of the key factors in the 1999 Championship-winning season had been the ability of the bowlers to knock over the opposition tail cheaply time after time. Saqlain had usually proved far too cunning for the average tailender, yet in the Hampshire match he had been unable to dislodge Francis or the partially-incapacitated Mascarenhas, despite beating the bat on a fair number of occasions. There was a feeling that he might be tired, or could have lost a little confidence, after Pakistan's tour to the West Indies, where he had not enjoyed consistent success, and it was also obvious that the knee he had injured during the 1999 World Cup final was still giving him considerable problems. Lesser men might have requested to be rested from the Hampshire match whereas Saqlain demonstrated his qualities as a team man by taking the field and delivering no fewer than seventy-eight overs!

The Pakistani spinner's physical condition was not the number one area of concern, however. More worrying was the fact that the top-order batting had not been firing, to date, with both Mark Butcher and Graham Thorpe surprisingly short of runs and, seemingly, confidence. The Thorpe situation, in particular, was interesting. Following his decision not to tour South Africa in the winter, it appeared that the England selectors had decided to make him wait for his return to the international scene, so his omission from the two-Test series against Zimbabwe had come as no great surprise to anyone. Surrey supporters knew that it was only a matter of time before he was recalled to the England set-up, however, and the triangular one-day international series seemed likely to see his return to the fold. Having said that, his output of runs had been disappointing and would doubtless have been troubling the national selectors. Despite this, I, like most Surrey fans, was hoping that the name G.P. Thorpe would feature in as many of the team's line-ups as possible during the season since it was obvious that he would eventually start scoring heavily and add considerably to the county's batting strength. We wanted him around but we needed him to regain his best form. Yet, as soon as that happened, everyone knew we would lose him to England. It was a no-win situation for the county.

The next game, against Derbyshire at Derby, appeared to offer an opportunity for both the team and individuals to regain some form and confidence. Dominic Cork's side - who I had predicted would finish bottom of the County Championship Division One, having only just sneaked into the top strata in controversial circumstances the previous September - had surprised everyone with a couple of good wins in the Benson And Hedges Cup North group during the early weeks of the season but had faded thereafter. They had yet to win either a Championship match or an NCL game after eight starts and, consequently, it seemed reasonable to expect their confidence to be at rock bottom. Our worries seemed quite trivial by comparison and our confidence level was likely to be on the rise following the Hampshire win and a good start in the NCL. Add to this the fact that we had happy memories of the ground after 1999's comprehensive win during the surge to the Championship title and it seemed that things were set up nicely. As we headed north, everyone was fully expecting Surrey to close the gap on the leading teams in the table.

COUNTY CHAMPIONSHIP - MATCH SIX

DERBYSHIRE versus SURREY
at The County Ground, Derby

First Day - Wednesday 7th June

Surrey 138; Derbyshire 181-9

The Teams And The Toss - *Alec Stewart, free from international duties, replaces Jon Batty in the Surrey line-up, while Jason Ratcliffe continues to deputise for the injured Ben Hollioake. Derbyshire opt to go into the game without a specialist spinner and, with the exception of Kevin Dean, still making a gradual comeback from a stress fracture of the back, the home side appears to be at full strength. Although the sun is shining as the captains toss up, the pitch appears, from the boundary, to be surprisingly dark in hue. Adam Hollioake calls correctly and decides to bat.*

Derbyshire open with the anticipated combination of Cork and Munton and it is immediately clear that both bowlers are obtaining plenty of sideways movement as the early overs produce an above-average quota of appeals. Although Mark Butcher and Ian Ward survive these initial scares, disaster is not far away as Munton strikes a double blow in his third over of the morning, bowling Butcher through the gate with an inswinger and then, two balls later, trapping Graham Thorpe lbw when offering no stroke to a similar delivery. So much for hopes of an early revival in the form of the two England left-handers.

The pitch certainly looks to be playing its part in Surrey's struggle, however, as Alec Stewart edges Cork to the third man boundary in his second over at the crease and the scoreboard gradually grinds to a halt. Although Surrey's honorary captain eventually gets it moving again with a meaty pull to the midwicket rope off Munton, the chastened bowler exacts swift revenge with his next delivery, rattling Stewart's stumps via an inside edge to reduce the visitors to a worrying 31-3.

Undeterred by the pitch and the quality of the bowling, Ali Brown starts positively and, though he looks less secure than Ward, he quickly passes his partner's score as Cork and Munton continue to pose problems.

With the Derbyshire duo being well supported by good ground fielding, the Surrey fifty doesn't materialise until the twenty-first over when Karl Krikken is unable to reach a swinging Cork delivery which goes for four byes. At this stage, Ian Ward is only on nine but the value of his steadfast approach is underlined in the next over when Paul Aldred, replacing Munton (10-4-20-3) at the grandstand end, strikes with his second ball as Brown bottom-edges an attempted pull stroke into his stumps. The reigning county champions are on the back foot again at 51-4 but once they see off Cork at the scoreboard end batting starts to look a little easier. With Aldred unable to add to his initial success and Matthew Cassar failing to locate a consistent line and length, Ward begins to reap the rewards for his early patience by picking off three boundaries in successive overs to move his score into the twenties. When Adam Hollioake then cuts and pulls fours off Aldred's replacement, Trevor Smith, in the closing overs of the session it appears that Surrey have almost neutralised the early advantage won for Derbyshire by Munton and Cork, who between them have delivered all but ten of the morning's thirty-two overs.

Lunch:- Surrey 89-4 (Ward 29*, Hollioake 16*) from 32 overs

During the interval it has emerged that Tim Munton's first-class bowling return for the season before today's play was three wickets at 94.66 runs apiece. Having doubled his wicket tally for the season in just ten overs this morning, he further enhances his 2000 record with another double-strike in his first over of the afternoon. The former Warwickshire bowler is understandably elated as Hollioake pushes his opening delivery straight to Dowman at short leg and then, five balls later, Jason Ratcliffe has his off stump pegged back by a ball which appears to jag back and keep wickedly low. Surrey's position is now rather precarious at 93-6 but, again, the pitch seems to be at least partly to blame for their struggles. There certainly appears to be inconsistency of bounce at the scoreboard end of the ground, with all the batsmen spending time prodding and 'gardening' around a good length both between and during overs. I had also noticed the incoming batsman, Martin Bicknell, out in the middle at lunchtime taking a careful look at the wicket and no doubt contemplating a lengthy spell when Derbyshire's turn comes to bat.

At the moment, Surrey's pressing need is for runs, however, and they are hard to come by against the home side's experienced opening attack. Cork, though wicketless at this point, has played a full part in the visitors' uncomfortable struggle and there is no doubt that Munton has enjoyed the lion's share of the good fortune on offer to date. This balance appears to be changing, though, as one wicket-taking opportunity is missed and another taken in the space of five balls. While second slip grasses a simple chance offered by Bicknell off Munton in the forty-second over, another fumble by the same fielder in the next over, with Cork the bowler and Ward the batsman, is picked up on the rebound by Di Venuto at first slip. Ward's excellent fighting effort had just about kept the Surrey ship afloat and his departure for forty-one spells serious danger at 109-7.

These fears prove justified and the boat lurches closer to the rocks just moments later when Bicknell follows his colleague back to the pavilion. Failing to capitalise on his earlier escape, he becomes Munton's sixth victim when his outside edge is well taken by Krikken standing up to the stumps and he goes for seven with the total unchanged.

The sinking feeling that there can now be no escape for Surrey is then confirmed as Ian Salisbury is adjudged lbw to Cork on the front foot and, after a few defiant blows to the boundary, Alex Tudor becomes the last of Munton's seven scalps when he drives over a full-length delivery and is bowled. Surrey are all out for a mere 138, thus missing out on all five batting points for the third time already this season, and a very happy Tim Munton leads his team-mates from the field with well-deserved figures of 19.5-7-34-7 to his name.

The burning question now is can Surrey's seam attack do similar damage to the Derbyshire batting? With the third seamer duties to be shared between Jason Ratcliffe and Adam Hollioake on a pitch which looks made - perhaps literally? - for the faster bowlers, the decision to play our two spinners and omit Carl Greenidge appears flawed.

Much is, therefore, expected of Messrs Bicknell and Tudor as they fire their opening salvos at Steve Stubbings and Matthew Dowman. Sadly for Surrey, Tudor disappoints early on, overstepping the crease twice in an opening over which costs ten precious runs and generally struggling to locate the right line and length. Bicknell, meanwhile, is reliability itself at the grandstand end and provides his side with a much-needed early break by having Stubbings caught behind from an attempted drive in the fifth over - 13 for 1. This encouraging start needs to be built upon rapidly but the home side's new Australian import, Michael Di Venuto, comes out with all guns blazing and drives Tudor powerfully through backward point and mid-off as the run rate is maintained at a healthy level. With Surrey's advantage already whittled down to ninety-seven by the tenth over of the innings, it therefore comes as a huge relief when Bicknell removes Di Venuto, courtesy of a sliced drive to Ian Ward at square cover, before he can do any more damage.

Despite this setback, Derbyshire continue to press on, posting fifty when Dowman drives a Bicknell no-ball to the cover boundary in the thirteenth over, prompting the introduction of Jason Ratcliffe. Luckily for the visitors, Tudor is now starting to hit his straps at the scoreboard end and, with tea almost upon us, he picks up wickets in successive overs - Matthew Cassar falls lbw when struck on the back pad by a ball nipping back, while Rob Bailey goes to the last ball before the break, brilliantly held by a diving Stewart low and right-handed in front of slip. This burst of two wickets for no runs has put the champions right back in the match.

Tea:- Derbyshire 62-4 (Dowman 22*) from 17.1 overs

During the interval, one important visitor to the ground has been conspicuous by his presence out in the middle. Mike Denness of the ECB's Pitches Liaison Committee has been taking a close look at the playing surface and Derbyshire must be fearing the worst.

Also during the break I speak to Iain Taylor, a fellow Surrey supporter who has been taking a stroll around the ground. He reports that he passed Dominic Cork and made the comment that it had been a good toss to lose, to which the Derbyshire captain apparently replied, 'Yes, but then we knew they would bat first whatever'. This strikes me as being an intriguing comment. Since they are clearly familiar with Surrey's tactics, I wonder whether the home side have succumbed to the temptation to prepare a deliberately damp, seamer-friendly surface? I get the feeling that we will be hearing a lot more about the state of this wicket over the course of the next couple of days.

Upon the players' return to the middle, Martin Bicknell is immediately reintroduced at the grandstand end and makes an almost instant impact, snaring Stephen Titchard at short leg with his second delivery. Derbyshire are now 65 for 5 and the visitors look to be on top as Tudor produces a marvellous over, during which he beats Dowman consistently outside the off stump, and Bicknell has a loud appeal for a catch at the wicket against Karl Krikken turned down. The unorthodox Derbyshire 'keeper mixes strokes of aggressive intent with a variety of air shots for several overs before his luck runs out when Tudor traps him on the crease and wins an affirmative leg-before verdict with the score on ninety-four. Krikken's brief innings has maintained the rather frenetic tempo of the innings, however, and with Dominic Cork now arriving at the wicket it seems unlikely that the pace will slacken. Sure enough, the Derbyshire skipper is immediately on the attack, lofting both of Surrey's opening bowlers over the covers for boundaries, while Dowman bides his time, mixing watchful defence with the occasional well-timed stroke of his own.

It soon becomes apparent that this fast-developing stand could pose a serious threat to the visitors and the decision not to field a specialist third seamer is looking increasingly likely to handicap their efforts. With Bicknell and Tudor having already sent down more than a dozen overs each and the home side closing in on Surrey's total, Adam Hollioake brings himself into the attack at the scoreboard end and employs Saqlain at the grandstand end.

We have now reached a crucial phase of the match and the scales tip heavily towards Derbyshire as the Surrey captain strays too frequently to leg and his premier spinner gifts the opposition ten valuable runs by overstepping the crease five times in three overs. This spell of uncharacteristically indisciplined cricket brings a plethora of milestones - Derbyshire cruise into the lead; the seventh-wicket partnership passes fifty; Dowman arrives at a most worthy fifty from 104 balls in 164 minutes; and the home team post their 150. Things appear to be going from bad to worse for the champions and, when Bicknell and Ratcliffe return to the fray in a double bowling change, a couple of sloppy misfields merely add to the impression that the visitors are running out of inspiration. Given the situation and Surrey's apparent lethargy it's little wonder that the pitch appears to have stopped misbehaving and batting suddenly looks a more straightforward business. Dowman continues to drive fluently through the covers and it seems that the home side will reach stumps with a healthy lead and several wickets intact until Alex Tudor is recalled for one last burst in place of Bicknell.

The young paceman's first over back finally provides some much-needed succour for Surrey when he first trims Dowman's bails with a fine delivery and then dismisses Paul Aldred first ball, the tail-ender top-edging a hook to long leg. The catcher, Jason Ratcliffe, then gets in on the act as a bowler when he traps Trevor Smith lbw with the final ball of the next over to enhance the visitors' previously flagging hopes. Three wickets have now fallen without addition to the score in the space of just nine balls and it looks a certainty that day one will end with both sides' first innings complete - a statistic which lends significant support to the view that the pitch has been below par for first-class cricket.

As it happens, the Derbyshire first innings is extended into day two when, a couple of balls into Tudor's next over, the umpires decide that the light has deteriorated sufficiently to suspend play. The time is 7.30pm and, with 2.4 overs still to bowl, we had been on course for one of the latest ever endings to a day of County Championship cricket. Derbyshire clearly take the first day honours, but Surrey's late strikes will have given them hope that they can continue their fightback tomorrow. As I leave the ground the pitch is under close scrutiny again.

Close:- Derbyshire 181-9 (Cork 35*, Munton 0*) from 47.2 overs

VIEW FROM THE DRESSING ROOM - ALISTAIR BROWN

Did we have concerns about the pitch at Derby as soon as we saw it?
AB - We knew it was damp but I wouldn't go so far as to say that we had immediate concerns. Once the game started, though, we realised that batting was going to be very difficult indeed.

From your point of view, what was the main problem with the pitch?
AB - There appeared to be something very fishy going on because the dampness tended to be only in the middle of the pitch. The bowlers' footholds and the net pitches were bone dry so they obviously have very funny rainfall in Derby! It looked to be a similar pitch to the one we'd played on at Chester-le-Street, although in that case the dampness was understandable because they'd had masses of rainfall and the whole of the ground was wet.

I know it's easy to say with hindsight, but wouldn't we have been better off selecting a third specialist seam bowler, maybe in place of Ian Salisbury, and then bowling first when we won the toss?
AB - We knew the pitch would be tough to bat on early in the game but I think we perhaps gambled on making about 200, bowling them out for the same sort of score and then coming through with the spinners in the second innings. It would also be fair to say that the wicket did quite a bit more than we thought it would do. Unfortunately, Sals didn't feature as a bowler because we didn't make a big enough first innings score and, as a result, we ended up with a shortened game - I think if the game had gone into the fourth day then Sals would have played a major part. If we had known it was only going to last just over two days then I think we would have played an extra seamer.

After we had been bowled out for 138, Derbyshire managed to take a first innings lead through a gritty Dowman effort and a positive knock by Dominic Cork. Was the pitch showing signs of easing at this stage?
AB - It did get slightly easier as it dried out, yes. Dowman batted pretty well, though he enjoyed the kind of luck with playing and missing which you need on that kind of pitch. The game was quite evenly poised when Corky came in and his score of about forty was a lot in the context of the game and it shifted the balance. I think he was virtually admitting that there was a problem with the pitch by running down the wicket to play a lot of his shots.

VIEW FROM THE DRESSING ROOM - ALEC STEWART

Do you think we selected the wrong team for this match?
AS - Yes, I think we definitely picked the wrong side - we can get blinded sometimes because we have two excellent spinners. Hindsight is a wonderful thing but I think we would have been better off going in with three specialist seamers, leaving out either a spinner or, more likely, a batsman. Since I was keeping wicket in the match we could have had five specialist bowlers filling positions seven to eleven. But I think that on a damp wicket we needed to play a third specialist seamer.

Second Day - Thursday 8th June

Surrey 138 and 218; Derbyshire 191 and 119-3

There is much speculation around the ground about the pitch and a possible points deduction for Derbyshire as the day's action gets under way. Surrey need to take the final wicket quickly and, after two boundaries from Cork, Martin Bicknell duly obliges when Munton edges a drive and is well taken behind the wicket by Alec Stewart. The home side's lead is fifty-three, which could prove quite handy unless the pitch has eased. We are about to discover whether or not it has.

The early indications are that it hasn't, since there is clear evidence of uneven bounce, notably when Mark Butcher takes a blow on the glove from Munton and then with Ian Ward's dismissal later in the same over. Ward perishes when he aims to leg only to find the ball lifting sharply on him and taking the outside edge on its way to third slip.

This is most certainly not what Surrey had required and the batsmen's concerns about the playing surface appear to show with an initially disastrous attempt at all-out attack. Having lofted his first delivery, from Munton, over extra cover for four and cut his fourth through point for another boundary, Graham Thorpe's innings is terminated by his fifth ball, a nasty lifter which drops down onto his stumps via his forearm.

The former Warwickshire captain now has nine wickets in his bag, out of a possible twelve, and Surrey are reeling at 24-2. It seems that things can't get much worse for the visitors at this point but they do, however, in the very next over from Dominic Cork as Mark Butcher's defensive stroke results in an edge to first slip where Rob Bailey holds a routine catch to spark further Derbyshire celebrations. Surrey are now well and truly on the ropes, twenty-five runs in arrears with only seven wickets left. Can the champions possibly turn this situation around?

They now have a mountain to climb but Alec Stewart and Ali Brown are clearly determined to make a fight of it and come out with all guns blazing. Having survived an early mix-up which had resulted in a missed run-out opportunity, Brown is soon forcing Cork to the cover boundary and taking Surrey into the lead with a square cut four off Paul Aldred, the Derbyshire captain's replacement at the scoreboard end.

After a spell of eight overs, Munton, like his skipper, takes a break from the action and the introduction of Trevor Smith quickly threatens to transform the match. In the course of two overs of assorted long-hops, Stewart and Brown plunder no fewer than four fours and a six with a variety of cuts, pulls and forces, raising a quick-fire half-century partnership in the process.

Appreciating the danger to his side, Cork sends Smith back to the outfield to contemplate figures of 2-0-23-0 and brings himself back into the fray. Initially, he fares little better than his colleague, however, his first over yielding pulled and driven boundaries to Brown as the visitors move closer to a position of parity. Stewart meanwhile continues the onslaught, a crunching cover drive to the boundary off Aldred bringing up the Surrey hundred in the twenty-fifth over of the innings.

Derbyshire are now the side under the cosh but the inspiration they so badly need at this critical stage is provided by their captain when Stewart appears to check a straight drive. Although the stroke is still middled and well timed by Surrey's honorary club captain, he is unable to keep the ball down and Cork sticks up a right hand to pluck an amazing catch out of thin air. The Derbyshire skipper celebrates, Stewart goes for a well-played forty-two and a very dangerous stand has been ended with the total at 108, much to the relief of the home side.

They are quickly reminded of the threat that Brown still poses, however, when he cuts Aldred high over cover's head for four in the session's final over.

Lunch:- Surrey 112-4 (Brown 44*, Hollioake 0*) from 27 overs

With his second-string seamers largely out of sorts, it's inevitable that Dominic Cork and Tim Munton are both back into the attack straight after the interval. Ali Brown continues to look in fine form, though, pushing Munton straight for two and then forcing him to the cover boundary in the afternoon's second over to reach a quite magnificent fifty from just 63 balls in 86 minutes. He promptly celebrates by driving the Derbyshire captain wide of mid-on for three and then thumping him over mid-on for the tenth four of his innings.

Although, at this juncture, batting again seems a less hazardous occupation, possibly as a result of the much-battered ball becoming softer, the pitch certainly hasn't eased completely, a point proved when Adam Hollioake takes a nasty rap on the knuckles from a rearing Cork delivery. This provokes an aggressive response from the Surrey skipper as he drives Munton beautifully, if uppishly, through the covers for two boundaries in quick succession. Cork reacts quickly to this attack from Hollioake, replacing his most experienced bowler with Matthew Cassar at the scoreboard end in an attempt to stem the tide that is now flowing in Surrey's favour. This move doesn't initially prove successful, however, as Brown raises the Surrey 150 with a pull to the deep midwicket boundary and then repeats the dose, this time behind square leg, in Cassar's second over to complete the fifth-wicket pair's fifty stand. The Derbyshire all-rounder quickly learns his lesson, though, and gains his revenge when Brown pushes at a ball of fuller length outside his off stump and edges a low catch to Karl Krikken behind the stumps. It's now 160-5, effectively 107-5, and the match is back in the balance.

While Brown and Cassar have been duelling at one end, the two captains have been fighting a contest of their own at the other, with Cork's testing line on or around off stump causing problems for Adam Hollioake. Despite beating the bat on a number of occasions, no reward is forthcoming for the Derbyshire skipper, however, and it's Cassar, in fact, who makes two further breakthroughs in successive overs to put his side back in control. He first disposes of Jason Ratcliffe, whose uneasy four-over stay at the crease is ended by a lifting delivery which he edges tamely to Krikken, then he follows up by claiming the prize scalp of Hollioake in his next over. The Surrey captain's dismissal for twenty-one, with the score advanced only as far as 171, comes about in disappointing fashion with a top-edged hook to his opposite number at long leg and as the crestfallen Hollioake departs to contemplate the stroke which has brought about his downfall, Cassar has now taken three for six in the space of nineteen deliveries to swing the match dramatically in Derbyshire's favour. The Surrey lead is just 118 at this stage but the strength of the team's lower-order batting gives the small group of away supporters hope that the opposition may yet have to chase a tricky fourth innings target in the region of 180 to 200.

This is soon looking very optimistic, however, as a further two wickets fall in the space of three eventful deliveries with the lead extended only as far as 125. The first of these two wounding blows is self-inflicted when a terrible mix-up results in the run out of Martin Bicknell. Having pushed a Cork delivery backward of square leg and turned for what appears to be a straightforward second run, Surrey's senior seam bowler is stunned to find that Alex Tudor has taken a different view of the situation and has settled for a single. By this point Bicknell, already fully committed to the run, is unable to turn back and the resulting throw to the bowler's end sees him hopelessly stranded in mid-pitch. This disastrous loss of a valuable wicket is then compounded two balls later when Tudor, having driven Cork's next delivery to the point boundary, plays the ball onto his stumps in attempting another off-side forcing stroke.

Although there appears to be only a very slim chance of Surrey escaping from the tight corner in which they now find themselves, Ian Salisbury and Saqlain Mushtaq continue to battle bravely, taking advantage of the fact that both Cassar and Cork are starting to tire after long unbroken spells to push the total up to, and then beyond, two-hundred. By the simple expedient of playing every ball on its merits the last-wicket pair manages to cause a few flutters in the Derbyshire camp, forcing Cork to take a well-earned breather after fifteen successive overs from the grandstand end and then seeing off Cassar at the scoreboard end.

This appears to represent a moral victory for the batsmen but the fresh bowlers are soon posing greater problems than their predecessors and it's not long before Paul Aldred ends the innings by deceiving Saqlain into chipping a simple catch to midwicket. Having at one stage been 160-4, Surrey are all out for a very disappointing total of 218, leaving Derbyshire to score just 166 to win. Although the visitors would have wanted to set a target of 200-plus, there is a feeling that this could still prove to be a tricky task for the home side - one that might even produce a very interesting finish sometime tomorrow.

Tea:- Between Innings

With such a small total to defend, Surrey need to produce a disciplined yet aggressive performance, with early wickets a necessity, as the match resumes after the break.

After a quiet start, the game bursts into life during the fourth over of the innings, delivered by Alex Tudor. In the space of two balls Surrey ride an emotional rollercoaster on a return trip to joy via despair, as Steve Stubbings, having chopped a ball into his stumps but been reprieved by the umpire's call of 'no-ball', then aims a scything cover drive at the very next delivery and nicks a straightforward catch to Alec Stewart. Tudor is off the hook for his front foot indiscretion and the hosts are immediately on the back foot at 8 for 1.

The new batsman, Michael Di Venuto, looks in no mood to be overawed by the situation, however, and, after cutting his first ball from Tudor to the point boundary, he moves rapidly on to twelve with two well-timed drives in the big fast bowler's fourth over.

At this early stage, runs are flowing much too freely from Surrey's point of view, so it comes as a huge relief when Bicknell redresses the balance by forcing Matt Dowman to play on in the next over of the innings. With the young left-hander having played so well in the first innings for his sixty-nine, the visitors are pleased to see him departing for just ten this time around with the score at 26-2.

Surrey now look to have the edge and Matt Cassar does nothing to steady the home fans' nerves as he is struck on the pads first ball, prompting a loud, but unsuccessful, appeal for lbw. Meanwhile, at the other end, Di Venuto appears absolutely nerveless and he dominates Tudor sufficiently for Adam Hollioake to withdraw his young pace ace from the firing line with figures of 6-0-26-1 to his name.

Unfortunately for the visitors, Jason Ratcliffe, the replacement for Tudor at the scoreboard end, is also unable to contain the Tasmanian and by the time the Derbyshire fifty rattles up in the fifteenth over Di Venuto's contribution is already an impressive thirty-six. Surrey appear to have a plan to feed the powerful left-hander's strokes square of the wicket on the off-side, since they appear to represent an area of weakness as well as strength, a point demonstrated by his first innings dismissal. With so few runs in the bank this looks to be a high-risk strategy, however.

Fortunately for Surrey, Matthew Cassar's frailty is rather easier and less expensive to expose. Never comfortable against spin bowling, the Derbyshire all-rounder survives for just six deliveries once Saqlain replaces Ratcliffe - although he tries to be positive, he misses an attempted slog sweep and departs lbw for a painstaking four. Thanks to Di Venuto's fluency, the third-wicket partnership has, nevertheless, yielded a very handy thirty-nine runs and it's clear to everyone in the ground that the home side holds a significant advantage while the Australian remains at the wicket. As if to emphasise this point he drives the returning Tudor through extra cover for the eighth boundary of his innings to reach a marvellous half-century from just 47 balls in seventy minutes.

At this stage Di Venuto appears to have a real hold over Tudor but the young quickie shows great spirit to fight back and rattle the Aussie's stumps in his next over. Sadly, he has overstepped the crease in doing so and the total advances by another two runs. This lucky escape, allied to the fact that he looks all at sea against Saqlain, at least sends Di Venuto into his shell and with the new batsman, Rob Bailey, also playing very resolutely the outside prospect of a Derbyshire win inside two days quickly disappears.

Surrey are clearly up against it now, though, and the hosts' hundred comes up with five overs left for play. By this time, Bicknell has returned in place of Tudor and he gives Bailey a real test in his final two overs of the day. Although the bowler has a loud appeal for a catch at the wicket turned down and induces two edges to third man, the former Northamptonshire and England batsman responds with a leg glance for four as the fourth-wicket stand passes fifty to leave Surrey staring down the barrel at close of play.

Close:- Derbyshire 119-3 (Di Venuto 57*, Bailey 27*) from 36 overs

VIEW FROM THE DRESSING ROOM - ALISTAIR BROWN

We eventually set Derbyshire 166 to win. With the pitch apparently easing, how confident were we that we could still win the match?

AB - We always believe we can win but we knew that we possibly weren't the favourites. We felt that if we could get them to, say, 50-4 then we would be in with a very good shout but things didn't work out for us and once they got past the opening spells from Martin Bicknell and Alex Tudor we felt that it wasn't going to be our day.

Third Day - Friday 9th June

Surrey 138 and 218; Derbyshire 191 and 167-3

Derbyshire beat Surrey by seven wickets
Derbyshire 15pts, Surrey 3

Day three dawns with the news that the Pitches Liaison Committee has announced that Derbyshire are to be deducted eight points for producing an unsatisfactory pitch. Needless to say, the matter dominates the conversation around the ground as we suffer a delayed start due to rain. I speak to a number of Derbyshire supporters and, whilst I can understand them being unhappy about the situation, I simply cannot fathom why many of them seem to be blaming Surrey for the points penalty. Mike Denness, David Hughes and Chris Wood, the Pitches Liaison Officers who made the final decision, are impartial arbiters appointed by the ECB and have no Surrey connections at all. I can only assume that the Derbyshire folk who are complaining about the visitors' role in the PLC's verdict might have been influenced by a scurrilous piece of supposition in the local daily newspaper where it was stated that '...it is a fair guess that Adam Hollioake, Surrey's captain, was critical of the conditions'. Even if that were the case, I see nothing wrong with him expressing an opinion because, when all is said and done, the actual

decision was that of the PLC, **not** the Surrey team or its captain - end of story.
Facing the possibility of finishing the match with a grand total of minus five points should they not complete their expected victory, Derbyshire make a blistering start once play gets under way at 11.30am. After both batsmen pick up a single in Martin Bicknell's opening over, Rob Bailey gives his side an enormous push in the direction of victory by blasting successive deliveries from Saqlain Mushtaq for six, the first over long-on and the second over long-off. Clearly it's not just the supporters who are feeling angry about the PLC's eight-point penalty!

Bailey's stunning assault has a dramatic and predictable effect. Not only does it deny Surrey the flying start they need to put pressure on their hosts but it also delivers a huge psychological blow and heads drop visibly.

Di Venuto then follows his colleague's lead with a violent square-driven boundary off Bicknell in an over costing seven runs and when the dose is repeated in the bowler's next over the white flag is quickly on its way up the flagpole. After one more over - a maiden - Bicknell immediately calls Carl Greenidge, the Surrey twelfth man, from the visitors' dressing room and leaves the field. The obvious conclusion to be drawn from this is that Bicknell is carrying an injury of some sort which he, quite rightly, sees no point in risking any further.

The end of the match comes quickly, in any case, with a welter of boundaries by Di Venuto off Jason Ratcliffe completing the Derbyshire duo's hundred partnership as well as the match. The remaining forty-seven runs required by the home side at start of play have been scored in just 35 minutes from a mere 53 deliveries and the Surrey team leaves the field looking extremely downcast, as one would expect.

On the way back to their dressing room they then have to run the gauntlet of a small group of Derbyshire supporters who are still, absurdly, venting their anger with the PLC's decision at the wrong people. Unfortunately, one or two Surrey players are sucked into a heated discussion which Keith Medlycott quickly and sensibly terminates. As if things weren't already bad enough, this darkens a gloomy day still further.

As the Derbyshire players celebrate their victory and the door to the nearby Surrey dressing room remains firmly closed, it's time for me to take stock and make some notes. The stunning annihilation at Chester-le-Street was a huge disappointment but this defeat seems to have hit everyone harder. At the start of the campaign, defeats against two of the prime candidates for relegation seemed unthinkable, yet that is exactly what has happened and our prospects of retaining the County Championship title have received a terrible setback.

For about an hour I sit outside the pavilion assimilating my thoughts and concerns. While the door to the Surrey dressing room remains shut, a few of the Derbyshire lads emerge on to the outfield for a game of football. Acknowledging some of their supporters, they shout 'We're going to stay up - fifth place, no problem'. I admire their optimism and certainly don't begrudge them their moment of glory but I still think they will be relegated.

That's one for the future, though, and I now have to pull myself back to the present time. After the humiliation at Chester-le-Street and the never-ending rain at both Taunton and Canterbury, I have become used to disconsolate walks back to my accommodation but this one is definitely the worst of the season so far. I hope it won't be too long before Surrey put a spring back into my step.

Surrey 138 and 218; Derbyshire 191 and 167-3
Derbyshire beat Surrey by seven wickets - Derbyshire 15pts, Surrey 3

DERBYSHIRE v SURREY at DERBY. Played from 7th - 9th June
Surrey won the toss   Umpires:- B. Dudleston & V.A. Holder

SURREY - First Innings

DERBYSHIRE bowling

Fall of wkt	Batsman	How Out	Score	Balls	4s	6s		O	M	R	W
1- 9	M.A. Butcher	b Munton	3	22	0	0	Cork	22	4	62	2
7- 109	I.J. Ward	c Di Venuto b Cork	41	122	4	0	Munton	19.5	7	34	7
2- 9	G.P. Thorpe	lbw b Munton	0	2	0	0	Aldred	4	2	13	1
3- 31	A.J. Stewart +	b Munton	14	33	2	0	Cassar	4	0	11	0
4- 51	A.D. Brown	b Aldred	12	22	0	0	Smith	2	0	11	0
5- 93	A.J. Hollioake *	c Dowman b Munton	16	27	3	0					
6- 93	J.D. Ratcliffe	b Munton	0	5	0	0					
8- 109	M.P. Bicknell	c Krikken b Munton	7	33	0	0					
10- 138	A.J. Tudor	b Munton	16	28	3	0					
9- 118	I.D.K. Salisbury	lbw b Cork	4	12	0	0					
	Saqlain Mushtaq	Not Out	8	10	1	0					
	Extras (5b, 2lb, 10nb)		17								
	TOTAL	(51.5 overs)	138								

DERBYSHIRE - First Innings

SURREY bowling

Fall of wkt	Batsman	How Out	Score	Balls	4s	6s		O	M	R	W
7- 181	M.P. Dowman	b Tudor	69	140	10	0	Bicknell	19.1	1	75	4
1- 13	S.D. Stubbings	c Stewart b Bicknell	3	11	0	0	Tudor	17	3	64	5
2- 41	M.J. Di Venuto	c Ward b Bicknell	16	17	2	0	Ratcliffe	7	2	21	1
3- 62	M.E. Cassar	lbw b Tudor	5	17	1	0	Hollioake	4	1	13	0
4- 62	R.J. Bailey	c Stewart b Tudor	0	6	0	0	Saqlain	3	0	13	0
5- 65	S.P. Titchard	c Salisbury b Bicknell	3	7	0	0					
6- 94	K.M. Krikken +	lbw b Tudor	17	26	2	0					
	D.G. Cork *	Not Out	44	79	7	0					
8- 181	P. Aldred	c Ratcliffe b Tudor	0	1	0	0					
9- 181	T.M. Smith	lbw b Ratcliffe	0	6	0	0					
10- 191	T.A. Munton	c Stewart b Bicknell	1	3	0	0					
	Extras (5lb, 4w, 24nb)		33								
	TOTAL	(50.1 overs)	191								

SURREY - Second Innings

DERBYSHIRE bowling

Fall of wkt	Batsman	How Out	Score	Balls	4s	6s		O	M	R	W
3- 28	M.A. Butcher	c Bailey b Cork	6	25	1	0	Cork	25	8	62	3
1- 12	I.J. Ward	c Aldred b Munton	10	21	1	0	Munton	15	2	53	2
2- 24	G.P. Thorpe	b Munton	8	5	2	0	Aldred	8.4	1	25	1
4- 108	A.J. Stewart +	c & b Cork	42	52	6	0	Smith	2	0	23	0
5- 160	A.D. Brown	c Krikken b Cassar	75	110	12	1	Cassar	12	0	46	3
7- 171	A.J. Hollioake *	c Cork b Cassar	21	57	3	0					
6- 164	J.D. Ratcliffe	c Krikken b Cassar	2	17	0	0					
8- 179	M.P. Bicknell	run out	4	13	0	0					
9- 183	A.J. Tudor	b Cork	7	12	1	0					
	I.D.K. Salisbury	Not Out	20	27	3	0					
10- 218	Saqlain Mushtaq	c Munton b Aldred	12	38	1	0					
	Extras (1b, 8lb, 2nb)		11								
	TOTAL	(62.4 overs)	218								

DERBYSHIRE - Second Innings

SURREY bowling

Fall of wkt	Batsman	How Out	Score	Balls	4s	6s		O	M	R	W
2- 26	M.P. Dowman	b Bicknell	10	29	1	0	Bicknell	18	5	52	1
1- 8	S.D. Stubbings	c Stewart b Tudor	0	11	0	0	Tudor	11	0	59	1
	M.J. Di Venuto	Not Out	92	133	14	0	Ratcliffe	2.5	0	25	0
3- 65	M.E. Cassar	lbw b Saqlain	4	26	0	0	Saqlain	13	5	24	1
	R.J. Bailey	Not Out	40	76	3	2					
	Extras (7lb, 2w, 12nb)		21								
	TOTAL	(44.5 overs)	167 - 3								

86

VIEW FROM THE BOUNDARY
(Compiled from notes made at the end of the match)

Where, for the moment, had it all gone wrong? In this match our team selection looked flawed from the start. This is emphasised by the fact that Ian Salisbury, one of our front-line bowlers, didn't bowl a ball in the match. Much though I hate to say it, as one of the leg-spinner's biggest supporters, I felt he should have been omitted in favour of Carl Greenidge, given the condition of the pitch at the start of the match. Clearly, Jason Ratcliffe was not sufficiently penetrative to play as the third seamer, impressive though he had been in the limited-overs form of the game to date. It was also obvious that, while he had been receiving a fair amount of criticism, the injured Ben Hollioake's value to the side with the ball was demonstrated in his absence. And we were still being denied the use of Mark Butcher's bowling through injury, too. There had been no word as to when Butch might be fit to bowl again but there was no doubting the fact that we had missed his skills as a swing-bowling fourth seamer in the early weeks of the season.

It seemed to me that our team selection then committed us to batting first, which always looked fraught with danger given a playing surface which started damp. This wouldn't have been such a risky decision had all our batsmen been in form. As it was, nobody in the batting line-up had consistently covered themselves in glory thus far, and the form of both Mark Butcher and Graham Thorpe, of all people, was continuing to give cause for concern in the short term. In their defence it had to be said that both players had been unlucky with some of their dismissals, notably Thorpe's in the second innings here.

Then there was the bigger picture to consider, along with the longer-term worries. The side was, understandably, looking a little short on spirit and confidence at the moment. Clearly, Keith Medlycott was about to undertake one of his biggest tests as a manager, having enjoyed almost non-stop success in his coaching career to date. It looked like a major job but everyone felt sure he would succeed.

We also had to think about what would happen if players continued to fail and had to be dropped. Which of the players in the second eleven, other than the prolific Nadeem Shahid, was pressing for a place? As I recorded my thoughts the team had just been beaten by Middlesex and, judging by the details printed in the press, no Surrey player had made much of an impression.

Perhaps my biggest worry, however, was the fitness of the bowlers. How much longer could Saqlain go on bowling over after over before his injured knee gave way completely? And, if it did, how long would he be out of action for? It looked to be a serious injury, judging by the way he was regularly hobbling from the field at the end of a day's bowling.

Then there was the new-ball pairing. The lack of a truly penetrative third seamer was placing a huge burden on Martin Bicknell and Alex Tudor, who were having to do the work of three bowlers. An injury to one, or even both, looked absolutely inevitable unless we could reduce their workload.

At the other end of the scale, I was concerned that Ian Salisbury was not getting **enough** bowling, as a result of games, like this one, being played on seamer-friendly surfaces. It's a well-known fact that spinners like to bowl a lot of overs to develop rhythm and confidence and Solly had not, to date, been able to bowl many long spells. Would he therefore be under-prepared and unable to do himself justice when we played on a pitch that did suit him?

Apart from these few things, everything was fine!

VIEW FROM THE DRESSING ROOM - ALEC STEWART

Were you convinced that Derbyshire's points deduction was justified?
AS - It was only justified if the Pitches Liaison Officers were going to be consistent throughout the season. You can't tell me that this was the worst wicket produced for a county game in the

country this year and, since only three pitches were marked down sufficiently to incur a points deduction all season, I wouldn't have penalised Derbyshire for this surface. That said, it's not the type of pitch we should be playing on. I like to ask this question - if you were staging a Test match at your ground is this the type of pitch you would produce? I don't believe for one minute that Derbyshire would have come up with that wicket if they had been hosting an international match, so I don't see why the standard of what they produce should be any lower for a county game.

So you would agree with the view I hold that there should really have been a lot more cases where points were deducted?
AS - Absolutely. I have a bee in my bonnet about the overall quality of pitches and practice pitches prepared in this country and, until we come up with better surfaces, the overall quality of our cricketers will not measure up to that of cricketers produced by, say, Australia or South Africa. Most of their facilities put ours to shame.

The locals seemed to blame Surrey for the points deduction. Why?!
AS - Well, I suppose it's inevitable that people look for excuses and someone to blame when their team is penalised. And then it didn't help that the Pitches Liaison Officers spoke to Surrey players in full view of the public. They merely came to us to ask our opinions but, in this kind of situation, it would have been more sensible to talk to us behind closed doors in order to avoid spectators and opposition players jumping to the wrong conclusions.

VIEW FROM THE DRESSING ROOM - ALISTAIR BROWN

Do you believe that the decision to dock Derbyshire eight points was justified?
AB - You never like to see anyone being deducted points but the question of how it apparently only rained in patches needs to be answered. I've read about how the umpires said it was a good wicket. I'd say that it **would have been** good but for the fact that it started wet, which meant that it was very, very sporty - the bounce and movement available to the seamers was extravagant. Obviously we can't be certain about what actually happened, whether it was by accident or design, but I would have to say that it **appeared** that they had watered the wicket. And the behaviour of the groundman concerned me, too - he was almost **too** nervous and apologetic. He kept telling me that it would have been a great wicket if only it hadn't rained and how they'd had fantastic pitches there all season - it was very suspicious. I do feel sorry for Derbyshire, though, because although they aren't the strongest side they've got some very likeable guys and hardworking players on their staff.

What was the dressing room reaction to this defeat?
AB - I thought our response was excellent. We wanted to practise at the ground on the Saturday but when we turned up we weren't allowed to get into our own dressing room or get any of our gear. So we changed in the car park at the front of the ground, did some fielding practice on the grass car parking area at the back and put in a really good session, which was excellent for team morale. I think we took a lot out of that day - it said "we're a top side, we enjoy playing together, we're going to work hard and things are going to happen for us soon." And that's how it worked out - we won the National League game the next day and we were back on the rails for the rest of the season.

We were now well off the pace in the title race. Were we still confident, with big games against our main rivals still to come, that we could turn things around?
AB - The fixture list was set up well for us, really - we still had the three 'big guns' to come, both

home and away, so it was up to us to win those games and if we did that then we knew we could close the gap very quickly.

VIEW FROM THE DRESSING ROOM - ADAM HOLLIOAKE

Were we concerned about the condition of the pitch right from the start?
AH - When we first looked at the pitch we could see that it was a damp seamer but we didn't think it was going to play as badly as it did. It's true to say that it did play much better on day two but it clearly wasn't the kind of wicket on which we should be playing professional county cricket. And even if a pitch does end up playing well that's not the point - if it starts damp or it isn't the best quality surface that can be produced then I think points should be docked before the game even starts, whoever the home team is. The intent is the most important factor in this matter. The competition regulations state that the pitch must start dry and, since everyone has covers, there is no excuse for games being played on anything other than a dry wicket.

We appeared to be guilty of selecting the wrong side for this match. Fair comment or not?
AH - There was definitely a case here for playing another seamer but when you have got two spinners as good as Salisbury and Saqlain then it's very hard to leave one of them out - even on pitches that don't suit them they have the quality to take wickets. I think the problem here was that we got bowled out for 138 - with that sort of total on the board you would struggle to win a game even if you had the best four bowlers in the world in your line-up. The pitch was difficult to bat on but our total was unacceptable.

Did our line-up commit us to batting first, when we might have been better off bowling?
AH - At Chester-le-Street the game had started on a similar kind of pitch and we decided to bowl when we won the toss. We then found that the ball made indentations in the surface which, when they dried out, made batting more difficult as the game went on. As a result, I decided to bat first here, only to find that the opposite thing happened and conditions actually got easier for batting - so it was really a case of us reading the pitch incorrectly.

Some of the local and national press and the Derby members seemed to blame you and Surrey for the fact that Derbyshire had eight points deducted. Why do you think that was?
AH - It baffles me! Both here and later in the season at Scarborough the situation was the same. At no stage did I approach a Pitch Liaison Officer - they came to me, they asked for my opinion and I said that I thought the pitch was poor. And that was about as far as it went. I find it unbelievable that anyone can seriously think that Adam Hollioake is the person who deducts the points. If someone does come at me with that argument then I tend to turn my back and walk away because I can't be wasting my time talking to people like that! At the end of the day the teams who produce poor pitches need to take a long hard look at themselves - if they provide a good wicket then they can save themselves a lot of problems.

After this defeat I was at the ground writing up my notes for over an hour yet I didn't see anyone emerge from our dressing room in that time. Did we have a team discussion about the match and our rather precarious position in the Championship?
AH - Yes, we did, and that was where our season turned around, really. We sat down for an hour and a lot of home truths were told. We'd gone back to whinging like the Surrey of old - we'd complained about the pitch, we'd complained about the weather, we'd complained about everything that was out of our control but, at the end of the day, we simply had to put all that aside and get out there and win games. Everyone agreed that we'd been selling ourselves short in training and in practice and, from there on in, we worked like hell until the end of the season.

KEITH MEDLYCOTT'S ASSESSMENT

Derby was a big disappointment, much more so than Durham. We went into the game with two spinners and you can always look back, with hindsight, and wonder whether or not it was the right decision. We felt, however, that the pitch was similar to the one in Durham, where the ball had left indentations in the damp surface, and that led us to believe that it would turn later in the game. That was, in fact, proved correct because Saqlain did get the ball to turn on the second day but by that time - having been sixty-five runs short of where we wanted to be at the end of our first innings - we were trailing in the match and we were never able to recover the lost ground. We had appreciated that it would be tough to bat on the first morning but we came up short because (a) they bowled exceptionally well; (b) there was excessive seam movement; (c) their wicket-keeper stood up to most of their seamers, which prevented our batsmen from using their feet to launch a counter-attack and (d) we simply didn't bat well enough.

A lot has been said about the pitch but I'm not convinced that Derbyshire wanted to produce a wet wicket. That said, we shouldn't be playing professional cricket on that kind of surface and there is clearly something wrong when you see top-order batsmen running down the pitch to the seamers in the first five overs of an innings - that's not the way we want to be going.

Despite our initial anger, I felt for their groundsman - I think he's an honest guy and he was very upset by the whole affair. What I did say to him, though, was that if I was a groundsman and I knew, for whatever reason, that the wicket was going to be wet at the start of a match, I would speak to the umpires and tell them that I needed another day to get it fit for play. I'm not sure whether anything could then be done in terms of delaying the start of the game by a day but if the pitch isn't dry when the first ball is bowled then, in my opinion, it deserves to be (a) reported and (b) hit with a points penalty.

As for ourselves, we had a serious discussion at the end of the game. At times things got a bit heated but, in the end, we came up with the answers that we wanted. We agreed that individual players had to put in more time on their own game, because the majority of people there in the dressing room were coming up short of expectations in their own skill department. A lot of the batting problems were down to the bad weather we had experienced but we couldn't keep using that as an excuse. We looked at ourselves very carefully and honest answers came out. As a result, we worked and prepared harder and, from that moment in the season, we never really looked back.

Other Division One Matches

The disappointment of Surrey's defeat and subsequent slide to fifth place in the table was compounded by victories for both Yorkshire and Lancashire, over Durham and Hampshire respectively. The white rose county was now twenty-eight points ahead of us and they also had a game in hand, while the team from the other side of the Pennines enjoyed a twenty-seven point advantage. There was clear cause for concern.

June 6-8
Liverpool:- **Lancashire beat Hampshire by an innings and 35 runs.** Lancashire 269 (Fairbrother 77 not out, Flintoff 73, Warne 4-61); Hampshire 95 (Smethurst 4-15) and 139 (Flintoff 4-18). **Lancashire 17pts, Hampshire 3**

June 6-9
Bath:- **Somerset beat Kent by two wickets.** Kent 261 (Dravid 90, Caddick 6-57) and 223 (Walker 61, Caddick 4-40); Somerset 295 (Parsons 62, Masters 5-55) and 193-8. **Somerset 17pts, Kent 5**

June 7-9
Chester-le-Street:- **Yorkshire beat Durham by six wickets.** Durham 189 (Hoggard 5-67) and 201 (Gough 6-63); Yorkshire 294 (Vaughan 94, Lehmann 79) and 97-4. **Yorkshire 17pts, Durham 3**

COUNTY CHAMPIONSHIP DIVISION ONE AT 9TH JUNE

Pos	Prev		P	Pts	W	D	L	Bat	Bowl	Last	Three	Res
1	2	Yorkshire	5	73	3	2	0	14	15	W17	D7	D10
2	3	Lancashire	6	72	3	3	0	11	13	W17	D8	D6
3	1	Leicestershire	6	57	1	4	1	16	13	D7	D9	D9
4	5	Somerset	5	54	2	2	1	11	11	W17	D5	L4
5	4	Surrey	6	45	1	3	2	10	11	L3	W18	D7
6	6	Derbyshire	6	43*	1	4	1	7	16	W7	D7	D7
7	7	Kent	5	39	1	3	1	2	13	L5	W15	D6
8	8	Durham	5	35	1	1	3	4	15	L3	L3	D10
9	9	Hampshire	6	29	0	2	4	3	18	L3	L4	D7

* Deducted 8pts for sub-standard pitch

REPEAT OF DURHAM RESILIENCE REQUIRED

The team now faced a familiar situation. As at Chester-le-Street, they had to put the disappointment of the Championship match behind them and lift themselves for the NCL Division Two encounter on the Sunday. Meanwhile, the Surrey fans who had made the trip north for both matches had the equally difficult task of finding ways to entertain themselves in Derby for a day and a half!

NCL DIVISION TWO - MATCH SIX

DERBYSHIRE SCORPIONS versus SURREY LIONS
at The County Ground, Derby on Sunday 11th June

Surrey Lions (198-7) beat Derbyshire Scorpions (197-9) by three wickets

Although the margin of victory suggests a fairly close finish, the Lions' three-wicket win was, in reality, pretty comfortable, with only one minor flutter when Adam Hollioake and Jason Ratcliffe fell in the same Dominic Cork over to reduce the eventual victors to 178-6. While Graham Thorpe, omitted from the England squad for the first West Indies Test earlier in the day, was still at the helm Surrey remained in control, however, and the loss of Alex Tudor with four runs still needed counted for nothing as the visitors cruised in with three overs to spare.

The match had started less than auspiciously for Surrey with Martin Bicknell not fit enough to be selected but, fortunately, his replacement, Ian Bishop, turned in an excellent opening spell of 7-1-19-1. This was just as well since Alex Tudor again suffered heavily at the hands of Michael Di Venuto, while Carl Greenidge, included in place of Ian Salisbury, was only entrusted with two overs as Derbyshire raced to 49-0 after just seven overs.

The Scorpions' sting was initially drawn by Bishop's inswinger, which bowled Di Venuto via his pads as he was running riot, and then again later by a very effective mid-innings spell from Jason Ratcliffe. Despite the misery economy of the medium pacer's unbroken stint from the grandstand end, the hosts still managed to reach 131-2 after twenty-six overs, largely thanks to Matthew Cassar's steady accumulation, before self-destructing when set to post a challenging total. Overs twenty-seven to thirty-six, delivered by a combination of Ratcliffe, Saqlain, Brown and Bishop, represented the key phase of the match with a mere eighteen runs being added to the total for the loss of two wickets. During this critical period Cassar was fourth out at 141 when he top-edged a sweep at Ali Brown's accurate off-spin to midwicket and thereafter the Scorpions lost wickets at regular intervals as the Lions took control. With the home side's lower-order unable to recover the situation, Saqlain took advantage of some desperate batting to claim three wickets in consecutive overs and Derbyshire's final total certainly looked below-par on what appeared to be a very good pitch.

The Lions began their pursuit of 198 in similar style to their hosts, with Ian Ward largely to the fore during an opening partnership of forty-nine in ten overs, before Mark Butcher fell lbw to Tim Munton. Alec Stewart then sparkled briefly to maintain the tempo and, as a result, Surrey were over halfway to their target with twenty-three overs remaining when Ward, having just reached fifty from 65 balls, was unfortunately run out by Kevin Dean's deflection of Graham Thorpe's drive onto the non-striker's stumps.

Cassar, enjoying a good match, battled bravely to keep his side in the game and if Di Venuto, in the gully, had accepted a straightforward chance offered by Ali Brown from only his fourth ball then things might have been different. As it was, Brown punished the error by compiling thirty-four in good time, pulling Munton for six and glancing him for four to raise a fifty partnership for the fourth wicket which effectively sealed the match. Although rarely at his very best, Thorpe always seemed likely to see his side home from this point and, despite Cork's late burst, Surrey's unbeaten National League record was never seriously threatened.

Surrey Lions (198-7) beat Derbyshire Scorpions (197-9) by three wickets

Surrey Lions 4pts

DERBYSHIRE SCORPIONS v SURREY LIONS at DERBY. Played on 11th June
Surrey Lions won the toss
Umpires:- B. Dudleston & V.A. Holder

DERBYSHIRE SCORPIONS

Fall of wkt	Batsman	How Out	Score	Balls	4s	6s
4- 141	M.E. Cassar	c Hollioake b Brown	56	97	5	0
1- 52	M.J. Di Venuto	b Bishop	31	25	5	0
2- 93	M.P. Dowman	b Hollioake	10	24	1	0
3- 135	S.P. Titchard	lbw b Ratcliffe	15	38	2	0
6- 177	R.J. Bailey	c & b Saqlain	23	41	0	1
5- 166	S.D. Stubbings	c Brown b Saqlain	7	14	0	0
7- 181	D.G. Cork *	b Hollioake	11	12	1	0
8- 185	K.M. Krikken +	b Saqlain	0	2	0	0
	P. Aldred	Not Out	8	9	1	0
9- 192	T.A. Munton	c Greenidge b Tudor	7	6	1	0
	K.J. Dean	Not Out	1	5	0	0
	Extras (7lb, 15w, 6nb)		28			
	TOTAL	(45 overs)	197- 9			

SURREY LIONS bowling

	O	M	R	W
Tudor	4	0	36	1
Bishop	9	1	22	1
Greenidge	2	0	11	0
Saqlain	9	0	36	3
Ratcliffe	9	1	25	1
Hollioake	8	0	42	2
Brown	4	0	18	1

SURREY LIONS

Fall of wkt	Batsman	How Out	Score	Balls	4s	6s
1- 49	M.A. Butcher	lbw b Munton	14	25	1	0
3- 102	I.J. Ward	run out	53	69	8	0
2- 87	A.J. Stewart +	lbw b Dean	19	20	3	0
	G.P. Thorpe	Not Out	45	74	2	0
4- 158	A.D. Brown	lbw b Cork	34	41	2	1
5- 178	A.J. Hollioake *	st Krikken b Cork	2	11	0	0
6- 178	J.D. Ratcliffe	lbw b Cork	0	3	0	0
7- 194	A.J. Tudor	b Cassar	7	6	1	0
	Saqlain Mushtaq	Not Out	2	3	0	0
	C.G. Greenidge	did not bat				
	L.E. Bishop	did not bat				
	Extras (4b, 7lb, 11w)		22			
	TOTAL	(42 overs)	198- 7			

DERBYSHIRE bowling

	O	M	R	W
Cork	8	1	31	3
Munton	9	0	53	1
Aldred	6	0	24	0
Dean	7	1	26	1
Cassar	9	0	35	1
Bailey	3	0	18	0

Other NCL Division Two Matches

Surrey's victory enabled them to keep pace with Nottinghamshire Outlaws, conquerors of the Hampshire Hawks, at the top of the table while the Glamorgan Dragons moved up to fourth with a 20-run win over the struggling Essex Eagles.

June 11
Trent Bridge:- **Nottinghamshire Outlaws beat Hampshire Hawks by eight wickets.** Hampshire 135 (Harris 5-35); Nottinghamshire 136-2 in 36.4 overs (Bicknell 58 not out). **Nottinghamshire Outlaws 4pts**

June 13
Cardiff:- **Glamorgan Dragons beat Essex Eagles by 20 runs.** Glamorgan 220 in 44.2 overs (Elliott 94, Maynard 50, Cowan 4-39); Essex 200 in 42.4 overs (Robinson 51). **Glamorgan Dragons 4pts**

NCL DIVISION TWO AT 13TH JUNE

Pos	Prev		P	Pts	W	T	L	N/R	Last	Three	Res
1	2	Nottinghamshire Outlaws	6	20	5	0	1	0	W	L	W
2	3	Surrey Lions	6	20	4	0	0	2	W	W	N/R
3	1	Warwickshire Bears	4	16	4	0	0	0	W	W	W
4	5	Glamorgan Dragons	6	14	3	1	2	0	W	T	W
5	4	Middlesex Crusaders	5	12	2	1	1	1	T	N/R	W
6	6	Essex Eagles	5	6	1	0	3	1	L	L	N/R
7	7	Durham Dynamos	5	4	1	0	4	0	W	L	L
8	8	Derbyshire Scorpions	4	0	0	0	4	0	L	L	L
9	9	Hampshire Hawks	5	0	0	0	5	0	L	L	L

7 A New Dawn?

We had reached a crossroads. Although we were only a third of the way through the season, Surrey's position in the Championship table was something of a worry, given the good starts that both Yorkshire and Lancashire had made to their campaigns.

I did feel that the white rose county might be in a slightly false position, however, since all of their five matches to date had been played on pitches likely to assist their powerful seam attack - three at Headingley, one at Chester-le-Street and the other at Derby. How would they cope when they had to perform on good batting tracks or turning pitches, the surfaces which would most probably expose their limitations? It was also true to say that their fixtures had been less than demanding, since they had, apart from Leicestershire, faced sides that were likely to finish at the wrong end of the table - Derbyshire (twice), Durham and Hampshire. Although Lancashire had enjoyed a similarly gentle start with fixtures against Hampshire (twice), Durham, Derbyshire, Kent and Leicestershire, I regarded them as more likely county champions because of their more-rounded attack and greater batting potential. Leicestershire could certainly not be discounted, either.

Amazingly enough, a few Surrey supporters were gripped by fears of relegation and they regarded my continued belief in the team's ability to come through with a strong run as misplaced optimism. When I reeled off the aforementioned details of the relatively easy fixtures that the roses counties had played to date, I was reminded that our own schedule had been no more demanding and that we had to play all the 'top' teams in the second half of the season. The doubters regarded that as bad news, whereas I looked at it from the opposite perspective in that each of those matches represented an opportunity not only to gain points for ourselves but also to deny them to our rivals. With six of these potential '24-plus pointers' to play, the advantage our rivals currently held over us could be narrowed and overturned very quickly.

Another factor that was very much in Surrey's favour was the home-to-away balance of their remaining fixtures. There was no doubting the fact that The Oval had become a real 'fortress' in recent years, with only Leicestershire having stormed the ramparts successfully in the County Championship since the start of the 1998 season. I felt it was therefore to our considerable advantage that we had six home games to come against only four away. Additionally, one of the home fixtures was at Guildford, where we had proved even more potent in recent years than we had at The Oval, while at least two of the away matches, against Leicestershire and Hampshire, were at grounds where the pitch was likely to prove true and fair. On a good surface, especially if the spinners stayed fit, I backed us to beat any side in the country.

For my optimism and positive outlook to prove justified, however, the team simply had to start winning matches immediately. At the start of the season I had estimated that, in its new two-division format of sixteen matches, nine or ten victories would be required to lift the County Championship crown. Surrey had one win from six games to date. If my calculations were to prove correct, we therefore needed to win eight of our last ten fixtures and, with the possibility of rain ruining a match or two somewhere along the line, that appeared to be a tough task. The forthcoming encounter with Somerset was looking increasingly like a must-win contest.

COUNTY CHAMPIONSHIP - MATCH SEVEN

SURREY versus SOMERSET
at The Oval

First Day - Wednesday 14th June

Surrey 338-5

The Teams And The Toss - *The Surrey side shows two changes from the defeat at Derby, with Alec Stewart (Test duty) and Jason Ratcliffe (dropped) replaced by Jon Batty and Nadeem Shahid. Having batted extremely well and amassed a good number of runs in the second eleven, Shahid's recall in place of Ratcliffe is clearly well-merited. Although their batting line-up looks to be at full strength, the visitors, deprived of the services of Andy Caddick (with England), Graham Rose and Matt Bulbeck (both injured), field a young attack, giving England Under-19 seamer, Peter Trego, his Championship debut. They also opt to include the 20-year-old former Essex paceman, Jamie Grove, ahead of the veteran off-spinner, Adrian Pierson. When the Somerset skipper, Jamie Cox, calls incorrectly at the toss Adam Hollioake has no hesitation in electing to bat.*

In good batting conditions, Surrey look to have gained an immediate advantage by winning the toss but they start badly when Ian Ward gets a faint touch to a legside delivery from Steffan Jones and departs to the fifth ball of the match.

This brings together Mark Butcher and Graham Thorpe, the two men who are currently most in need of time at the wicket and runs to their name. Neither batsman looks particularly out of touch in the opening stages, though, as Thorpe instantly drives Jamie Grove to the cover boundary and Butcher unfurls a textbook off-driven four off Jones in the following over. Although some of the early bowling is undoubtedly loose, allowing the two left-handers to rattle up thirty-nine runs inside the first eight overs, both opening bowlers eventually regain a measure of control and Jones, in particular, produces some dangerous deliveries.

After seven indifferent overs from Grove at the Vauxhall end, Peter Trego, just two days past his nineteenth birthday, takes his place in the attack and starts his Championship career with a maiden over. The harsher realities of county cricket are illustrated to him in his second over, however, when Butcher pulls him for a brace of fours, the first of which raises both the Surrey fifty and the half-century partnership.

By this time Jones has completed nine overs, forcing Jamie Cox into a change at the pavilion end which sees the introduction of Michael Burns. Although little more than a limited-overs fill-in bowler, the medium-pacer almost comes up with a wicket in his third over when Butcher drives at an innocuous delivery wide of off stump and breathes a sigh of relief as Keith Parsons at first slip grasses a routine catch. This is a bad blow for a Somerset attack that has already looked, at best, pedestrian.

Trego and Burns give way to Parsons and Blackwell as lunch approaches but this new pairing looks no more likely to produce a breakthrough as Butcher and Thorpe take full advantage of a welcome opportunity to play themselves into form.

Lunch:- Surrey 95-1 (Butcher 45*, Thorpe 40*) from 36 overs

Upon the resumption, Jamie Cox sensibly pairs the two bowlers who are most likely to provide him with a breakthrough - his fastest and most penetrative bowler, Steffan Jones, and his left-arm spinner, Ian Blackwell. Although this combination of pace and spin yields just nineteen runs in the first eleven overs of the session, forcing the scoring rate below two-and-a-half runs per over, neither bowler makes much impression as both batsmen record half-centuries - Thorpe first from 120 balls in 154 minutes, then Butcher five overs later from 150 balls in 178 minutes. Inevitably, with the Surrey pair now well set, the shackles begin to loosen as Jones tires and Blackwell is replaced by Grove. Cox even gives his own off-spin an airing but to little effect as Thorpe brings up the 150 total and partnership with a rasping square cut off Grove.

The Somerset captain goes on to bowl five tidy overs before he recalls young Trego at the pavilion end with expensive results. In an over costing ten runs, Butcher pulls him to the backward square leg boundary to put the second-wicket stand into the record books as the highest for Surrey against Somerset, then Thorpe helps himself to a couple of fours in the young tyro's next two overs.

With both batsmen now looking in much better touch, the field is spreading and the visitors' position is looking really bleak until Grove suddenly brightens the gloom a little by removing Butcher eighteen runs short of his century. The delivery which brings succour for his side is not the greatest, being quite short and wide, but the batsman gets a bottom edge to his attempted cut and Rob Turner completes the catch behind the stumps.

Grove's joy is short-lived, however. Having denied Butcher a ton in his previous over, he then dishes up two loose deliveries to allow Thorpe a safe passage through to his. A clip through square leg for four and a drive wide of mid-on for three see the Surrey and England man through to three figures in 257 minutes from exactly 200 balls. It's great news for the county side, and also the national side, that Thorpe is finally back in the runs and there's a feeling amongst the Surrey faithful that this could prove to be a significant innings in many ways, not least in the context of this particular match.

Tea:- Surrey 212-2 (Thorpe 108*, Shahid 6*) from 72 overs

With a considerable amount of cloud having built up during the afternoon, poor light dogs the early part of the day's final session. Even though Nadeem Shahid takes two boundaries from the second over, bowled by Steffan Jones from the Vauxhall end, the umpires, guided by the fact that all five lights are aglow on the scoreboard, give the batsmen the opportunity to leave the field. After a brief discussion, Thorpe and Shahid opt to continue and they promptly demonstrate that they are having no trouble seeing the ball by thrashing nineteen runs from the next three overs! Shahid, looking in magnificent form, continues his racing start by cutting and driving Burns through the off-side for boundaries then Thorpe pulls Jones for a mighty six over square leg as Surrey streak towards their second batting point.

Unfortunately for the home side, Jones then puts a spanner in the works by winning two lbw verdicts in the space of three balls. Thorpe is the big fast bowler's first victim, his marvellous innings ended by what looks, at best, a marginal decision, then Ali Brown is comprehensively defeated by a ball of very full length. This second dismissal prompts another umpires' conference about the light and, predictably enough, Surrey accept the offer this time, since Somerset suddenly have an outside chance of getting back into the game with their hosts 242 for 4.

Luckily enough, the light improves rapidly, only three overs are lost and normal service is resumed almost immediately with Adam Hollioake forcing Jones through point and lifting him over extra cover for boundaries. It seems implausible that the Surrey captain can maintain his lightning start but, after two edgy moments when the ball flies first to the third man fence and then just short of slip, he is soon locating the middle of his bat again, crashing successive balls from Burns through backward point and extra cover. The returning Ian Blackwell is afforded no respect, either, as first Hollioake and then Shahid drive him back over his head for boundaries which prompt Cox to replace him immediately with Marcus Trescothick. To give Somerset credit, their ground fielding remains sharp, even in the face of this violent assault, though it has

EARLY SEASON EXTRAS 1

(Richard Spiller)

(Marcus Hook)

(Richard Spiller)

TOP - A well-populated Oval pavilion with the 1999 County Champions pennant flying proudly alongside the Union Jack
MIDDLE - Martin Bicknell and Alec Stewart appeal successfully for lbw against James Hockley of Kent
BOTTOM - A relaxed and relieved Alex Tudor poses with the ball after the tense two-run win over Hampshire

EARLY SEASON EXTRAS 2

(Marcus Hook)

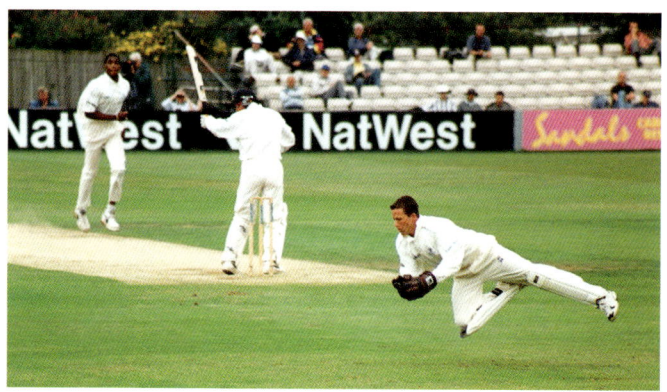

(Reg Elliott)

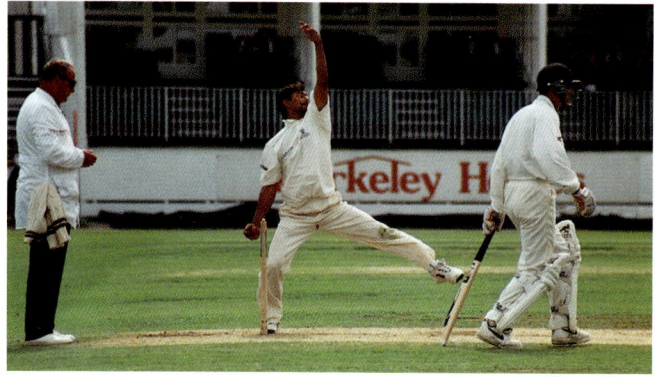

(Reg Elliott)

TOP - One for the picture board on 'A Question Of Sport' ? It's Rahul Dravid, bowling for Kent at The Oval
MIDDLE - Jon Batty is forced to perform acrobatics to take a wayward Alex Tudor delivery at Southampton
BOTTOM - Ever wondered why Saqlain oversteps the crease more often than the average spinner? This excellent photo from Southampton provides the answer - his delivery stride is more like that of a fast bowler than a spinner

TOP SPINNERS ON SHOW IN HAMPSHIRE ENCOUNTERS

TOP - A delighted Saqlain celebrates the wicket of John Stephenson in Hampshire's second innings at The Oval
MIDDLE - Ian Salisbury cuts Shane Warne through the covers during Surrey's second knock in the same game
BOTTOM - In the match at Southampton, Giles White's second innings of 73 is ended by Ian Salisbury
All photos by Reg Elliott

THE OAKHAM STORY - PART ONE

FROM THE TOP - (1) Ali Brown launches into an elegant straight drive; (2) Jon Batty drives through mid-off against the backdrop of the main school building as Surrey attempt to recover from 125-5; (3) It's 181-6 as Batty's drive finds the safe hands of Chris Lewis; (4) Brown receives warm applause from the crowd and congratulations from Alex Tudor upon reaching his double century

All photos by Reg Elliott

THE OAKHAM STORY - PART TWO

FROM THE TOP - (1) Saqlain pulls Darren Maddy high over midwicket for four as Surrey's last wicket partnership prospers; (2) Ali Brown cuts Anil Kumble backward of square; (3) Adam Hollioake takes a great catch at third slip to dismiss Darren Maddy early in Leicestershire's first innings; (4) It's that man Brown again! Aftab Habib edges his first ball to second slip and Leicestershire are 27-4 in their first innings.
All photos by Reg Elliott

THE OAKHAM STORY - PART THREE

FROM THE TOP - (1) The scoreboard tells the story - it's not ready for Darren Maddy's departure to a catch by Jon Batty from the first ball of Leicestershire's second innings; (2) Leicestershire are crumbling to defeat at 40-4 as Aftab Habib is left hopelessly stranded by Saqlain's wrong 'un and stumped by Jon Batty; (3) The 56-4 on the scoreboard is about to become 56-5 as Ali Brown makes no mistake with a catch at second slip to remove Ben Smith; (4) A job well done, the Surrey team celebrates on the pavilion verandah as the rain starts to lash down
All photos by Reg Elliott except (4) Michael Cunnew

CAREER MILESTONES

(John Banfield)

(Richard Spiller)

TOP - Jon Batty leaves the field having completed his maiden first-class century in the match against Somerset
BOTTOM - Adam Hollioake presents Ian Ward with a very well-deserved county cap

SURREY C.C.C. SQUAD - 2000 SEASON

BACK (L to R):- Carl Greenidge, Gareth Batty, Mark Patterson, Philip Sampson, Kevin Barrett, Michael Carberry

MIDDLE (L to R):- Keith Booth (Scorer), John Gloster (Physio), Dale Naylor (Physio), Gary Butcher, Rupesh Amin, Ian Bishop, Jonathan Batty, Ian Ward, Keith Medlycott (Cricket Manager), Alan Butcher (Coach)

FRONT (L to R):- Alex Tudor, Jason Ratcliffe, Alistair Brown, Saqlain Mushtaq, Graham Thorpe, Alec Stewart (Honorary Club Captain), Adam Hollioake (Captain), Martin Bicknell, Mark Butcher, Ian Salisbury, Nadeem Shahid, Ben Hollioake

Photo by Tony Eva - Sports Pictures

to be said that their limited attack gives them the appearance of a good one-day side playing four-day cricket.

Looking a better bet than some of his specialist bowling colleagues, Trescothick does manage to restore a degree of order at the pavilion end with his medium-pace swing bowling but his good work is then quickly undone by a wretched two-over spell from Jamie Grove which costs twenty-one runs. His first over sees Shahid picking off two successive boundaries which bring up the fifty partnership in a shade over twelve overs and the batsman's own sparkling half-century in ninety minutes from 67 balls. Then, with Surrey having gone past the three-hundred mark in the next over from Trescothick, the hapless Grove's second over yields three fours to Hollioake by way of a pull, an on-drive and a cut.

The Surrey captain looks in marvellous touch and set for a quick-fire fifty at this stage but his entertaining knock is cut off in its prime when a top-edged cut at a wide Trescothick delivery is very well pouched right-handed by Rob Turner diving away in front of first slip. Although Hollioake is surely disappointed with his dismissal, he does at least have the consolation of knowing that his swashbuckling 79-run partnership with Shahid has snuffed out any potential Somerset fightback and rushed his side into a position of immense power. With Surrey's former Essex batsman underlining the home side's dominance by plundering two successive fours in an over by Keith Parsons, the reigning champions eventually end a dominant day on 338-5, having scored almost two-hundred runs in boundaries and taken a big stride towards achieving their objective of a morale-boosting victory.

Close:- Surrey 338-5 (Shahid 77*, Batty 2*) from 101 overs

VIEW FROM THE DRESSING ROOM - NADEEM SHAHID

The early weeks of the season must have been very frustrating for you, since you couldn't get into the first team even though you were scoring plenty of runs in the second eleven.
NS - Yes, it was a frustrating time. Having worked really hard in Australia during the winter I was hoping for a break but it didn't come. All I could do was score as many runs as possible in the second eleven in order to put pressure on the first team guys and to ensure that I was in good form when my chance finally came along.

Although I don't personally agree with the view, some pundits would like to see the abolition of second eleven county cricket. Without second eleven cricket do you think you could have come back into the first team and made such an immediate impact?
NS - The value of second eleven county cricket is in the fact that you are playing almost every day of the week. This gives you the opportunity to work on your game and, if you play well enough, to get runs under your belt and into good form. The fact that I was playing well when my first team chance came along enabled me to grab the opportunity and make the most of it. Second eleven cricket should certainly not be abolished as the gap in the standard between first-class cricket and club cricket is enormous. I think the people who want to get rid of county second elevens are basing their ideas on the Australian set-up. Their club cricket is stronger than our second team cricket but we have to stick with our current system until our leagues become a lot stronger.

This was an interesting game for your return to the first eleven as the team had just lost at Derby. Did you pick up on any signs of slightly depressed morale after our stumbling start in the Championship?
NS - Not at all, the spirit in the dressing room was as good as ever. This group of players is far

too experienced to allow themselves to become depressed or down so early in the season. We did need to turn our Championship fortunes around, though, which made this an even bigger game for me on my return to the side.

You must have been delighted to score seventy-seven in your first innings back.
NS - Of course, but it was just as important to me that I had batted very positively, especially in the fading light. I should really have gone on to complete a century on the second day, so that took a little bit of the shine off for me.

VIEW FROM THE DRESSING ROOM - IAN SALISBURY

We got away to a good start in this game thanks to excellent knocks from Messrs Butcher, Thorpe and Shahid. The first two had been short of runs and the third had been out of the side, so I felt their efforts were especially impressive. Would you agree with that view?
IS - This was probably the first really good pitch we'd played on all season and I think that was part of the reason for us coming good. Those three guys all batted really well - Butch and Thorpey showed great mental strength after Derby, whereas Nad came in with a fresh attitude.

Second Day - Thursday 15th June

Surrey 548; Somerset 111-6

Steffan Jones gives his side an early fillip on the second morning of the match, plucking Nadeem Shahid's off stump out of the ground with the first ball of his second over. The bustling fast bowler's high-quality opening spell, during which he beats Martin Bicknell several times without reward, is not matched by Jamie Grove, however, and the pressure on Surrey's seventh-wicket pair gradually eases.

Having given his all in conceding just two runs in his first six overs of the day, Jones suddenly appears to flag and he pays a heavy price as the batsmen hit back. After being cut and hooked to the boundary by Jon Batty in his seventh and eighth overs, Bicknell then flays him for three successive fours in the next to raise both the fifty partnership and the Surrey four-hundred.

This blistering attack proves to be the final act not only for Jones, who retires to the outfield with his figures for this spell badly dented, but also for Bicknell, whose innings ends with the first ball bowled by the Somerset paceman's replacement at the Vauxhall end. Peter Trego is the man who makes the breakthrough for the visitors, picking up his maiden Championship wicket with a full-length delivery that deceives and bowls Bicknell for thirty-four to end the seventh-wicket stand at sixty.

Any thoughts the fielding side might have harboured about ripping through Surrey's lower-order are quickly dashed, however, when Alex Tudor immediately unfurls a beautiful straight drive and Batty follows up with a stinging square cut off Trescothick. Batting looks a reasonably straightforward business, in fact, as the limitations of the Somerset attack are exposed in much the same way as they had been on day one. While Trescothick completes a five-over spell at the pavilion end before giving way to Burns, for just one over, and then Blackwell, Trego keeps going at the Vauxhall end. All the bowlers suffer some degree of punishment as Batty and Tudor turn up the heat, both men reeling off some pleasing strokes as a half-century partnership arrives in just 46 balls, but Trego's persistence pays off when Tudor hits across the line of another near yorker-length delivery and falls lbw.

Although the pace slackens just a little in the remaining overs up to lunch, as Blackwell obtains a fair degree of turn and Trego induces an occasional false stroke, Jon Batty passes a succession of personal milestones. Having completed his first County Championship half-century (from 100 balls in 136 minutes) since June 1998 when sweeping Blackwell to the midwicket boundary, he goes on to surpass his highest Championship score (63 v Hampshire at Southampton, 1998) and then equal his personal best score in first-class cricket (64 not out v Sri Lanka 'A' at The Oval, 1999) during the final over of the session.

Lunch:- Surrey 482-8 (Batty 64*, Salisbury 8*) from 135 overs

Blackwell and Burns form the first bowling combination of the afternoon and they keep things relatively quiet for a while, though Batty moves past his previous best first-class score and into the seventies with a pair of well executed cuts and Surrey eventually surpass five-hundred, courtesy of Ian Salisbury's on-driven boundary off Blackwell. Having been battered for 558 in the corresponding fixture in 1999, the Somerset bowlers must be getting heartily sick of bowling at The Oval. It must certainly be unusual for a team to concede a total of over five-hundred against the same opposition in consecutive seasons.

While wondering if this represents some kind of record, Batty is moving ever closer to a maiden first-class century and, consequently, the possibility of history repeating itself is growing, since the 26-year-old wicketkeeper's current batting partner, Ian Salisbury, had achieved this very feat in the previous season's encounter with Somerset. Unfortunately, with Batty on seventy-nine, the prospects of this cricketing coincidence occurring are dimmed as Salisbury advances on Blackwell and drives a catch to deep mid-off.

Batty's task is suddenly more difficult on two scores. As well as being left with only one partner, albeit a very competent number eleven in Saqlain, the pressure is increased slightly by the recall of Steffan Jones in place of Burns at the Vauxhall end. Thankfully, the Surrey 'keeper remains unruffled by this scenario and progresses serenely into the nineties during a Blackwell over in which he follows a cover-driven two with a brace of sweeps worth four and two runs respectively.

Almost inevitably there are one or two scares as the century draws closer, notably when Saqlain almost holes out to cover from a checked drive and then when Batty, on ninety-four, gloves an attempted hook at Jones just over the head of a leaping Rob Turner. Everyone with Surrey at heart breathes a huge sigh of relief as the ball flies to the boundary but then shuffles back to the edge of their seat again when a single from the next delivery takes the home wicketkeeper on to ninety-nine.

Saqlain now has to face three deliveries from Jones and, having kept out the first two, he pushes the final ball into the covers and sets off for a run. He has barely moved two strides down the wicket when Batty's cry of 'No' is augmented by similar advice to stay put from just about every occupant of the pavilion! Fortunately, Saqlain gets the message and then watches from the non-striker's end as Batty sweeps the second ball of Blackwell's new over to deep backward square leg to reach the magical three figures after 220 minutes and 173 balls at the crease. The home crowd applauds this personal milestone enthusiastically and Saqlain offers congratulations to his jubilant partner before skying a catch behind the bowler from the very next delivery.

As Batty hurries from the field to get padded and gloved up to keep wicket, the pavilion rises to him again for his outstanding effort in seeing Surrey through from 321-5 to 548 all out. It speaks volumes for the team's depth of batting that no fewer than six partnerships in the innings have exceeded fifty and that this imposing total has been built despite two of the top five batsmen failing to score. Somerset now face the very demanding task of making 399 to avoid the follow-on and will have to bat for a tricky sixteen overs before tea.

Although the chances of Cox and Trescothick surviving the opening assault from Bicknell and Tudor look rather remote as the innings commences, both Somerset men battle bravely, despite having spent almost five complete sessions in the field. With the pitch still playing extremely well, Trescothick makes a positive start, driving both bowlers to the long-off boundary, and he also looks the more secure of the two batsmen as his captain endures one or two uncomfortable moments, including an appeal for a catch at the wicket off Tudor. To their immense credit, the Somerset openers manage to survive the initial thrusts from the Surrey new-ball pairing and reach tea unscathed, having also played out the final four overs of the session from Adam Hollioake and Saqlain.

Tea:- Somerset 49-0 (Cox 26*, Trescothick 19*) from 16 overs

For twenty minutes after the resumption all goes well for the visitors as the initial efforts of Hollioake and Saqlain are repelled with no hint of a problem. Somerset even seem to be making light of their daunting requirement to reach 399 as Cox clips a full-toss from the Pakistani off-spinner to the square leg boundary to push the total up to seventy-three without loss. The turning point of the innings comes later in the same over, however, when the Somerset captain is trapped on the back foot, plumb in front of the stumps, by an off-break.

Sensing his opportunity, Adam Hollioake immediately recalls Martin Bicknell at the pavilion end and, two isolated strokes from Trescothick excepted - a slog-sweep for six off Saqlain and a square cut for four off Bicknell - the runs dry up completely as Surrey take control. Although Bicknell reaps no reward for a fine four-over spell, Saqlain passes Piran Holloway's outside edge on countless occasions and the pressure on the batsmen continues to grow once Salisbury's introduction in the thirty-first over makes for an all-spin attack. This is clearly not to the liking of the left-handed Holloway, who is so becalmed that it takes an edged defensive stroke against Salisbury to get him off the mark some forty minutes after his arrival at the crease. The crowd consequently offers up some ironic applause which the batsman acknowledges in good humour.

There are very few Somerset smiles in evidence anywhere around the ground for the rest of the session, however, as the spinners rip through the visitors' middle-order in double-quick time. Ian Salisbury makes the initial breaches by taking wickets with successive deliveries, first penetrating Trescothick's loose drive with a well-flighted leg-break and then having Peter Bowler taken at short leg from a googly. These two wickets are the high spots of a quite marvellous over which ends with six fielders around the bat and Somerset wobbling at 95-3.

With the spinners calling all the shots, the batsmen are quite simply transfixed and unable to respond as the maiden overs stack up and Holloway's strokeless one-run vigil ends in unusual circumstances after seventy minutes at the crease - a top-edged sweep strikes the back of the leg slip fielder as he takes evasive action and rebounds sufficiently for an alert Jon Batty to complete a rather fortunate catch - Somerset are now 96 for 4.

Having reached ninety-five with just one man out, the odds on six wickets being down before Somerset registered their hundred would have been phenomenal, yet that turns out to be the case as Saqlain follows his spin partner's lead by taking two wickets in two balls in the next over. Keith Parsons is his first victim, chopping the ball onto his stumps as he attempts to cut a ball which is too full and too straight for the shot, then Peter Trego records a golden duck on debut when he pads up to an off-break and departs lbw. Stunned by these blows, Somerset are suddenly staggering towards the precipice at 98-6 and their nerves are frayed further when Rob Turner plays and misses at the hat-trick ball before raising three figures with a total miscue through cover for two runs.

At this point, with five overs left for play and fielders clustered around the bat, there remains an outside possibility that Somerset might be bowled out before the close. Burns and Turner clearly have their work cut out but they battle through in relative comfort until the latter survives a straightforward chance to Thorpe at second slip from the penultimate ball of the day bowled by Salisbury. With two days left for play and the Surrey spinners in great form it's hard to imagine this error turning out to be too costly, however.

Saqlain (3-36) and Salisbury (3-9) duly lead their team-mates from the field after another spin masterclass and the old firm looks set to put the home side back on track in their quest for back-to-back County Championship titles.

Close:- Somerset 111-6 (Burns 12*, Turner 3*) from 49 overs

VIEW FROM THE DRESSING ROOM - JON BATTY

You must have been delighted to record your maiden first-class century in this match. What do you remember most about your innings and the reaching of the landmark?
JB - It was the high spot of my season and, along with the Championship titles, is the highlight of my career so far. Perhaps surprisingly, I don't recall too much about the innings apart from realising that I was in 'the zone'. I remember when Saqi came in to bat I was a little uncertain as to whether I should go for it or just keep batting normally. I quickly decided that I should just carry on playing normally because Saqi is obviously a very capable batsman. Then I recall being on ninety-four, gloving a four over Rob Turner, and suddenly realising how close I was! Luckily, I didn't have too much time to get nervous about completing the hundred.

Unfortunately, you didn't have much time to savour the moment, since you had to dash off and pad up ahead of Somerset's innings. Any regrets about that?
JB - No, that's all part of being in a team, and being a wicketkeeper - I had to go out and do a hugely important job, and I wouldn't want it any other way. I still managed to have a glass of champagne with all the boys after play, anyway!

VIEW FROM THE DRESSING ROOM - IAN SALISBURY

The lower order was fantastic again in this game, led by Jon Batty with his maiden first-class century - I'm sure you would agree that it's one of the great strengths of this team
IS - It's something we pride ourselves on and we set ourselves high standards. For example, in this game even though Bickers, Tudes and I all got twenties and thirties, I think we were disappointed that we hadn't gone on to make bigger scores as the wicket was good and we all got out playing attacking shots - we have to be striving for scores of seventy and eighty. Jon Batty was desperate to do well and he played excellently. Although I let him down by getting out with him still twenty runs short of his hundred, Saqi was a good man to have coming in at eleven, so we were confident that he would still get there.

They started their first innings after five sessions in the field. Is it more the mental fatigue or the physical fatigue that makes batting so difficult after such a long time in the field?
IS - There's a physical side to it, of course, but the mental side is possibly even tougher - they knew the wicket would turn for me and Saqi and they knew there was no weak link in our attack. But perhaps the biggest problem when you face a score like 548 is knowing that the best you can do is draw the game because that tends to put you in a negative frame of mind before you start.

Marcus Trescothick batted well in the first innings, as he had done at Taunton and also at The Oval last year. I guess the Surrey lads must have felt that he deserved his chance when he was called up by England?
IS - Although he'd scored runs against us he'd had a fair bit of luck early on at Taunton and he'd twice got out to me through playing a bad shot, once down there and then again in the first innings here. We certainly thought he could play but we hadn't seen the best of him. When he played in the one-dayers and the Tests for England he exceeded our expectations by showing great composure and brilliance which we had never seen from him before. It was very refreshing to see the way he played and everyone was very impressed and pleased for him.

JON BATTY'S MAIDEN FIRST-CLASS CENTURY
Original run chart as compiled by Keith Seward

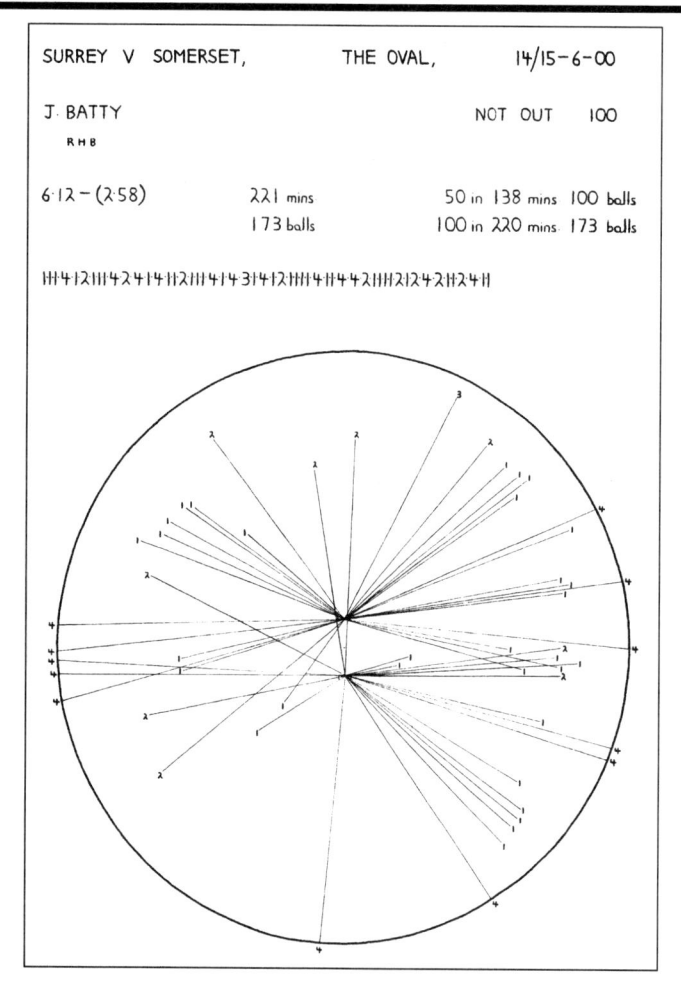

SURREY V SOMERSET,   THE OVAL,   14/15-6-00

J. BATTY   NOT OUT   100
RHB

6·12 - (2·58)   221 mins   50 in 138 mins 100 balls
                 173 balls   100 in 220 mins 173 balls

HH 4 121114 2 4 14 112111 4 14 3 14 12 HH 4 H 4 4 2 HH 2124 2 H 24 H

VIEW FROM THE DRESSING ROOM - NADEEM SHAHID

Saqlain's reappearance had clearly lifted the team. How highly do you rate him?
NS - Saqi is an extraordinary cricketer and his appearance not only lifts our team but, just as importantly, it also stirs enormous fear in the opposition's changing room. One of his greatest assets is his ability to both keep the runs down and take wickets at the same time.

I guess some of the guys were very pleased to see **you** *back, too, for the simple reason that they wouldn't have to field at short leg any more!*
NS - Of course the guys were pleased to see me back! Although most people don't like to field at short leg, for obvious reasons, I personally find it great fun fielding there to Saqi and Solly - watching batsmen trying to 'pick' them is extremely interesting!

Third Day - Friday 16th June

Surrey 548; Somerset 145 and 190

Surrey beat Somerset by an innings and 213 runs
Surrey 20pts, Somerset 2

The visitors' extremely slim hopes of avoiding the follow-on recede still further in the first over of the day when Rob Turner top-edges a sweep and is well caught by Alex Tudor running round towards deep backward square leg - the score is now 113 for 7.

Although Somerset's number nine, Ian Blackwell, attempts to play positively, Michael Burns remains pretty much strokeless in the early stages, bar a square cut off Salisbury which races away to the fence at point. The passive approach rarely succeeds against quality spinners, however, and the point is proved here when Burns is brought to book by Saqlain in the ninth over of the morning - having failed to get either forward or back, he becomes the Pakistani's third leg-before victim of an innings which has now subsided to 122-8. When Steffan Jones then departs seven balls later, defeated by a Salisbury googly and also adjudged lbw, Somerset's innings is all but over at 123-9.

Appreciating that there is now no hope of escape, the last-wicket pair opts for all-out attack and their positive approach yields two overs of rich entertainment, along with a degree of success. Having watched Blackwell pull Saqlain for six and then loft the next delivery over cover for four, Jamie Grove follows up by driving Salisbury straight back to the pavilion railings and then over long-on for six.

Everyone knows that the fun won't last, though, and it takes Saqlain just two more deliveries to end the innings as Blackwell's attempt to repeat his pull stroke of the previous over merely results in a skied return catch to the bowler off the top edge. The visitors are all out for 145 and Saqi finishes with a haul of 6-47 after another mesmeric display of spin bowling. Their job well done, the Surrey spin twins lead their team from the field of play with Somerset facing a truly demoralising first innings deficit of 403 runs and inevitable defeat - though no-one is prepared to predict this with total certainty, given the way the previous home Championship match had finished!

After the events of their first innings it's clear that a solid opening partnership will be no guarantee of success for Somerset as they commence their second knock. This is just as well since they don't even start well this time around! The innings is only in its fourth over when Alex Tudor strikes a valuable blow for the county champions by removing Marcus Trescothick. Having just miscued a pull stroke high over the slips for his third boundary, the big left-hander drives at a delivery of much fuller length and edges to third slip, where Adam Hollioake holds on to a good, sharp catch. Trescothick is out for thirteen, Somerset are 13-1 and Surrey are immediately back in the box seats.

They do encounter sterner resistance in the rest of the session, however, as Jamie Cox finds the boundary with handsome drives on no fewer than five occasions and Piran Holloway looks a little more comfortable, having taken a mere fifteen minutes to break his second-innings duck. After seven good overs apiece from Bicknell and Tudor, the spinners are back in tandem for the final four overs before the break but, on this occasion, they are unable to produce instantaneous results.

Lunch:- Somerset 56-1 (Cox 31*, Holloway 8*) from 18 overs

The spinners resume after the interval and, within minutes of the second-wicket pair completing a fifty partnership, Ian Salisbury strikes a crucial blow by removing Jamie Cox, the one man capable of playing a big enough and long enough innings to deny Surrey their expected victory. The vital second breakthrough comes about when Salisbury fizzes a fine leg-break past Cox's outside edge and the ever-sharp Batty removes the bails with the batsman marginally out of his ground - Somerset, 66-2, still trail by 337 runs and the writing is on the wall.

Holloway and Bowler proceed to push and prod fairly aimlessly for twelve overs, adding just seventeen runs, before the former Warwickshire left-hander's second unconvincing effort of the match is ended by an error of judgement as he pads up to a Salisbury leg-break and goes lbw.

Having seen the futility of passive resistance, the new batsman, Keith Parsons, does at least attempt to play a few strokes and even Bowler breaks out momentarily to sweep Saqlain for a boundary which raises the Somerset century. Danger is always lurking around the corner, though, and the visitors' fate is almost sealed when Adam Hollioake's decision to switch the spinners' ends produces rapid results.

Saqlain's second over from the pavilion end yields the wicket of Parsons, snapped up by the Surrey skipper at silly point, while a Salisbury one-two shortly afterwards brings the prospect of a three-day victory into sight. It's the leg-spinner's googly which provides him with his third and fourth wickets of the innings - Burns is beaten and 'gated' on the drive, while Rob Turner fails to move his feet and succumbs to the umpire's finger - 120-6.

As if to acknowledge the fact that they have now reached the point of no recovery, Bowler and his new partner, Blackwell, unleash some hearty strokes in the final overs before tea, though the latter has a lucky escape when Batty just fails to hang on to a top edge off Saqlain. It's of little consequence in the general scheme of things, however, and as the players leave the field it's just a matter of when, as opposed to whether, Surrey will tie up an emphatic victory.

Tea:- Somerset 141-6 (Bowler 28*, Blackwell 8*) from 60 overs

Although Bowler continues in positive vein after tea, driving Saqlain to the boundary and then cutting Salisbury for another four to take his side through to 150, the only area of interest left for Somerset is whether or not they can take the game into day four.

Their prospects of achieving this are dimmed in the first over of the session, however, when the vastly experienced former Leicestershire and Derbyshire batsman prods a catch to Adam Hollioake at silly point to present Salisbury with his fifth wicket. Bowler looks most unhappy with the umpire's decision but he has to go, leaving his side tottering towards their inevitable defeat at 155-7.

An already dire position then deteriorates further four overs later when Salisbury makes it six of the best by snaring Peter Trego in identical fashion to Bowler, though this time there can be no doubt about the dismissal. The Surrey leg-spinner still has both his Surrey-best and career-best bowling figures in his sights at this point and, with Saqlain a little below par, he appears to have a great chance of improving on one or both of these stats.

He has to wait six overs for his next success, however, as Blackwell and Jones put bat to ball in adding twenty-eight runs before the latter tries to drive a leg-break through midwicket and spirals a leading edge to Saqlain at backward point.

With the batsmen having crossed while the ball was in the air, Jamie Grove, the Somerset number eleven, is now left to face the Pakistani off-spinner and, since the match is already won, the majority of Surrey supporters find themselves almost willing him to survive the over so that Salisbury can have a chance of picking up his eighth wicket. As luck would have it, Grove actually manages to pinch a single to mid-off to put himself on strike for the leg-spinner's next over.

Can Salisbury take his chance? You bet! It takes just four balls, too, as Grove hits over a delivery of yorker length and hears the death-rattle of his stumps being rearranged behind him. A delighted Salisbury celebrates with his team-mates and then leads them from the field as the public address confirms that the former Sussex bowler's second innings figures of 8-60 represent his best return in first-class cricket, beating the 8-75 he returned for his previous county against Essex at Chelmsford in 1996. Furthermore, he has taken twelve wickets in a match for the first time in his career, making his 12 for 91 another new mark. It's not just the statistics that have been so impressive in this match, though. Having not bowled a single ball at Derby, Salisbury's performance has been absolutely brilliant in terms of both control and his ability to produce wicket-taking deliveries. Many good judges at The Oval find it baffling that Chris Schofield has been awarded an England contract ahead of him and on this display it would be impossible for even his harshest critic to disagree.

From a wider perspective, there is one burning question that has to be asked - does this utterly comprehensive win against a side well-known for their fighting qualities represent a new dawn for Surrey's 2000 Championship campaign? I believe it does, since several of my Derby worries have been eased considerably during the three days of this match - key batsmen, Mark Butcher and Graham Thorpe, now have runs to their name; Nadeem Shahid has instantly and almost effortlessly transferred his second eleven form into a first team match; Ian Salisbury has finally got a long spell of bowling under his belt and produced his best-ever bowling performance; and the previously over-worked opening bowlers have had a fairly quiet match, with Martin Bicknell sending down just seventeen overs and Alex Tudor a mere thirteen. On top of all these things, we've also had Jon Batty's maiden first-class century, which is clearly a huge bonus.

Suddenly, in the space of just one match, everything is looking rosy again. This upward trend has to be continued in the next Championship encounter with Hampshire at Southampton, though, since a series of vital fixtures follows that game.

Surrey 548; Somerset 145 and 190
Surrey won by an innings and 213 runs. Surrey 20pts, Somerset 2

SURREY v SOMERSET at THE OVAL. Played from 14th - 16th June

Surrey won the toss   Umpires:- R. Julian & G. Sharp

SURREY - First Innings

Fall of wkt	Batsman		How Out	Score	Balls	4s	6s
2- 191	M.A. Butcher	c Turner	b Grove	82	212	12	0
1- 1	I.J. Ward	c Turner	b Jones	0	4	0	0
3- 242	G.P. Thorpe		lbw b Jones	118	227	15	1
6- 343	Nadeem Shahid		b Jones	77	103	13	0
4- 242	A.D. Brown		lbw b Jones	0	2	0	0
5- 321	A.J. Hollioake *	c Turner	b Trescothick	39	46	8	0
	J.N. Batty +		Not Out	100	173	12	0
7- 403	M.P. Bicknell		b Trego	34	61	5	0
8- 457	A.J. Tudor		lbw b Trego	27	25	6	0
9- 516	I.D.K. Salisbury	c Jones	b Blackwell	23	60	2	0
10- 548	Saqlain Mushtaq	c Holloway	b Blackwell	11	24	2	0
	Extras (5b, 8lb, 7w, 20nb)			40			
	TOTAL		(154.3 overs)	548			

SOMERSET bowling

	O	M	R	W
Jones	37	11	103	4
Grove	24	3	113	1
Trego	22	4	79	2
Burns	20	3	70	0
Parsons	7	2	23	0
Blackwell	26.3	3	99	2
Cox	5	1	8	0
Trescothick	13	1	40	1

SOMERSET - First Innings

Fall of wkt	Batsman		How Out	Score	Balls	4s	6s
1- 73	J. Cox *		lbw b Saqlain	34	63	5	0
2- 95	M.E. Trescothick		b Salisbury	45	110	6	1
4- 96	P.C.L. Holloway	c Batty	b Salisbury	1	65	0	0
3- 95	P.D. Bowler	c Shahid	b Salisbury	0	1	0	0
5- 98	K.A. Parsons		b Saqlain	1	18	0	0
8- 122	M. Burns		lbw b Saqlain	17	49	2	0
6- 98	P.D. Trego		lbw b Saqlain	0	1	0	0
7- 112	R.J. Turner +	c Tudor	b Saqlain	3	17	0	0
10- 145	I.D. Blackwell		c & b Saqlain	16	40	1	1
9- 123	P.S. Jones		lbw b Salisbury	0	4	0	0
	J.O. Grove		Not Out	12	14	1	1
	Extras (7b, 3lb, 2w, 4nb)			16			
	TOTAL		(63.2 overs)	145			

SURREY bowling

	O	M	R	W
Bicknell	10	3	24	0
Tudor	6	3	25	0
Hollioake	5	2	8	0
Saqlain	25.2	11	47	6
Salisbury	17	6	31	4

SOMERSET - Second Innings

Fall of wkt	Batsman	How Out		Score	Balls	4s	6s
1- 13	M.E. Trescothick	c Hollioake	b Tudor	13	17	3	0
2- 66	J.Cox *	st Batty	b Salisbury	36	65	6	0
3- 83	P.C.L. Holloway		lbw b Salisbury	24	90	0	0
7- 155	P.D. Bowler	c Hollioake	b Salisbury	37	136	6	0
4- 111	K.A. Parsons	c Hollioake	b Saqlain	12	31	2	0
5- 118	M. Burns		b Salisbury	3	10	0	0
6- 120	R.J. Turner +		lbw b Salisbury	1	7	0	0
	I.D. Blackwell		Not Out	32	62	4	0
8- 161	P.D. Trego	c Hollioake	b Salisbury	4	12	0	0
9- 189	P.S. Jones	c Saqlain	b Salisbury	9	21	1	0
10- 190	J.O. Grove		b Salisbury	1	8	0	0
	Extras (4b, 2lb, 2w, 10nb)			18			
	TOTAL		(75.4 overs)	190			

SURREY bowling

	O	M	R	W
Bicknell	7	2	21	0
Tudor	7	3	25	1
Saqlain	30.4	9	60	8
Salisbury	30	7	75	1
Brown	1	0	3	0

VIEW FROM THE DRESSING ROOM - NADEEM SHAHID

I thought Ian Salisbury was brilliant throughout the match. Is he now bowling as well as you have ever seen him?
NS - Certainly. He's probably at his very best right now - not only is his bowling very consistent but his batting down the order often provides us with crucial runs.

We were now up and running again to an extent. I assume we must have viewed the upcoming games with Leicestershire, Lancashire and Yorkshire as crucial if we were to get back in the title race?
NS - Yes, a lot of emphasis was put on those games as we knew that the eventual champions would come from these three sides plus ourselves. As a team, and as individuals, we were very focused on those matches.

VIEW FROM THE DRESSING ROOM - IAN SALISBURY

You did the early damage in the first innings and then Saqi swept the lower-order away. Your spin twin's reappearance had clearly given the side a boost.
IS - I was a bit disappointed because I bowled well early on to get the first wickets and then he came along, went mad and didn't give me much more of a chance! But that's the great quality of both of us - we bowl as a pair but we are always competing with one another, too. He's an amazing bowler, great to bowl with and a very good mate. It must be a great pleasure for all Surrey fans to have the chance to watch him bowl.

Then, in the second innings, it was your turn. It must have been a great feeling to come up with a career-best in a match the team badly needed to win?
IS - There's a lot of luck involved. In the first innings I probably bowled as well as Saqi and he got six wickets to my four, then, in the second knock, I had a bit more luck than he did and ended up with eight to his one. It was funny that, until this game, no-one really knew how well Saqi and I were bowling because we hadn't bowled that much - now we knew!

Alex Tudor and Martin Bicknell had bowled a lot of overs in the early weeks of the season and I, for one, was worried that it would result in one, or both, of them breaking down. They must benefit physically from us having two quality spinners in that they get games like this one where they have a much lighter workload?
IS -You weren't the only one who was worried about them breaking down! In that respect, this

game came along at just the right time for them if they were going to get through the rest of the season. They had bowled an awful lot of overs up to this point, partly because they'd been bowling so well and partly because the pitches in the early weeks of the season were such that spinners couldn't get into the game much.

Did everyone now believe that we were right back in contention for the title, especially with big games against Leicestershire, Lancashire and Yorkshire to come?
IS - We had started the season so slowly with all the rain and the defeat at Chester-le-Street. Then we had that vital win over Hampshire, went to Derby feeling confident and then got knocked over again. It was therefore vitally important that we got back on track again quickly and the way we did it here, with our bowlers bowling well and our batsmen now coming back into form, made us very confident, as a side, that good things were around the corner. It was good that we had the leading teams still to play because it meant that every game from now on was going to be a really big game and really good fun to play in.

KEITH MEDLYCOTT'S ASSESSMENT

After Derby, the Somerset game was an important one to win and having got runs on the board we were always in a strong position. It was good to see the batsmen making runs because that is vital for us. If we can win the toss and then put together a good score then we are always going to have a good chance of winning the match.

Other Division One Matches

Two further pitch controversies dogged this round of matches. At Basingstoke, Durham were tumbled out for a total of 176 runs in the match while at Headingly thirty-four wickets fell for just 423 runs on a pitch which apparently both looked and played very poorly. PLC representatives consequently visited both grounds. Hampshire's defence was helped by the fact that they had totalled 340 in their only innings but it was more difficult to understand how Yorkshire escaped censure. They did, however, and their fifteen-point win increased their lead at the top of the table since Lancashire sat out this series of games. Derbyshire's belief that the smaller counties were more likely to be docked points than those with Test Match grounds gained further credence as a result of Yorkshire's good fortune and their mood was further darkened by a crushing defeat at Grace Road. Leicestershire moved up to second place in the table with this win and the 'big four' now filled the top four positions.

June 14-16
Basingstoke:- **Hampshire beat Durham by an innings and 164 runs.** Hampshire 340; Durham 83 (Warne 4-34) and 93 (Warne 4-22). **Hampshire 18pts, Durham 3**

Headingley:- **Yorkshire beat Kent by six wickets.** Kent 129 (Sidebottom 5-27) and 82 (Sidebottom 6-16); Yorkshire 149 and 63-4. **Yorkshire 15pts, Kent 3**

June 14-17
Leicester:- **Leicestershire beat Derbyshire by ten wickets.** Leicestershire 310 (Habib 164, Dean 4-47) and 47-0; Derbyshire 133 (Ormond 6-50) and 223 (Wells 4-58). **Leicestershire 18pts, Derbyshire 3**

COUNTY CHAMPIONSHIP DIVISION ONE AT 17TH JUNE

Pos	Prev		P	Pts	W	D	L	Bat	Bowl	Last	Three	Res
1	1	Yorkshire	6	88	4	2	0	14	18	W15	W17	D7
2	3	Leicestershire	7	75	2	4	1	19	16	W18	D7	D9
3	2	Lancashire	6	72	3	3	0	11	13	W17	D8	D6
4	5	Surrey	7	65	2	3	2	15	14	W20	L3	W18
5	4	Somerset	6	56	2	2	2	11	13	L2	W17	D5
6	9	Hampshire	7	47	1	2	4	6	21	W18	L3	L4
7	6	Derbyshire	7	46*	1	4	2	7	19	L3	W7	D7
8	7	Kent	6	42	1	3	2	2	16	L3	L5	W15
9	8	Durham	6	38	1	1	4	4	18	L3	L3	L3

* Deducted 8pts for sub-standard pitch

NO CHANGE AT THE TOP IN NCL DIVISION TWO

Two NCL matches were played on Sunday 18th June but neither had a bearing on the top positions as Hampshire Hawks and Derbyshire Scorpions each recorded their first win of the season. Middlesex Crusaders would have gone fourth but for their surprise defeat at Lord's.

Basingstoke:- **Hampshire Hawks beat Durham Dynamos by 18 runs.** Hampshire 222-5 (Stephenson 83); Durham 204 in 44 overs (Lewis 55 not out, Collingwood 51, Mullally 4-40). **Hampshire Hawks 4pts**

Lord's:- **Derbyshire Scorpions beat Middlesex Crusaders by 15 runs.** Derbyshire 186-8 (Cork 64); Middlesex 171 in 43.5 overs (Langer 56). **Derbyshire Scorpions 4pts**

SURREY ENJOY A STROLL BY THE BEACH AT EXMOUTH

The draw for the third round of the Nat West Trophy had presented Surrey with a trip to either Devon or Staffordshire and I have to admit that I, for one, was quite pleased when Devon prevailed in round two, leaving us with a visit to Exmouth. The game was always likely to be one-sided, of course, but the thought of a short break by the sea was very appealing. And when I say 'by the sea' I mean that quite literally, since the very attractive Exmouth Cricket Club ground turned out to be just a short pebble's throw from the beach - only a road and two pavements separated the ground from the sand dunes!

The match itself became something of a stroll for Surrey once Martin Bicknell, bowling his allotted overs in one spell at the start of the innings, had removed the top three men in the Devon order - Bobby Dawson, Gareth Townsend and Nick Folland - inside the first fifteen overs. Although the youthful fourth-wicket pairing of Matt Wood, 19, and David Lye, 21, batted well to stave off any threat of humiliation, the home side never looked capable of posting a big total. This was largely due to the tidy efforts of Saqlain Mushtaq and Ian Salisbury, who bowled in tandem from the 27th to the 46th over to return figures of 10-0-36-2 and 10-0-30-0 respectively. After Lye's exit for 56 in the forty-first over and Wood's departure for 43 just two overs later, the crowd was entertained by some merry slogging from the helmetless Andy Procter (21 not out) which took Devon close to the 200 mark.

This total was never likely to cause any problems for a Surrey side at full strength but for Alex Tudor. After the early loss of Mark Butcher, adjudged caught behind for five in the fourth over, the second-wicket pair of Ali Brown and Alec Stewart took the score up to 103 before the former was bowled when missing a pull. Stewart and Graham Thorpe (46 not out) then guided Surrey safely through to a fourth round meeting with Sussex at The Oval.

SCOREBOARD - NAT WEST TROPHY - THIRD ROUND

Devon 194-6 from 50 overs (D.F. Lye 56, M.P. Bicknell 3-19)
Surrey 198-2 from 44 overs (A.J. Stewart 70 not out, A.D. Brown 59)
Surrey won by eight wickets

Umpires: D.L. Burden and M.J. Kitchen

Man Of The Match - D.F. Lye (Devon)

NCL DIVISION TWO - MATCH SEVEN

WARWICKSHIRE BEARS versus SURREY LIONS
at Edgbaston on Friday 23rd June

Surrey Lions (166-3) beat Warwickshire Bears (162-7) by seven wickets

Just two days after their win at Exmouth, Surrey produced an outstanding performance in the top-of-the-table NCL Division Two clash under the floodlights at Edgbaston to beat the Warwickshire Bears by seven wickets and move to the top of the league table.

The Lions proved more proficient than their hosts in every facet of the game, bowling and fielding tightly to restrict the Bears to a below-par total of 162-7 and then snuffing out the opposition's hopes with an excellent batting effort to seal victory with almost four overs to spare.

The home side batted first on winning the toss but, despite the fact that they reached fifty for the loss of Graeme Welch inside fourteen overs, they were never able to dominate as Martin Bicknell (7-1-23-1) and Alex Tudor (5-2-19-0) turned in accurate opening spells. Jason Ratcliffe and Saqlain Mushtaq then tightened the screws further with some outstandingly straight and testing bowling which kept the scoring rate down at three-and-a-half per over and produced panic in the Warwickshire middle-order. Dominic Ostler, after a particularly desperate struggle against Saqlain, was eventually undone by the off-spinner's "wrong 'un" in attempting to get down the track and when David Hemp departed, lbw offering no stroke, to the next delivery the Bears were clearly losing their way at 93-3 in the twenty-seventh over. Although Nick Knight had, by now, passed fifty he was being made to fight for every run and the pressure on him increased when Tudor returned to the fray in the thirtieth over and soon accounted for Trevor Penney with a brilliant slower ball.

The Lions' excellent bowling on an awkward pitch was well supported by athletic fielding throughout and, as the overs began to run out, Ben Hollioake pegged back Neil Smith's off stump with a well-disguised off-break to reduce the hosts to 127-5. Although Dougie Brown did his best to raise the tempo, it was already clear that the Bears' final total would not provide Surrey with the sternest of challenges when Knight departed with the score at 146 in the forty-second over. Even at this late stage Warwickshire, with wickets in hand, could only manage sixteen runs from the final twenty-one deliveries of the innings as both Bicknell and Ben Hollioake completed excellent spells to go with those of their colleagues.

A target of 163 looked well within the capabilities of a strong Surrey batting line-up and Neil Smith's decision to open the bowling with Ashley Giles' left-arm spin hinted at desperation.

Although the former Surrey Young Cricketer removed Mark Butcher in the fifth over, courtesy of a dubious lbw verdict, Alec Stewart drove him straight for six and then through extra cover for four in his next over to bring the Bears' experiment to a sudden halt. By despatching a high percentage of deliveries to the boundary, the second-wicket pairing of Brown and Stewart gave the Lions a racing start and, though the former was badly missed by Smith at mid-off two balls after smashing Ed Giddins into the pavilion for six, there were few scares as a fifty partnership rattled up in just seventy-one deliveries.

Surrey were so much in control of proceedings that they were easily able to ride out the loss of Brown, to a wretched leg-before decision with the total on 94, and Thorpe, as the result of an unfortunate mix-up with Stewart at 129, to cruise home in comfort. Warwickshire were looking a pretty dispirited outfit long before the end as their one-hundred percent record was shattered and the Lions roared to the top of the table. Following another brilliant limited-overs innings, Alec Stewart was adjudged Sky Sports' Man Of The Match.

Surrey Lions (166-3) beat Warwickshire Bears (162-7) by seven wickets

Surrey Lions 4pts

WARWICKSHIRE BEARS v SURREY LIONS at EDGBASTON. Played on 23rd June
Warwickshire Bears won the toss   Umpires:- J.W. Holder & A.A. Jones. Third Umpire:- V.A. Holder

WARWICKSHIRE BEARS

Fall of wkt	Batsman	How Out	Score	Balls	4s	6s
6- 146	N.V. Knight	c Thorpe b Bicknell	82	129	6	0
1- 25	G. Welch	c Ward b Bicknell	13	22	2	0
2- 93	D.P. Ostler	st Stewart b Saqlain	25	53	1	0
3- 93	D.L. Hemp	lbw b Saqlain	0	1	0	0
4- 115	T.L. Penney	lbw b Tudor	5	13	0	0
5- 128	N.M.K. Smith *	b B.C. Hollioake	4	13	0	0
	D.R. Brown	Not Out	21	27	0	0
7- 150	A.F. Giles	c Ratcliffe b B.C. Hollioake	1	6	0	0
	M.A. Sheikh	Not Out	2	6	0	0
	K.J. Piper +	did not bat				
	E.S.H. Giddins	did not bat				
	Extras (6lb, 3w)		9			
	TOTAL	(45 overs)	162 - 7			

SURREY LIONS bowling

	O	M	R	W
Bicknell	9	1	29	2
Tudor	9	2	41	1
Ratcliffe	9	0	34	0
Saqlain	9	1	24	2
B.C. Hollioake	9	0	28	2

SURREY LIONS

Fall of wkt	Batsman	How Out	Score	Balls	4s	6s
1- 19	M.A. Butcher	lbw b Giles	2	7	0	0
2- 94	A.D. Brown	lbw b Giles	45	62	6	1
	A.J. Stewart +	Not Out	72	116	6	1
3- 129	G.P. Thorpe	run out	17	34	2	0
	A.J. Hollioake *	Not Out	13	30	1	0
	B.C. Hollioake	did not bat				
	I.J. Ward	did not bat				
	J.D. Ratcliffe	did not bat				
	M.P. Bicknell	did not bat				
	A.J. Tudor	did not bat				
	Saqlain Mushtaq	did not bat				
	Extras (3b, 2lb, 8w, 4nb)		17			
	TOTAL	(41.1 overs)	166 - 3			

WARWICKSHIRE bowling

	O	M	R	W
Giles	9	1	43	2
Welch	9	2	24	0
Brown	7	0	30	0
Giddins	3	0	20	0
Sheikh	7.1	0	25	0
Smith	6	0	19	0

NCL DIVISION TWO AT 23RD JUNE

Pos	Prev		P	Pts	W	T	L	N/R	Last	Three	Res
1	2	Surrey Lions	7	24	5	0	0	2	W	W	W
2	1	Nottinghamshire Outlaws	6	20	5	0	1	0	W	L	W
3	3	Warwickshire Bears	5	16	4	0	1	0	L	W	W
4	4	Glamorgan Dragons	6	14	3	1	2	0	W	T	W
5	5	Middlesex Crusaders	6	12	2	1	2	1	L	T	N/R
6	6	Essex Eagles	5	6	1	0	3	1	L	L	N/R
7	8	Derbyshire Scorpions	5	4	1	0	4	0	W	L	L
8	7	Durham Dynamos	6	4	1	0	5	0	L	W	L
=	9	Hampshire Hawks	6	4	1	0	5	0	W	L	L

8 Onwards And Upwards

As the Surrey team headed down to Southampton for the return National League and Championship fixtures against Hampshire, it was clear that the most crucial period of the season was almost upon us. While the National League position was most encouraging, especially after the outstanding win at Edgbaston, there was still much to be done in the Championship, with crunch battles coming thick and fast throughout July and early August. Following on from Southampton the next four games were Leicestershire (Oakham School), Yorkshire (Oval), Leicestershire (Guildford) and Lancashire (Oval). This schedule offered a great opportunity to move swiftly back into contention for the title, especially with three of the games being played at home. The key was for everyone to stay fit and in form over this vital period and the only area of slight concern was the announcement that Graham Thorpe's international exile had been ended by his call-up for the triangular one-day series against Zimbabwe and the West Indies from 6th to 22nd July. Although everyone was pleased for Thorpe it did mean that he would almost certainly miss all of the aforementioned big games. The strength of the Surrey squad would clearly be tested again during the weeks ahead but, for now, everyone had to concentrate on the games against a Hampshire side still struggling desperately, especially on the batting front.

NCL DIVISION TWO - MATCH EIGHT

HAMPSHIRE HAWKS versus SURREY LIONS
at The County Ground, Southampton on Tuesday 27th June

Surrey Lions (116) beat Hampshire Hawks (73) by 43 runs

Surrey got their six days in Southampton off to a stunning start by claiming a most unlikely 43-run victory in a truly remarkable match which emphasised the visitors' renewed confidence after their demolition of Somerset as well as the frailties of the low-flying Hawks.
Electing to bat after winning the toss, the Lions recovered well after losing Ali Brown to the seventh ball of the match, thanks to the efforts of Mark Butcher and Ian Ward, who both scampered well between the wickets and took advantage of an erratic opening burst from Simon Francis.
The loss of three quick wickets, two of them to Alan Mullally at the start of a fine spell, swung the game back in Hampshire's favour, however, as Surrey slumped to 44-4. The briefest of recoveries then followed as Ben Hollioake and Jason Ratcliffe added nineteen runs before another catastrophic collapse saw the Lions slump to 75-8. Although there was an element of bad luck about three of the dismissals - Ratcliffe run out at the non-striker's end when Shaun Udal deflected Hollioake's drive onto the stumps; Batty caught by the ever-alert Aymes after jamming a full-length delivery down onto his boot; and Tudor ludicrously adjudged lbw to a low Warne full toss with his front leg way down the wicket - Surrey were, nevertheless, staring down the barrel at this point.
Fortunately for the visitors, Ben Hollioake was still in occupation and playing a mature and responsible innings, using his feet well to the spinners and driving Warne for one towering straight six as the last two wickets took the total past the meagre ninety-four that the Hawks had managed in the first game at The Oval and then beyond three figures. Disappointingly, there were still seven overs left to bowl when Hollioake's disciplined effort, and the Lions' innings, was ended by a brilliant legside stumping by Aymes off Mascarenhas. A final score of 116 looked woefully inadequate and it was obvious that Surrey's bowlers would need to produce something very special to rescue their team's unbeaten NCL record.

In order to prey on the nerves of Hampshire's out-of-form batsmen the Lions needed to strike early and they did so in style when Martin Bicknell knocked back Giles White's off stump with the second ball of the innings. Dimi Mascarenhas then fell to the final ball of the over, steepling a catch to extra cover where Alex Tudor completed a fine catch, as Surrey made a dream start. Great bowling by the Lions' opening pair was to produce two further breakthroughs before twenty runs were on the board - Robin Smith had his forward defensive stroke penetrated and his middle stump removed by Tudor, while Derek Kenway fell lbw on the front foot to Bicknell. Now we had a game on our hands!

Suddenly the runs and wickets dried up as John Stephenson and Jason Laney battened down the hatches, eschewing all risks and seeing off Bicknell (9-4-14-3) at the city end. At this point, Adam Hollioake faced a big decision. Did he bring on Ian Salisbury, Ben Hollioake or Jason Ratcliffe to support Saqlain, who had already taken over from Tudor at the Northlands Road end? While the seamers might be more likely to keep the scoring rate down, his team needed wickets and Salisbury would clearly be more likely to oblige in this respect. Almost inevitably, Hollioake took the attacking option, chose his leg-spinner and for an uncomfortable period, as Salisbury started indifferently and the Hawks pair took the score up to and beyond fifty, it looked like being the wrong move.

In the space of seven deliveries the picture changed completely, however, as Stephenson had his off stump pegged back by a Salisbury googly, Shane Warne paid a heavy price for hitting across the line against Saqlain and Adie Aymes fell, second ball, to a superb pick-up and direct hit throw from Tudor at extra cover. This was just one example of some superb Surrey fielding which kept Hampshire under pressure throughout their entire innings and it reduced the hosts to 60-7.

The Division Two leaders were now, almost unbelievably, favourites to win the match and when Saqlain removed both Udal and Mullally in the space of four balls just two overs later it looked all over bar the shouting. Memories of the last-wicket stand in the Championship match at The Oval meant that no-one was taking anything for granted, however, and it was only when Salisbury had Laney caught at short fine leg from a top-edged sweep with the Hawks still forty-four runs short of their target that the Lions' players and fans were able to celebrate an incredible fightback to victory. The unbeaten record was intact, thanks to bold captaincy by the Surrey skipper, a fine innings by his younger brother and another outstanding display in the field.

From a Hampshire point of view, this defeat was a disaster. Although much of the bowling had been pretty impressive, their batting had looked totally bereft of confidence and their fielding display was marred by two missed caught-and-bowled chances - Mascarenhas reprieved Butcher on sixteen and, most significantly, Warne allowed Ben Hollioake a life on fifteen - which cost them dearly in the final analysis. They had a major task on their hands to pick themselves up in time for the upcoming County Championship clash.

Surrey Lions (116) beat Hampshire Hawks (73) by 43 runs

Surrey Lions 4pts

HAMPSHIRE HAWKS v SURREY LIONS at SOUTHAMPTON. Played on 27th June
Surrey Lions won the toss   Umpires:- M.J. Harris & B. Leadbeater

SURREY LIONS   *HAMPSHIRE HAWKS bowling*

Fall of wkt	Batsman	How Out	Score	Balls	4s	6s		O	M	R	W
3- 40	M.A. Butcher	c Smith b Mascarenhas	21	27	3	0	Francis	4	0	23	0
1- 3	A.D. Brown	lbw b Mascarenhas	0	3	0	0	Mascarenhas	8	1	21	3
2- 40	I.J. Ward	c Warne b Mullally	14	24	1	0	Mullally	9	1	20	2
4- 44	A.J. Hollioake *	c Aymes b Mullally	3	8	0	0	Warne	9	2	32	2
10- 116	B.C. Hollioake	st Aymes b Mascarenhas	37	77	1	1	Udal	8	1	18	2
5- 63	J.D. Ratcliffe	run out	9	22	0	0					
6- 73	J.N. Batty +	c Aymes b Warne	6	13	0	0					
7- 74	M.P. Bicknell	c Aymes b Udal	0	4	0	0					
8- 75	A.J. Tudor	lbw b Warne	0	6	0	0					
9- 97	I.D.K. Salisbury	b Udal	13	25	1	0					
	Saqlain Mushtaq	Not Out	7	19	0	0					
	Extras (2lb, 4w)		6								
	TOTAL	(38 overs)	116								

HAMPSHIRE HAWKS   *SURREY LIONS bowling*

Fall of wkt	Batsman	How Out	Score	Balls	4s	6s		O	M	R	W
1- 0	G.W. White	b Bicknell	0	2	0	0	Bicknell	9	4	14	3
5- 57	J.P. Stephenson	b Salisbury	23	72	2	0	Tudor	7	2	7	1
2- 5	A.D. Mascarenhas	c Tudor b Bicknell	4	4	1	0	Saqlain	9	4	12	3
3- 15	R.A. Smith *	b Tudor	5	21	0	0	Salisbury	7.4	0	38	2
4- 18	D.A. Kenway	lbw b Bicknell	2	9	0	0					
10- 73	J.S. Laney	c Saqlain b Salisbury	29	65	3	0					
6- 60	S.K. Warne	lbw b Saqlain	1	3	0	0					
7- 60	A.N. Aymes +	run out	0	2	0	0					
8- 67	S.D. Udal	c B.C. Hollioake b Saqlain	1	4	0	0					
9- 67	A.D. Mullally	lbw b Saqlain	0	3	0	0					
	S.R.G. Francis	Not Out	1	11	0	0					
	Extras (2lb, 5w)		7								
	TOTAL	(32.4 overs)	73								

Other NCL Division Two Matches

Since Surrey's victory at Edgbaston, the Nottinghamshire Outlaws had recorded victories over both the Essex Eagles and the Derbyshire Scorpions to move back to the top of the table, while the Warwickshire Bears had slumped to a surprising home defeat at the hands of the Eagles. The Lions' win over the Hawks therefore resulted in a ten-point gap developing between the top two and the rest of the pack, with the Outlaws topping the table only as a result of having recorded more victories than the Lions. It was already looking quite clear that there were several very poor limited-overs teams in the division, with the bottom three counties already out of the picture for promotion and the Essex Eagles struggling to stay in the hunt.

June 24
Cardiff:- **Glamorgan Dragons beat Hampshire Hawks by 51 runs.** Glamorgan 236-7 (Maynard 67); Hampshire 185-9 (Udal 51 not out). **Glamorgan Dragons 4pts**

Trent Bridge:- **Nottinghamshire Outlaws beat Essex Eagles by four wickets.** Essex 177-9 (Irani 52, Lucas 4-38); Nottinghamshire 179-6 in 42.3 overs. **Nottinghamshire Outlaws 4pts**

June 25
Chester-le-Street:- **Middlesex Crusaders beat Durham Dynamos by 53 runs.** Middlesex 233 in 44.2 overs (Strauss 90); Durham 180 in 40.1 overs (Speak 53 not out, Laraman 6-51). **Middlesex Crusaders 4pts**

Edgbaston:- **Essex Eagles beat Warwickshire Bears by 24 runs.** Essex 163-7; Warwickshire 139 in 40.2 overs. **Essex Eagles 4pts**

June 26
Derby:- **Nottinghamshire Outlaws beat Derbyshire Scorpions by 30 runs.** Nottinghamshire 212-8 (Bicknell 90, Cork 4-40); Derbyshire 182 in 42.3 overs (Cork 51, Lucas 4-27). **Nottinghamshire Outlaws 4pts**

NCL DIVISION TWO AT 27TH JUNE

Pos	Prev		P	Pts	W	T	L	N/R	Last	Three	Res
1	2	Nottinghamshire Outlaws	8	28	7	0	1	0	W	W	W
2	1	Surrey Lions	8	28	6	0	0	2	W	W	W
3	4	Glamorgan Dragons	7	18	4	1	2	0	W	W	T
4	3	Warwickshire Bears	6	16	4	0	2	0	L	L	W
5	5	Middlesex Crusaders	7	16	3	1	2	1	W	L	T
6	6	Essex Eagles	7	10	2	0	4	1	W	L	L
7	7	Derbyshire Scorpions	6	4	1	0	5	0	L	W	L
8	8	Durham Dynamos	7	4	1	0	6	0	L	L	W
9	8	Hampshire Hawks	8	4	1	0	7	0	L	L	W

CHAMPIONSHIP PROGRESS HAS TO BE MAINTAINED

Surrey clearly held all the psychological aces as the two teams prepared for a County Championship encounter that both sides needed to win - the hosts to haul themselves away from the relegation zone and the visitors to maintain the improved form shown in the Somerset match ahead of a hoped-for surge to the top of the table.

Reasonably enough, the local Daily Echo had slammed Hampshire's performance in the National League match, carrying the headline 'PATHETIC', followed by a sub-headline stating 'Hampshire Are The Pits'. Robin Smith was quoted as saying 'I don't think we can stoop any lower than we have done today' after the NCL debacle and he admitted that he didn't know how to turn his side's fortunes around - 'I'm not a magician. Its very sad. After twenty years at this club I can't ever remember being as desperately disappointed as this.'

Surrey now had to take full and ruthless advantage of Hampshire's disarray in the Championship match.

COUNTY CHAMPIONSHIP - MATCH EIGHT

HAMPSHIRE versus SURREY
at The County Ground, Southampton

First Day - Thursday 29th June

Surrey 331; Hampshire 6-0

<u>The Teams And The Toss</u> - Despite scoring an excellent seventy-seven on his return to first team action against Somerset, the unfortunate Nadeem Shahid makes way for the fit-again Ben

Hollioake to resume his place in Surrey's Championship line-up. The side is otherwise unchanged. In an attempt to strengthen their batting, Hampshire select Andrew Sexton and Derek Kenway ahead of Jason Laney and John Stephenson, ironically their two top-scorers in the NCL rout, while Simon Francis continues to deputise for the injured Peter Hartley in the bowling attack and Shaun Udal plays as a second spinner. Adam Hollioake predictably elects to take first use of the pitch upon winning the toss.

The game opens in quite lively fashion as both Mark Butcher and Ian Ward clip boundaries through midwicket before the latter has a lucky escape, surviving an overhead catching opportunity to Will Kendall at first slip off Alan Mullally in the third over. While Butcher immediately looks confident, undoubtedly buoyed by his innings against Somerset, Ward never truly settles and eventually falls ten overs later when he edges the same bowler to the same fielder. Positioned this time at second slip, Kendall gratefully hangs on the catch to atone for his earlier error and Surrey are 37 for 1.

Graham Thorpe is the new batsman for Surrey and he starts very positively, driving Mullally to the rope at cover and then pulling him behind square for a second boundary in the same over. Having now completed eight overs, the former Leicestershire fast bowler is immediately withdrawn from the attack to allow Simon Francis a crack from the Northlands Road end after an initial four-over burst from the city end. The young seamer consistently pitches too short, however, and Thorpe takes the opportunity to continue his flying start by cutting, pulling and hooking three fours in three overs.

With the score racing up into the seventies at three-and-a-half runs per over, Robin Smith makes the obvious and sensible move of turning back to Mullally at the Northlands Road end and introducing Shane Warne at the city end. Surprisingly, the Australian leg-spinner makes an indifferent start, allowing Thorpe to feast on a series of juicy full-tosses and long-hops and, in the process, to raise a fifty partnership which he has dominated. Meanwhile, Butcher appears to have lost his way at the other end and, having added only three runs to his score in the previous twelve overs, he becomes Mullally's second victim of the morning when adjudged lbw with the score at 100.

After his two wayward opening overs Warne has now settled into his rhythm and asks some testing questions of the batsmen in the closing stages of the session.

Lunch:- Surrey 105-2 (Thorpe 44*, A.J. Hollioake 4*) from 34 overs

Alan Mullally's opening over of the afternoon session is an action-packed affair. Having been called for a wide at the start of the over, he is very much on target with his fourth delivery which defeats Thorpe's drive and knocks back the batsman's leg stump. This is a major disappointment for Surrey but it doesn't inhibit Ali Brown, who clips his first delivery through square leg for two runs and then despatches a no-ball to the extra cover boundary.

The pace of events doesn't slacken too much, either, especially when Mullally is rather curiously withdrawn after just three overs and replaced by Shaun Udal, who had delivered just one over in the morning session. The Hampshire off-break bowler is immediately subjected to some rough treatment as Hollioake advances down the track to drive for three through extra cover and Brown follows up by lifting a handsome six over long-off, resulting in a lost ball. Although he then survives a very sharp chance to the right hand of Warne at slip in Udal's next over, Brown continues his assault on the off-spinner, finding the boundary on two further occasions with a cut and a sweep. The latter stroke raises Surrey's 150 in the forty-fourth over and leaves Udal with figures of 3-0-24-0 since his reintroduction.

Warne has thus far escaped punishment since lunch but his turn is to come as the aggressive Hollioake-Brown pairing begins to set about him. The Surrey skipper is the Aussie's first assailant, lofting him for three off-side boundaries in an over which sees the fourth-wicket duo's fifty stand completed at almost a run a ball. With two of Hollioake's strokes having only just cleared the heads of fielders, a frustrated Warne is not impressed but he can have few complaints in his next over when Brown pounds him for three successive fours with a brace of cuts and an extra cover drive. Having maybe given the leg-spinner too much respect at The Oval this apparently calculated assault represents good cricket and makes for absorbing viewing.

To the credit of the Hampshire spinners, they do manage to drag the scoring rate back a little over the course of the next few overs but when Brown drives Udal wide of mid-on for the boundary which takes him to an excellent fifty at exactly a run a ball in just 61 minutes (7 fours, 1 six) and Hollioake then lifts Warne almost effortlessly over long-off for a superb six, Robin Smith feels obliged to take action. In a double change, Mullally returns at the Northlands Road end to replace a chastened Warne (15-5-52-0) while Mascarenhas replaces Udal (8-1-38-0) at the city end. This move brings no immediate improvement for Hampshire, though, as Brown takes eight from the left-armer's opening over to bring up the visitors' two-hundred and Hollioake cuts Mascarenhas for two fours to complete a quite magnificent century partnership in 20.1 overs.

Surrey now look nicely placed to record a large total in quick time but the situation changes rapidly with the loss of two wickets in the space of four balls. The rollicking fourth-wicket stand ends with a brilliant catch at short extra cover by Kendall off Mascarenhas, which accounts for Adam Hollioake just three runs short of fifty, before brother Ben holes out to mid-on when facing Mullally. While the Surrey skipper's stroke had been well timed and middled, his sibling's second-ball exit followed the tamest of chip shots, presumably brought about by a touch of indecision.

As a result of these quick-fire breakthroughs, Surrey's commanding 216-3 has now become 217-5 and Hampshire's fightback continues seven overs later when Mascarenhas, aided by another marvellous piece of fielding, brings Brown to book for seventy-one with the total advanced to 231. Adrian Aymes is Hampshire's hero on this occasion, pulling off a breathtaking legside stumping to end a richly-entertaining knock and provide his London-born team-mate with his second wicket of the innings.

With parity now almost restored to the match, the Hampshire captain shuffles his bowlers again, restoring his spinners to the attack, but Jon Batty and Martin Bicknell bat safely through to tea, collecting another batting bonus point en route.

Tea:- Surrey 253-6 (Batty 15*, Bicknell 8*) from 72 overs

To the surprise of many, given that the game appears to be delicately poised, Robin Smith pairs Warne with the inexperienced Francis, rather than Mullally, upon the resumption. While the young pace bowler proves largely ineffective before making way for Udal at the city end, Hampshire's Aussie legend begins to cause problems by switching to the round-the-wicket attack which had proved so successful in the earlier encounter at The Oval.

This move produces quite dramatic results as he sends three men back to the pavilion within twenty-four balls. Unfortunately for the home side, Warne's middle victim is his own team-mate, Adrian Aymes, who is struck a nasty blow in the face when Alex Tudor pads up to a legside delivery, leaving the veteran wicketkeeper momentarily unsighted. On a more positive note, he yorks Jon Batty with the score at 270 and follows up by hitting Tudor's off stump with a fine leg-break just fourteen runs later. Surrey have now lost five wickets in adding sixty-eight runs and are suddenly in danger of failing to post three-hundred.

Both Martin Bicknell and Ian Salisbury are good players of spin bowling, however, and they quickly allay this fear with a boundary apiece before Bicknell launches Udal over long-on for a mighty six to prompt a belated recall for Mullally. The England left-armer is immediately on the mark, too, but Salisbury blocks him out successfully at one end while his partner again demonstrates that Warne's leg-breaks hold no fear for him, sweeping three fours in consecutive overs and also adding an imperious straight-driven boundary on the way to an excellent half-century compiled in just a few minutes under two hours from 97 balls. By now the Hampshire 'leggie' is showing signs of frustration again but he is spared further punishment when Mullally brings the innings to a close with two wickets in two balls, Salisbury being taken behind the wicket by Kenway, deputising for the indisposed Aymes, and Saqlain edging to Warne at first slip. The former Leicestershire paceman thus ends with six wickets to his name after another good display against Surrey.

Having been in complete control at 216-3, the reigning champions' final total of 331 represents something of a disappointment, yet it probably seems quite awesome to a Hampshire team with serious worries about their batting.

Considering their current lack of form and confidence in this department, they are doubtless delighted to survive the two overs that they are required to face before the close of play.

Close:- Hampshire 6-0 (White 3*, Sexton 3*) from 2 overs

VIEW FROM THE DRESSING ROOM - ADAM HOLLIOAKE

You appeared to relish your duels with Shane Warne in both Championship matches against Hampshire - I guess that is the kind of challenge that you most enjoy.
AH - He's a great bowler and a great competitor, so it's inevitable that any time I come up against him I want to do well. I've played against him quite a lot over the years and one of us usually comes out well on top of the other, so it's good fun and I enjoy the battle.

During this game it appeared to me that our batsmen were determined to be extremely positive against Warne. Was it a conscious team policy to show him less respect than we had in both the Benson And Hedges Cup and Championship games at The Oval?
AH - Definitely. He wasn't spinning the ball as much as we had expected and we knew that it would make life a lot easier for Hampshire if we allowed him to settle and keep bowling at one end for a long period of time. We therefore had a policy to go after him and be positive when facing him... and I think that plan worked well for us.

Second Day - Friday 30th June

Surrey 331 and 134-3; Hampshire 167

Hampshire's hopes of a sound start are dashed during a testing opening to day two as both openers fall prey to Martin Bicknell. Andrew Sexton goes first, brilliantly taken one-handed down the legside by Jon Batty from a genuine leg glance in the sixth over of the morning, then Giles White shuffles across his stumps and departs lbw just two overs later - it's 17 for 2 and the champions are immediately holding the whip hand.

Although both Surrey bowlers are looking dangerous and giving absolutely nothing away, Bicknell is withdrawn after five overs to allow him a rest before he takes over from Tudor at the city end. This seems to be a sensible move but, unfortunately, Bicknell's replacement, Ben Hollioake, is unable to find any rhythm and Robin Smith batters him ruthlessly in a three-over spell costing twenty-four runs. In Hollioake's final over, the former England batsman picks off three boundaries - one driven straight, the other two cut square - and in no time at all Hampshire have sailed past fifty.

At this point Bicknell reappears in place of Tudor and Saqlain takes over from Hollioake but the Surrey 'dream team' surprisingly fails to stem the flow of runs. Kendall cuts and pulls the off-spinner for two fours in an over and Smith follows up with a brace of boundaries in the next over from Bicknell, though it must be said in the bowler's defence that one comes via a thick edge over the slips. Surrey's swing king then suffers further frustration in his following over when he bowls Kendall with a fine yorker only to hear the umpire calling a no-ball.

Despite coming close to a wicket on these two occasions, Adam Hollioake removes Bicknell from the attack after just four overs and turns to an all-spin offensive, switching Saqlain to the city end in the process.

Bingo! The new combination brings instant results and the game takes another dramatic turn. Having added sixty-seven runs at four-an-over, both participants in the third-wicket partnership depart within six balls of one another, Smith lbw to a big Saqlain off-break as he attempts to cut and Kendall taken by Thorpe at slip off Salisbury via Batty's gloves.

Hampshire are now struggling again at 84-4 and, with the Surrey spinners taking complete control, it is no surprise when a fifth wicket falls with lunch beckoning. Adrian Aymes is the man to go, adjudged lbw when trapped on the crease by a very well-disguised quicker ball from Saqlain, though the Hampshire 'keeper's reaction to the umpire's decision suggests that he feels he has got an inside edge.

Lunch:- Hampshire 89-5 (Kenway 2*, Mascarenhas 1*) from 33 overs

A real war of attrition develops after lunch as Kenway and Mascarenhas hang on grimly against the Surrey spinners. Only fourteen runs are added in the opening twelve overs of the afternoon before both batsmen momentarily break free with a boundary apiece off Salisbury. For Mascarenhas this turns out to be a final act of defiance, however, as Saqlain has him caught by Mark Butcher at silly point in the very next over to reduce Hampshire to a desperate 113-6, still 218 runs adrift of Surrey's total.

The new batsman at the wicket is Shane Warne and he immediately announces his arrival by slog-sweeping Salisbury to the midwicket boards. As at the Oval earlier in the season, he looks determined to get on top of the bowling and the Australian's presence seems to encourage his partner, too, since Kenway suddenly appears from his shell to drive and pull two fine boundaries. During a short phase of dominance by the batsmen, Warne produces his slog-sweep again to thrash a Saqlain delivery over the rope at deep midwicket before the spin twins start to reassert their authority.

Once they are back on top again Saqlain and Salisbury show no mercy as they sweep through the lower-order. The initial breakthrough comes when Kenway falls to the fourth leg-before verdict of the innings, seemingly hit on the back pad by Saqlain's 'other' ball, then Warne is undone by the same type of delivery and stumped by Batty, having danced down the wicket and failed to regain his ground.

At 150-8, the innings is now all over bar the slogging. Alan Mullally's innings lasts just eight balls and includes three fours - one swept, one edged and one flicked over square leg - before he is bowled behind his legs by another Saqlain "wrong 'un", while Francis cuts his first ball, from Salisbury, to the point boundary and then falls to a sharp catch by the Surrey skipper at silly point from his second. In the final analysis, Hampshire have declined from 84-2 to 167 all out, largely as a result of the efforts of Saqlain, who finishes with 6 for 51 from twenty-two testing overs.

The visitors have therefore established a commanding first innings lead of 164 and, with the pitch already assisting the spinners, the question now is whether or not Adam Hollioake will choose to enforce the follow-on.

Tea:- Between Innings

With seven sessions still available for play, Surrey decide to bat again and build on their already imposing advantage. The openers make a fairly positive start, too, as both Mark Butcher and Ian Ward find the cover boundary during the course of the early overs from Mullally and Francis. The ball only beats the outside edge on rare occasions and the closest Hampshire come to a wicket is when Ward edges Francis just wide of a diving second slip in the twelfth over. Surrey's lead has already extended past two-hundred by this point, though, and the fifty opening partnership comes up shortly afterwards when Ward drives Warne straight down the ground for a boundary in the Aussie legend's opening over.

In an apparently desperate last throw of the dice, Robin Smith keeps Mullally going for eleven overs, the last four in tandem with Warne, but no breakthrough is forthcoming. Both left-handers seem comfortable even against Hampshire's ace leg-spinner, mixing careful defence with the occasional drive through the covers or back past the bowler, and it's only when Udal joins Warne in an all-spin attack that the picture changes slightly.

With the total on ninety-two and his personal tally standing at forty-two, Ward gets an outside edge to Aymes off Warne to provide the home side with a morsel of comfort and, as a result, the brakes are suddenly applied to a very healthy scoring rate. Just four singles accrue from the next six overs until Butcher cuts Udal backward of square for a boundary which takes Surrey past three figures and the batsman through to a well-played fifty in 125 minutes from 101 balls.

It's been a hard day for Hampshire but as we move into the final stages they do at least find some succour when Graham Thorpe advances on Udal and skies a catch to deepish cover with the lead up to 280. Since there are only five overs left for play at the fall of this wicket, Surrey send a nightwatchman, in the form of Saqlain Mushtaq, to the crease. The Pakistani spin king's approach to this role turns out to be rather unorthodox, however - having swept Warne to the rope backward of square leg, he despatches Udal over the deep midwicket boundary for six and then back over his head for four before being given out lbw to the Aussie leg-spinner in the final over of the day. This very entertaining innings of seventeen at almost a run a ball ends a very good day for Surrey in some style. With the visitors' advantage already standing at 301 Hampshire most certainly have their backs to the wall and Adam Hollioake's men look set to build on their success against Somerset in the previous match.

Close:- Surrey 134-3 (Butcher 60*) from 41.5 overs

VIEW FROM THE DRESSING ROOM - MARK BUTCHER

Our batsmen appeared to be more positive against Warne in this game than they had been during the games earlier in the season - was this a pre-determined game plan?
MB - I'm not sure that it was actually a conscious decision but I remember that we talked about the fact that he does get a lot of wickets with deliveries that look like heavy-spun leg-breaks but actually go straight on - we felt, therefore, that the right-handers should keep their front pad out of the way and concentrate on playing at the ball. That's certainly what the guys did in the first innings and they then took it one step further by hitting the ball over the top of the infield! I think our approach shocked them a bit and it meant that Alan Mullally had to come back and bowl more. Although he bowled well, it meant he'd got more overs on the clock by the time the second innings came around.

Third Day - Saturday 1st July

Surrey 331 and 228-6 declared; Hampshire 167 and 265-9

Day three starts fairly sedately as Robin Smith pairs Mullally and Warne, presumably in the hope that they might pull off a cricketing miracle. Consequently, Mark Butcher and Adam

Hollioake play every ball on its merits, though still managing the occasional boundary to push the Surrey total beyond 150 in the first half-hour.

After a short four-over blast, Mullally gives way to Dimi Mascarenhas at the city end and the Surrey captain shows some aggressive intent by driving consecutive deliveries from Warne down the ground to the sightscreen. Needless to say, the Aussie legend isn't too impressed by this and when Butcher pulls him to square leg for another boundary in his next over he promptly fires down two successive bouncers. Having apparently got the frustration out of his system, Warne's demeanour then improves immeasurably when he removes both of his first innings tormentors in his following over. Adam Hollioake goes to the first ball, stumped at the second attempt after a headlong charge down the track, then Ali Brown follows his skipper back to the pavilion four balls later when Giles White snaps up a bat-pad catch at silly point. Surrey are 182-5, though, as far as the wickets are concerned, it's all largely academic stuff at this stage.

Apart from assessing the timing of the visitors' declaration, the major point of interest is now Mark Butcher's push for a century. Although he enjoys one slice of good fortune in the nineties when he edges Mascarenhas over the slips for four runs, the magical milestone arrives when he drives a Warne full-toss through backward point for three. His hundred has come from 210 balls in 245 minutes and during this innings Butcher has surely proved to many doubters that his weakness against quality spin bowling has been somewhat exaggerated.

Once the celebrations for a fine knock have died down, Udal replaces Mascarenhas and the Surrey batsmen pick off singles at will as their lead builds towards four-hundred. They lose Ben Hollioake, perhaps harshly adjudged lbw when struck on a well-advanced front pad by a full-length delivery from Warne, with the score at 218 before rain brings an early lunch at 12.50pm.

Since 393 appears to represent a mere fantasy target for a side whose batting is currently in disarray, the best guess is that Adam Hollioake's declaration will come during the interval.

Lunch:- Surrey 228-6 (Butcher 116*, Batty 1*) from 71.1 overs

As anticipated, the visitors declare at their lunch score and, with five sessions of play left in the match, weather permitting, we will clearly get a result one way or the other, with Surrey most definitely the red-hot favourites.

They look likely to justify this tag, too, as the early stages of the Hampshire innings are characterised by much playing and missing. The inexperienced Andrew Sexton certainly appears to find first team cricket something of a struggle and the wily Bicknell eventually defeats him with an inswinger in the ninth over to win an lbw verdict - Hampshire 25 for 1.

Fortunately for the hosts, White and Kendall are able to see off the remainder of the opening spells from Surrey's new-ball pair and they even take advantage of some indifferent overs from Alex Tudor to push the total beyond fifty.

The biggest test is now about to begin, though, as a double change sees Saqlain taking up the attack at the city end and Ian Salisbury appearing at the Northlands Road end.

For Hampshire the early signs are not good as Saqlain's second delivery spits wickedly at White, prompting worried glances at the pitch from both batsmen. Kendall's personal concerns about the playing surface quickly become irrelevant, however, as a breakdown in communications results in him being run out in the next over. Having pushed a delivery from Salisbury into a sizeable gap at midwicket, Kendall turns for a second run but is sent back by his partner and fails to beat Adam Hollioake's return to the non-striker's end. It's a terrible waste of a wicket for the home side, reducing them to 56-2, and, perhaps more significantly, it also opens the door for the Surrey spinners. Salisbury needs no second invitation to take advantage of the situation, either, quickly pinning Robin Smith lbw for just three as he pads up to a googly.

There is now a justifiable feeling that Hampshire could fold quickly against the visitors' spin duo but White remains steadfast and his new partner, Derek Kenway, adopts an initially aggressive approach by punching and forcing both Saqlain and Salisbury down the ground.

Interestingly, Adam Hollioake reacts to Kenway's stirring start by recalling Alex Tudor in place of Saqlain. The big fast bowler had enjoyed considerable success against the Hampshire youngster in the encounter at The Oval but, on this occasion, Kenway survives four good hostile overs and the Surrey skipper quickly reverts to his off-spinner. Much to Hollioake's chagrin the 22-year-old Fareham-born batsman then immediately slog-sweeps Saqlain for six over midwicket! Fortunately, this counts for little since Salisbury immediately traps him on the back foot with a googly which keeps low and leaves the umpire with a straightforward decision. Kenway departs for twenty-three and Hampshire are well and truly in the mire at 101-4.

If they are to survive the day they can now ill afford to lose another wicket before tea but they do exactly that when Mascarenhas, after less than a quarter-of-an-hour at the crease, drives a catch back to Saqlain at head height. It seems to be just a matter of time now - can Surrey finish the match after tea or not?

Tea:- Hampshire 120-5 (White 46*, Warne 7*) from 38 overs

The second over of the final session, bowled by Saqlain, produces a staggering nineteen runs, including a mighty legside pick-up from Giles White which takes him through to a 169-minute half-century from 103 balls.

Any ideas that this expensive over might represent the start of a significant Hampshire counter-attack are soon dispelled, however, as the spinners rapidly regain control. This is clearly not to Shane Warne's liking, so, after four largely passive overs, he moves back on to the attack, whipping Salisbury through midwicket for three and then cutting Saqlain to the rope at point to raise the fifty partnership for the sixth wicket.

The Australian's attempts to dominate bring about his downfall in his fellow leg-spinner's next over, though, as an ambitious slog-sweep results in a miscue and a very good catch by Ben Hollioake running back towards deep midwicket. With Warne gone for twenty-three and Hampshire now 161 for 6, a three-day defeat is looming for the home side.

Although the picture is very bleak for his team, Giles White fights on with commendable spirit, sweeping a clearly below-par Saqlain for another boundary then despatching him high over the rope at midwicket for the second time in the session.

While the off-spinner appears to be struggling somewhat, it's fortunate for Surrey that his 'twin' is proving a real handful at the Northlands Road end. During an exceptionally well-controlled spell of leg-spin bowling, Ian Salisbury eventually unseats White, whose attempt to find the boundary with another sweep ends with his off stump pegged back and his innings terminated at seventy-three.

With the last specialist batsman now departed after an impressive effort, everyone expects Surrey to cruise home in style but Adie Aymes and Shaun Udal provide stern resistance, taking the score beyond two-hundred with a sensible mix of solid defence and attractive strokeplay. Alex Tudor and Martin Bicknell are both given short spells at the city end in place of the off-colour Saqlain, but neither manages to provide a breakthrough so, after ten overs, Adam Hollioake reverts to an all-spin attack.

Surrey fans know that one of Saqlain's many qualities is his ability to bounce back well after a disappointing spell, so it is almost inevitable, therefore, that his return to the fray quickly brings the desired breakthrough - Udal, trapped lbw on the back foot just two balls after the Pakistani off-spinner had changed to an around-the-wicket attack. It's just as well for Surrey that Saqi has come back in style since Salisbury appears to tire and loses a little of his earlier control as the schedule time for close of play nears.

When it arrives, with just two Hampshire wickets standing, it's no surprise to anyone that the visitors elect to claim the extra half-hour in an attempt to force a three-day victory. Aymes and Mullally clearly have no intention of giving the game away, though, and they resist manfully until Saqlain lures Mullally into giving a return catch with just eight deliveries remaining.

Hard though they try, Surrey prove unable to seal their victory in the final over of the session, leaving the match to spill over into day four. Poor weather is forecast but Hampshire will need a monsoon to deny the reigning champions their third win of a campaign which looks to be gathering momentum.

Close:- Hampshire 265-9 (Aymes 43*, Francis 0*) from 78 overs

VIEW FROM THE DRESSING ROOM - MARK BUTCHER

Following on from your eighty-two against Somerset at The Oval, you must have been very happy to return to something like your best form with this hundred after struggling a little with indifferent form and some bad luck during the early weeks of the season?

MB - This innings gave me a lot of pleasure, coming as it did against Shane Warne, who has got me out a few times in Test Matches and earned me some stick for not playing spin especially well. I felt I played him very well here and I thought this was a very professional innings because I had to concentrate hard and work hard throughout. And it was particularly satisfying having come off a bit of a bad run.

I noticed that you spent a lot of time in the nets with Ian Salisbury before play started. I guess it must be a great help having people like Sals and Saqi to practise against?

MB - Yes, in the Surrey dressing room everyone tries to help everyone else improve their game. Since I knew I could, potentially, be facing a lot of overs from Warney in this match, I asked Sals if he would come and bowl to me in the nets and he was only too happy to help. Interestingly, because the Hampshire batsmen were likely to be seeing a lot of our spinners, I remember that Shane Warne was over at the nets on the first two mornings waiting to bowl to their guys... but no-one turned up. Quite understandably, he was rather annoyed, having gone out of his way to help his team-mates.

Fourth Day - Sunday 2nd July

Surrey 331 and 228-6 declared; Hampshire 167 and 272

Surrey beat Hampshire by 120 runs
Surrey 18pts, Hampshire 3

Although Adrian Aymes reaches a well-deserved half-century from 106 balls in the second over of the morning, he falls lbw on the back foot to Saqlain in the following over to confirm Surrey's expected victory.

By a strange quirk of fate, both spinners finish with four wickets for eighty-four as Adam Hollioake's men record their third County Championship win in four games, this one by the margin of 120 runs.

HAMPSHIRE v SURREY at SOUTHAMPTON. Played from 29th June - 2nd July
Surrey won the toss   Umpires:- K.E. Palmer & A.G.T. Whitehead

SURREY - First Innings

Fall of wkt	Batsman	How Out		Score	Balls	4s	6s
2- 100	M.A. Butcher		lbw b Mullally	34	81	6	0
1- 37	I.J. Ward	c Kendall	b Mullally	15	42	2	0
3- 107	G.P. Thorpe		b Mullally	44	74	9	0
4- 216	A.J. Hollioake *	c Kendall	b Mascarenhas	47	82	7	1
6- 231	A.D. Brown	st Aymes	b Mascarenhas	71	83	9	1
5- 217	B.C. Hollioake	c Smith	b Mullally	1	2	0	0
7- 270	J.N. Batty +		b Warne	26	65	2	0
	M.P. Bicknell		Not Out	56	103	7	1
8- 284	A.J. Tudor		b Warne	5	29	0	0
9- 331	I.D.K. Salisbury	c Kenway	b Mullally	7	37	1	0
10- 331	Saqlain Mushtaq	c Warne	b Mullally	0	1	0	0
	Extras (4b, 7lb, 8w, 6nb)			25			
	TOTAL		(99.2 overs)	331			

HAMPSHIRE bowling

	O	M	R	W
Mullally	24.2	6	75	6
Francis	14	2	58	0
Mascarenhas	14	4	34	2
Udal	16	2	63	0
Warne	31	12	90	2

HAMPSHIRE - First Innings

Fall of wkt	Batsman	How Out		Score	Balls	4s	6s
2- 17	G.W. White		lbw b Bicknell	6	30	0	0
1- 10	A.J. Sexton	c Batty	b Bicknell	5	17	0	0
4- 84	W.S. Kendall	c Thorpe	b Salisbury	23	68	4	0
3- 84	R.A. Smith *		lbw b Saqlain	36	53	7	0
7- 147	D.A. Kenway		lbw b Saqlain	30	98	4	0
5- 87	A.N. Aymes +		lbw b Saqlain	2	16	0	0
6- 113	A.D. Mascarenhas	c Butcher	b Saqlain	12	47	1	0
8- 150	S.K. Warne	st Batty	b Saqlain	17	37	1	1
	S.D. Udal		Not Out	3	13	0	0
9- 162	A.D. Mullally		b Saqlain	12	8	3	0
10- 167	S.R.G. Francis	c A.J. Hollioake	b Salisbury	4	2	1	0
	Extras (1lb, 16nb)			17			
	TOTAL		(63.3 overs)	167			

SURREY bowling

	O	M	R	W
Tudor	9	1	26	0
Bicknell	10	2	25	2
B.C. Hollioake	3	0	24	0
Saqlain	22	4	51	6
Salisbury	19.3	7	40	2

SURREY - Second Innings

Fall of wkt	Batsman	How Out		Score	Balls	4s	6s
	M.A. Butcher		Not Out	116	221	14	0
1- 92	I.J. Ward	c Aymes	b Warne	42	72	5	0
2- 113	G.P. Thorpe	c Sexton	b Udal	9	36	1	0
3- 134	Saqlain Mushtaq		lbw b Warne	17	19	2	1
4- 180	A.J. Hollioake *	st Kenway	b Warne	24	41	3	0
5- 182	A.D. Brown	c White	b Warne	0	4	0	0
6- 218	B.C. Hollioake		lbw b Warne	10	32	0	0
	J.N. Batty +		Not Out	1	3	0	0
	Extras (5lb, 2w, 2nb)			9			
	TOTAL		(71.1 overs)	228 - 6 dec			

HAMPSHIRE bowling

	O	M	R	W
Mullally	15	4	48	0
Francis	6	0	22	0
Warne	29.1	3	90	5
Udal	13	3	40	1
Mascarenhas	8	1	23	0

HAMPSHIRE - Second Innings

Fall of wkt	Batsman	How Out	Score	Balls	4s	6s
7- 187	G.W. White	b Salisbury	73	146	4	2
1- 25	A.J. Sexton	lbw b Bicknell	5	22	0	0
2- 56	W.S. Kendall	run out	15	25	2	0
3- 63	R.A. Smith *	lbw b Salisbury	3	10	0	0
4- 101	D.A. Kenway	lbw b Salisbury	23	42	2	1
5- 110	A.D. Mascarenhas	c & b Saqlain	2	12	0	0
6- 161	S.K. Warne	c B.C. Hollioake	b Saqlain	23	34	3	0
10- 272	A.N. Aymes +	lbw b Saqlain	50	108	5	1
8- 230	S.D. Udal	lbw b Saqlain	24	51	3	0
9- 265	A.D. Mullally	c & b Saqlain	10	28	1	0
	S.R.G. Francis	Not Out	0	8	0	0
	Extras (13b, 17lb, 6w, 8nb)		44			
	TOTAL	(80.2 overs)	272			

SURREY bowling

	O	M	R	W
Bicknell	10	2	27	1
Tudor	14	1	46	0
Saqlain	23.2	1	84	4
Salisbury	32	4	84	4
Brown	1	0	1	0

KEITH MEDLYCOTT'S ASSESSMENT

We'd now got into the winning habit with a run of about half-a-dozen games, including the one-dayers, so we were feeling very positive and upbeat. After this win everyone was now looking forward with relish to the big forthcoming Championship matches against Leicestershire, Yorkshire and Lancashire.

Other Division One Matches

Surrey's win moved them up to third in the table, while Lancashire's thrashing of Yorkshire evened things up at the top. Although the roses counties both maintained a points and games advantage over the reigning champions, suddenly there appeared to be much less ground to make up. Was it significant, and a sign of things to come, that Yorkshire's defeat came on an Old Trafford pitch which gave plenty of encouragement to the spinners?

June 28-30
Darlington:- **Durham beat Derbyshire by an innings and 79 runs.** Derbyshire 151 (Betts 7-30) and 249 (Titchard 87 not out, Dowman 61, Munton 52, Brown 6-40); Durham 479-9dec (Katich 114, Collingwood 111, Speak 78, Betts 55). **Durham 20pts, Derbys 2**

June 28-July 1
Maidstone:- **Somerset drew with Kent.** Somerset 475 (Bowler 108, Trescothick 90, Blackwell 69); Kent 261 (Dravid 88) and 338-3 (Fulton 115, Dravid 95, Wells 60 not out, Key 54). **Somerset 11pts, Kent 8**

June 29-July 1
Old Trafford:- **Lancashire beat Yorkshire by nine wickets.** Yorkshire 164 (Blakey 56) and 151 (Keedy 4-47); Lancashire 269 (Hegg 58) and 47-1. **Lancashire 17pts, Yorkshire 3**

COUNTY CHAMPIONSHIP DIVISION ONE AT 2ND JULY

Pos	Prev		P	Pts	W	D	L	Bat	Bowl	Last Three		Res
1	1	Yorkshire	7	91	4	2	1	14	21	L3	W15	W17
2	3	Lancashire	7	89	4	3	0	13	16	W17	W17	D8
3	4	Surrey	8	83	3	3	2	18	17	W18	W20	L3
4	2	Leicestershire	7	75	2	4	1	19	16	W18	D7	D9
5	5	Somerset	7	67	2	3	2	15	16	D11	L2	W17
6	9	Durham	7	58	2	1	4	9	21	W20	L3	L3
7	8	Kent	7	50	1	4	2	4	18	D8	L3	L5
8	6	Hampshire	8	50	1	2	5	6	24	L3	W18	L3
9	7	Derbyshire	8	48*	1	4	3	7	21	L2	L3	W7

* Deducted 8pts for sub-standard pitch

NCL RESULTS STRENGTHEN SURREY'S POSITION

The Surrey Lions and the Nottinghamshire Outlaws took a firmer grip at the top of NCL Division Two when Middlesex Crusaders lost at Chelmsford and Glamorgan Dragons fought out a Duckworth-Lewis calculated tie with the Warwickshire Bears. It was starting to look like the division might be splitting into three sub-sections, with Surrey and Nottinghamshire at the top, a group of four counties vying for the other promotion slot in the middle and three no-hopers at the bottom.

July 2
Darlington:- **Durham Dynamos beat Derbyshire Scorpions by 95 runs.** Durham 182-6 in 37 overs (Katich 67 not out, Speight 55); Derbyshire 87 in 24 overs (Phillips 3-4). **Durham Dynamos 4pts**

Chelmsford:- **Essex Eagles beat Middlesex Crusaders by seven wickets.** Middlesex 213-9 (Roseberry 72); Essex 214-3 in 37 overs (S.G. Law 104 not out). **Essex Eagles 4pts**

Swansea:- **Glamorgan Dragons tied with Warwickshire Bears (Duckworth-Lewis method).** Glamorgan 167-4 in 38 overs (Elliott 84 not out); Warwickshire 201-7 in 38 overs. **Glamorgan Dragons 2pts, Warwickshire Bears 2pts**

NCL DIVISION TWO AT 2ND JULY

Pos	Prev		P	Pts	W	T	L	N/R	Last	Three	Res
1	1	Nottinghamshire Outlaws	8	28	7	0	1	0	W	W	W
2	2	Surrey Lions	8	28	6	0	0	2	W	W	W
3	3	Glamorgan Dragons	8	20	4	2	2	0	T	W	W
4	4	Warwickshire Bears	7	18	4	1	2	0	T	L	L
5	5	Middlesex Crusaders	8	16	3	1	3	1	L	W	L
6	6	Essex Eagles	8	14	3	0	4	1	W	W	L
7	8	Durham Dynamos	8	8	2	0	6	0	W	L	L
8	7	Derbyshire Scorpions	7	4	1	0	6	0	L	L	W
9	9	Hampshire Hawks	8	4	1	0	7	0	L	L	W

9 Ali Brown's Glorious Schooldays

With the most crucial phase of the season now upon us, everyone was hoping that the Surrey team could maintain their winning run, starting at Oakham School against Leicestershire. I had heard many good reports about the Rutland venue, which was being used for a first-class fixture for the first time since 1938, and I was, like many other Surrey fans, very much looking forward to taking in a new ground in a new part of the country. It was also to be hoped that the two most recent holders of the County Championship title would produce a feast of cricket to put the county of Rutland back on the cricketing map.

The pre-match scenario was certainly promising - third in the table versus fourth, with both sides needing to win in order to stay in touch with the roses counties who were occupying the top two positions. There were questions to be answered, too. Were Leicestershire serious title contenders after the departures of Mullally, Nixon and Millns in the close season? Could Surrey maintain their surge up the table? This match would give us some clues, so everything was set fair for an absorbing battle.

Before everyone could make the trip to Oakham, however, there was the small matter of a Nat West Trophy fourth round match against Sussex to fit in - and this posed a problem for me. Owing to the rather crowded fixture list, the eve of the Championship match with Leicestershire had been doubled up as the reserve day for the Nat West game. My usual practice of travelling to an away venue on the afternoon prior to the match was, therefore, scuppered, since I had to allow for the possibility of the Sussex contest being rain-affected and running over into the reserve day.

As things turned out, it was just as well that I booked myself on an evening, as opposed to afternoon, train from London to Oakham.

SUSSEX SWEPT ASIDE IN NATWEST

With rain allowing just two overs to be bowled on the first scheduled day of the match, Surrey's progress to the quarter-finals of the Nat West Trophy was delayed until early evening on the reserve day.

Their safe passage was rarely ever in doubt during a game which they largely dominated, save for one spell when the Sussex third-wicket pairing of Montgomerie and Bevan looked capable of taking their side through to a competitive total. After 37 overs, the Sussex score stood at 143-2 but the very next ball saw Bevan taken behind the wicket by Stewart off Salisbury and a terminal decline set in thereafter, with the final thirteen overs yielding just forty-nine runs for the loss of seven wickets. Though it was Adam Hollioake who picked up the bulk of the wickets during an intelligent spell of six overs at the death, much credit for Sussex's struggles went to Martin Bicknell (10-1-26-1) and the spinners, who each returned figures of 1-30 from their ten-over allocations.

Requiring 193 to win, Surrey lost Ali Brown in the fifth over of their reply as Robin Martin-Jenkins and James Kirtley made life uncomfortable in the early stages but Mark Butcher and Alec Stewart continued their recent good form to gradually ease the pressure. Although Stewart (31) was dismissed by Martin-Jenkins (2-28) in the lanky seamer's second spell with the total on ninety-two, the required run rate rarely rose much above four an over and by the time I had to depart in order to catch my train to Oakham a mere seventeen runs were required from five overs. Although, as I later discovered, Ian Ward made his exit shortly after mine, the inevitable Surrey victory was eventually sealed with fourteen deliveries to spare.

A mouth-watering home quarter-final with Lancashire was the reward for Keith Medlycott's men.

SCOREBOARD - NAT WEST TROPHY - FOURTH ROUND

Sussex 192-9 from 50 overs (M.G. Bevan 60, R.R. Montgomerie 53, A.J. Hollioake 3-23)
Surrey 196-3 from 47.4 overs (M.A. Butcher 87 not out)
Surrey won by seven wickets

Umpires: G.I. Burgess and J.H. Harris

Man Of The Match - M.A. Butcher (Surrey)

OAKHAM - FIRST IMPRESSIONS ARE FIRST-CLASS

My first impressions of the town of Oakham, albeit in rapidly fading light, were extremely favourable and I soon found my way to my accommodation, in a beautiful bungalow, with the help of a map supplied by the landlady. The Oakham Cricket Club ground, a picture in itself, backed onto my bedroom but, as I was to discover, the Oakham School ground was something else altogether.

Everything seemed extremely promising and my only worry ahead of the first day's play was the effect on the Surrey players of a late-evening dash to Oakham following the Sussex game - not the best preparation for an important County Championship fixture.

Although our hosts had been able to complete their Nat West match on the first scheduled day, they'd had problems of their own, suffering a humiliating collapse against the holders, Gloucestershire. Requiring just twenty to win from five overs with five wickets in hand, Leicestershire had somehow contrived to lose by ten runs with almost two overs still to be bowled. Maybe the handicap we had suffered because of our late finish would be matched by Leicestershire's sense of deep disappointment at throwing away a clear winning position.

COUNTY CHAMPIONSHIP - MATCH NINE

LEICESTERSHIRE versus SURREY
at Oakham School

First Day - Friday 7th July

Surrey 334-8

The Teams And The Toss - *The Surrey team shows just one change from Southampton, with Nadeem Shahid returning to the line-up in place of Graham Thorpe, who is on duty with England in the one-day international triangular tournament, while Leicestershire field what appears to be their strongest eleven. On a disappointingly chilly and grey morning, Adam Hollioake calls correctly and elects to bat.*

With the school building providing a dominant backdrop and the boundary skirted by trees and smart white plastic seats, the setting is magnificent as the players emerge from the pavilion onto a beautifully manicured outfield. Since an early inspection of the pitch has revealed an almost white surface which looks equally immaculate it's clear that everything I had been told about the Oakham School ground has proved to be correct. All we need now is an improvement in the weather and, hopefully, a Surrey win!

Things don't start well for the visitors, however, as they lose their first wicket, without a run on the board, to the sixth delivery of the match. Mark Butcher, fresh from his unbeaten eighty-seven the previous afternoon, top edges a cut at James Ormond and is well held above his head by Vince Wells at first slip. I had only just remarked to a friend that, in the circumstances, I half expected Butcher to either score plenty - if he was still feeling in the groove so soon after his Sussex knock - or nothing - if he was over-confident or felt tired after his efforts of the previous day. I have, therefore, been proved correct but in the wrong way from a Surrey viewpoint.

With Leicestershire having received this early boost to their confidence, it's very surprising to see Phillip DeFreitas starting the second over of the match with just two slips in place and a third man back on the boundary, especially since the batsmen are having to establish themselves on a pitch which looks to have plenty of pace and bounce. Consequently, stalemate develops, with just one run scored between the third and the eighth overs as Ian Ward and Nadeem Shahid dig in.

The scoreboard is eventually pressed into service again when Shahid clips Ormond through midwicket for two, and the visitors' total finally moves into double figures in the tenth over when Ward manages to drive DeFreitas straight for three. This stroke turns out to be Ward's last contribution to the Surrey cause, however, as Jimmy Ormond wins an lbw verdict against him in the next over. From my viewing position, square of the wicket, it looks to be a debatable decision by the umpire since Ward is not only batting outside his crease but has also got a good stride in. Although these decisions do have a tendency to even out over the course of a season, it's hard to see it that way at this moment in time since Surrey are now 11-2 and struggling.

This rather bleak situation soon deteriorates further since Adam Hollioake's stay at the crease, though eventful, turns out to be extremely brief. Having immediately glanced Ormond to the fine leg boundary and then watched Nadeem Shahid force DeFreitas away through the covers and mid-on for four, two and three runs, Hollioake is undone by a good delivery from Ormond which results in an edge to third slip, where Chris Lewis picks up a fine low catch to leave Surrey in real trouble at 25 for 3.

To the surprise of many, DeFreitas immediately gives way to Anil Kumble at the town end and a questionable move soon appears badly flawed as the Indian leg-spinner drops a little too short in his first spell and pays the price with cut and pulled boundaries by Shahid.

The turning point of the session comes shortly afterwards, however, when Ormond is forced to take a rest after a very impressive opening burst of 10-3-20-3. The former England 'A' paceman, still only 22 years of age, has looked decidedly quick and dangerous whereas his replacement, Chris Lewis, comes in off a very short run and is immediately greeted with an upper-cut four by Shahid which raises the visitors' fifty.

Suddenly the whole picture changes as Wells replaces Kumble, Shahid throttles back and Ali Brown, after a relatively sedate start, moves up through the gears to take command. Drives, cuts and pulls flow from the broad Brown bat as the fifty partnership for the fourth wicket arrives inside thirteen overs to restore some balance to the game.

With the county champions fighting back so strongly, the Leicestershire captain resorts to a double bowling change, restoring Kumble to the attack at the town end and introducing Darren Maddy's medium pace at the playing field end. Neither bowler is able to disturb either Surrey's or Brown's progress, though, as the team's hundred and the individual's sparkling fifty (from 74 balls in 81 minutes) come up in successive overs. Consecutive boundaries, off-driven and pulled, by Brown off Kumble in the final over of the morning merely serve to underline the power of Surrey's comeback.

Lunch:- Surrey 112-3 (Shahid 36*, Brown 59*) from 38 overs

In increasingly pleasant weather, Leicestershire respond positively through DeFreitas and Ormond after lunch. Having been largely ineffective in his morning spell, it takes DeFreitas just two deliveries to lure Shahid into a loose drive which results in an edge to Neil Burns behind the stumps and then, in the next over from Ormond, Brown snicks the ball at catchable height between the Leicestershire 'keeper and first slip. Neither fielder moves a muscle as the ball flies to the boundary and the batsman's score advances to sixty-three.

While everyone is still pondering how crucial this miss might turn out to be, the home side strikes again when Ben Hollioake chips a simple catch to Habib at midwicket off DeFreitas. It's a very disappointing way for the Surrey all-rounder to go, being almost a carbon copy of his first innings dismissal at Southampton, and it reduces the visitors to a fairly sickly 125-5.

Although DeFreitas has the two wickets to fall since lunch, it's still Ormond who appears to pose the greater threat as Leicestershire attempt to hammer home their advantage. Brown and Jon Batty battle bravely to repel the best efforts of the strongly-built paceman, however, and it is again noticeable that the pressure on the batsmen eases considerably with his departure from the attack after almost an hour.

With DeFreitas now beginning to tire at the town end and Ormond's replacement, Vince Wells, unable to locate a consistent line and length, Ali Brown is soon back in full flow and moving relentlessly towards his first Championship century of the season. Three off-side boundaries off Wells in two overs take him through to ninety-nine and a single to backward square leg then brings up three figures from 139 balls in 168 minutes. It's been a fabulous effort by Brown in difficult circumstances and it is fully appreciated by the sizeable contingent of Surrey supporters on the ground. Both the player and the fans know that there is still a lot of work to be done, however, since the pitch looks to be playing beautifully and Surrey are still well short of the two-hundred mark.

The need for Brown to build on his century is quickly underlined, in fact, when the visitors lose two further wickets in quick succession, at 181 and 190. Jon Batty is the first to go, his valuable supporting knock in a stand of fifty-six ended by a sliced drive to gully in the second over of a new spell from Maddy, then Martin Bicknell dabs fatally outside the off stump when faced by Lewis.

Surrey's position now looks critical but it doesn't stop the apparently nerveless Brown from registering the first six of his innings, courtesy of a pull over midwicket off Maddy, in the over immediately following Bicknell's dismissal. Although the visitors' eighth-wicket pair safely negotiates the final six overs of the afternoon, it's been Leicestershire's session, with four wickets captured at a cost of 101 runs. The day's final period now looks increasingly important to the shaping of the match.

Tea:- Surrey 213-7 (Brown 115*, Tudor 7*) from 72 overs

Predictably enough, Leicestershire's opening bowlers are back in harness immediately after the break but Ormond, having bowled eighteen overs during the first two sessions, understandably appears to have lost a little of his sharpness and DeFreitas also looks rather laboured. Consequently, confronted by a very aggressive and dominant Ali Brown, the bowlers wilt. Although the Surrey man does edge one Ormond delivery over the slips and offers a sharp overhead catching chance to Habib at midwicket off DeFreitas on 129, it's pretty much all Brown for the opening hour of the session. It's not a happy period for Leicestershire's former Lancashire, Derbyshire and England seamer as he is battered for five boundaries in the space of two overs, during which Brown's 150 comes up from 203 balls in 249 minutes. Alex Tudor meanwhile contents himself with a supporting role, giving his partner the strike as often as possible and watching in wonder from the other end. With Surrey's former England one-day international batsman striking the ball so well on a pitch that clearly suits him, the total races past 250 and the balance of power in the match seems to be shifting quite dramatically.

In an attempt to arrest the slide, Vince Wells makes another double bowling change, turning to Chris Lewis at the playing field end and Anil Kumble at the town end, but this has no effect whatsoever for the first few overs as Brown picks up two fours from each bowler and takes the eighth-wicket partnership up to a hundred. This milestone has been reached in just over twenty-three overs, with Tudor's contribution being just eleven. This is one of those occasions where the statistics don't tell the whole story, however, since the big paceman's supporting role has been of immense value to both his partner and his team.

By now the field is spread far and wide and, partly as a result of this, but also because Lewis and Kumble settle into their best spells of what has been a disappointing day for both of them, the scoring rate dips considerably. With both batsmen quite prepared to bide their time, the total advances slowly with a succession of singles for around eight overs. The Surrey three-hundred arrives during this period, though, and, with recovery almost complete, Tudor celebrates by cutting Lewis violently over point for only his second boundary in twenty-nine overs at the crease.

Brown, by this stage, has found the rope no fewer than twenty-five times and he is steadily closing in on the second County Championship double-century of his career. Eschewing all risks and picking up a series of easy singles to the fielders at long-on and long-off, there never appears to be any chance of the Beckenham-born batsman failing to reach the mark and when he clips his 257th ball backward of square leg for three he moves through to 202 after 325 minutes at the wicket. As with just about everything else at this charming ground, the crowd is top-class and they offer up generous applause for Brown's masterful effort which has well and truly turned the tide against their team. From a Surrey viewpoint, the hope now is that the eighth-wicket pair can survive until tomorrow to take their team through to a full hand of batting points and a commanding total.

It isn't to be, however, as Tudor's marvellous effort is ended three overs from the close when he miscues a pull at the returning Wells and sees Maddy pull off an excellent catch, running back from midwicket. Surrey's young fast-bowling star returns, crestfallen, to the pavilion after what is probably one of the most valuable innings of twenty-two he will ever play, having helped to steer his side from a perilous 190-7 to the prosperity of 331-8. He should certainly be proud of his performance.

Having provided Leicestershire with a much-needed breakthrough, the home captain's decision to bring himself back for the final two overs from the town end has proved inspired and he almost lands the big fish, too, in the day's last over - Brown glances, wicketkeeper Burns dives far away to his left, ball hits glove, ball doesn't stick. It is, theoretically, a chance, although we can safely say that it's unlikely to prove as costly as the missed opportunity when Brown's snick bisected Burns and first slip just after lunch with the batsman on fifty-nine!

He might have given a couple of chances during his stay at the wicket but nothing can tarnish an outstanding day for Surrey's 30-year-old middle-order powerhouse and he leaves the field to a further warm ovation from everyone. We all know we have witnessed a very special innings which has transformed the visitors' fortunes in this extremely important match.

Although the spectators' day is now over, it seems that Ali Brown's isn't as he astounds us by running onto the outfield just minutes after the close to join his colleagues in a game of football!

Close:- Surrey 334-8 (Brown 211*, Salisbury 0*) from 104 overs

VIEW FROM THE DRESSING ROOM - ALISTAIR BROWN

What was going through your mind when we were 190-7?
AB - Well, I certainly didn't imagine that we would end up scoring 505! But I don't believe that this Surrey side has a tail - we have a lot of very good players, who are all capable of coming in and scoring runs when we need them. Batsmen numbers seven to eleven have come in and

helped us on many occasions and I would imagine that we average between 100 and 150 for our last four wickets in recent times. So I had a lot of confidence in the players who were still to come in and they all played very well on what was a good wicket.

Second Day - Saturday 8th July

Surrey 505; Leicestershire 134-9

A new day brings a new ball for Leicestershire but it makes no difference to Ali Brown as he glances and square-drives Jimmy Ormond for successive boundaries in the opening over of the morning. This gives the visitors the perfect stirring start and Ormond's new-ball partner, Philip DeFreitas, finds life no easier as Ian Salisbury reels off two boundaries of his own with superb off-side drives to take Surrey past 350.

Leicestershire clearly need to polish off the innings as quickly as possible and they take a step in that direction in the eighth over of the day when Salisbury appears surprised by a lifting delivery from DeFreitas and gloves a catch to Darren Maddy at second slip. The Surrey leg-spinner departs for twelve with the score now 364-9 and Saqlain Mushtaq enters the fray along with a shower of rain, which soon drives the players from the field.

Play is held up for ten minutes, giving everyone time to speculate as to whether or not Surrey will be able to make it to their final batting point, which is still some thirty-six runs away. The consensus view is that anything is possible with Ali Brown still in occupation and whatever score is achieved will certainly be many more than the visiting supporters had imagined when the score was 190-7!

Upon the resumption, Brown continues on his merry way with a straight-driven four off Ormond while Saqlain starts brightly with a pair of drives for three off DeFreitas. The former England bowler is consequently replaced by the Leicestershire captain at the town end, a move which appears much to Saqlain's liking as he takes two steps down the wicket and pulls the ball dismissively over square leg for four.

At this stage, much to everyone's amazement, the Surrey number eleven is outscoring his well-established partner and he continues in the same vein by driving Ormond to the rope at extra cover and then repeating the shot when Kumble replaces the young fast bowler for the next over at the playing field end. It's a marvellous effort by Saqlain, who has moved on to twenty-one by the time Brown forces a single to deep cover to raise the four-hundred. This team milestone is then quickly followed by a personal milestone as Brown completes an outstanding 250 from 331 balls in 429 minutes with a straight-driven two off Wells.

Surrey are now in complete command and their position is further aided by a loose opening over from Darren Maddy when he takes over from his skipper at the town end of the ground. The fifty partnership for the last wicket arrives during an over costing ten, in which Saqlain's pull over wide mid-on for four is greeted by the public address system bursting into life with 'Good shot, Saqi boy!' As at Chester-le-Street in 1998, it seems that one of the Surrey players has momentarily hijacked the tannoy! This humorous moment is probably lost on Maddy, however, as his second over proves no better than his first, with Saqlain lofting him back over his head for two further boundaries. Fortunately, the beleaguered Wells, who by now is fielding on the boundary in front of me, is still able to see the funny side of an increasingly dire situation for his team by turning to the crowd and asking whether anyone wants to have a bowl!

After two overs costing twenty runs, it's no surprise to see Maddy replaced immediately by DeFreitas for the last few overs of the session at the town end. Although he keeps a slightly tighter rein on things, he happens to be the bowler as three further landmarks are achieved. First, Ali Brown records a new highest score in first-class cricket of 266, courtesy of a single to long-off, then Saqlain's pull to midwicket brings his highest score for Surrey (46), and, finally, the visitors move on to 450. Saqlain has now scored as many runs in this one innings as he did in the whole of the previous County Championship campaign, although it must be said that his opportunities with the bat were limited to just eight innings in 1999.

I'm not sure whether this statistic has leaked through to DeFreitas but there's no doubting the fact that his frustration gets the better of him in the final over of the session as he bowls four bouncers at Saqlain and is quite correctly no-balled twice, for the illegal third and fourth short deliveries. This is definitely not a good way for the home side to go to lunch.

Surrey, meanwhile, will be delighted to have scored 120 runs for the loss of just one wicket in the session, largely thanks to a last-wicket stand which has so far added ninety runs.

Lunch:- Surrey 454-9 (Brown 269*, Saqlain 46*) from 136 overs

Much to the disappointment of Surrey players and fans, the start of the afternoon session is delayed by some twenty-five minutes after a further burst of rain.

Once play does get underway, however, Saqlain sweeps Kumble to the fine leg boundary in the second over to register his first Surrey half-century, a brilliant effort compiled in 97 minutes from 87 balls. This merely adds to Leicestershire's misery and their sense of despair is then deepened in the next over when Ormond somehow manages to grass a most simple caught-and-bowled chance which Brown pops back to him on 270. The young fast bowler is absolutely distraught and sinks to his hands and knees in the middle of the wicket, while his colleagues look on in disbelief. To add insult to injury, the century partnership then arrives in the following over, Brown and Saqlain having been together for just twenty-nine overs.

A combination of Wells and Kumble, operating to deep-set fields, eventually slows the run rate without ever threatening to end the last pair's fun and Brown gradually creeps closer to the magical three-hundred with another series of singles and twos. He finally moves into the two-hundred-and-nineties with a savage square cut to the rope off Wells and later in the same over Saqlain clips through midwicket for two to bring five-hundred up on the scoreboard.

Over the course of the next few overs Brown nudges his score up to 295, within touching distance of cricketing immortality, when Wells suddenly produces a fine delivery to clip the top of Saqlain's off stump and, simultaneously, end Surrey's innings, Leicestershire's ordeal and Brown's dreams. Even though he has performed magnificently, the Pakistani off-spinner looks more disappointed than his team-mate as the two Surrey batsmen leave the field to a well-deserved ovation. Brown had, after all, been seventy-one runs short of three-hundred when the ninth wicket fell and, at that moment in time, he can hardly have expected to get this close to one of the ultimate goals in a cricketer's career. The team has to come first, in any case, and by compiling two stands of 141, for the eighth and last wickets, Surrey have, largely as a result of Brown's magic, turned 190-7 into 505 all out.

This leaves Leicestershire facing a huge test of character since they require 356 to avoid the follow-on and they must be exhausted and demoralised after seeing a great position in the match slip away from them in truly astonishing fashion.

Although they start well, with Darren Maddy racing into double figures inside the first three overs through a series of sweetly-struck drives, things turn sour very quickly after Alex Tudor makes the first break for Surrey in the fourth over. When Iain Sutcliffe edges a defensive jab at a good delivery from the tall Surrey paceman it's almost inevitable that the ball should fly to none other than Brown at second slip and equally predictable that he should hang on safely to set the home side off on the wrong foot at 12 for 1. Things are about to get far worse, however.

Having become becalmed after his promising start, Maddy is the second man to go, his defensive edge off Martin Bicknell very well held by Adam Hollioake swooping low to his right at third slip with the total unchanged. As if this isn't bad enough for Leicestershire, a double strike of catastrophic proportions then follows with the loss of, arguably, their two best batsmen in the space of three deliveries. The first of these dismissals is unquestionably self-inflicted as Ben Smith pushes the fifth delivery of the tenth over towards mid-on and calls his skipper through for what looks to be an impossible single. Ian Salisbury, lurking at midwicket, is quickly onto the ball and throws down the non-striker's stumps from close range with Smith hopelessly short of the crease. From Leicestershire's point of view this was, as I recorded in my notes, 'Stupid!'

Vince Wells, now on strike after the run-out fiasco, plays out the final ball of the over and then watches in horror as Aftab Habib falls, first ball, to the opening delivery of the next over from Bicknell. It's a fine delivery which does the damage and the resulting outside edge is again safely pouched at second slip by that man Brown. At 27 for 4, the hosts are in complete disarray and the Surrey new-ball bowlers are looking consistently dangerous.

Just three overs now remain until tea and it appears imperative that Leicestershire lose no further wickets before the break. As it happens, they lose three! Darren Stevens is the first of this hapless triumvirate, adjudged lbw when offering no stroke to the first ball of Tudor's seventh over, then, seven balls later, Chris Lewis is rapped on the pads by Bicknell and, having made no forward movement, suffers the same fate as his colleague. The home team is in dire straits at 49-6 and the smattering of polite applause which greets their fifty following a DeFreitas leg glance moments later seems to possess an almost sarcastic overtone.

It's been an amazing session for Surrey and, quite appropriately in the final over before tea, the icing is put on the cake with the dismissal of Wells, who, after the most edgy and scratchy of starts, finally locates the middle of his bat... and drives a catch, at head height, straight to Saqlain Mushtaq at mid-off.

Bicknell and Tudor, with three wickets each after a sensational opening effort, will clearly enjoy their twenty-minute rest and will be looking forward to launching another assault on the Leicestershire lower-order after the break.

Tea:- Leicestershire 51-7 (DeFreitas 2*) from 15.1 overs

After a quiet start to the day's final session, Phillip DeFreitas makes his intentions clear with a calculated assault on the Surrey opening bowlers, first cutting, dabbing and pulling fours in an over from Bicknell which costs fourteen and then upper-cutting Tudor to the boundary in an over costing nine.

Maybe as a result of this sudden counter-attack, or possibly because both his pacemen have now completed a hefty eleven overs, Adam Hollioake immediately makes a double change to introduce his spinners. This move doesn't initially stem the flow of runs, though, as DeFreitas and Burns sweep and cut Leicestershire to three figures and the latter then drives Salisbury to the rope at point to complete a bold fifty partnership at a rate of five runs per over. The minor fightback soon receives a major setback, however, when DeFreitas props forward to Saqlain and provides the Surrey skipper with a bat-pad catch at silly point. A brave innings of thirty-eight from 46 balls is thus terminated and the home side sink further into the mire since, at 106-8, they are still 399 runs in arrears.

Although the spirit of DeFreitas lives on briefly after his departure, with Kumble and Burns picking up a boundary apiece off Saqlain, the day's play thereafter descends, perhaps inevitably, into a state of stalemate. With Surrey having produced a performance more powerful than they could possibly have hoped for in the early stages and the opposition having greatly underachieved, suddenly there is an air of reality about the play on what is undoubtedly a very good pitch. The fantasy cricket has, temporarily we hope, been cast aside and the batsmen resist more steadfastly as the spinners exert control, conceding a mere thirty runs from the final twenty-three overs of the day. This final period of play is not entirely satisfactory from a Leicestershire point of view, however, since they lose Kumble twenty balls from the close.

It perhaps sums up the home side's day that the batsman's dismissal comes about when he plays a delivery from Salisbury onto his stumps.

Since the hosts trail by 371 runs with just one first innings wicket left to fall, Surrey will now be confident of completing a very important victory sometime over the course of the next two days, the only possible cloud on their horizon being a very unsettled weather forecast.

Close:- Leicestershire 134-9 (Burns 24*, Ormond 2*) from 48 overs

ALISTAIR BROWN'S 295 NOT OUT - AT-A-GLANCE STATISTICS

RATE OF SCORING

Over	Milestone	Balls	Mins	6s	4s	Breakdown	Balls	Mins	6s	4s
13	In at 25-3	0	0	0	0					
36	50	74	81	0	5	First 50	74	81	0	5
59	100	139	168	0	12	Second 50	65	87	0	7
78	150	203	249	1	18	Third 50	64	81	1	6
99	200	257	325	1	24	Fourth 50	54	76	0	6
124	250	331	429	1	28	Fifth 50	74	104	0	4
147	295	392	517	1	32	Final 45	61	88	0	4

WHERE THE RUNS WERE SCORED

	Zone 1	Zone 2	Zone 3	Zone 4	Zone 5	Zone 6	TOTAL
0-100	17	20	16	16	23	8	100
101-202	15	4	11	33	27	12	102
203-295	19	14	4	14	25	17	93
TOTAL	51	38	31	63	75	37	295

Zone 1 - Straight hit round to extra cover
Zone 2 - Extra cover round to point
Zone 3 - Behind square on the off side
Zone 4 - Behind square on the leg side
Zone 5 - Square leg round to wide mid-on
Zone 6 - Wide mid-on round to straight hit

WHO THE RUNS WERE SCORED OFF

	Ormond	Kumble	Lewis	Wells	Maddy	DeFreitas	TOTAL
0-100	22	19	11	29	4	15	100
101-202	18	23	17	0	15	29	102
203-295	24	23	0	19	8	19	93
TOTAL	64	65	28	48	27	63	295

THE TEN HIGHEST INDIVIDUAL SCORES FOR SURREY IN FIRST-CLASS CRICKET

Score	Batsman	Opposition	Venue	Year
357*	R. Abel	Somerset	The Oval	1899
338	W.W. Read	Oxford University	The Oval	1888
316*	J.B. Hobbs	Middlesex	Lord's	1926
315*	T.W. Hayward	Lancashire	The Oval	1898
306*	A. Ducat	Oxford University	The Oval	1919
295*	A.D. BROWN	LEICESTERSHIRE	OAKHAM SCHOOL	2000
294*	D.M. Ward	Derbyshire	The Oval	1994
292*	A. Sandham	Northamptonshire	The Oval	1921
291	I.A. Greig	Lancashire	The Oval	1990
290*	A. Ducat	Essex	Leyton	1921

VIEW FROM THE DRESSING ROOM - ALISTAIR BROWN

I would assume that this innings would rank some way ahead of your 265 at Lord's in 1999, since it transformed an important game at a crucial stage?
AB - Very much so. At Lord's we'd already clinched the Championship, it was a very, very good batting wicket and we'd had a reasonable start. Here we were 25-3 against a side who I couldn't recall beating away from home for some considerable time, with Jimmy Ormond bowling very well on a wicket with a lot of pace and bounce. So it was a major game in which to make a big score.

I was very impressed by the bowling of Jimmy Ormond in this match - it sounds as if you were, too.
AB - I thought he was probably the best bowler I came up against all year. That might seem a strange thing to say, having made 295 in this match, but I felt he bowled exceptionally well - he bowled with good pace, he swung the ball around and with a bit more luck could have ended up with a few more wickets. I was also impressed by the fact that he bowled with a lot of heart during a couple of ten-over spells and he was always a handful.

There was some stunning bowling at the start of their innings to reduce them to 51-7.
AB - I would say that this was a perfect first-class wicket, with something for everyone. It was good for batting on because the ball came on to the bat, yet the pace and bounce also made it good to bowl on if you could swing the ball and put it in the right place consistently. We bowled outstandingly well and, having been pretty deflated by the way we came back from 190-7, they must have thought that it really wasn't their day when our opening bowlers then got amongst them.

Third Day - Sunday 9th July

Surrey 505; Leicestershire 143 and 184

Surrey beat Leicestershire by an innings and 178 runs
Surrey 20pts, Leicestershire 3

As the third day's action gets under way there are two things to note. Firstly, it has emerged that Alistair Brown's 295 not out had comfortably surpassed the previous highest individual score ever made in Rutland - 252 by former England captain, Percy Chapman, in a house match at Uppingham School in 1918 - and, of greater relevance to the remainder of the current match, Alex Tudor looks unlikely to play any further part since he has a side strain.

While this is clearly a blow for Surrey, it looks more likely to present a problem in future games as opposed to this one, and it is to be hoped that the injury will not keep the young fast bowler on the sidelines for too long.

Tudor's absence is certainly not felt in the day's opening period as the spinners attempt to finish off the Leicestershire first innings. Although it takes them almost ten overs to split the last pair, only nine runs have been added when Neil Burns prods Saqlain to Adam Hollioake at silly point after a stubborn 135-ball innings of thirty. The home side are all out for 143 and they will, therefore, commence their second innings needing the small matter of 362 runs to avoid an innings defeat. To have any hope of achieving this, the county champions of 1996 and 1998 will need to build their second knock around solid foundations.

What they most certainly *don't* need is for Darren Maddy to edge the first delivery of the innings from Martin Bicknell to Jon Batty behind the stumps. It's the stuff of nightmares for the former England batsman and for Leicestershire and it gives an ecstatic Surrey team the perfect start.

The home skipper, Vince Wells, therefore joins Iain Sutcliffe for the second ball of the innings with some serious remedial work to be done. It's a real struggle early on, too, as Bicknell consistently passes the outside edge and Ben Hollioake, opening the attack in Tudor's place, looks the part from the playing field end. Leicestershire are in a deep, deep hole but, after a run of five successive maidens from the third to the seventh over inclusive, the batsmen gradually expand their repertoire to push the score up to twenty.

Whether it has any effect on what follows is impossible to tell, but, after a dozen overs, Surrey complain about the condition of the ball and the umpires agree to a change. Within three overs of this taking place both batsmen are back in the pavilion - Wells after bottom-edging a pull at Bicknell into his stumps and Sutcliffe following a thick-edge to the 'keeper from an off-side slash at Hollioake, having cut the previous delivery square for four. At 26-3 there already appears little hope for Leicestershire.

Ben Smith and Aftab Habib, two men capable of playing a long innings - witness The Oval, 1998 - do represent a potential danger, however, and Smith looks to play positively right from the off, slog-sweeping Ian Salisbury for four and six in the leg-spinner's first two overs after taking over from Bicknell at the town end.

Fortunately for Surrey, Habib's attempts to play Saqlain in a similarly aggressive manner bring about his demise in the off-spinner's first over from the playing field end. Charging down the wicket to the Pakistani's fifth ball, he is comprehensively beaten by what appears to be the 'other' ball and stumped by a distance. It's a great result for the visitors to have removed the dangerous Habib just two overs before the lunch break and the reigning champions have, consequently, taken a huge step towards sealing a much-deserved victory in this match.

Lunch:- Leicestershire 42-4 (Smith 10*, Stevens 2*) from 22 overs

The rain that the weathermen had been threatening finally arrives during the interval and, as a result, no further play is possible until 4pm, following an early tea.

While Saqlain continues his spell from the playing field end, Martin Bicknell returns at the town end and the first five overs of the session are full of interest as home side rattles up twenty-nine runs for the very significant loss of Ben Smith. The Leicestershire batsman's departure to a catch at second slip provides Bicknell with ample compensation for two earlier flashing cuts to the boundary and leaves the hosts in a sorry state at 56 for 5.

Undeterred by the loss of his partner, Darren Stevens produces some well-timed strokes all around the wicket and, in partnership with Chris Lewis, takes Leicestershire up to three figures in good time, seeing off Bicknell and Saqlain in the process. Are we at last to see a period of quality batting and sustained defiance from the home team?

The good news for Leicestershire is that the introduction of Ben Hollioake and Salisbury brings another surge in the scoring rate. The down side is that it also produces another wicket for Surrey when Chris Lewis edges a drive at Hollioake to the diving Batty. It's now 118-6 and the reigning champions have the scent of another three-day victory in their nostrils.

On a grey afternoon in more ways than one for Jack Birkenshaw's team, Stevens at least continues to provide a ray of sunshine, with a straight-driven four and an on-driven three seeing him through to a very well-played half-century from just 61 balls. He continues to dominate, too, driving Hollioake through the covers and then taking two further boundaries off Salisbury, while the new batsman, Phillip DeFreitas, settles in at the other end.

The 24-year-old strokemaker is unable to sustain his effort, however, as the return of Saqlain for Hollioake brings about his downfall. To be fair to the batsman it is an exceptional delivery that terminates his fine innings at sixty-eight and revives Surrey's hopes of completing their job with a day to spare - he shoulders arms to a ball well wide of off stump and then watches in horror as a heavily-spun off-break fizzes back to trim his off bail.

Although the game is now all but over, DeFreitas appears keen to enjoy himself and entertain the crowd with some aggressive strokeplay. Having been missed at second slip off Salisbury in the over following Stevens' dismissal, he drives the leg-spinner to the long-off boundary, slog-sweeps Saqlain for six over midwicket and then sweeps Salisbury for a second four. The first boundary in this sequence has, incidentally, seen Leicestershire's total of runs for the match finally pass Ali Brown's 295... for the loss of a mere *seventeen* wickets!

While this statistic is doing the rounds and providing much amusement for Surrey supporters, the man himself comes on to bowl, in order to switch the spinners' ends. Although Brown enjoys no success at all in his solitary over, twice being square cut for four by Neil Burns, his captain's move works wonders for the visitors. Under increasingly threatening skies and with drizzle starting to fall, Saqlain provides his team with the eighth Leicestershire wicket when he gets an off-break to turn and bounce and take the outside edge of Burns' defensive bat on its way through to Jon Batty.

As the home 'keeper makes his way back to the pavilion the rain is getting heavier and, suddenly, we have the prospect of the match going into day four. This wouldn't be a problem but for the fact that tomorrow's weather forecast is fairly dire. It's now a race against both the clock and the rain.

Salisbury, having bowled well but without much luck throughout, draws a blank in the next over, so the focus shifts back to Saqlain as Surrey's sense of urgency increases. Three balls, plus a no-ball, pass without success before the Pakistani spin wizard finds the key to unlock the door to victory, having Anil Kumble snapped up by Adam Hollioake at silly point via bat and pad. The Surrey players and supporters are ecstatic, the batsman departs looking unconvinced about his dismissal and just one wicket remains.

As Jimmy Ormond takes guard in what is, by now, quite unpleasant rainfall, the view of the Surrey faithful is that Saqi will slip in his quicker ball in an attempt to nail the Leicestershire number eleven before his eyes grow accustomed to the deepening gloom.

Sure enough, his second ball to Ormond, the final delivery of the over, is very quick and full of length and hits the batsman on the boot. All the fielders go up for the appeal, the umpire's finger follows and Surrey have won in almost unbelievable circumstances. While Ormond stands and stares in apparent disbelief at the decision for a few seconds, the victorious visitors troop joyously from the field, led by the amazing Saqlain, who has finished with 5-35, including a final spell of 6-2-13-4, to sweep his team to a first County Championship victory away to Leicestershire since 1993 and the first anywhere against the Foxes since 1996. With both Yorkshire and Lancashire struggling in their matches it is even looking likely that Keith Medlycott's men will be sitting proudly on top of the Championship table come tomorrow night. Incredible!

Surrey celebrations, for players and fans alike, are somewhat muted by the rain, however, and as I make my way from the ground just ten minutes after the end of the game the heavens open and I get drenched. Do I care? Of course not!

Surrey 505; Leicestershire 143 and 184
Surrey won by an innings and 178 runs. Surrey 20pts, Leicestershire 3

LEICESTERSHIRE v SURREY at OAKHAM SCHOOL. Played from 7th - 9th July
Surrey won the toss
Umpires:- A. Clarkson & J.W. Holder

SURREY - First Innings / LEICESTERSHIRE bowling

Fall of wkt	Batsman	How Out		Score	Balls	4s	6s		O	M	R	W
1- 0	M.A. Butcher	c Wells	b Ormond	0	6	0	0	Ormond	34	4	92	3
2- 11	I.J. Ward		lbw b Ormond	6	31	0	0	DeFreitas	29	6	115	3
4- 113	Nadeem Shahid	c Burns	b DeFreitas	37	108	5	0	Kumble	35	5	101	0
3- 25	A.J. Hollioake *	c Lewis	b Ormond	4	6	1	0	Lewis	18	2	60	1
	A.D. Brown		Not Out	295	392	32	1	Wells	17.5	1	65	2
5- 125	B.C. Hollioake	c Habib	b DeFreitas	2	14	0	0	Maddy	15	2	59	1
6- 181	J.N. Batty +	c Lewis	b Maddy	19	60	0	0					
7- 190	M.P. Bicknell	c Burns	b Lewis	5	13	1	0					
8- 331	A.J. Tudor	c Maddy	b Wells	22	108	2	0					
9- 364	I.D.K. Salisbury	c Maddy	b DeFreitas	12	37	2	0					
10- 505	Saqlain Mushtaq		b Wells	66	129	8	0					
	Extras (3b, 10lb, 2w, 22nb)			37								
	TOTAL		(148.5 overs)	505								

LEICESTERSHIRE - First Innings / SURREY bowling

Fall of wkt	Batsman	How Out		Score	Balls	4s	6s		O	M	R	W
2- 12	D.L. Maddy	c A.J. Hollioake	b Bicknell	10	23	1	0	Bicknell	11	3	41	3
1- 12	I.J. Sutcliffe	c Brown	b Tudor	1	5	0	0	Tudor	11	6	34	3
7- 51	V.J. Wells *	c Saqlain	b Tudor	13	34	2	0	Salisbury	18	8	29	1
3- 27	B.F. Smith		run out	3	13	0	0	Saqlain	17.2	8	25	2
4- 27	A. Habib	c Brown	b Bicknell	0	1	0	0					
5- 44	D.I. Stevens		lbw b Tudor	6	11	0	0					
6- 49	C.C. Lewis		lbw b Bicknell	3	4	0	0					
8- 106	P.A.J. DeFreitas	c A.J. Hollioake	b Saqlain	38	46	6	0					
10- 143	N.D. Burns +	c A.J. Hollioake	b Saqlain	30	135	3	0					
9- 131	A. Kumble		b Salisbury	10	49	1	0					
	J. Ormond		Not Out	5	28	0	0					
	Extras (2b, 12lb, 10nb)			24								
	TOTAL		(57.2 overs)	143								

LEICESTERSHIRE - Second Innings / SURREY bowling

Fall of wkt	Batsman	How Out		Score	Balls	4s	6s		O	M	R	W
1- 0	D.L. Maddy	c Batty	b Bicknell	0	1	0	0	Bicknell	15	4	44	3
3- 26	I.J. Sutcliffe	c Batty	b B.C. Hollioake	14	38	2	0	B.C. Hollioake	15	4	48	2
2- 22	V.J. Wells *		b Bicknell	9	43	0	0	Salisbury	14	4	41	0
5- 56	B.F. Smith	c Brown	b Bicknell	20	35	3	1	Saqlain	15	4	35	5
4- 40	A. Habib	st Batty	b Saqlain	4	18	1	0	Brown	1	0	8	0
7- 149	D.I. Stevens		b Saqlain	68	80	11	0					
6- 118	C.C. Lewis	c Batty	b B.C. Hollioake	24	51	2	0					
	P.A.J. DeFreitas		Not Out	25	59	3	1					
8- 182	N.D. Burns +	c Batty	b Saqlain	8	26	2	0					
9- 184	A. Kumble	c A.J. Hollioake	b Saqlain	0	9	0	0					
10- 184	J. Ormond		lbw b Saqlain	0	2	0	0					
	Extras (5b, 3lb, 4nb)			12								
	TOTAL		(60 overs)	184								

VIEW FROM THE DRESSING ROOM - ALISTAIR BROWN

Were you surprised that Leicestershire didn't put up greater resistance second time around and by the margin of victory?

AB - They are a very good side and they never give in easily but you have to say that we bowled extremely well, kept the pressure on them and took all the chances that came our way, which can make a big difference. I feel this was retribution, in a way, for the way they treated us at The Oval in 1998, when they did much the same thing to us that we did to them here!

I suppose we have to admit that we had a little bit of good fortune towards the end of the day with a couple of umpiring decisions and the way in which we just beat the rain?
AB - I'm a firm believer in fate and sometimes things are just meant to happen. Much as it was with the two-run victory against Hampshire and the win over Somerset at The Oval in 1999, this was just someone telling us that it was going to be our year. We kept hoping the rain would hold off and then Saqi put in a couple of quicker balls and we were lucky enough to get the decisions. But it's fair to say that we'd put a lot into this game and done everything right so I think we deserved the breaks in the end. Let's not forget either that rain on the last day denied us what I thought was a certain victory at Leicester the previous year after Butch made his 259. So I think this was payback time - it was just meant to be.

I thoroughly enjoyed my stay in Oakham and I guess it's a fair bet that you did too!
AB - Everything about Oakham was perfect for first-class cricket - the conditions, the practice facilities, the atmosphere and, of course, the excellent pitch. I'd like to see more cricket played there and more grounds like it around the country. I felt everything was first-class - and that would still have been my opinion even if I had scored nought.

With five of our last seven games at home, were we now confident that we were right back in the frame to retain the Championship title?
AB - We knew that we had a lot of big games still to come but we were now on a roll, we were confident, we were playing well and winning was becoming a habit.

KEITH MEDLYCOTT'S ASSESSMENT

This was a very good performance indeed. After recovering from a poor start, we allowed Leicestershire back into the game in our first innings with some indifferent shots but Ali Brown came up with an absolutely fantastic individual performance, backed up superbly by the lower-order. I thought that both Alex Tudor and Saqlain Mushtaq played innings of immense character and worked very hard for their team-mate at the other end. What impressed me most was how disappointed those guys were that they hadn't seen Browny through to a well-deserved 300, even though they had helped get the team past 500 and into a powerful position. Tudes, in particular, was distraught to get out near the end of the first day having worked so hard for Browny and that kind of thing speaks volumes for our team spirit.

We had another example of this in Leicestershire's second innings when Tudes was injured and Ben Hollioake took the new ball to great effect. It was very pleasing for all of us to see Ben put his hand up there and really look the business.

And at the end of the match it was good to hear Adam saying that we'd played well but that we were still only performing at eighty percent. "There's still more to come," he said, and we will keep striving for one-hundred percent, because you've always got to seek perfection. Just imagine what we could achieve and how good we could be if we can attain that.

Other Division One Matches

Were the tides turning suddenly in Surrey's favour? Had the Leicestershire match carried over to day four then it would have resulted in a draw, since it rained almost all day long in the Oakham area - I should know, I was still there! Meanwhile, Yorkshire and Lancashire, who both looked in danger of defeat for long periods of their rain-affected games against struggling Durham and Derbyshire respectively, only managed to scrape together seven points apiece. As a consequence of these results, Surrey moved to the top of the County Championship table, although they had still played one game more than both of their roses rivals. Could this round of matches prove to be the turning point in the race for the title?

July 7-10
Derby:- **Derbyshire drew with Lancashire.** Derbyshire 307 (Stubbings 64, Smith 53 not out, Cork 52) and 80-4; Lancashire 172 (Cork 6-41). **Derbyshire 10pts, Lancashire 7**

Taunton:- **Hampshire drew with Somerset.** Hampshire 142 (P.S. Jones 4-45, Rose 4-47) and 319-5 (Kendall 161, Kenway 54); Somerset 368 (Holloway 113, Burns 56, Warne 4-91). **Somerset 11pts, Hampshire 7**

Headingley:- **Durham drew with Yorkshire.** Durham 314 (Lewis 66, Speak 61 not out, Katich 55, Sidebottom 5-66); Yorkshire 129 (Brown 4-33) and 386-4dec (Lehmann 136, Vaughan 118). **Durham 10pts, Yorkshire 7**

\multicolumn{11}{c	}{COUNTY CHAMPIONSHIP DIVISION ONE AT 10TH JULY}
Pos	Prev		P	Pts	W	D	L	Bat	Bowl	Last Three Res
1	3	Surrey	9	103	4	3	2	23	20	W20 W18 W20
2	1	Yorkshire	8	98	4	3	1	14	24	D7 L3 W15
3	2	Lancashire	8	96	4	4	0	13	19	D7 W17 W17
4	4	Leicestershire	8	78	2	4	2	19	19	L3 W18 D7
=	5	Somerset	8	78	2	4	2	19	19	D11 D11 L2
6	6	Durham	8	68	2	2	4	12	24	D10 W20 L3
7	9	Derbyshire	9	58*	1	5	3	10	24	D10 L2 L3
8	8	Hampshire	9	57	1	3	5	6	27	D7 L3 W18
9	7	Kent	7	50	1	4	2	4	18	D8 L3 L5
\multicolumn{11}{l	}{* Deducted 8pts for sub-standard pitch}

10 Tykes Trumped And Dragons Slain

My four days in Oakham had been hugely enjoyable, in every respect, and I knew they were unlikely to be bettered this season - unless, of course, Surrey were to continue their winning streak for long enough to be able to retain the Championship title with a crushing win over Yorkshire on the tykes' home soil at a permanently sunny Scarborough. But enough of this Surrey fan's fantasy...

The performance at Oakham had been dream-like in any case, with Ali Brown's amazing innings followed by an outstanding display of bowling and fielding which had seen a team with quality and depth in their batting twice dismissed for under two-hundred. Interestingly, the last Championship game to have been played at Oakham, back in 1938, had followed an almost identical pattern to this one, with the visitors on that occasion, Kent, making over five-hundred (with B.H. Valentine scoring a double-century) and then twice bowling Leicestershire out cheaply to win by an innings. It was to be hoped that these huge defeats, some sixty-two years apart, wouldn't deter the midlands county from returning to play further matches at a most pleasant ground in a lovely town.

Judging by their display in the most recent game, Leicestershire looked as if they could be discounted as contenders for the 2000 Championship, though they would doubtless be gunning for an 'equalising' victory in the forthcoming fixture at Guildford to revive their challenge.

That left Yorkshire and Lancashire, teams we still had to play twice, as our main opponents and, though each had a game in hand, I felt we were now probably favourites to retain our crown. My predictable optimism was based on a run-in that featured five home games out of seven. Even though our remaining away games were at Scarborough and Old Trafford, I was confident that we could win the preceding home games against our main rivals to give ourselves a psychological advantage. Could the team now put my theory into practice as Yorkshire, whose form had dropped away, as many had expected, came to The Oval for a vital top-of-the-table clash between the two historical giants of English county cricket?

COUNTY CHAMPIONSHIP - MATCH TEN

SURREY versus YORKSHIRE
at The Oval

First Day - Wednesday 12th July

Surrey 226; Yorkshire 33-1

The Teams And The Toss - *The injured Alex Tudor is replaced by Carl Greenidge in the Surrey line-up, though the home side is otherwise unchanged. Yorkshire, like their hosts, are without two players - Darren Gough and Craig White - on duty with England and also miss the injured Gavin Hamilton and Paul Hutchison, though it is unlikely that both men would have played in any case. James Middlebrook is Yorkshire's choice of spinner for the match. Surrey elect to bat first when Adam Hollioake wins the toss.*

Under cloudy skies, Surrey make an understandably cautious start against the England pace pairing of Chris Silverwood and Matthew Hoggard, while David Byas' posting of just two slips looks excessively negative. As luck would have it, Yorkshire still manage to pick up an early wicket, though, when Mark Butcher tickles a legside delivery from Hoggard through to Richard Blakey in the sixth over with the score on just five.

Nadeem Shahid is the new man at the crease and he begins brightly by steering and driving a brace of boundaries in Silverwood's fifth over, the first shot prompting Byas into finally placing a third slip. Meanwhile, at the other end, Ian Ward gets off the mark, after some forty minutes, with two glorious strokes in the same Hoggard over - an elegant off-drive to the rope at the Vauxhall end is followed by a crisp clip to the boards at midwicket.

With both sides striving for early control of the match, the cricket is, naturally, keen and competitive, but Surrey edge ahead slightly through the sensible batting of the second-wicket pair. Shahid is certainly the more dominant partner and he produces the majority of the boundary strokes, including a pull off Hoggard and then a cut and a cover drive off Silverwood to raise the home county's fifty in the twenty-second over.

Although he has looked in great touch, Shahid becomes the second Surrey man to fall, three overs later with the score at sixty-six, undone by an astonishingly good delivery from Ryan Sidebottom, Silverwood's replacement at the pavilion end. Having driven the left-armer through mid-on and the covers earlier in the over, the former Essex man has his off stump rocked back by a big, late inswinging yorker which gives him no chance and probably rates as one of the deliveries of the season.

With an excellent innings of thirty-six and a very important partnership of sixty-one now ended, Surrey have to dig in to ensure they don't lose another wicket before lunch and they are helped greatly in this respect by the almost immediate withdrawal of Sidebottom, after an impressive eight-over spell, and the pairing of Gary Fellows' gentle medium-pace with James Middlebrook's ordinary-looking off-spin. Apart from an optimistic appeal for a catch at the wicket by Middlebrook against Ward when he gets a ball to turn and bounce a little, the final stages of the session see Surrey consolidating on a decent start.

Lunch:- Surrey 77-2 (Ward 26*, A.J. Hollioake 4*) from 34 overs

Having batted through the morning with great control to see off the new ball, Ian Ward is an early casualty in the second over after lunch when a late inswinger from Hoggard defeats an attempted drive and raps him on his pads in front of the stumps. Umpire Cowley agrees with the bowler's view that the batsman is out and Surrey are pegged back to 82-3.

This breakthrough brings Ali Brown to the wicket and, in an interesting move, David Byas, having given Middlebrook the first over of the session from the pavilion end, immediately recalls Silverwood in his place. It would appear that this a deliberate ploy by the Yorkshire captain to confront Brown with his fastest bowler, although the move actually very nearly brings the wicket of Adam Hollioake. Having driven Silverwood to the cover boundary, the Surrey skipper then redirects the inevitable short delivery that follows straight to Hoggard at long leg. It appears to be a simple catch, straight down the fielder's throat, but he elects to take the ball at a lower height than necessary and consequently grasses the chance. This is indeed a bad miss, with Hollioake on eleven and his side on 86-3, and the home captain then adds insult to injury by driving successive deliveries for four in Silverwood's next over. When Brown follows up by pulling the last ball high over midwicket for another boundary to bring up Surrey's hundred the Yorkshire quickie must be starting to think that it's not his day. This is not the case, however, since he has his revenge in the next over when Brown can only deflect a lifting delivery to the Yorkshire skipper at second slip - Surrey are 105-4 and the visitors appear to hold a slight, but definite, advantage.

Hoggard and Silverwood are now really pounding in as they try to tip the balance further in their side's favour but it's not until Sidebottom returns to the fray that things really start to happen. The left-armer's reappearance in place of Silverwood for the forty-seventh over of the innings brings an immediate result for Yorkshire as Ben Hollioake clips a leg stump half-volley straight to Gary Fellows at square leg and departs for just eight with the score at 127.

If Surrey are wobbling now then they are positively staggering just six overs later after the loss of two further wickets for twenty-one runs. Jon Batty goes first at 144, his judgement flawed and punished as he pads up to what looks like a pretty straight delivery from Hoggard, then Adam Hollioake follows his colleague back to the pavilion four runs later when his tentative push at a ball angled across him by Sidebottom results in an outside edge to Richard Blakey behind the stumps.

Although Surrey are now in all sorts of trouble, the Yorkshire skipper also has a slight problem. With Silverwood having only recently completed a spell, Hoggard having delivered nine overs off the reel since lunch and Sidebottom already four overs into a new stint, how can he maintain the pressure on the batsmen? His solution is to block up the Vauxhall end with Fellows bowling a line wide of off stump, supported by a seven-two field, and hope that Sidebottom can make further inroads from the pavilion end. The first part of Byas's plan actually works pretty effectively but when his front-line paceman proves unable to shift either Bicknell or Salisbury after three further overs the visiting captain is forced to turn to Middlebrook's fairly flat and none-too-threatening off-breaks. As a result, the pressure eases slightly, the batsmen claw back a little of Yorkshire's considerable advantage and Byas switches his bowlers with great rapidity in the final half-a-dozen overs before tea. Silverwood returns for two unimpressive overs, during which both batsmen glance him to the boundary, then Lehmann and Vaughan are given a spin, but to no effect as Surrey reach the interval breathing just a touch more easily.

Tea:- Surrey 192-7 (Bicknell 28*, Salisbury 17*) from 72 overs

Bicknell and Salisbury continue their fine rebuilding effort after the break, with Bicknell clipping successive Hoggard deliveries to the fence at square leg to raise both the Surrey two-hundred and the fifty partnership, and Salisbury cutting Sidebottom to the rope at backward point. The balance of the game is now swinging back towards equality, a fact that Byas acknowledges by setting increasingly defensive fields, as the eighth-wicket stand passes seventy and a second batting point begins to appear on the horizon.

At this point, however, Yorkshire reassert their authority in dramatic fashion with a burst of three wickets in eighteen balls to lop off the champions' tail. The Surrey slide starts with Bicknell's departure for forty-five, trapped leg-before by a Sidebottom off-cutter, and continues when Saqlain shuffles too far across his wicket and has his leg stump knocked back to complete a well-deserved five-wicket bag for the promising young left-armer. When Hoggard then pegs back Carl Greenidge's off stump in the very next over, Surrey are suddenly all out for 228 and the visitors leave the field, led by Sidebottom (5-40) and Hoggard (4-70), doubtless feeling very satisfied with their efforts.

With twenty overs left for play, Surrey would clearly like to pick up a couple of wickets before the close and Martin Bicknell certainly pulls out all the stops in his opening spell without gaining any reward. As well as seeing Byas edge just short of the slips twice in his first over, he sees Michael Vaughan missed by Ali Brown at second slip in his third - the score is one, the batsman is not off the mark, the chance is low to the fielder's left, the bowler is not amused.

From the pavilion end, Carl Greenidge plays his part, too, as both Yorkshire openers look unconvincing in the early stages, though Vaughan eventually gets the measure of the young fast bowler by pulling and clipping him for three legside fours in the space of two overs.

This prompts a double bowling change and, eventually, the pairing of Saqlain and Salisbury for the last three overs of the day. Immediately there are clear signs of danger ahead for Yorkshire as Byas looks wracked with uncertainty. Despite looking so ill-at-ease, it appears as if the visitors' captain will survive to the close, however, until Salisbury outfoxes him with the day's penultimate delivery, a googly which takes the leading edge of the bat and dollies the ball into the air on the off-side. As Adam Hollioake plunges forward from silly point to hold a good catch inches from the turf so the Surrey team recovers a little of the ground lost earlier in the day.

Close:- Yorkshire 33-1 (Vaughan 21*) from 19.5 overs

VIEW FROM THE DRESSING ROOM - NADEEM SHAHID

We struggled with the bat in our first innings against Matthew Hoggard and Ryan Sidebottom, who both look good prospects to me. What's your opinion of them?
NS - They are definitely both high-class bowlers, but for different reasons. Hoggard bowls an immaculate line and length, whilst Sidebottom is always at you, swinging the ball both ways. The massive inswinging yorker that Sidebottom bowled me with in the first innings was certainly an absolute beauty.

VIEW FROM THE DRESSING ROOM - ALISTAIR BROWN

What was your view of Matthew Hoggard and Ryan Sidebottom, two bowlers who have impressed me every time I've seen them bowl?
AB - They are both very good bowlers and if they can stay clear of injuries then I think we'll be seeing a lot more of those two. Hoggard is similar to Jimmy Ormond in that he has the ability to swing the ball at a very sharp pace, he bowls a good full length and is always asking questions of you. Sidebottom bowled very well, too, and swung the ball around consistently.

VIEW FROM THE DRESSING ROOM - IAN SALISBURY

How disappointed were we with our first innings total of 226?
IS - Although it wasn't a bad pitch it wasn't easy to bat on, especially against their quality seamers, and our score could have been a lot worse but for Bickers and I clawing it back from a potential 160 all out. We felt it was definitely a below-par total but with our bowling attack we know that we are never out of the game. So long as we bowled them out for a score not too much bigger than ours, we felt confident that we could easily outscore them in the second innings, especially as they had to bat last against the turning ball.

Second Day - Thursday 13th July

Surrey 226 and 1-1; Yorkshire 242

Overnight rain and morning showers leave the ground unfit for play until 1.30pm and then, with the score advanced to 45-1 after just seventeen minutes' action, the players are forced off the field for another quarter-of-an-hour by a further brief shower.

Upon the resumption, Michael Vaughan and Richard Blakey take Yorkshire past fifty despite a good, controlled spell by Martin Bicknell which precedes the pairing of the Surrey spin twins again. While Ian Salisbury appears, understandably, to have struggled with the inevitably wet ball right from the start of the day's play, Saqlain seems to have no such problems when introduced at the Vauxhall end and he brings almost instant joy to the home team when Blakey bat-pads the off-spinner's second ball to Nadeem Shahid at short leg. Yorkshire 64 for 2.

With Darren Lehmann, currently the leading run-scorer in the Championship, now joining Vaughan in the middle, we have the visitors' two best batsmen pitted against the country's top spin combination and the match appears to be entering an important phase. While Lehmann, a batsman renowned for his ability against spin, comes through a couple of uncertain moments early on, Vaughan sweeps and pulls Salisbury to the boundary to reach a 122-ball half-century. It's a characteristic of the England batsman's innings thus far that he has taken advantage of any loose deliveries and scored heavily from them but, while he is merely good in this respect, Lehmann is among the very best and he proceeds to demonstrate the fact with a murderous assault on Salisbury. Three successive deliveries in the leg-spinner's next over disappear for 4-6-4 as a cut follows two sweeps and when Saqlain is driven for three by Lehmann and pulled for four by Vaughan in the next over it's clear that Yorkshire have planned to take the attack to the spinners. The hundred rushes up during this period and the fifty partnership, compiled in eleven overs, follows shortly afterwards when Vaughan pulls and cuts successive Salisbury long hops to the boundary. It's a shock to the system for Surrey fans to see their leg-spinner receiving such rough treatment but it's also fair to say that he has been well below par today. Despite this, Hollioake sensibly decides to keep faith with Salisbury, though he is finally forced to pull him out of the firing line when Lehmann again gets after him in the next over, with a cut to the fence followed by lofted drives for four and six.

While Salisbury contemplates today's spell of 12.1-0-72-0 and the Surrey faithful contemplate the strong possibility of a substantial first innings deficit for their team, Martin Bicknell returns at the Vauxhall end and Saqlain switches to the pavilion end. This combination has an initial calming effect before Lehmann briefly cuts loose again to reach a quick-fire fifty from just 45 balls in 71 minutes with a late-cut four off Saqlain. Having enjoyed no luck whatsoever in the innings to date, Bicknell then endures further frustration in the following over when an edge from Vaughan, on sixty-seven at the time, somehow bisects Brown and Butcher in the slips at catchable height on its way to the boundary. The match position is starting to look a little bleak for Surrey now and the reprieved batsman promptly rubs salt into Bicknell's wound by pulling him for a boundary which takes the visitors' total past 150.

Inspiration is clearly needed from somewhere and, luckily for Surrey, a change of fortune for Bicknell enables him to provide it just in the nick of time. Although the wicket of either Yorkshire batsman would be acceptable, given the state of the game, it's actually the prize scalp of Lehmann that Bicknell captures, courtesy of a miscued pull which dollies a simple catch to Salisbury at mid-on. Having been guilty of an over-ambitious shot, the Australian left-hander drags himself dolefully from the field while the public address announcer informs the crowd that the wicket which has given Surrey renewed hope is the 800th of Martin Bicknell's distinguished first-class career. A well-merited round of applause follows, but the celebrations for both the wicket and Bicknell's personal milestone are quickly put aside, since the visitors are still very well placed at 158 for 3, despite Lehmann's departure for fifty-five.

Almost inevitably, the tempo of the innings now drops markedly and just seventeen runs are added in the final eight overs before tea. Only one of these runs is scored by Vaughan and I can't help but think that he is making a tactical error by seemingly withdrawing into his shell at this critical stage of proceedings.

Tea:- Yorkshire 175-3 (Vaughan 76*, McGrath 13*) from 59 overs

With Lehmann safely out of the way, the Surrey spin twins are reunited after tea for what looks to be a vital session of play. If Yorkshire can build a lead with wickets in hand by the end of the day then they will be in a very healthy position, while all Surrey can do, realistically, is try to limit the opposition's first innings lead to as few runs as possible. The Yorkshire batting line-up certainly gives the champions hope, since the lower middle-order lacks in experience and the tail appears weak, but the fourth-wicket pairing of Vaughan and McGrath will need shifting first.

Unfortunately, from a Surrey point of view, the latter of this pair looks to be in decent form during the early overs of the session, taking three threes from Salisbury with a pair of cuts and an on-drive and pushing his side ever closer to the home county's total. The game, in fact, appears to be running away from Surrey again until Saqlain provides succour with another crucial breakthrough at 189-3. It's Saqi's 'deadly dart', a very much quicker delivery bowled with no great change of action, that brings the all-important wicket of Vaughan, who is beaten for pace, trapped on the crease and adjudged lbw. The England batsman's eighty has been a fine knock but I feel that he has let the initiative slip in the later stages of his innings - a dangerous thing to do against this Surrey team.

With the lower middle-order now exposed, the feeling that the balance of power could change very rapidly proves justified as the hosts capture two more wickets and miss two chances to take a third, all in the space of four overs. Matthew Wood goes at 194, edging a well-pitched Salisbury leg-break to Adam Hollioake at second slip, McGrath falls four runs later when he nicks Saqlain to the younger Hollioake at first slip and, in between these dismissals, a very nervous Gary Fellows makes a dreadful start by offering a difficult catching chance off each spinner before scoring.

While the young all-rounder prompts equal measures of nervous laughter and anguished frustration from the Surrey faithful as he continues to live a charmed life by finding gaps in the field with a leading edge and then a top-edged sweep, his new partner, James Middlebrook, looks surprisingly composed. Perhaps drawing strength from his team-mate's apparent confidence, Fellows does eventually settle down, however, and he finally begins to locate the middle of his bat as he takes boundaries off both bowlers in successive overs. When Middlebrook then follows suit, courtesy of a cut off Salisbury and a sweep off Saqlain, Yorkshire move into the lead and they are once again looking capable of building a worthwhile advantage. Adam Hollioake reacts to this possibility by recalling the trusty Bicknell and switching his Pakistani spin genius to the pavilion end... with the desired result. Suddenly the flow of runs dries up and, after three scoreless overs, Middlebrook is undone by Saqlain's quicker ball, his off stump knocked back by a yorker-length delivery almost before he has got his bat down. After a valuable partnership of thirty-seven by the Fellows-Middlebrook combination, it's now 235-7 and the visitors' frail tail is on display... but not for long!

Within five overs the Yorkshire innings is complete - Chris Silverwood and Ryan Sidebottom both fall leg-before to Saqlain, the former rapped on the back pad by another 'dart' and the latter pushing forward without offering a stroke, and then Ian Salisbury nips in with an lbw wicket of his own when Matthew Hoggard shoulders arms to a googly. This sudden, but not unexpected, slump, which has seen the last four wickets go for the addition of a mere seven runs, has left Yorkshire all out for 242, a lead of just sixteen. The chief architect of their demise has been the trusty Saqlain with 6-63, though Bicknell has played his part and Salisbury has shown great resilience to bounce back quickly from his mauling at the hands of Darren Lehmann.

The day should now be ending on a real high for Surrey but two late incidents - one towards the end of Yorkshire's innings and one at the start of Surrey's reply - cast a slight shadow over the team's determined fightback. The first had occurred when Martin Bicknell limped off the field after just one ball of his twenty-fifth over with what appeared to be a knee injury, leaving Ian Salisbury to complete the over and pick up the final wicket. The second comes in the first of the two overs that Surrey have to face before the close of play when Mark Butcher pads up to the third delivery from Silverwood and is palpably lbw as the ball swings back into his pads.

Losing Butcher is a bad enough blow, but the Bicknell injury could be far more damaging to the team in the long term. The physio's report will be eagerly and nervously awaited.

Close:- Surrey 1-1 (Ward 0*, Salisbury 1*) from 2 overs

VIEW FROM THE DRESSING ROOM - ALISTAIR BROWN

When Yorkshire were 158-2 we looked to be really struggling, with Vaughan very patient and Lehmann very powerful. How concerned were you with our position at that stage?
AB - Yorkshire are a very good side with some great swing bowlers but I do feel they rely too heavily on Darren Lehmann to score their runs. If he gets runs then the other players tend to prosper as well, but if you can get him out cheaply then there's a bit of pressure on the rest of their batting to score some runs and they are often found to be lacking. Getting him out in this innings, with a rather soft dismissal after he had played so well, was a big turning point. Once we got past him then we knew there was a very good chance that we would knock them over for a similar score to ours.

Saqi blew away their tail with a faster ball which was described as 'a bullet ball' by the reporter in the Yorkshire Post. Was that delivery a new addition to Saqi's already impressive armoury in 2000?
AB - Yes, it was, and it keeps me on my toes at slip because if the batsman nicks it then I could end up 'wearing' the ball if I'm not paying full attention! Fortunately, he usually bowls it very well and very straight.

VIEW FROM THE DRESSING ROOM - JON BATTY

Since the end of the 1999 season, Saqi had developed a new, much quicker, delivery which paid dividends for him in this match. It's incredible how he seems to keep adding new deliveries to his armoury - does that present problems for you as a wicketkeeper?
JB - Saqi is a truly world class bowler and it has been a huge honour for me to watch him from close quarters over the past four seasons. He is constantly striving to become a better bowler, trying to learn new tricks as well as perfect the ones he already has up his sleeve, and, as a result, I have to work closely with him and develop as he does.

VIEW FROM THE DRESSING ROOM - IAN SALISBURY

As a supporter, I was very worried when Yorkshire reached 158-2. How did it feel for you guys out in the middle?
IS - You shouldn't have been worried - you know you should always trust us! To be fair, Vaughan, who impressed us greatly in this innings, and Lehmann played very well. Lehmann got after me and, for once, I don't suppose Saqi and I looked very potent. Normally we come up with a wicket somehow but I think we'd lost our game plan slightly on this occasion, so we had to rely on Bickers coming back to get rid of Lehmann - but that's just an example of the way that our bowlers work as a unit. Once we'd broken that stand we got things back under control and bowled them out fairly rapidly.

Third Day - Friday 14th July

Surrey 226 and 320-7; Yorkshire 242

If ever there was a day when the early overs were of paramount importance to the shaping of a game then it's today. Surrey simply cannot afford to lose a handful of early wickets against the fired-up Yorkshire pace attack and a huge task lies ahead of the top-order batsmen plus the nightwatchman, Ian Salisbury.

In conditions closer to those expected at Headingley in April than in the south-east of England in July, Surrey start steadily before a brief shower halts play after thirty-five minutes. During this initial period of play the reigning champions have added just eighteen runs - the most significant contribution being four overthrows when the batsmen steal a quick single - but, crucially, Ward and Salisbury have stood firm against everything thrown at them by Silverwood, Hoggard and, latterly, Sidebottom.

Around twenty-five minutes' play is lost during the rain break and it takes Yorkshire seven overs after the restart to make their first breakthrough of the day with the score at twenty-eight. Having started with four successive maidens, it's Ryan Sidebottom who finally ends Salisbury's stout resistance with a touch-and-go lbw decision, the ball appearing to pitch very close to the line of leg stump. The departing nightwatchman has done a great job for his team in repelling the visitors' best efforts for almost seventeen overs and his contribution to the cause is recognised by the knowledgeable and appreciative Surrey members who applaud longer and louder than would normally be expected after an innings of twelve.

The value of Salisbury's knock is soon underlined, in fact, when David Byas is forced to turn to James Middlebrook at the pavilion end, his three front-line seamers having all contributed a burst of at least six overs. Cleverly, Nadeem Shahid doesn't allow the young off-spinner any chance to settle, twice making ground to drive the ball over mid-on for four and also sweeping fine for two. It looks like a tactical masterstroke and Ian Ward maintains the pressure on Middlebrook by whipping him through midwicket for three in his next over. Having batted with great patience and calm assurance throughout the morning, Ward is suddenly breaking loose and he takes his team past fifty shortly afterwards when he cuts an apparently tiring Silverwood to the rope at cover and then clips him through midwicket for three. He then emphasises the fact that it's been Surrey's session by cutting Middlebrook to the boundary backward of point on the stroke of lunch to leave the hosts forty-six runs ahead after a hard, competitive and absorbing morning's cricket.

Lunch:- Surrey 62-2 (Ward 33*, Shahid 13*) from 30 overs

Ryan Sidebottom bowls the first over from the pavilion end after lunch, which is much as expected, since this looks to be a key period in the game. David Byas' choice of bowler at the Vauxhall end is something of a surprise, however - although Matthew Hoggard hasn't bowled a ball in anger since about 12.20pm, the Yorkshire captain opts for James Middlebrook. This gives the Surrey batsmen a little time to play themselves back in and Shahid shows his gratitude by raising the fifty partnership for the third wicket with an extra cover drive to the boundary off Sidebottom. Having delivered just four overs, the left-arm seamer is then replaced by Gary Fellows.

This seems a very strange move indeed but, just as everyone is wondering whether Byas has taken leave of his senses, his bowlers pick up a wicket each in consecutive overs. With the score at 84-2, Ian Ward, after a valiant and valuable effort, top edges a cut at Middlebrook to Richard Blakey and then, with just one run added, Adam Hollioake falls to Fellows in identical fashion. Suddenly the game looks wide open again.

Situations like this never seem to faze Ali Brown, however, and having smashed Fellows to the extra cover boundary in his third over at the crease he then drives Middlebrook for a towering six over wide long-on in his fourth. This stroke raises the Surrey hundred and heralds the immediate reintroduction of Chris Silverwood.

After two ineffective overs, during which he bangs the ball in too short to be dangerous, Silverwood is switched to the Vauxhall end and paired with the returning Hoggard. This combination very nearly brings the wicket Yorkshire crave when Brown, on 21, smashes Hoggard into the covers and sees Michael Vaughan just fail to hang on to a reasonable catching chance, diving away to his right. The fielder and his team are then given time to contemplate this missed opportunity as another shower brings a fifteen-minute break in play with the score at 120-4.

Upon the resumption, Surrey make further rapid progress, with Shahid immediately forcing Hoggard to the cover fence and Brown pulling Silverwood to the boundary at deep backward square leg. When Brown then drives Hoggard for four through extra cover in an over costing eleven he completes a fine half-century partnership with Shahid, which looks to be tipping the scales in the home county's favour. Yorkshire will clearly not be relishing the thought of batting last against Saqlain and Salisbury, especially if they need to chase a total much in excess of two-hundred. That sort of target is looking increasingly likely, however, as Shahid arrives at a most worthy fifty from 104 balls in 149 minutes during an over in which he twice pulls the recalled Fellows for four.

With his front-line pacemen apparently all bowled out and no quality spinner in his line-up, Byas now finds himself backed into a corner and, by introducing Darren Lehmann's occasional left-arm spin, he is forced to concede further ground. It's clear that tea can't come soon enough for the Yorkshire skipper as Brown takes full toll of the tasty morsels on offer from the visiting bowlers. Having reached his fifty from just 52 deliveries in 67 minutes with two cuts to the boundary off Lehmann, he drives Fellows wide of mid-on for the sixth four of his innings and picks up his second six with a huge straight hit onto the pavilion balcony. During the course of this pre-tea carnage, Shahid and Brown have recorded a century partnership in nineteen overs and succeeded in putting Yorkshire very much on the rack.

Tea:- Surrey 197-4 (Shahid 64*, Brown 71*) from 65 overs

Having surprisingly bowled only four overs during the course of the middle session, in one spell immediately after lunch, Ryan Sidebottom is back after tea in what looks like a last throw of the dice for Yorkshire. Sensibly enough, Shahid and Brown opt to play him with caution while milking Middlebrook at the other end. By this method they push the Surrey lead beyond two-hundred before Shahid falls lbw to the off-spinner while trying to work the ball to leg. Although the batsman will be disappointed to miss out on a century, the home supporters recognise his eighty-run contribution to their team's very promising position with a warm ovation upon his return to the pavilion.

Far from reining back the Surrey scoring rate, this wicket brings forth a sudden flood of runs as the total advances by twenty-eight in four overs. Ben Hollioake, though he sparkles only briefly, becomes the first batsman in the match to score freely off Sidebottom, reeling off three sumptuous drives in the space of two overs, while Brown makes hay against Middlebrook, lofting him over extra cover for four to move on to ninety-two before driving him high over wide long-off in the following over to complete a breathtaking 106-ball century after just 130 minutes at the wicket. As the crowd rises to applaud an excellent innings, Brown must be getting that Friday feeling, having scored 211 not out at Oakham exactly seven days previously.

With Surrey now 241 runs to the good, the loss of two wickets to Middlebrook for eight runs at this point is of no great concern - Hollioake's cameo ends when he falls leg-before in similar fashion to Shahid, while Jon Batty top-edges a sweep high to midwicket. Of far greater interest and relevance, however, is the emergence of Martin Bicknell, accompanied by a runner, at the fall of the seventh wicket. Clearly his knee injury isn't bad enough to prevent him batting, but, since he is unable to run freely, it looks unlikely that he will be doing much, if any, bowling tomorrow. If that is the case then one would imagine that the home side will want to extend their lead still further in the remaining playing time, rather than declare and put Yorkshire in for a few overs tonight.

And so it proves. With Byas relying on Middlebrook, Lehmann and Fellows to deliver the final fifteen overs of the day, Surrey advance their total by a further fifty-five runs with barely a false stroke. It says much for the visitors' negative state of mind at this stage that Lehmann is called four times for legside wides by umpire Cowley and, with the pressure now off, Brown takes the opportunity to ease his way to 130 by the close of play.

Close:- Surrey 320-7 (Brown 130*, Bicknell 25*) from 97 overs

VIEW FROM THE DRESSING ROOM - IAN SALISBURY

We looked to be in a spot of bother when we were 85-4. Were we feeling a bit uncomfortable at that stage?
IS - Funny though it might sound, we weren't too displeased with 85-4 because our game plan was working well. We had batted for a lot of overs at that point so we'd seen off the new ball and forced their three main bowlers to do a lot of work. As their fast bowlers hadn't had much rest after bowling quite a bit in the first innings, we knew that Yorkshire would then be forced to bowl Fellows and Middlebrook for quite a number of overs. That was what happened and Browny and Nad took advantage of the situation by scoring quickly and batting magnificently well.

VIEW FROM THE DRESSING ROOM - NADEEM SHAHID

We looked to be in some trouble at 85-4 in our second innings. Looking back, do you think that your partnership with Ali Brown represented the decisive phase of the match?
NS - Yes, I think it was a definite turning point because, until then, we were always just behind them in the game. Browny and I just tried to stay positive all the time as we knew that their seam bowlers would tire eventually.

VIEW FROM THE DRESSING ROOM - ALISTAIR BROWN

I thought Ian Ward and Ian Salisbury did a good job for us at the start of the day when seeing off the early overs from the Yorkshire seamers. Fair comment?
AB - Certainly. Ian Ward didn't get a huge score but I thought he played very well - his was a very important innings and sometimes it's not the top run-scorer who should get all the credit, this being a case in point. He's a class player and he gave us the base that we needed.

Did you feel that your 144-run partnership with Nadeem Shahid represented the turning point of the match?
AB - I remember that when I came in to bat they were very chirpy and Darren Lehmann said "Come on lads, they're 70 for 4 and they're struggling". I therefore felt that we should try to be positive in order to take the initiative away from them. Then, shortly after I arrived in the middle, I hit Middlebrook for six, which prompted Lehmann to say something along the lines of "He's come in to throw it away". That immediately told me that they were running scared because it was almost exactly the comment *I* would make to *him* in that situation if my real feelings were "I hope he doesn't go on and take this game away from us"! So that was more of a turning point for me because I could see their confidence just dropping a little bit and ours increasing. Nad and I were determined to be very positive in any case. He's a very good player, he's good fun to bat with and he's always up for a challenge - he gets very excited when you start playing positively because he can't wait to join in!

It was very noticeable in both innings that as soon as you arrived at the crease Chris Silverwood was brought on to bowl. Were you aware of this and, if so, do you know of any reason why David Byas adopted this tactic? Does Silverwood have a particularly good record against you or were they hoping to bounce you out, maybe?

AB - I'm not really sure what that was about - I've faced Chris many times and I've never noticed anything before. He's a very good, quick bowler although I think he sometimes tends to bowl too short - I get the feeling that David Byas perhaps encourages him to bang it in short and tries to work him up into a frenzy. And if someone can play the short ball then Byas isn't quite sure what to do next - that 'let's knock his head off' kind of tactic is a bit old-fashioned these days. But if that's the policy he wants to pursue and if he feels that some players need to have the ball banged in short at them then that's up to him, I don't have a problem with that - I'm certainly not fussed about who I face when I come in to bat.

Fourth Day - Saturday 15th July

Surrey 226 and 345-8 declared; Yorkshire 242 and 126

Surrey beat Yorkshire by 203 runs

Surrey 16pts, Yorkshire 4

Adam Hollioake surprises a few people by batting on at the start of the day but at least it gives Surrey fans the encouraging sight of Martin Bicknell batting without a runner and appearing to have no difficulties in moving between the wickets as twenty-five runs are added in four overs. Only eight of these runs come in boundaries, however, since Byas posts all but three men on the rope - it's a rarely-seen field setting as it would, of course, be illegal in one-day cricket. The declaration comes as soon as Bicknell skies an attempted hook back to the bowler, leaving Yorkshire to score 330 in a minimum of ninety overs to win. Realistically, barring an astounding knock from Darren Lehmann, they have no hope of achieving this and the only relevant question is whether or not Surrey can take ten wickets in the time left.

Bicknell's presence in the attack clearly makes this more likely and he starts superbly, beating the bat on numerous occasions and conceding only an edged four to Byas in his first four overs, before finally finding joy when he finds the top of Vaughan's off stump in the ninth over of the innings. Since the England batsman appears to have covered everything, it's hard to understand how the ball has penetrated his defence but the sight of the bails on the ground is clear evidence that it has and the visitors are 21 for 1 with their linchpin batsman heading back to the pavilion.

Vaughan's departure brings Anthony McGrath to the crease in a change of batting order. It appears to be a positive move to bring the powerful striker up from number five but it has a down side, too, in that it pushes Richard Blakey, never a good player of spin, down to a position in the order where he will almost certainly have to start against Saqlain and Salisbury. On balance, it seems a marginal decision and the former England Under-19 batsman almost makes it look completely foolish when he edges his second delivery just wide of third slip. His captain is not so fortunate, however, finding the safe hands of Ali Brown at second slip later in the same over with the score on twenty-five. It's been a miserable match for David Byas and his team is now in real danger of slipping into desperate trouble with lunch still forty-five minutes away. In fact, they even have a scare before Bicknell's magnificent sixth over is complete, as Darren Lehmann squirts his second delivery perilously close to the squarer of the two gully fieldsmen that Adam Hollioake has posted.

Having survived this heart-stopping moment, Lehmann plays with greater comfort in the run-up to the interval, though he is outscored by McGrath, who actually looks the more positive of the two batsmen as he produces some pleasant strokes on both sides of the wicket. The Surrey captain's pairing of his spinners for the final two overs of the session gives the batsmen a foretaste of what is to come, however.

Lunch:- Yorkshire 55-2 (McGrath 22*, Lehmann 12*) from 21 overs

Surrey have to wait only eight balls for their first breakthrough after the interval, McGrath falling to a bat-pad catch at silly point by Adam Hollioake off Saqlain Mushtaq without a run added to the lunch score. With very little reliable batting now left to support him, the pressure on Lehmann increases significantly and some outstandingly accurate and testing spin bowling steadily squeezes the life out of Yorkshire. Just ten singles come from eleven overs as scoring opportunities become almost non-existent and everyone knows that something or someone is going to crack. Fortunately for Surrey, it's Lehmann. Unable to restrain himself any longer, he advances on Salisbury and, perhaps beaten in the flight, miscues a drive low to wide mid-on, where Ali Brown swoops to pick up a good catch. As the South Australian left-hander departs for the pavilion, with the scoreboard reading 65 for 4, just about everyone in the ground appreciates the significance of his demise and the giant step Surrey have just taken towards a very important victory.

For the benefit of those who are still in doubt, Salisbury makes everything much clearer with another wicket in each of his next two overs. As Blakey perishes, back on his stumps and defeated by a googly, and Wood follows, well snapped up at second slip from a top-edged cut, the Surrey leg-spinner completes a burst of three wickets for one run in twelve balls and Yorkshire sink to a miserable 68-6. The visitors' very slim hopes of victory had disappeared with Lehmann and now, just four overs later, even the draw is looking highly unlikely, thanks to a combination of classy spin bowling and hesitant, indecisive batting.

Since they are now facing a hopeless situation, Fellows and Middlebrook pursue a more positive approach, with limited success. Fellows takes twelve from a Saqlain over, including a slog-sweep for six, and Middlebrook ten from the next over bowled by Salisbury, before Surrey's Pakistani magician brings both to book in the space of four balls as the Yorkshire innings disintegrates before our very eyes. Fellows is the first to fall, taken at short leg by Nadeem Shahid with the score just into three figures, then Middlebrook drives a simple catch to mid-on with just one run added to the total.

With the visitors' dreams now turned to dust, all that remains is for Chris Silverwood to blast two angry sixes and a four off Salisbury before Saqlain completes the destruction and a five-wicket haul by repeating his two-wickets-in-four-deliveries trick - Silverwood, for the second time in the match, is despatched lbw by a 'bullet ball' and Hoggard trapped likewise on the front foot. This final wicket completes a match-clinching burst of 4-9 in fourteen balls by Saqlain and seals Surrey's first County Championship victory over Yorkshire since 1995.

To enthusiastic acclaim from the pavilion, Saqlain - who has taken 11 for 104 in the match - and Salisbury lead their team from the field with Surrey's position at the top of the table now considerably strengthened.

**Surrey 226 and 345-8dec; Yorkshire 242 and 126
Surrey won by 203 runs. Surrey 16pts, Yorkshire 4**

SURREY v YORKSHIRE at THE OVAL. Played from 12th - 15th July

Surrey won the toss
Umpires:- N.G. Cowley & P. Willey

SURREY - First Innings

Fall of wkt	Batsman	How Out		Score	Balls	4s	6s
1- 5	M.A. Butcher	c Blakey	b Hoggard	5	21	1	0
3- 82	I.J. Ward		lbw b Hoggard	28	105	3	0
2- 66	Nadeem Shahid		b Sidebottom	36	58	6	0
7- 148	A.J. Hollioake *	c Blakey	b Sidebottom	48	85	5	0
4- 105	A.D. Brown	c Byas	b Silverwood	7	14	1	0
5- 127	B.C. Hollioake	c Fellows	b Sidebottom	8	18	1	0
6- 144	J.N. Batty +		lbw b Hoggard	1	6	0	0
8- 221	M.P. Bicknell		lbw b Sidebottom	45	90	4	0
	I.D.K. Salisbury		Not Out	29	79	3	0
9- 223	Saqlain Mushtaq		b Sidebottom	1	9	0	0
10- 226	C.G. Greenidge		b Hoggard	3	7	0	0
	Extras (5b, 8lb, 2nb)			15			
	TOTAL		(81.5 overs)	226			

YORKSHIRE bowling

	O	M	R	W
Silverwood	16	5	64	1
Hoggard	21.5	3	70	4
Sidebottom	20	8	40	5
Fellows	12	2	16	0
Middlebrook	8	1	19	0
Lehmann	2	2	0	0
Vaughan	2	1	4	0

YORKSHIRE - First Innings

Fall of wkt	Batsman	How Out		Score	Balls	4s	6s
1- 33	D. Byas *	c A.J. Hollioake	b Salisbury	9	52	0	0
4- 189	M.P. Vaughan		lbw b Saqlain	80	203	10	0
2- 64	R.J. Blakey +	c Shahid	b Saqlain	10	28	1	0
3- 158	D.S. Lehmann	c Salisbury	b Bicknell	55	55	7	2
6- 198	A. McGrath	c B.C. Hollioake	b Saqlain	26	44	0	0
5- 194	M.J. Wood	c A.J. Hollioake	b Salisbury	4	7	1	0
	G.M. Fellows		Not Out	24	62	3	0
7- 235	J.D. Middlebrook		b Saqlain	14	49	2	0
8- 237	C.E.W. Silverwood		lbw b Saqlain	1	6	0	0
9- 241	R.J. Sidebottom		lbw b Saqlain	0	13	0	0
10- 242	M.J. Hoggard		lbw b Salisbury	0	3	0	0
	Extras (4b, 11lb, 4nb)			19			
	TOTAL		(86.4 overs)	242			

SURREY bowling

	O	M	R	W
Bicknell	24.1	8	40	1
Greenidge	6	3	18	0
B.C. Hollioake	2	1	1	0
Saqlain	30	8	63	6
Salisbury	24.3	2	105	3

SURREY - Second Innings

Fall of wkt	Batsman	How Out		Score	Balls	4s	6s
1- 0	M.A. Butcher		lbw b Silverwood	0	3	0	0
3- 84	I.J. Ward	c Blakey	b Middlebrook	39	126	2	0
2- 28	I.D.K. Salisbury		lbw b Sidebottom	12	58	0	0
5- 229	Nadeem Shahid		lbw b Middlebrook	80	156	9	0
4- 85	A.J. Hollioake *	c Blakey	b Fellows	1	4	0	0
	A.D. Brown		Not Out	140	162	10	3
6- 257	B.C. Hollioake		lbw b Middlebrook	13	13	2	0
7- 265	J.N. Batty +	c Fellows	b Middlebrook	1	9	0	0
8- 345	M.P. Bicknell		c & b Silverwood	40	75	4	0
	Extras (2b, 5lb, 10w, 2nb)			19			
	TOTAL		(100.5 overs)	345 - 8 dec			

YORKSHIRE bowling

	O	M	R	W
Silverwood	15.5	4	51	2
Hoggard	11	3	35	0
Sidebottom	18	7	38	1
Middlebrook	33	5	119	4
Lehmann	10	1	34	0
Fellows	13	2	61	1

YORKSHIRE - Second Innings

Fall of wkt	Batsman	How Out		Score	Balls	4s	6s
2- 24	D. Byas *	c Brown	b Bicknell	7	35	1	0
1- 21	M.P. Vaughan		b Bicknell	10	25	1	0
3- 55	A. McGrath	c A.J. Hollioake	b Saqlain	22	37	2	0
4- 65	D.S. Lehmann	c Brown	b Salisbury	17	66	0	0
6- 68	M.J. Wood	c A.J. Hollioake	b Salisbury	5	51	0	0
5- 67	R.J. Blakey +		lbw b Salisbury	0	4	0	0
7- 100	G.M. Fellows	c Shahid	b Saqlain	18	33	1	1
8- 101	J.D. Middlebrook	c Salisbury	b Saqlain	11	18	2	0
9- 124	C.E.W. Silverwood		lbw b Saqlain	18	11	1	2
	R.J. Sidebottom		Not Out	6	9	1	0
10- 126	M.J. Hoggard		lbw b Saqlain	2	3	0	0
	Extras (4b, 6lb)			10			
	TOTAL		(48.4 overs)	126			

SURREY bowling

	O	M	R	W
Bicknell	8	4	17	2
Greenidge	6	2	18	0
Saqlain	17.4	5	41	5
B.C. Hollioake	2	0	4	0
Salisbury	15	4	36	3

ALISTAIR BROWN'S 140 NOT OUT AGAINST YORKSHIRE
Original run chart as compiled by Keith Seward

SURREY V YORKSHIRE,   THE OVAL,   14/15-7-00

A. BROWN   NOT OUT   140
  RHB

2·40 - (11·13)   209 mins   50 in 66 mins 52 balls
                      162 balls   100 in 130 mins 106 balls

4·2·6·1·1·1·3·2·1·1·4·2·4·1·2·2·1·1·1·2·1·1·2·1·4·4·1·3·1·4·6·1·4·2·1·1·1·1·1·1·1·1·1·4·2·6·1·1·1·1·1·4·2·1·1·3·1·4·1·1·1·2·1·1·1·2·1·2·1·3·1

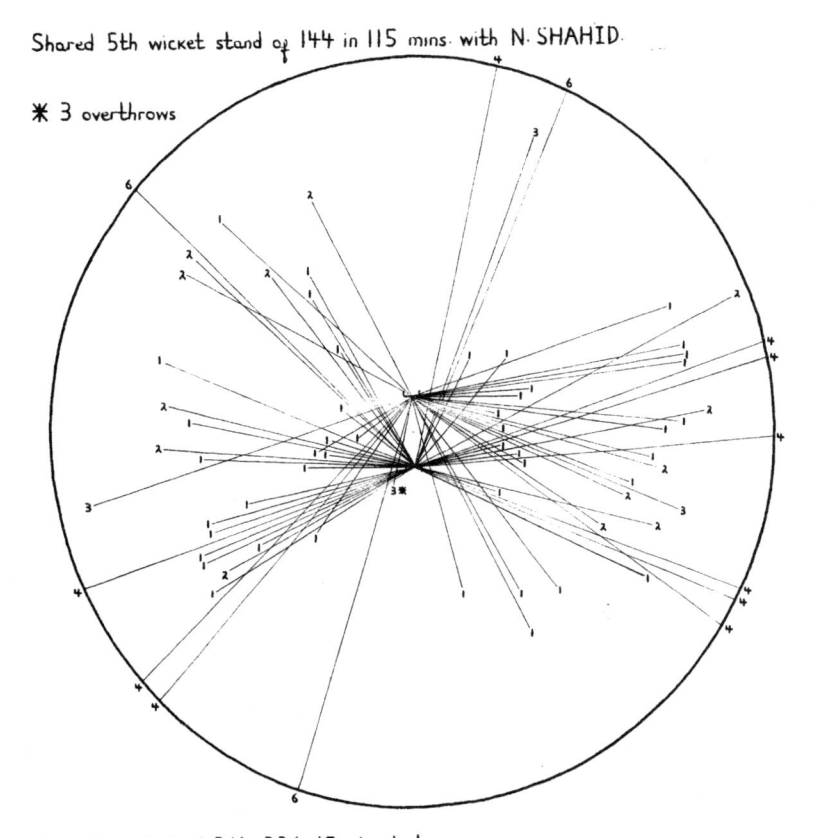

Shared 5th wicket stand of 144 in 115 mins. with N. SHAHID.

✳ 3 overthrows

Rain stopped play: 3·11 - 3·26. 15 mins lost.

VIEW FROM THE DRESSING ROOM - NADEEM SHAHID

It was clear that Darren Lehmann was going to be the key man again in Yorkshire's second knock but he was tied down by the spinners and eventually holed out to midwicket. From your position at short leg, can you sense when a batsman is getting impatient and frustrated and did you get that feeling in this particular case?

NS - Lehmann is certainly a classy player and we knew his wicket was crucial because he is a very dominant player, but we always felt that he would take a risk if we could tie him down. I can definitely sense what the batsman is feeling when I am fielding at short leg and in this case I knew it was just a matter of time before he played a big shot.

Having now won four Championship games in succession, I guess the players must have been starting to feel very confident that we would go on to retain the title?

NS - We were definitely on a roll now but we knew that things could change very quickly, so everybody remained focused. I think this was due to the harsh lessons we had learned in the past, most notably in 1998.

VIEW FROM THE DRESSING ROOM - ALISTAIR BROWN

Would it be fair to say that the game was really won when Lehmann was out, after some great bowling by Solly and Saqi?

AB - Pretty much so. When our two spinners get together I think they are the best in the world. Everyone talks about Saqi, with good reason, but I think Solly is the most under-rated spinner in world cricket - I stand at a slip to him most of the time and I can tell you that he is a class act. But both spinners bowled brilliantly, they frustrated him and he ended up getting out to a fantastic diving catch at midwicket... which I milked as much as I could!

VIEW FROM THE DRESSING ROOM - IAN SALISBURY

Darren Lehmann was clearly their key man. After getting some rough treatment from him in the first innings, you must have been especially delighted when you had him caught by Browny second time around.

IS - We were helped on our way by Bickers, who took the top off their batting with the wickets of Vaughan and Byas, which meant that Saqi and I were able to come on and attack numbers three and four. It was obvious that Lehmann was going to be the danger again so we bowled to a game plan we had devised, part of which was to keep him quiet with more defensive fields. He's not worried by having five men around the bat, he's still going to go for his shots, whatever. So we both kept it tight, stuck to our plan and waited for his patience to snap. It did eventually and I was the one lucky enough to be bowling at the time.

After this win did we now feel confident that we would go on to retain the title?

IS - We knew that we'd now got our noses in front and that we were playing really good cricket, so we had to keep playing the same way and keep the run going. By this stage of the season we were so excited by the way we were playing that it was a case of 'bring on the next big game'.

KEITH MEDLYCOTT'S ASSESSMENT

This was clearly a very important victory over one of the top sides and again we played some great cricket for long periods of the match. It is very tough to be at one-hundred percent over the course of a whole four-day game, though - even Australia, who are a fantastic model to aspire to, rarely manage to achieve that.

Other Division One Matches

Surrey's win, coupled with Lancashire's poor display against Somerset at Taunton, allowed the reigning champions to open up a sixteen point lead at the top of the table. The roses counties each had a game in hand, however, so they were still, potentially, ahead of Surrey in the race for the title. Leicestershire's hopes of getting back into the picture had been revived by a convincing win over Durham.

July 12-14
Leicester:- **Leicestershire beat Durham by 217 runs.** Leicestershire 222 (Smith 111 not out, Wood 5-60) and 259 (Maddy 77, Brown 5-70); Durham 171 (Kumble 4-32, Ormond 4-44) and 93 (Ormond 5-34, Kumble 4-23). **Leicestershire 16pts, Durham 3**

July 12-15
Derby:- **Kent beat Derbyshire by eight wickets.** Derbyshire 181 (Stubbings 72, Cork 58) and 269 (Titchard 74, Patel 6-77); Kent 280 (Key 83, Dravid 55, Munton 6-54) and 171-2 (Fulton 66 not out). **Kent 17pts, Derbyshire 3**

Taunton:- **Lancashire drew with Somerset.** Lancashire 239 (Atherton 113, Parsons 5-13) and 417-9dec (Crawley 120, Ganguly 99); Somerset 565 (Cox 171, Burns 108, Bowler 95, Turner 75). **Somerset 11pts, Lancashire 7**

COUNTY CHAMPIONSHIP DIVISION ONE AT 15TH JULY

Pos	Prev		P	Pts	W	D	L	Bat	Bowl	Last	Three	Res
1	1	Surrey	10	119	5	3	2	24	23	W16	W20	W18
2	3	Lancashire	9	103	4	5	0	14	21	D7	D7	W17
3	2	Yorkshire	9	102	4	3	2	15	27	L4	D7	L3
4	4	Leicestershire	9	94	3	4	2	20	22	W16	L3	W18
5	4	Somerset	9	89	2	5	2	23	22	D11	D11	D11
6	6	Durham	9	71	2	2	5	12	27	L3	D10	W20
7	9	Kent	8	67	2	4	2	6	21	W17	D8	L3
8	7	Derbyshire	10	61*	1	5	4	10	27	L3	D10	L2
9	8	Hampshire	9	57	1	3	5	6	27	D7	L3	W18

* Deducted 8pts for sub-standard pitch

LIONS READY FOR KEY NCL PROMOTION BATTLE

The Surrey Lions' first NCL match following a two-week break brought about by the ongoing One-Day International Triangular Tournament pitted them against the Glamorgan Dragons, who had gradually moved up to third place in the table after a poor start to their campaign, including that first-match defeat at the hands of the Lions in Cardiff. With both teams halfway through their sixteen-match programme and Surrey eight points better off, this really did look to be a key game. While Glamorgan had the opportunity to cut the gap to a mere four points, a win for the Lions would open up a twelve-point chasm that the Dragons would surely struggle to close in their remaining seven games. This was a real eight-pointer, therefore, and a Surrey victory would represent a huge step forward in the club's promotion campaign.

NCL DIVISION TWO - MATCH NINE

SURREY LIONS versus GLAMORGAN DRAGONS
at The Oval on Sunday 16th July

Surrey Lions (268-5) beat Glamorgan Dragons (201) by 67 runs

A stunning innings of 111 from just 98 balls by Surrey skipper, Adam Hollioake, with brilliant support from Ian Ward, put the Lions almost out of sight by the halfway point of this important NCL encounter and the Glamorgan Dragons were never able to mount a serious challenge, eventually losing by the very substantial margin of sixty-seven runs.

Although the game had started badly for the home side, with Alex Wharf removing Mark Butcher's middle stump and Nadeem Shahid's off stump inside the first three overs with just nine runs on the board, it was pretty much all Surrey thereafter. The recovery was initiated by Ian Ward and Ali Brown, who added sixty-three runs in good time to get their side back on track before Brown's loose drive to mid-on brought the Lions' captain to the wicket in the fourteenth over.

After an unspectacular and, at times, uncertain start, during which he survived a straightforward catch to Steve James at midwicket off Robert Croft when on eighteen, Hollioake steadily upped the tempo, initially through scampering breathtaking singles with the speedy Ward. Before long, both batsmen were finding the gaps in the field with ease and as the power of Hollioake's strokeplay took him through to a 54-ball half-century Glamorgan's fielding simply wilted and the scoring rate soared. Although no bowler escaped punishment, the Surrey skipper was particularly severe on the left-arm spin of Dean Cosker, twice launching him into the pavilion for six as he raced from fifty to a hundred in a mere thirty-eight deliveries. Meanwhile, Ward, though overshadowed by his skipper, continued to play the perfect supporting innings, finding the boundary on five occasions himself and running the Dragons ragged with increasingly audacious stolen singles. Consequently, the Welshmen were looking very dispirited well before the end of the Lions' innings and even after the Surrey skipper's departure with seven balls of the innings remaining their misery was not complete as the younger Hollioake and Jason Ratcliffe flayed Owen Parkin for fourteen runs in the final over.

Needing to score at a run a ball to secure an unlikely victory, Glamorgan were well contained in the vital first fifteen overs by an accurate seven-over spell from Martin Bicknell, after Carl Greenidge had removed the dangerous Matthew Elliott in the sixth over.

Saqlain Mushtaq and Jason Ratcliffe then piled further pressure on the Dragons during valuable holding spells which brought the wicket of Keith Newell with the score on sixty-five, before Ben Hollioake burst into the action by striking two decisive blows in his first over, the twenty-fifth of the innings. Having dismissed Steve James lbw with his fourth delivery, a rapid yorker, he then removed the hard-hitting Michael Powell two balls later with a well-disguised slower off-cutter to leave Glamorgan reeling on the ropes. Four men were now gone with 155 runs still required from twenty overs and, faced with this almost impossible task, it was no surprise that the lower-middle order crumpled in the face of more clever bowling from the Hollioakes. Although Croft and Cosker threw the bat merrily in the later stages, the result had looked a formality long before Ben Hollioake completed a well-deserved four-wicket haul and Greenidge yorked Cosker to end the innings in style.

Surrey Lions (268-5) beat Glamorgan Dragons (201) by 67 runs

Surrey Lions 4pts

SURREY LIONS v GLAMORGAN DRAGONS at THE OVAL. Played on 16th July
Surrey Lions won the toss   Umpires:- N.G. Cowley & P. Willey

SURREY LIONS

Fall of wkt	Batsman	How Out	Score	Balls	4s	6s
1- 2	M.A. Butcher	b Wharf	2	3	0	0
	I.J. Ward	Not Out	90	119	5	0
2- 9	Nadeem Shahid	b Wharf	5	10	1	0
3- 72	A.D. Brown	c James b Dale	26	33	3	0
4- 253	A.J. Hollioake *	b Dale	111	98	11	2
5- 264	B.C. Hollioake	c Wharf b Parkin	11	6	1	0
	J.D. Ratcliffe	Not Out	4	1	1	0
	J.N. Batty +	did not bat				
	M.P. Bicknell	did not bat				
	Saqlain Mushtaq	did not bat				
	C.G. Greenidge	did not bat				
	Extras (13lb, 6w)		19			
	TOTAL	(45 overs)	268-5			

GLAMORGAN bowling

	O	M	R	W
Wharf	9	1	37	2
Parkin	9	0	70	1
Dale	9	0	43	2
Croft	9	0	41	0
Cosker	7	0	47	0
Newell	2	0	17	0

GLAMORGAN DRAGONS

Fall of wkt	Batsman	How Out		Score	Balls	4s	6s
2- 65	K. Newell	c A.J. Hollioake	b Ratcliffe	32	44	4	0
1- 21	M.T.G. Elliott	c Batty	b Greenidge	9	13	1	0
3- 113	S.P. James *		lbw b B.C. Hollioake	36	63	2	0
4- 114	M.J. Powell	c A.J. Hollioake	b B.C. Hollioake	31	29	4	0
6- 130	A. Dale	c Butcher	b A.J. Hollioake	9	11	1	0
5- 130	A.W. Evans		run out	5	15	0	0
7- 147	A.D. Shaw +	c Ratcliffe	b B.C. Hollioake	6	12	0	0
9- 180	R.D.B. Croft	c Ratcliffe	b B.C. Hollioake	24	23	2	1
8- 178	A.G. Wharf		lbw b Saqlain	4	18	0	0
10- 201	D.A. Cosker		b Greenidge	17	15	2	0
	O.T. Parkin		Not Out	5	6	0	0
	Extras (13lb, 4w, 6nb)			23			
	TOTAL		(41.2 overs)	201			

SURREY LIONS bowling

	O	M	R	W
Bicknell	7	0	16	0
Greenidge	7.2	0	43	2
Saqlain	7	0	31	0
Ratcliffe	5	0	29	1
B.C. Hollioake	9	0	42	4
A.J. Hollioake	6	0	27	1

Other NCL Division Two Matches

Victories by both the Warwickshire Bears and the Middlesex Crusaders over lowly opposition had given Surrey's win over Glamorgan even greater significance, since a win for the Dragons would have resulted in the whole of the chasing pack closing in on the Lions. As it was, only the Nottinghamshire Outlaws remained within touching distance.

July 16
Derby:- **Warwickshire Bears beat Derbyshire Scorpions by 45 runs.** Warwickshire 150 in 45 overs (Dean 4-30); Derbyshire 105 in 40.5 overs (Smith 3-10, Brown 3-13). **Warwickshire Bears 4pts**

Southgate:- **Middlesex Crusaders beat Durham Dynamos by 1 run.** Middlesex 173 in 43.4 overs (Killeen 4-18); Durham 172-9 in 45 overs (Katich 70 not out). **Middlesex Crusaders 4pts**

NCL DIVISION TWO AT 16TH JULY

Pos	Prev		P	Pts	W	T	L	N/R	Last	Three	Res
1	2	Surrey Lions	9	32	7	0	0	2	W	W	W
2	1	Nottinghamshire Outlaws	8	28	7	0	1	0	W	W	W
3	4	Warwickshire Bears	8	22	5	1	2	0	W	T	L
4	3	Glamorgan Dragons	9	20	4	2	3	0	L	T	W
=	5	Middlesex Crusaders	9	20	4	1	3	1	W	L	W
6	6	Essex Eagles	8	14	3	0	4	1	W	W	L
7	7	Durham Dynamos	9	8	2	0	7	0	L	W	L
8	8	Derbyshire Scorpions	8	4	1	0	7	0	L	L	L
=	9	Hampshire Hawks	8	4	1	0	7	0	L	L	W

SHAHID AND BROWN PUT YORKSHIRE ON THE RACK

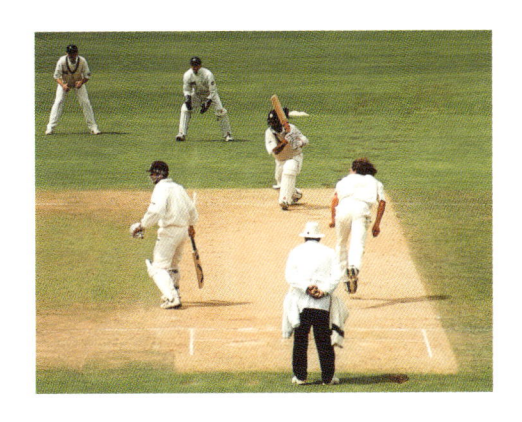

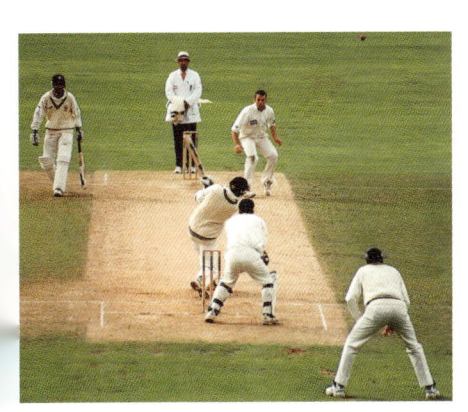

TOP - Nadeem Shahid drives Ryan Sidebottom through extra cover...
MIDDLE - ...and pulls Gary Fellows over square leg
BOTTOM - Ali Brown launches James Middlebrook over wide long-off for the six that took him to his century
All photos by Reg Elliott

DECISIVE MOMENTS AS YORKSHIRE FLOP

TOP - Michael Vaughan has his bails trimmed by Martin Bicknell - 21 for 1
MIDDLE - Ian Salisbury shows his delight after Darren Lehmann holes out to wide mid-on - 65 for 4
BOTTOM - Richard Blakey is palpably lbw to a Salisbury googly - 67 for 5
All photos by Reg Elliott

WARD ANCHORS SURREY AT WOODBRIDGE ROAD

TOP - Ian Ward strikes the ball gloriously through the covers
MIDDLE - Neil Burns jumps for joy as Ben Hollioake is snapped up by Iain Sutcliffe off James Ormond
BOTTOM - Ian Ward clips through midwicket as he closes in on his century
All photos by Steve Porter of The Surrey Advertiser

BICKERS' GLORY DAYS AT GUILDFORD

(Steve Porter of The Surrey Advertiser)

(Reg Elliott)

(John Banfield)

TOP - Bowling to Leicestershire's century-maker, Ben Smith, during his first innings 7 for 72
MIDDLE - Phil DeFreitas becomes Martin Bicknell's thirteenth victim as Mark Butcher pulls off an excellent catch on the third morning
BOTTOM - History has been made and Bicknell leads his team from the field

HONOURS EVEN IN BICKNELL v BICKNELL CLASH

TOP - Darren drives Martin through extra cover
BOTTOM - Martin gets one past Darren's outside edge
Both photos by Terry Habgood of The Surrey Advertiser

TUDOR ROUTS LANCASHIRE FOR 120

TOP - Makeshift opener Glen Chapple edges to Mark Butcher at second slip
MIDDLE - Graham Lloyd snicks his second ball to Jon Batty
BOTTOM - Gary Keedy's edge is picked up by Ben Hollioake at fourth slip to give Alex Tudor his sixth wicket
All photos by Reg Elliott

NATIONAL LEAGUE SNAPSHOTS

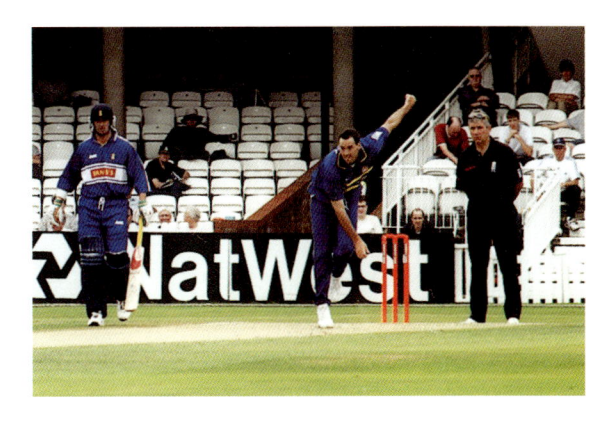

TOP - Martin Bicknell in full flow against the Derbyshire Scorpions at The Oval
MIDDLE - Ali Brown's bails are sent flying by Paul Aldred in the same match
BOTTOM - The blond bombshell! Jason Ratcliffe, a key member of the National League line-up,
in action against the Nottinghamshire Outlaws at Trent Bridge
All photos by Marcus Hook

GARY BUTCHER'S FABULOUS FOUR IN FOUR BALLS

1. The ball that started it all   2. Munton, caught Bicknell   3. Dean, caught Bicknell
4. The umpire's arm begins to rise - Wharton - lbw   5. The innings is over - but not the celebrations
(Photos by Peter C Frost)

11 Bickers' Finest Hours

As the Guildford festival week arrived, Surrey's Championship campaign was gathering momentum but there was no room for complacency since the team was only halfway through the series of four key games against their main rivals, with Leicestershire next to play. Jack Birkenshaw's team had recovered some of the ground lost at Oakham with an emphatic win against Durham at Grace Road and everyone fully appreciated that they would be hell-bent on revenge for their humiliation just two weeks previously. Recent history suggested that Leicestershire faced a tough task, though, since the Guildford Cricket Club ground in Woodbridge Road had become an impregnable fortress for Surrey in recent years, with a run of five successive County Championship wins, dating back to 1995.

Everything was certainly set up for a fantastic festival, with the four-day fixture being followed by the National League visit of second-placed Nottinghamshire Outlaws for a top-of-the-table clash on the Sunday. A feast of cricket lay ahead of us.

COUNTY CHAMPIONSHIP - MATCH ELEVEN

SURREY versus LEICESTERSHIRE
at Guildford

First Day - Wednesday 19th July

Leicestershire 313-9

The Teams And The Toss - *With Alex Tudor still unfit and Carl Greenidge again deputising, Surrey field an unchanged side for the first time this season... but only just. Ian Salisbury, having missed the NCL game against the Glamorgan Dragons because of a shoulder injury, passes a late fitness test but it is rumoured that he is unlikely to be able to bowl on the first day of the match. Leicestershire, meanwhile, show one change from the side that was so soundly thrashed at Oakham School, with Dominic Williamson in for Chris Lewis. Since the pitch looks up to its usual very high standard, Vince Wells has no hesitation in batting when he calls correctly at the toss.*

The game gets off to a very sedate start with Bicknell and Greenidge versus Maddy and Sutcliffe yielding just five runs in the first six overs. It is immediately obvious that this is a good toss for Vince Wells to have won, however, since the pitch looks a beauty, a fact which is underlined by Adam Hollioake's decision to dispense with Carl Greenidge's short leg fielder after just two deliveries.

Following the openers' cautious start, Iain Sutcliffe finally gives the visitors' innings some impetus by penetrating Greenidge's off-side field with two drives in the eighth over before Bicknell hits back for Surrey, striking twice in two overs to cheer the home supporters. Darren Maddy's dire run of dismissals at the hands of the Surrey swing maestro continues when his loose drive results in an edge to Jon Batty behind the wicket with the score on sixteen while Darren Stevens, having snicked the previous delivery over the slips for four, checks a drive and pops the simplest of return catches back to a very grateful bowler with the score advanced by ten. This represents a marvellous start for Surrey and the home county's position almost improves further when Ben Smith, coming in at number four, sees his defensive jab at Bicknell result in a thick edge to the third man boundary.

By the twelfth over Ben Hollioake has replaced Greenidge at the railway end and, after eight excellent overs from the pavilion end, Bicknell gives way to Saqlain Mushtaq. It's a further indication of the quality of the pitch that Hollioake operates with just two slips, and even Saqlain is only prepared to post two close fielders - a slip and a silly point - initially.

With the innings gradually stabilising, Smith reels off a couple of his trademark square cuts and eventually takes his side through to fifty with a pull to the rope at backward square leg off Hollioake. Another pull stroke almost brings about his downfall four overs later, however, when he checks the shot and offers an overhead chance to Greenidge at square leg with his score on eighteen and the total on fifty-nine. Although the young opening bowler makes a fine effort, knocking the ball up and successfully grabbing the rebound as he dives backwards, the ball bounces out of his hands as he hits the ground and Smith survives. It's bad luck on Hollioake, whose opening spell has, generally speaking, been pretty impressive.

As lunch approaches, with Saqlain having switched to the railway end and Bicknell back in the attack for Hollioake, the third-wicket pair registers a fifty partnership when Smith edges the Guildford-born swing bowler just wide of a diving second slip to the third man boundary. It's already abundantly clear that the bowlers are going to need all the luck they can get on this fine track and there would appear to be a heavy workload ahead for Messrs Bicknell and Saqlain - the doubts about the condition of Ian Salisbury's shoulder have been confirmed by the sight of the leg-spinner throwing the ball in under-arm throughout the morning session

Lunch:- Leicestershire 80-2 (Sutcliffe 32*, Smith 34*) from 32 overs

With the exception of a fine forcing stroke to the cover boundary by Smith from Bicknell's first delivery, the second session of the day starts in similar fashion to the first, with very little of note happening for half-a-dozen overs. The first significant event of the afternoon then turns out to be a third wicket for Bicknell and for Surrey when the outside edge of Sutcliffe's defensive bat directs the ball into the midriff of Ali Brown at second slip - Leicestershire 95 for 3.

After making this breakthrough, Surrey's senior seamer delivers another two overs before taking a breather with seventeen overs from the pavilion end already under his belt. Unfortunately, his replacement, Ben Hollioake, is less impressive than in his morning spell, straying too frequently to leg and allowing the visitors to gain the upper hand again, with Smith reaching his half-century from 96 balls in 140 minutes and Aftab Habib playing a couple of elegant strokes through midwicket and square leg. The home side had clearly been gambling on winning the toss and batting first when they selected Salisbury with his shoulder problem and the leg-spinner's absence from Surrey's attack consequently leaves very few options for Adam Hollioake, whose own two-over spell from round the wicket with a defensive field is terminated as the Smith-Habib alliance notches its fiftieth run. Having seen enough of these two batsmen to last a lifetime at The Oval in 1998, Surrey fans are therefore much relieved when Saqlain suddenly provides his side with a much-needed fourth wicket by snaring Habib at short leg in the following over with the score now advanced to 146.

Any hopes that this wicket might lead to one or two more are snuffed out quickly, however, as Smith continues to put away the occasional bad ball in fine style, cutting and forcing Greenidge to the rope at point in the course of an otherwise accurate four-over spell from the pavilion end by the young Surrey paceman. Smith's partner, the Leicestershire captain, Vince Wells, has meanwhile found both his timing and the boundary rather elusive, yet he has played a good enough supporting role for the fifth-wicket stand to reach fifty when Smith cuts the returning Bicknell for four to move his personal tally to ninety. Although he has been brought back at the pavilion end for a mere three overs before tea, Bicknell incredibly, yet almost inevitably, still manages to strike another blow for his side in this time, trapping Wells lbw in his second over as the batsman attempts to play the ball to leg. The local lad now has four wickets to his name and would clearly be the man of the day so far but for the continued presence at the crease of Ben Smith, who moves on to ninety-two, and raises the Leicestershire two-hundred, in the next over from Saqlain.

Since only two more overs remain to be bowled in the session and the first is to be delivered by the in-form Bicknell, there wouldn't be too many people expecting Smith to reach three figures ahead of the break, yet that is exactly what happens. There are no 'nervous nineties' problems for the Corby-born middle-order man as he moves to ninety-six with a forcing stroke to the cover boundary, goes to ninety-eight with a clip through midwicket and then arrives at his century courtesy of another back-foot forcing stroke through extra cover for two. Smith's fine ton, containing fifteen fours, has come from 182 balls in 254 minutes, and it is the first individual Championship hundred conceded by Surrey in the 2000 season to date. This is, therefore, a very significant achievement by the Leicestershire batsman and his innings has ensured that the visitors are in a comfortable position in the match as the interval arrives.

Tea:- Leicestershire 213-5 (Smith 102*, DeFreitas 1*) from 72 overs

Surrey make a dream start to the day's final session when Smith edges Bicknell's fourth delivery to Mark Butcher, the sole slip, without addition to his tea score. It's a vital break for the home team and it gives Bicknell his second five-wicket haul of the season, after failing to achieve the feat at all in 1999.

There is plenty of scope to add to this bag of victims, too, with four wickets still to fall, and five does indeed become six just four overs later when the Leicestershire 'keeper, Neil Burns, nicks the ball to his opposite number with the score at 226. This is sensational stuff from Bicknell and he comes within an ace of picking up a seventh wicket in his following over, inducing another catch to the wicketkeeper, from Phillip DeFreitas, only to have his ecstasy translated into agony by umpire Mallender's cry of 'no ball'.

On a beautiful day and with the pitch playing splendidly, Surrey can now justifiably claim to be well on top, although there is still potential danger in the lack of top quality support bowling for Bicknell and Saqlain, who, by this stage, have delivered fifty-two of the seventy-seven overs bowled. Apart from missing an occasional over when changing ends, the Pakistani off-spinner has, in fact, bowled straight through from the seventeenth over of the day and has done a wonderful containing job for his skipper. Both Surrey bowlers must be tired, however, and when Bicknell again takes his sweater after a six-over post-tea stint, DeFreitas and Dominic Williamson gradually begin to rebuild the wreckage of the Leicestershire innings.

The sheer brilliance of Bicknell's bowling is underlined - and the efforts of some of the earlier batsmen put into perspective - as the eighth-wicket pair compiles a fifty partnership with relatively few alarms. The most disappointing feature of this stand, from Surrey's point of view, is that they have contributed nineteen of the fifty runs in extras, while the total number of sundries for the innings has, in the meantime, reached an unwanted half-century.

As this dangerous-looking partnership has been developing, Ian Salisbury has been seen doing a lot of shoulder-twirling and, with Saqlain looking a spent force after a marathon spell of thirty-five overs, the leg-spinner duly enters the fray, in place of his spin twin, with fifteen overs remaining in the day's play. Almost inevitably, this change nearly brings the crucial breakthrough as Salisbury finds Williamson's outside edge, only for the chance to go begging as the ball somehow fails to stick in either the gloves of Batty or the hands of Butcher at slip.

While Salisbury continues to show no obvious ill effects from his injury, Ben Hollioake completes a rather unlucky five-over burst from the pavilion end by seeing Williamson top-edge an attempted hook to the boundary, and Greenidge gives his all for three overs without looking likely to make the break that his team needs. Leicestershire meanwhile pass three-hundred in the ninety-fourth over and, with Williamson driving fluently through the covers on the way to his career-best Championship score, it begins to look as if the visitors might end the day with a slight advantage until a double bowling change yields double dividends for Adam Hollioake. The Surrey skipper brings himself into the attack at the pavilion end with four overs to play and the final delivery of his first over produces an edged drive from Williamson which Jon Batty appears to catch well, low down to his right. Neither the striker nor his partner, DeFreitas, are convinced that the ball has carried to the 'keeper, however, and it takes a considerable amount of debate - some of it, largely involving DeFreitas, looking to be rather heated - before the umpires rule that the batsman is out. While Williamson departs the scene very reluctantly and excruciatingly slowly, the former England seamer continues to rail at all and sundry, including the umpires.

All-in-all it's a pretty unattractive scenario and DeFreitas' petulance then appears to bring about his downfall from the very next ball bowled. Having recalled Saqlain for one last effort in place of Salisbury, the Surrey captain's decision is wholly vindicated when he picks up a low catch at backward point from DeFreitas' angry miscued square slash. The equilibrium of the game appears to have been restored and the Surrey team leaves the field owing a huge debt of gratitude to Martin Bicknell (26-5-70-6) and Saqlain Mushtaq (37-8-92-2) for sixty-three overs of very hard graft.

Close:- Leicestershire 313-9 (Kumble 0*, Ormond 1*) from 104 overs

VIEW FROM THE DRESSING ROOM - MARTIN BICKNELL

It looked a very good pitch indeed at Woodbridge Road so I guess we were disappointed to lose the toss and have to field first?
MB - The pitch looked an absolute belter, as it has done for the past five or six years in particular, but we weren't as disappointed as we might have been to lose the toss, given the recent history of Guildford. For the last few years the side that has won the toss and batted first has been in all sorts of trouble early on with the ball swinging around quite a lot. So it was no surprise to us that the ball started swinging from ball one of this game.

You started as you were to go on with a couple of early wickets. Did you have any indication, at that stage, of your fortunes for the rest of the match - did you feel in an especially good rhythm, for example?
MB - It's always nice to pick up a couple of wickets early on because that sets you up well for the rest of the game and I certainly felt that I was in a really good rhythm and that the ball was coming out nicely. When you turn up at Guildford, as a bowler, you think there's not much there for you, what with a great wicket, short boundaries and a fast outfield, but the one thing that's generally in your favour is that the ball does swing, which is handy for me since that is obviously what I specialise in. So that was very much in my favour throughout the match.

We only conceded one century in the 2000 Championship - Ben Smith's 102 in this match. I guess that all our bowlers must be very proud of that statistic?
MB - Yes, very much so - and we've got to the stage now where we begrudge anybody getting a hundred against us. But Ben Smith played very well - he got stuck in and it was very hard to dislodge him.

Were we happy with our overall performance in containing Leicestershire to 312-9 on the first day?
MB - We felt we'd done really well - on what was quite a warm day we thought we'd stuck to our task and bowled well for most of the day. We were then backing ourselves to go past them and make a big score.

You shouldered a very heavy load, along with Saqlain, on the first day. Tudes was out injured and I believe Solly had been advised not to bowl on the first day because of a shoulder injury?
MB - That's right, Solly wasn't supposed to bowl at all on day one, but then, to be fair, he doesn't often bowl that much in the first innings of games anyway. It was a bit of a risk for us to play him but we thought we could get through okay - Saqi and I knew that we would be bowling a lot of overs and that the other bowlers would be capable of filling in around us.

VIEW FROM THE DRESSING ROOM - IAN WARD

I would imagine that you must have been keen to bat first on what looked like a lovely Woodbridge Road track?
IW - Yes, it's always a good pitch at Guildford and the festival week is usually blessed with good weather and a nice atmosphere, too. Our game plan is always to try and win the toss, bat first on a good pitch, build a big total and then let the spinners get to work as the wicket deteriorates, so it was a bit disappointing not to get first use of a good pitch but you have to deal with these things - and in the end we dealt very well with them in this game.

Ben Smith chalked up the only century scored against us in the 2000 Championship in this match - I guess that speaks volumes for the amazing efforts of the bowlers again this season?
IW - You don't win the Championship without the bowlers making a massive contribution - it's not an easy task to take twenty wickets to win a match. And not only do our bowlers take wickets, they score runs as well, so it's fair to say that our four main bowlers have really all stuck their hands up and grabbed the Championship for us in two consecutive years now.

Second Day - Thursday 20th July

Leicestershire 318 and 33-6; Surrey 288

There are no prizes for guessing which two bowlers are in harness as Surrey strive to finish the Leicestershire first innings as swiftly as possible on the second morning! Just five runs are added in four overs before Martin Bicknell strikes with the first ball of his third over of the day, having Anil Kumble taken behind the wicket to end with a haul of seven wickets for seventy-two runs. It's been an awesome display of fast-medium swing bowling in conditions which have favoured the batsmen and as he again leads the team from the field he will doubtless be hoping that he can put his feet up for a day or so while the batsmen build a big total.

Alas, things don't start well for either Mark Butcher or umpire Neil Mallender as the Surrey left-hander is adjudged to have feathered the third ball of the innings, a legside delivery from James Ormond, through to the wicketkeeper. Sometimes, even from the distance of the boundary, you just know that an umpire's decision is wrong and this is a case in point - the appeal seems unconvincing and the raising of the finger even more so. That said, it has to be admitted that umpiring is a very tough job when the ball is being propelled towards the batsman at the kind of speed that can be generated by a bowler of Ormond's pace.

Fortunately for Surrey, Ian Ward and Nadeem Shahid respond well to this early setback, safely negotiating Ormond's initial four-over blast from the pavilion end and then picking off a string of boundaries in the four overs, from DeFreitas and Wells, that elapse before he returns at the railway end. In the young fast bowler's absence the score has rattled past fifty at almost five runs an over, with Shahid having so far found the boundary five times to Ward's four.

With Wells' three overs having yielded seventeen runs, DeFreitas switches ends, too, but it's still Ormond who looks the more threatening bowler in these early stages, the sturdy speedster striking Ward on the body a couple of times before 'box-ing' the unfortunate Shahid. The batsmen battle on bravely, though, and, while Ward keeps the scoreboard ticking with well taken singles, it's his partner who dominates by driving DeFreitas for two fours and then following up with a brace of off-side boundaries off Ormond.

With lunch only minutes away, things are looking good for the home side but the old ploy of trying an over of spin before the break works wonders for Wells as Shahid spoons Kumble's final delivery tamely to Ben Smith at midwicket. It's a great shame that a fine, positive innings of forty-seven has ended with an apparently indecisive stroke, especially since it evens up the match position once again.

Lunch:- Surrey 93-2 (Ward 37) from 24 overs*

DeFreitas and Kumble open proceedings for Leicestershire upon the resumption, with the former managing to get several deliveries past the outside edge of Ian Ward's bat and the latter enjoying a good contest with the new batsman, Adam Hollioake. The Surrey captain drives the Indian leg-spinner through the covers for four and then pulls him to the midwicket boundary two overs later but, sandwiched between these impressive strokes, there is a strong suspicion of a dropped catch by Burns behind the wicket with Hollioake on twelve.

As things turn out, this apparent miss doesn't prove costly since Jimmy Ormond accounts for the home skipper soon afterwards with his first delivery after replacing Kumble at the railway end. Unable to resist the challenge of a bouncer, Hollioake hooks the ball straight to DeFreitas at long leg and departs for eighteen with the total at 123.

Although Alistair Brown almost immediately pulls Leicestershire's young quick bowler to the rope at midwicket, Surrey suddenly hit the buffers for a period as Ward's sticky patch against DeFreitas continues and Ormond puts in another very sharp burst. Despite his temporary difficulties, Ward maintains his level of concentration impressively and eventually moves through to a valuable fifty from 129 balls in 174 minutes with a single to square leg as the game remains nicely poised. The visitors do win a minor victory of sorts shortly afterwards, however, when Brown sustains a nasty crack on the wrist in attempting another pull at Ormond and, after lengthy treatment, opts to retire hurt on five with the score standing at 138 for 3.

This brings the out-of-form Ben Hollioake to the crease with just ninety-one Championship runs, at an average of 9.10, to his name. These statistics seem hard to believe as he immediately drives Ormond down the ground for a most majestic boundary but, thereafter, runs prove much harder to come by as the Leicestershire opening bowlers continue to plug away with commendable accuracy.

DeFreitas and Ormond are unable to keep going for much longer, though, and, having delivered fourteen overs in harness, Vince Wells is eventually forced into a double change which sees Kumble and Williamson recalled to the attack.

This relieves some of the pressure on the batsmen and Ward, enjoying a little more freedom against the new bowlers, soon picks up a couple of boundaries to move his score into the seventies. Hollioake then follows up with a brace of fours through the on-side and, since batting is now looking reasonably straightforward and the fourth-wicket pair is propelling Surrey towards two-hundred, Wells is obliged to act again. After an initial move to switch Kumble to the pavilion end, he decides to recall Ormond at the railway end to bowl some off-breaks and reaps an almost instant reward when Hollioake is well caught by Sutcliffe at short leg from the young paceman's fifth delivery in this new style. Needless to say, the bowler and his team-mates are jubilant and the skipper gets a hefty pat on the back.

With Ali Brown's further participation in the innings, and indeed the match, uncertain at this stage, Leicestershire are now very much in contention again and they take another step towards equality when Kumble quickly removes Jon Batty, who, much like Shahid before him, pops up a simple catch to midwicket and goes for three to leave Surrey on 209-5.

Much to the relief of the home county's fans, the question as to whether Brown will be able to bat again is now answered by the sight of him emerging from the pavilion. There appears to be no serious damage to Surrey's middle-order mainstay, either, as he quickly drives Kumble to the extra cover boundary, while Ward moves into the nineties with a similar stroke at the expense of Ormond.

Tea is now almost upon us but it doesn't stop Brown from lofting the part-time 'offie' back over his head for another boundary - gaining a measure of revenge for the damage inflicted upon his wrist in the process - nor from enjoying further success during a bizarre final over of the session from Kumble. After Ward moves on to ninety-six with a glanced single and Brown picks up two runs through extra cover, the Indian leg-spinner proceeds to concede almost a full set of extras - a no-ball, four byes and a legside wide - before Brown pulls the final delivery to square leg for four. As the players leave the field Surrey look to be in control again and Ian Ward is in the now familiar position of heading off for a break just short of a century.

Tea:- Surrey 247-5 (Ward 96*, Brown 21*) from 65 overs

DeFreitas and Ormond (faster version!) are back in tandem after tea as Leicestershire strive to regain the ground they lost in the closing overs before the break. While Ward progresses to ninety-nine with three singles in the first five overs of the session, Brown on-drives both bowlers to the boundary as Surrey close to within sixty runs of the opposition's total. With the field brought in to block Ward's easiest route to three figures, he puts the crowd on tenterhooks by flashing nervously at a rather wide DeFreitas delivery before finally driving wide of mid-on for three to complete his second Championship hundred of the season from 206 balls in just two minutes under five hours. His terrific effort has, like Smith's century on day one, underpinned an otherwise undistinguished batting display by his team. Unlike Leicestershire, the hosts do still have power to add to their total of 265, however, since they still have five wickets in the bank.

Unfortunately for Surrey, five wickets soon becomes four, however, when Brown top-edges a cut at the final delivery of the next over from Ormond and departs for thirty-four with the total on 266.

And then four becomes three. After Ward drives DeFreitas to the boundary over the head of the man at cover, Martin Bicknell falls lbw to the second ball he faces from Ormond. The impressive young Leicestershire paceman has completed a well-deserved five-wicket haul and Surrey's prospects of gaining a significant first innings lead are receding at 270-7.

Things are rapidly going from bad to worse for the home side now and the chances of them enjoying any advantage at all at the end of their innings then evaporate almost completely in the very next over when Ward's attempt to loft DeFreitas over the off-side field for a second time results only in a catch to Habib at cover. This hard-earned wicket for the persevering DeFreitas has, at a stroke, terminated an excellent innings of 107 and reduced Surrey to 272-8.

It is now obvious to everyone that this is a serious game-changing collapse, with three wickets having vanished in four overs, and it quickly becomes four in five when Saqlain becomes Ormond's sixth victim of the innings just five balls later. The comparison between the lower-order's efforts here and at Oakham couldn't be more marked as the Surrey spin maestro gift-wraps his wicket with a wild attempted pull shot that merely skies the ball high to Habib at point. Saqlain out for one, Surrey 273-9.

The only glimmer of resistance from the tail on this occasion comes with a flurry of three boundaries from the final pair. Salisbury cuts and pulls successive fours off Ormond and then Carl Greenidge unleashes a magnificent hooked boundary in the big quickie's next over. After forty minutes of sheer misery for the home supporters, during which their team has slipped from 266-5 to 273-9, this classical stroke from the Surrey number eleven, son of the former

West Indian Test great, at least brings smiles back to a few faces, since it is followed instantly by a voice in the crowd chanting 'Are you Gordon in disguise?'!

Unfortunately, Greenidge adds only a single to his score before Kumble claims him lbw, a big forward stride failing to save the batsman from the umpire's finger. The final Surrey total is, therefore, a very disappointing 288, leaving Leicestershire with a useful, though not particularly significant, thirty-run lead, when it really had seemed that the home county was set fair for a lead of maybe 100-plus. While everyone with Surrey at heart digests this rather unpalatable fact, Jimmy Ormond leads his team from the field with a well-merited 6 for 87 analysis to his name. It represents a fine effort from a very promising young bowler.

With fourteen overs remaining for play, Surrey's best hope now is to pick up the consolation prize of a couple of wickets before the close to balance up the contest again, and there's a clear feeling that a crucial phase of the match lies ahead as the Surrey team takes to the field.

The opening over sees Martin Bicknell bowling to one of his county 'bunnies', Darren Maddy, and the Surrey swing bowler gets the home crowd buzzing almost instantly by uprooting the former England batsman's off stump with his sixth ball. It looks to have been a special delivery which has sent Maddy packing and completed a 2000 sequence against Bicknell of 10, 0, 3, 0 - two catches to the wicketkeeper, one catch to third slip and, now, a clean bowled.

This is just the start that the reigning champions needed and things get even better for them in Bicknell's second over when the left-handed Iain Sutcliffe loses his middle stump to a ball which appears to swing back through the gate as he attempts to drive. It's 7 for 2 and Surrey are coming right back into the match, much to the delight of their supporters.

With the game suddenly back in the balance, a quiet spell of play ensues as the batsmen try to re-establish some degree of control for their side and the bowlers maintain a disciplined line and length in an attempt to force an error. This period of inactivity doesn't last too long, however, and it turns out to have been the calm that precedes the storm. Once Darren Stevens has broken out against Bicknell with two boundaries - one to square leg, one down the ground - and a clip to square leg for two, the Surrey storm erupts.

Stevens pays a heavy price for taking those ten runs from Bicknell's fifth over as a flashing edge to the first ball of the bowler's next over results in a catch to Mark Butcher at second slip. It's the former Guildford C.C. bowler's tenth wicket of the match and it pegs Leicestershire back to 31-3.

Then, four balls later, it's 31-4 as nightwatchman, Neil Burns, becomes Bicknell's eleventh victim, falling lbw as he is defeated by inswing. The crowd erupts again, excited by the realisation that Surrey now have the upper hand in the match, and when the new batsman, Aftab Habib, plays and misses at his first ball a collective gasp goes up all around the ground. A haul of four wickets in this final session is clearly beyond Surrey's wildest dreams - and there are still three overs left to bowl!

Leicestershire negotiate the first of these overs safely enough as Greenidge racks up a fourth consecutive maiden but, four balls into the day's penultimate over, disaster strikes for the visitors again with the loss of Habib, taken by Butcher at second slip off the remarkable Bicknell. The innings is in tatters at 33 for 5 and Surrey's senior seamer now has five-out-of-five and a bag of twelve wickets in a match for the first time in his career. It's stunning stuff and the atmosphere in the ground is absolutely electric for the bowler's last two deliveries of the day. Despite this, Vince Wells manages to play out the remainder of the over and as the public address announcer reads out Martin Bicknell's end-of-day figures of 7-2-24-5 every single one of his team-mates rushes over to high-five him and the crowd offers up an amazing ovation.

How can Carl Greenidge possibly follow this as he runs in to deliver the final over of an unbelievable session of cricket? His task seems impossible but he finds the perfect answer when he manages to swing his second delivery back into Ben Smith as the batsman shoulders arms - the ball thuds into Smith's pad, the players go up in appeal, the crowd joins in, and the umpire agrees... it's out! Phenomenal! Leicestershire are 33-6, the Surrey players celebrate joyously, the supporters are in ecstasy and Martin Bicknell leaves the field a hero, with applause ringing in his ears.

Just over an hour ago the match looked to be tilted slightly in the visitors' favour and Surrey fans were in despair after their team's dramatic collapse. Now, the home team has the game almost won and the supporters are on cloud nine. An incredible final session of the day has seen eleven wickets fall for just seventy-four runs, largely as a result of some outstanding bowling from Messrs Ormond and Bicknell, and a game has been transformed, not once, but twice. Unfortunately for Leicestershire, but happily for Surrey, the second transformation looks likely to prove decisive!

Close:- Leicestershire 33-6 (Wells 0*) from 13.2 overs

VIEW FROM THE DRESSING ROOM - MARTIN BICKNELL

As a fellow opening bowler, how did you rate Jimmy Ormond?
MB - I was very impressed - he's a big strong lad, he's quick, he swings the ball away and he looks to have good control, so I think he's got a big future in the game. He's not had a good run with injuries so far in his career, but if he does then I think there's a huge possibility that he will play for England in the not-too-distant future.

Although we collapsed at the end of the day I guess it turned out to be a blessing in disguise?!
MB - We were very disappointed to have collapsed as we did as it was one of the few times all season where the lower-order didn't make a contribution. We played some very average shots and we knew we were short of runs, so it was a real 'downer'. At that stage we really envisaged day three becoming a long hard struggle because the pitch wasn't turning as such and there was nothing much there for the seamers. But fourteen overs was a good period of time to bowl for and we knew that a couple of wickets would get us back in the game. It just turned out to be an amazing session!

You clearly enjoy bowling to Darren Maddy! Any reason why he should be such a regular Bicknell victim?
MB - Both times when we played Leicestershire the ball did swing and I find that he's a bit vulnerable when the ball swings away because he does tend to push at the ball a bit outside off stump. The shot he played in the first innings at Guildford wasn't too clever but I managed to find a rip-snorter for him in the second innings that very few people would have been able to play. It came out beautifully and from the moment I let go of it I knew it was going to be a very good ball - it started to swing just before it pitched and it hit the top of his off stump and knocked it out. There's no better sight than that for a bowler.

I guess it was almost a repeat of Guildford 1999, third evening, with the players and the crowd really up for it and a good atmosphere in the ground? You said to me last year that during that period in the 1999 game 'we knew we were doing something special'... but that wasn't a patch on this. This period effectively decided the game, didn't it?
MB - Adam Hollioake said to me that it was one of the most incredible experiences of his cricketing career yet, at the time, it all just seemed very unreal to me. It was very strange - I got the first two wickets with really good deliveries and after that I didn't feel that I bowled especially well, certainly not as well as in the first innings. I wasn't really comfortable with how I was bowling, I didn't feel I had a great deal of rhythm and I was still feeling a bit tired after my bowling in the first innings, yet everything happened for me - the ball swung a bit and they

played a couple of loose shots after the two initial good balls. Adam also told me that he thought it was the quickest I'd bowled all season and that he felt I was going to get a wicket with every ball - but it didn't feel that way to me. All very strange.

VIEW FROM THE DRESSING ROOM - IAN WARD

Did we feel that Leicestershire's first innings total of 318 was a little below par?
IW - We were very pleased with our efforts because that sort of score at Guildford, with its short boundaries and fast outfield, would only be worth about 270 on most grounds - and, generally speaking, if you win the toss and bat then you would be disappointed with 270. It also meant that we could get in to bat while the pitch was still firm and playing well.

After Mark Butcher had been out in unfortunate circumstances, you and Nadeem Shahid got us off to a good start. I thought that Nad took his chance really well after getting back into the first team - I guess it demonstrated the strength in depth of the squad again?
IW - Absolutely. It's very difficult when you're in and out of the side in cricket, or any sport for that matter, and we've had a few guys, myself included, over the past few years who have sometimes found themselves back in the second eleven even after a good first team performance, which is obviously very frustrating and disappointing. But you have to show a bit of character, as Nad did here - he played exceptionally well and very positively. He was in early after Butch got a pretty ordinary decision, but he and I managed to get stuck in, the runs flowed and that set us up nicely for the rest of the innings.

Although we collapsed at the end of the day I guess it proved to be a blessing in disguise as Bickers ripped through their top order in the fourteen overs that remained. What can you say about that amazing period of play?
IW - The first thing I must say is that if I'd done my job properly and played through to the close with Solly then we wouldn't have been treated to the sight of Bickers destroying them in those last fourteen overs. I suppose every now and again you get your just deserts as a bowler - there have been days when he's run up and beaten the outside edge countless times, had decisions go against him, had catches dropped and bowled beautifully for just one or two wickets but, on this occasion, he got it absolutely spot-on and got everything he deserved. It was just sensational and an absolute pleasure to be out there on the field when he did it.

Third Day - Friday 21st July

Leicestershire 318 and 87; Surrey 288 and 119-0

Surrey beat Leicestershire by ten wickets
Surrey 17pts, Leicestershire 6

At the end of Surrey's first innings yesterday evening the match had looked set to go well into day four but now we are faced with an early finish as the 1998 county champions start day three leading by sixty-three runs with just four wickets to fall.

In truth, the match appears to be almost in the bag for Surrey since the pitch is still looking immaculate as Martin Bicknell and Carl Greenidge attempt to carry on where they had left off the previous evening. They are in for an initial shock, though. Making their intentions very clear, right from the off, Vince Wells and Phillip DeFreitas launch a stunning offensive which, in the space of three overs, brings five boundaries, the most amazing of which is a lofted square drive for six by Wells off Bicknell. This apparent do-or-die effort by the Leicestershire duo fails to completely unsettle the bowlers, however, as Greenidge sees an edge by DeFreitas fly off to the third man boundary and Bicknell appears to trap Wells plumb lbw, only to be denied by a no-ball call.

After another short burst of scoring by DeFreitas off Greenidge, which includes two well-struck off-side fours, Bicknell is back in business in the eighth over of the morning. His thirteenth wicket of the match comes when DeFreitas' flashing outside edge is brilliantly picked up by Mark Butcher diving low to his left at second slip. Forty-seven runs have been added by Leicestershire in a mere seven overs this morning but the departure of the former England seamer for twenty-four almost ends the Foxes dreams of an incredible recovery.

Their final glimmer of hope is then extinguished just two balls later when Bicknell takes his personal wicket tally to a fabulous fourteen by removing the Leicestershire skipper with the aid of another sharp catch, this time by Ali Brown at first slip. The Surrey team celebrates and the crowd, though much smaller today because of the possibility of an early finish, shows full appreciation for the incredible Bicknell. How much further can he go? Sixteen is the goal but surely that's asking too much?

After Anil Kumble drives his first delivery from Bicknell to the rope at long-off there's a lull in the action for three overs before Saqlain Mushtaq replaces Greenidge at the railway end. With the Pakistani spin wizard into the attack, and numbers nine and ten at the crease, it's clear that Bicknell will have to act fast if he wants to increase his tally of wickets... and he does.

The third ball of his very next over brings the wicket of Kumble, who advances and drives airily to Ben Hollioake at point to become victim number eight in the innings, fifteen in the match and fifty for the summer, making Bicknell the first man in the country to this milestone in the 2000 season.

But can he still go one better? He can! The Surrey swing king ends the Leicestershire innings two balls later by knocking back Jimmy Ormond's off stump and he thereby increases his final haul of wickets to a very sweet sixteen. Martin Bicknell has written his name large in the record books. The players rush to rejoice with the sixteen-wicket man of the moment, the crowd goes wild with delight, the statisticians start leafing through the record books and Surrey know that they require just 118 runs to pull off a very important victory in the race for the title. Although many Surrey supporters immediately realise that Bicknell's second innings figures of 9 for 47 represent a County Championship best, only narrowly failing to beat his best first-class return of 9 for 45 against Cambridge University at The Oval in 1988, the thing that nobody appreciates until later is that his match figures of 16 for 119 are the best in England since Jim Laker's 19 for 90 in the Old Trafford Test of 1956! This is an act of real cricketing history that we have seen played out in front of us.

As the crowd cheers and applauds the modest Bicknell from the field, you get the feeling that everyone is simply lost in admiration for an extraordinary feat of fast-medium bowling in conditions which, swing excepted, have favoured the batsmen throughout. Those of us who are here to witness this performance can consider ourselves truly fortunate.

Once all the excitement has died down, the Surrey openers emerge with a major job to do. If they can see off the opening spells of Ormond and DeFreitas then Surrey should be virtually home and dry, since a solid start should make the victory target of 118 a mere formality.

Perhaps lifted and driven on by the emotion generated by their colleague's monumental bowling display, Butcher and Ward start confidently and when both men pick up an off-side boundary apiece in Ormond's third over you can almost see the Leicestershire team's last vestige of optimism draining away. At the end of the over the young fast bowler then leaves the field, presumably suffering from some kind of injury, and with him, you feel, goes the visitors' minuscule chance of winning the match and, quite possibly, also the Championship.

By the simple expedient of picking off the occasional boundary and taking short singles wherever possible, the Surrey openers move their side ever closer to victory as Vince Wells rests DeFreitas and pairs Kumble with Williamson. There are no real alarms along the way to a fifty partnership but this is hardly surprising since the pitch remains a belter, a fact that further emphasises the outstanding quality of Martin Bicknell's record-breaking performance.

Lunch:- Surrey 53-0 (Butcher 18*, Ward 29*) from 19 overs

Any thoughts that Leicestershire might not have thrown in the towel are quickly dispelled after lunch by the sight of Phillip DeFreitas purveying his off-spin from the pavilion end. A series of misfields in the early overs just adds to the impression of a demoralised and well-beaten side going through the motions, though, to be fair to the visitors, they never allow the scoring rate to reach three an over.

Since Ormond hasn't reappeared after the interval and Kumble is not called upon to bowl, Darren Maddy gets a chance to turn his arm over as Ward picks up singles almost at will, looking very much a man in form. While Butcher actually finds the boundary with greater frequency, it's his partner who scores at the faster rate and completes his second fifty of the match from 96 balls as the end becomes nigh.

Surrey are finally helped on their way to their sixth consecutive County Championship win at Woodbridge Road by some less-than-impressive occasional spin bowling from Iain Sutcliffe and by 2.55pm the county champions have completed a ten-wicket win which seemed absolutely impossible less than twenty-four hours earlier when they had been bowled out thirty runs in arrears of the opposition. But then we know who to thank for that!

Leicestershire 318 and 87; Surrey 288 and 119-0
Surrey won by ten wickets. Surrey 17pts, Leicestershire 6

SURREY v LEICESTERSHIRE at GUILDFORD. Played from 19th - 21st July
Leicestershire won the toss   Umpires:- V.A. Holder & N.A. Mallender

LEICESTERSHIRE - First Innings   SURREY bowling

Fall of wkt	Batsman	How Out		Score	Balls	4s	6s		O	M	R	W
1- 16	D.L. Maddy	c Batty	b Bicknell	3	24	0	0	Bicknell	28.1	5	72	7
3- 95	I.J. Sutcliffe	c Brown	b Bicknell	37	119	5	0	Greenidge	12	2	35	0
2- 26	D.I. Stevens		c & b Bicknell	6	7	1	0	B.C. Hollioake	19	5	74	0
6- 214	B.F. Smith	c Butcher	b Bicknell	102	191	15	0	Saqlain	39	9	93	2
4- 146	A. Habib	c Shahid	b Saqlain	20	41	3	0	A.J. Hollioake	4	2	8	1
5- 199	V.J. Wells *		lbw b Bicknell	15	57	2	0	Salisbury	6	1	9	0
9- 312	P.A.J. DeFreitas	c A.J. Hollioake	b Saqlain	27	88	2	0					
7- 226	N.D. Burns +	c Batty	b Bicknell	4	17	1	0					
8- 312	D. Williamson	c Batty	b A.J. Hollioake	47	76	6	0					
10- 318	A. Kumble	c Batty	b Bicknell	2	17	0	0					
	J. Ormond		Not Out	2	25	0	0					
	Extras (4b, 23lb, 26nb)			53								
	TOTAL		(108.1 overs)	318								

SURREY - First Innings   LEICESTERSHIRE bowling

Fall of wkt	Batsman	How Out		Score	Balls	4s	6s		O	M	R	W
1- 2	M.A. Butcher	c Burns	b Ormond	0	3	0	0	Ormond	29	6	87	6
8- 272	I.J. Ward	c Habib	b DeFreitas	107	215	14	0	DeFreitas	25	7	76	1
2- 93	Nadeem Shahid	c Smith	b Kumble	47	75	9	0	Wells	4	0	25	0
3- 123	A.J. Hollioake *	c DeFreitas	b Ormond	18	26	3	0	Williamson	6	0	17	0
6- 266	A.D. Brown	c Burns	b Ormond	34	70	6	0	Kumble	17	1	68	3
4- 198	B.C. Hollioake	c Sutcliffe	b Ormond	21	57	3	0					
5- 209	J.N. Batty +	c Habib	b Kumble	3	6	0	0					
7- 270	M.P. Bicknell		lbw b Ormond	0	2	0	0					
	I.D.K. Salisbury		Not Out	10	16	2	0					
9- 273	Saqlain Mushtaq	c Habib	b Ormond	1	4	0	0					
10- 288	C.G. Greenidge		lbw b Kumble	6	23	1	0					
	Extras (12b, 3lb, 4w, 22nb)			41								
	TOTAL		(81 overs)	288								

LEICESTERSHIRE - Second Innings   SURREY bowling

Fall of wkt	Batsman	How Out		Score	Balls	4s	6s		O	M	R	W
1- 0	D.L. Maddy		b Bicknell	0	6	0	0	Bicknell	12.5	3	47	9
2- 7	I.J. Sutcliffe		b Bicknell	7	5	1	0	Greenidge	11	6	35	1
6- 33	B.F. Smith		lbw b Greenidge	8	37	2	0	Saqlain	1	0	2	0
3- 31	D.I. Stevens	c Butcher	b Bicknell	14	22	3	0					
4- 31	N.D. Burns +		lbw b Bicknell	0	4	0	0					
5- 33	A. Habib	c Butcher	b Bicknell	2	5	0	0					
8- 81	V.J. Wells *	c Brown	b Bicknell	17	23	2	1					
7- 80	P.A.J. DeFreitas	c Butcher	b Bicknell	24	23	5	0					
	D. Williamson		Not Out	1	10	0	0					
9- 87	A. Kumble	c B.C. Hollioake	b Bicknell	5	14	1	0					
10- 87	J. Ormond		b Bicknell	0	2	0	0					
	Extras (3lb, 2w, 4nb)			9								
	TOTAL		(24.5 overs)	87								

SURREY - Second Innings   LEICESTERSHIRE bowling

Fall of wkt	Batsman	How Out	Score	Balls	4s	6s		O	M	R	W
	M.A. Butcher	Not Out	47	122	8	0	Ormond	3	1	14	0
	I.J. Ward	Not Out	61	116	6	0	DeFreitas	15	2	30	0
							Williamson	7	2	17	0
							Kumble	3	1	5	0
							Wells	4	1	13	0
							Maddy	3	0	11	0
							Stevens	3	0	8	0
	Extras (3b, 6lb, 2nb)		11				Sutcliffe	1.3	0	12	0
	TOTAL	(39.3 overs)	119 - 0								

173

MARTIN BICKNELL'S RECORD-BREAKING PERFORMANCE

INNINGS ANALYSIS - 9 for 47

Career-best in the County Championship
beating 7 for 52 against Sussex at The Oval, 1991

Best in first-class cricket at Woodbridge Road, Guildford
beating Tony Lock's 9 for 77 for Surrey against Oxford University, 1960

Best in the County Championship at Woodbridge Road, Guildford
beating Peter Loader's 7 for 36 for Surrey against Hampshire, 1957

Best for Surrey against Leicestershire
beating 8 for 44 by Henry Lockwood at Leicester, 1898 and Bill Hitch at Leicester, 1913

Best in the County Championship since Richard Johnson's 10 for 45
for Middlesex against Derbyshire at Derby, 1994

MATCH ANALYSIS - 16 for 119

Career-best in the County Championship
beating 11 for 108 against Sussex at Hove, 1993

Best in first-class cricket at Woodbridge Road, Guildford
beating Tony Lock's 12 for 148 for Surrey against Oxford University, 1960

Best in the County Championship at Woodbridge Road, Guildford
beating Peter Loader's 11 for 70 for Surrey against Hampshire, 1957

Best for Surrey against Leicestershire
beating 15 for 113 by Tom Richardson at The Oval, 1896

Best in England since Jim Laker's 19 for 90
for England v Australia at Old Trafford, 1956

Best in first-class cricket, globally, since Anil Kumble's 16 for 99
for Karnataka v Cerala at Terricherry, 1994-95

Best in the County Championship since Tony Lock's 16 for 83
for Surrey v Kent at Blackheath, 1956

Best in the County Championship by a seam bowler since Cliff Gladwin's 16 for 84
for Derbyshire v Worcestershire at Stourbridge, 1952

SCOREBOOK EXTRACT - MARTIN BICKNELL's 9-47 AT GUILDFORD
(Reproduced by kind permission of Surrey C.C.C. Scoring by Keith Booth)

[Scorebook page showing bowling analysis of Martin Bicknell's 9-47 against Leicestershire, 2nd innings, dated Thursday 20 / Friday 21 July 2000 at Guildford. Batsmen include Sutcliffe, Maddy, Smith, Stevens, Burns, Habib, Wells, DeFreitas, Williamson, Kumble, Saqlain, Ormond. Bowlers include Bicknell, Greenidge, Saqlain. Close of 2nd day at 7/21; 3rd day resumes.]

VIEW FROM THE DRESSING ROOM - IAN WARD

Guildford is now a real 'fortress' for Surrey, isn't it?
IW - We certainly enjoy going there because there's always a great atmosphere, enhanced by the crowd being so close to the action, and the conditions - a good true pitch, a fast outfield and some help for the spinners later on as the wicket breaks up - really suit our style of play.

VIEW FROM THE DRESSING ROOM - MARTIN BICKNELL

I guess it couldn't have been any better - home ground, sixteen wickets, Surrey win, Championship-best innings and match figures etc. Were you able to fully appreciate, at the time, what you had achieved?
MB - The feeling in the dressing room at the close of play was one of elation, it was really buzzing. When the innings started we faced an uphill struggle in the match, and possibly the Championship, but by the time we left the field at the end of the second day we felt that we'd got out of jail and won the match - it was incredible. Then, having already got twelve wickets, I went home that evening knowing that something special was happening and I didn't really sleep well that night because I was on such a high. I think my wife and children could sense that something big was about to happen, too, so they all came down to the game the following day - something they wouldn't normally do. It was an awesome experience and, because of all the components that you mentioned, obviously the most memorable game of my career.

How surprised were you to discover that you had recorded the best match analysis since Jim Laker's 19 for 90 in 1956?
MB - I certainly hadn't realised that my achievement was that significant. As I drove home on the second evening, I definitely wasn't thinking about getting sixteen wickets - I thought that if I could get another two and get up to fourteen then it would be pretty special but to take the last four was just awesome. But I still thought that there must be lots of people ahead of me.

Were we now feeling that we were very well placed to retain our Championship title?
MB - Yes, I think we were. Apart from Lancashire, we'd now seen all the other teams and I remember saying to Adam (Hollioake) that we'd got nothing to fear and that I didn't think there was any side who had got enough to win the Championship - we had again got the side to win it, if we played anything like our best. We'd felt Leicestershire were strong contenders but we'd demolished them at Oakham School and after this game they were out of the hunt. That left Yorkshire and Lancashire and we always backed ourselves to beat Yorkshire because they weren't in the greatest form. We felt the home game with Lancashire was going to be the key.

KEITH MEDLYCOTT'S ASSESSMENT

Martin Bicknell's bowling was outstanding throughout the whole match - he kept running in and beating the bat consistently on what was an excellent pitch. Martin fully deserved all the plaudits he got and I couldn't have been more pleased for him.

It was very interesting for me to study the Leicestershire team as I sat on top of the pavilion with them during that final period of play on the second day. During the 1999 match at Guildford it was amazing to see how, even with a first innings lead of 150-odd, Hampshire never really believed they would win the match and here, on this occasion, it was noticeable how tense the Leicestershire players were as they started their second innings. They knew that if they could get through that final hour or so then they would be in a good position and you could sense the tension. Once Bickers started to get amongst them I could see the pressure building and building on them - every time you make a breakthrough people have to move, they have to get pads on and things happen.

Other Division One Matches

Despite their excellent win over Leicestershire, Surrey's lead at the top of the table had actually been cut by three points, since both roses counties had won their games with a full hand of twenty points, as opposed to the reigning champions' seventeen. Durham had actually given Lancashire a good run for their money at Old Trafford, whereas Somerset had twice subsided meekly at Scarborough on an apparently well-grassed pitch.

July 19-21
Scarborough:- **Yorkshire beat Somerset by an innings and 6 runs.** Somerset 182 and 212 (Hoggard 5-50); Yorkshire 400 (Byas 84, Lehmann 77). **Yorkshire 20pts, Somerset 3**

July 19-22
Portsmouth:- **Kent beat Hampshire by six wickets.** Hampshire 320 (Laney 81) and 136 (White 80 not out, Patel 5-46); Kent 252 (Dravid 137) and 205 (Dravid 73 not out). **Kent 17pts, Hampshire 6**

Old Trafford:- **Lancashire beat Durham by six wickets.** Durham 370 (Katich 129) and 206 (Keedy 6-56); Lancashire 445 (Crawley 117, Lloyd 86, Ganguly 65, Atherton 64) and 132-4 (Atherton 64 not out). **Lancashire 20pts, Durham 4**

Pos	Prev		P	Pts	W	D	L	Bat	Bowl	Last	Three	Res
1	1	Surrey	11	136	6	3	2	26	26	W17	W16	W20
2	2	Lancashire	10	123	5	5	0	19	24	W20	D7	D7
3	3	Yorkshire	10	122	5	3	2	20	30	W20	L4	D7
4	4	Leicestershire	10	100	3	4	3	23	25	L6	W16	L3
5	5	Somerset	10	92	2	5	3	23	25	L3	D11	D11
6	7	Kent	9	84	3	4	2	8	24	W17	W17	D8
7	6	Durham	10	77	2	2	6	16	29	L6	L3	D10
8	9	Hampshire	10	63	1	3	6	9	30	L6	D7	L3
9	8	Derbyshire	10	61*	1	5	4	10	27	L3	D10	L2

* Deducted 8pts for sub-standard pitch

TOP-OF-THE-TABLE NCL CLASH TOPS OFF FESTIVAL WEEK

After the excitement and drama of Martin Bicknell's amazing record-breaking performance in the County Championship match, everyone had a day to recover before the vital clash between the two leading sides in the NCL Division Two, Surrey Lions and Nottinghamshire Outlaws. The Outlaws had surprised me greatly by doing so well in the competition as I felt their line-up didn't look particularly well suited to one-day cricket. They had performed very poorly in the northern qualifying group of the Benson and Hedges Cup at the start of the season and, to me, their batting and fielding, on paper at least, seemed poor in a limited-overs context. Having then taken a closer look at the eight matches they had played to date, it was noticeable that seven had been against the sides currently occupying the bottom four places in the division - and they had won the lot. Their other fixture, away to the Warwickshire Bears, had ended in defeat. They had, of course, yet to face the Lions, so this match looked likely to be the best test yet of their promotion credentials. I strongly fancied Surrey to win.

NCL DIVISION TWO - MATCH TEN

SURREY LIONS versus NOTTINGHAMSHIRE OUTLAWS
at Guildford on Sunday 23rd July

Surrey Lions (273-3) beat Nottinghamshire Outlaws (146) by 127 runs

A magnificent century from Graham Thorpe at a packed Woodbridge Road ground enabled the Surrey Lions to strengthen both their promotion and title challenges with a comprehensive 127-run mauling of the Nottinghamshire Outlaws on a glorious summer's afternoon.

Coming in at 10-1 in the third over, the England left-hander initially played a supporting role to the in-form Ian Ward but once ignited by a burst of three classy boundaries in David Lucas' fifth over there was no stopping him. Despite an outstanding first spell of five overs for just nine runs from Andrew Harris, the Lions roared to a hundred inside twenty overs, Thorpe completed a fine fifty just six balls later and, when Ward went for a well-played fifty-one in the thirtieth over, the carnage really began with the entrance of Ali Brown.

By now, Thorpe was well into his stride and looking in excellent form as he rushed to a magnificent century, including fourteen fours, from just 99 balls during a stand of 74 in 56 balls with Brown. Aided by a sub-standard fielding effort from a very unathletic Nottinghamshire outfit, the Lions passed two-hundred in the thirty-fifth over as Brown compiled a quick-fire 37 from just 24 balls before losing his middle stump to Lucas with the score at 223 and six overs of the innings remaining.

In the circumstances, the Outlaws did well to restrict Surrey to fifty runs in this closing period and they would have done even better but for the bad luck suffered by Paul Franks in the final over. Much to the amusement of the home fans, the visitors' England 'A' paceman shattered the stumps of both Thorpe and Adam Hollioake with successive deliveries but failed to be credited with a wicket on either occasion since the first delivery was a no-ball and the second was the resulting 'free-hit' ball. To add insult to injury, a single was run in each instance as the ball ricocheted away from the stumps!

The main feature of the opening stages of Nottinghamshire's pursuit of an unlikely 274 to win was the eagerly-anticipated Bicknell versus Bicknell clash. It would probably be fair to say that it ended in something akin to a nil-nil draw, with Martin getting a few deliveries past his brother's outside edge and Darren producing a couple of nice strokes before running himself out in trying to steal a bye to Jon Batty, who recovered well to throw down the stumps after an initial fumble.

Despite the fact that Jason Gallian struck the ball beautifully during an innings of forty-two from 47 balls, the visitors could never quite get up with the required run rate and some decidedly desperate batting in the face of magnificent spells from Saqlain Mushtaq and Jason Ratcliffe saw the upper- and middle-order swept away in the space of eleven action-packed overs. Having subsided dramatically from 66-1 to 111-7, there was no way back for the Outlaws and the Hollioake brothers tidied up the tail with the minimum of fuss as Surrey ran out winners by a huge margin to confirm the belief that they were the best side in the division.

Surrey Lions (273-3) beat Nottinghamshire Outlaws (146) by 127 runs

Surrey Lions 4pts

SURREY LIONS v NOTTINGHAMSHIRE OUTLAWS at GUILDFORD. Played on 23rd July
Surrey Lions won the toss Umpires:- V.A. Holder & N.A. Mallender

SURREY LIONS

Fall of wkt	Batsman	How Out		Score	Balls	4s	6s
1- 10	M.A. Butcher	c Reiffel	b Lucas	6	11	1	0
2- 149	I.J. Ward	run out		51	95	5	0
	G.P. Thorpe	Not Out		126	127	14	0
3- 223	A.D. Brown		b Lucas	37	24	6	0
	A.J. Hollioake *	Not Out		21	19	1	0
	B.C. Hollioake	did not bat					
	J.D. Ratcliffe	did not bat					
	J.N. Batty +	did not bat					
	M.P. Bicknell	did not bat					
	Saqlain Mushtaq	did not bat					
	C.G. Greenidge	did not bat					
	Extras (11lb, 8w, 13nb)			32			
	TOTAL	(45 overs)		237 - 3			

NOTTS OUTLAWS bowling

	O	M	R	W
Lucas	9	0	68	2
Franks	9	0	50	0
Harris	9	2	33	0
Reiffel	6	0	41	0
Tolley	9	0	44	0
Gallian	3	0	26	0

NOTTINGHAMSHIRE OUTLAWS

Fall of wkt	Batsman	How Out		Score	Balls	4s	6s
1- 57	D.J. Bicknell	run out		14	31	2	0
2- 66	J.E.R. Gallian *	c Ward	b Ratcliffe	42	47	8	0
3- 70	J.E. Morris	c Ratcliffe	b Saqlain	7	22	1	0
5- 87	P. Johnson		b Saqlain	9	12	1	0
4- 76	U. Afzaal	c A.J. Hollioake	b Saqlain	3	9	0	0
6- 91	C.M.W. Read +		b Ratcliffe	8	7	1	0
7- 111	C.M. Tolley	lbw b Ratcliffe		7	20	1	0
8- 141	P.R. Reiffel	c Greenidge	b B.C. Hollioake	18	28	2	0
	P.J. Franks	Not Out		14	29	1	0
9- 145	D.S. Lucas	lbw b A.J. Hollioake		4	4	1	0
10- 146	A.J. Harris	lbw b B.C. Hollioake		1	4	0	0
	Extras (7lb, 10w, 2nb)			19			
	TOTAL	(35.2 overs)		146			

SURREY LIONS bowling

	O	M	R	W
Bicknell	7	0	26	0
Greenidge	5	0	28	0
Ratcliffe	9	0	39	3
Saqlain	9	1	25	3
B.C. Hollioake	3.2	0	13	2
A.J. Hollioake	2	0	8	1

Other NCL Division Two Matches

With Surrey's other principal rivals, the Warwickshire Bears, going down to a shock defeat at the hands of the Durham Dynamos, this vital victory over the Outlaws left the Lions in pole position for promotion - it looked like another two wins would probably ensure Division One NCL cricket in 2001 - and quite possibly the Division Two title as well. There was still more work to be done, but things were looking very good.

July 23
Chelmsford:- **Essex Eagles beat Derbyshire Scorpions by 6 runs.** Essex 203-8 (Munton 3-24); Derbyshire 197 in 44.5 overs (D.R. Law 3-41). **Essex Eagles 4pts**

Portsmouth:- **Middlesex Crusaders beat Hampshire Hawks by four wickets.** Hampshire 190-9; Middlesex 192-6 in 44.2 overs (Roseberry 54). **Middlesex Crusaders 4pts**

Edgbaston:- **Durham Dynamos beat Warwickshire Bears by 50 runs.** Durham 198-6 (Katich 64); Warwickshire 148 in 40.1 overs. **Durham Dynamos 4pts**

NCL DIVISION TWO AT 23RD JULY

Pos	Prev		P	Pts	W	T	L	N/R	Last	Three	Res
1	1	Surrey Lions	10	36	8	0	0	2	W	W	W
2	2	Nottinghamshire Outlaws	9	28	7	0	2	0	L	W	W
3	4	Middlesex Crusaders	10	24	5	1	3	1	W	W	L
4	3	Warwickshire Bears	9	22	5	1	3	0	L	W	T
5	4	Glamorgan Dragons	9	20	4	2	3	0	L	T	W
6	6	Essex Eagles	9	18	4	0	4	1	W	W	W
7	7	Durham Dynamos	10	12	3	0	7	0	W	L	W
8	8	Derbyshire Scorpions	9	4	1	0	8	0	L	L	L
=	8	Hampshire Hawks	9	4	1	0	8	0	L	L	L

12 Red Rose Revenge

Since the desperate debacle at Derby, the team had now recorded five successive wins in the County Championship and thirteen victories off the reel in total - five Championship, five National Cricket League, two Nat West Trophy and a limited-overs friendly match against New Zealand 'A'. As a result of this fantastic run, Surrey's season had been transformed in dramatic style and the club was now chasing three trophies.

While looking very well placed for glory in the NCL and now in a good position in the Championship, perhaps the key match in the chase for a potential treble was the forthcoming Nat West Trophy quarter-final against Lancashire at The Oval. Although I fancied us strongly to win the four-day contest which, as fate would have it, followed a week later, I wasn't quite so sure about the limited-overs clash, despite the fact that the red rose county was fighting a relegation battle in Division One of the NCL. Admittedly, we had been very impressive in remaining unbeaten in Division Two but there appeared to be no really strong one-day teams in our league, as had been demonstrated by second-placed Nottinghamshire Outlaws! Even though it seemed likely that we would have a head start in terms of confidence, Lancashire had the potential, at full strength, to give us a very hard game.

YOU KNOW WHEN YOU'VE BEEN FLINTOFF-ED!

Alas... Surrey's treble dreams were wrecked in the Nat West Trophy quarter-final by an innings of extraordinarily powerful strokeplay by Andrew Flintoff after a below-par performance with the bat from the home side. The young England all-rounder smashed an incredible unbeaten 135, including four sixes and nineteen fours, from just 110 deliveries as he toyed with the Surrey attack, which was, crucially, missing Martin Bicknell, absent with a back strain.

The day started well for the home county when they won the toss and batted, reaching eighty in the first twenty overs through the efforts of Ian Ward (28) and Alec Stewart (49). Lancashire had chosen to field three spinners and open the bowling with Saurav Ganguly, a move which initially looked flawed as the Indian struggled to contain the Surrey openers but proved to be correct as Schofield, Keedy (1-40) and Yates (2-40) got to work on a pitch which offered a much greater degree of turn than expected. Apart from Graham Thorpe, who played well in making an accomplished fifty-five, no batsman was able to make any headway against the spinners and wickets were regularly tossed away with desperate and inappropriate strokes. A decent run-a-ball effort by Ian Salisbury (21 not out) in the closing overs at least pushed the score past two-hundred, although the general consensus of opinion was that this was perhaps twenty or thirty runs short of being a good total.

When Alex Tudor then spectacularly extracted Michael Atherton's off stump with the third ball of Lancashire's reply, Surrey's total suddenly looked more impressive but it was a sign of things to come when Flintoff clipped his first delivery to the midwicket boundary. Although Tudor produced a good opening spell, his new-ball partner, Carl Greenidge, was soon despatched for three fours in an over and Jason Ratcliffe suffered similar rough treatment when the last two balls of his second over after replacing Greenidge disappeared into the pavilion. The second of these two sixes took the big Lancastrian through to a forty-ball half-century and with just twelve overs completed the visitors already had seventy-one runs on the board.

The immediate introduction of the Surrey spin twins almost had the desired effect for Adam Hollioake when Flintoff edged Salisbury just past the grasping hands of Ali Brown at slip and then somehow survived a huge appeal for lbw when trapped plumb in front of his stumps by a googly but, by this stage, Lancashire were already nearly halfway to their target.

Continuing to pick off a boundary almost every over, Flintoff eventually arrived at a breathtaking century in just eighty-eight balls and continued to make hay when the Hollioake brothers replaced the spinners in the attack. Although Ganguly fell to a catch at slip the ball after completing a cultured 84-ball half-century in the last over of Tudor's second spell, the game was long gone for Surrey and Flintoff fittingly completed Lancashire's victory with a massive fourteen overs to spare by pulling Ali Brown to the midwicket fence.

This very easy win for the visitors proved something of a shock for the Surrey team and their supporters and provided conclusive evidence, to those who doubted it, of Flintoff's phenomenal power and natural ability. It was to be hoped that he couldn't reproduce this kind of form in the following week's vital Championship fixture between the reigning champions and the only side still able to boast an unbeaten record in the 2000 competition.

SCOREBOARD - NAT WEST TROPHY QUARTER-FINAL

Surrey 210-7 from 50 overs (G.P. Thorpe 55, C.P. Schofield 4-41)
Lancashire 214-2 from 36 overs (A. Flintoff 135 not out, S.C. Ganguly 51)
Lancashire won by eight wickets

Umpires: G. Sharp and D.R. Shepherd

Man Of The Match - A. Flintoff (Lancashire)

ROSES RIVALS PRODUCE PERFECT DRAW

Despite sitting out the round of Championship matches that followed the Nat West quarter-finals, Surrey had a great deal of interest in events at Headingley, where rivals-in-chief, Yorkshire and Lancashire, went head-to-head. The home side clearly had the better of the first three days before a last-day washout consigned the match to a draw. Although this kept both counties well in contention, with Yorkshire just three points behind us and Lancashire now four adrift, it did at least mean that we retained our top spot in the table. With games in hand now used up, we could see just how tight things were at the top - and how vital the forthcoming Surrey versus Lancashire clash was going to be.

July 28-31
Chester-le-Street:- **Durham drew with Somerset.** Durham 292 (Lewis 115) and 73-3; Somerset 280 (Bowler 107, Rose 82 not out, Wood 5-88). **Durham 9pts, Somerset 9**

Canterbury:- **Derbyshire drew with Kent.** Derbyshire 279 (Dowman 77) and 293-0 (Titchard 141 not out, Stubbings 135 not out); Kent 251-9dec (Nixon 80 not out, Patel 60, Dean 8-52). **Kent 9pts, Derbyshire 9**

Headingley:- **Lancashire drew with Yorkshire.** Lancashire 267 (Hegg 75) and 127-2; Yorkshire 376 (Lehmann 83, Byas 81). **Yorkshire 11pts, Lancashire 9**

COUNTY CHAMPIONSHIP DIVISION ONE AT 31ST JULY

Pos	Prev		P	Pts	W	D	L	Bat	Bowl	Last	Three	Res
1	1	Surrey	11	136	6	3	2	26	26	*W17*	*W16*	*W20*
2	3	Yorkshire	11	133	5	4	2	24	33	D11	*W20*	*L4*
3	2	Lancashire	11	132	5	6	0	21	27	D9	*W20*	D7
4	5	Somerset	11	101	2	6	3	25	28	D9	*L3*	D11
5	4	Leicestershire	10	100	3	4	3	23	25	*L6*	*W16*	*L3*
6	6	Kent	10	93	3	5	2	10	27	D9	*W17*	*W17*
7	7	Durham	11	86	2	3	6	18	32	D9	*L6*	*L3*
8	9	Derbyshire	11	70*	1	6	4	12	30	D9	*L3*	D10
9	8	Hampshire	10	63	1	3	6	9	30	*L6*	D7	*L3*

* Deducted 8pts for sub-standard pitch

THE LIONS' POSITION GROWS STRONGER IN THE NCL

Having been outplayed by the Surrey Lions at Guildford, the Nottinghamshire Outlaws came badly unstuck against another of their promotion rivals, the Warwickshire Bears, one week later at Trent Bridge. This result suited the resting Lions nicely, since it left them eight points clear at the top of the table, with only Glamorgan Dragons, some sixteen points adrift, having a game in hand. Since our rivals still had a number of games to play against one another, promotion was looking increasingly certain and the league title a real possibility.

July 30
Southampton:- **Hampshire Hawks beat Essex Eagles by six wickets.** Essex 158-9 (Peters 51); Hampshire 162-4 in 42.2 overs. **Hampshire Hawks 4pts**

August 1
Trent Bridge:- **Warwickshire Bears beat Nottinghamshire Outlaws by 95 runs.** Warwickshire 244-6 (Ostler 79 not out, Knight 50); Nottinghamshire 149 in 43.5 overs (Bicknell 61). **Warwickshire Bears 4pts**

NCL DIVISION TWO AT 1ST AUGUST

Pos	Prev		P	Pts	W	T	L	N/R	Last	Three	Res
1	1	Surrey Lions	10	36	8	0	0	2	*W*	*W*	*W*
2	2	Nottinghamshire Outlaws	10	28	7	0	3	0	*L*	*L*	*W*
3	4	Warwickshire Bears	10	26	6	1	3	0	*W*	*L*	*W*
4	3	Middlesex Crusaders	10	24	5	1	3	1	*W*	*W*	*L*
5	5	Glamorgan Dragons	9	20	4	2	3	0	*L*	*T*	*W*
6	6	Essex Eagles	10	18	4	0	5	1	*L*	*W*	*W*
7	7	Durham Dynamos	10	12	3	0	7	0	*W*	*L*	*W*
8	8	Hampshire Hawks	10	8	2	0	8	0	*W*	*L*	*L*
9	8	Derbyshire Scorpions	9	4	1	0	8	0	*L*	*L*	*L*

COUNTY CHAMPIONSHIP - MATCH TWELVE

SURREY versus LANCASHIRE
at The Oval

First Day - Wednesday 2nd August

Surrey 191-6

The Teams And The Toss - With Alex Tudor recovered from his side strain and Martin Bicknell sufficiently recovered from his back problem to take his place in the team, Surrey are able to field their strongest available eleven for this vital match. Lancashire's only notable absentee is broken thumb victim, Peter Martin, though Saurav Ganguly has to pass a late fitness test on a groin strain picked up in the previous week's Roses match. John Crawley calls incorrectly at the toss, giving Surrey first use of the wicket.

The Surrey openers make a cautious start as Glen Chapple, from the pavilion end, and Michael Smethurst, from the pavilion end, find some early movement and manage to beat the outside edge of the bat on a number of occasions. It is, therefore, hard to understand why Crawley starts with, and maintains, a defensive field with a third man in place at both ends.

Ward and Butcher appear to be establishing sound foundations for their team as they reach ten without loss after nine overs, but the lively Smethurst suddenly brings about a dramatic transformation with three wickets in eleven balls at a personal cost of one run. Ward falls first in the 23-year-old paceman's fifth over, chasing a wide half-volley and seeing his edge fumbled by Warren Hegg into the hands of Andrew Flintoff at first slip, then Butcher departs seven balls later, courtesy of an outside edge to Neil Fairbrother at third slip. Surrey are now 11-2 and in Smethurst's seventh over they slip deeper into trouble at 12-3 when Nadeem Shahid falls lbw, beaten by inswing and hit on the back pad.

It's all going the way of the tall seamer at this stage and he clearly believes he has a fourth wicket moments later when he strikes Ali Brown on the pad and goes racing towards his team-mates in a state of high jubilation. Unfortunately, having not bothered to look around to check, he has missed the fact that the umpire has ruled 'not out' and he is consequently made to look rather foolish... to put it mildly.

The pressure on Surrey's fourth-wicket pair is eased a little at this point as Chapple gives way to Joe Scuderi, and Adam Hollioake responds to the new bowler by driving him to the cover boundary three times in two overs. Chapple's return is not long delayed, however, since he replaces Smethurst at the pavilion end after an impressive opening burst of 9-5-7-3 from the Oldham-born seam bowler.

The former England 'A' paceman's reappearance is certainly welcomed by Brown who, having spent twenty-five minutes on nought, suddenly bursts into life with three boundaries in three overs. This is sufficient to see off Chapple for a second time and his replacement, Gary Keedy, initially fares no better against Brown, with the full toss that starts his opening over driven wide of mid-on for four and the long-hop that ends it being cut away to the extra cover fence.

With Brown now seemingly in control as he drives Keedy over mid-off to bring up the fifty partnership for the fourth wicket, the early damage to the Surrey innings is gradually being repaired and the introduction of Flintoff for Scuderi at the Vauxhall end does nothing to slow an increasing scoring rate. Hollioake and Brown pick up two more boundaries apiece in the closing overs before the interval, three off Flintoff and one off Keedy, to bring the contest almost level again.

Lunch:- Surrey 87-3 (A.J. Hollioake 29*,Brown 40*) from 35 overs

184

Smethurst and Chapple resume for Lancashire after the interval, again with very defensive fields - only two slips, no gully, third man - which seems surprising since Surrey are still in a rather vulnerable position at this stage. Ali Brown does his best to change this, however, three boundaries in quick succession taking Surrey's score into three figures and the batsman through to a half-century, from 76 balls in 99 minutes, containing no fewer than eleven fours. Unfortunately for the home side, Brown's innings is cut off in its prime just two overs later when Smethurst lures the batsman into a drive which results in an edge to Flintoff at first slip - Surrey are 108-4 and Lancashire have managed to gain a slight advantage again.

Given the delicate balance of the match, this would clearly be a good time for the out-of-form Ben Hollioake to come good and he starts well, cutting and driving the newly-introduced Chris Schofield for two threes and then unfurling a perfect on-driven four off Smethurst. His elder brother is meanwhile living a little dangerously, coming perilously close to giving Schofield a return catch before offering a tough, but catchable, chance to Chapple at mid-on off the same bowler. The errant fielder is then given an almost immediate opportunity to make amends when he replaces Smethurst at the pavilion end and he comes close when the Surrey captain edges him through a vacant second slip position. As bowler and captain rue their overly-defensive field setting, the ball speeds to the boundary to complete a valuable fifty for Hollioake senior after 119 balls and 146 minutes at the crease.

With Ben continuing to look in better touch than at any previous stage of the season and Adam gradually playing his way out of his sticky patch, the Hollioake brothers' partnership starts to look rather threatening for a Lancashire side that appears to have lost a degree of focus since lunch. As Chapple takes another break, to be replaced by Scuderi, and Schofield continues to purvey his leg-breaks skilfully but without reward, the score moves steadily past 150 and, before long, the fifty partnership arrives following a rare misfield from a Lancashire side whose ground fielding has been largely very impressive to date.

The visitors' need for a breakthrough is becoming more urgent by the minute so Crawley, strangely reluctant to use his spinners in tandem, recalls Keedy in place of Schofield. As it happens, the wicket Lancashire crave comes in the very next over from Scuderi when Ben Hollioake, only half-forward, is adjudged lbw for twenty-four with the score at 164. The young all-rounder's surprised and disappointed reaction to the umpire's decision confirms feelings on the pavilion balcony that he had got an inside-edge to the delivery, making his departure after a good start all the more unfortunate. He has to go, however, and the red rose county has again hit back just as the balance of the game was starting to tip towards Surrey.

Seemingly unaffected by his brother's demise, the home skipper immediately blasts Keedy for a towering six over long-off and, in company with the new batsman, Jon Batty, recommences the battle to regain the initiative for his side. Scuderi has had no joy at all when bowling to Hollioake so far and the pattern continues as the Surrey captain drives wide of mid-on for three and then square cuts to the point boundary to move on to eighty. The next delivery, a wide half-volley, looks likely to be punished, too, but Hollioake doesn't quite get to the pitch of the ball as it offers to swing away and the resulting outside edge is well pouched by Warren Hegg diving away in front of first slip. It's a bad blow for Surrey and a major fillip for Lancashire to see the back of Hollioake, who has played a valiant captain's innings, and when rain brings an early tea just two overs later the visitors appear to hold a slight advantage again.

Unfortunately, we are denied any further play as the rain fails to abate after the break and play is called off for the day at 5.45pm. We should at least be in for an interesting morning session tomorrow.

Tea and Close:- Surrey 191-6 (Batty 3*, Bicknell 3*) from 68 overs

VIEW FROM THE DRESSING ROOM - NADEEM SHAHID

I guess this was another case of the skipper coming to the fore when we most needed him?
NS - Yes, we'd had a very poor start and Adam led from the front and really took the attack to Lancashire. It wasn't just the number of runs he scored that lifted the team, it was also the way in which he scored them. He certainly does have a knack of scoring runs when they are most needed.

Second Day - Thursday 3rd August

Surrey 310

Rain frustrates everyone again with only 6.2 overs possible before lunch. Surrey can at least take heart from the fact that they advance their score by fifteen without further loss.

Lunch:- Surrey 206-6 (Batty 9*, Bicknell 11*) from 74.2 overs

The afternoon session proves to be just as disappointing for the players and supporters of both teams. Play resumes at 2.15pm after an early lunch but we are restricted to just five largely uneventful overs before the rain returns.

Tea:- Surrey 213-6 (Batty 11*, Bicknell 13*) from 79.2 overs

After an early tea, the match is able to resume at 4.25pm with thirty-three overs left for play. Crawley immediately hands the ball to Scuderi and Chapple and, much to the Lancashire captain's delight, his former England 'A' seamer makes an initial breakthrough in the fourth over - clean bowling Batty with the score advanced to 217 - and then comes close to another wicket in his next over when Bicknell gets a leading edge back down the pitch. Although the ball only just carries to Chapple in his follow-through, the bowler's attempt to complete the catch is far from impressive and allows the batsman a reprieve on nineteen with the total standing at 220.

Having completed four overs, Scuderi then gives way to Smethurst at the pavilion end and the scoring rate receives a sudden boost as eleven runs, including a cover-driven four by Bicknell and a pulled boundary from Salisbury, accrue from the new bowler's opening over. After the excellent control of his early overs in the match this comes as something of a surprise but he is soon back on the mark in his second over and collects his fifth wicket of the innings when Bicknell top-edges an attempted cut to first slip, where Flintoff makes an awkward low catch look absurdly easy.

Although Surrey are now 237-8, with hopes of a substantial total and further potentially vital batting points receding, it is undoubtedly to their advantage that John Crawley now faces something of a dilemma, brought about by an apparent absence of forward planning. The new ball is due in six overs time yet his opening bowlers, Chapple and Smethurst, having already delivered seven and four overs respectively in their current spells, will clearly be tiring by the time the new 'cherry' arrives. Does the Lancashire skipper keep them going in the hope that they knock over the last two wickets before the new ball becomes available or does he rest them and fill in with his other bowlers for a while? He decides on the latter option, bringing Keedy and Schofield into the attack immediately, and pays a heavy price as Salisbury and Tudor take advantage of a number of short deliveries to plunder twenty-six runs from the final six overs with the old ball.

To no-one's surprise, Chapple and Smethurst are recalled straight away but, with the total having advanced to 274, Surrey have stolen the initiative. Tudor now takes over the leading role, crashing Chapple through the covers for four and then pulling Smethurst wide of mid-on for another boundary as an extremely valuable fifty partnership comes up in just over twelve overs and the home side edges closer to their third batting point at 300.

Although they are still six runs short of their goal when Salisbury becomes Smethurst's sixth victim of the innings, falling lbw when hitting across his front pad, a square cut to the rope by Tudor off the recalled Scuderi in the following over takes Surrey past a milestone that they had looked unlikely to reach after their disastrous start on the first morning. With only four overs remaining for play at this point, Tudor opts, sensibly enough, to maintain his aggressive approach and picks up two further boundaries off Scuderi before being cleaned up by a yorker-length delivery from the returning Flintoff.

A final score of 310 seems to represent a good effort by the county champions but if they are to squeeze an important victory out of this match they will need to bowl and field extremely well during the remaining two days of the match - and also hope for better weather.

Third Day - Friday 4th August

Surrey 310 and 227-4 declared; Lancashire 120 and 19-0

From the moment that the teams for this match had been announced I had been wondering who was going to open the batting for Lancashire. It seemed certain that John Crawley would be one of the openers - a rather strange move, to my mind, given his capabilities against spin bowling in the middle-order - but who would his partner be? Since there was no other recognised specialist opener in the visitors' eleven and all their strokeplayers - Flintoff, Lloyd, Fairbrother - looked wholly unsuited to the role, most people had assumed that Saurav Ganguly would take on the job. We are in for a surprise then as the players take the field at the start of day two.

Much to our amazement it is Glen Chapple who accompanies his captain to the crease - an incredible decision, considering the quality of new-ball bowling that he will be up against, and a ploy that I feel has little or no chance of proving successful.

The Lancashire innings closely follows the pattern of Surrey's in the early stages, with an explosion of wickets following a sedate start. The stand-in opener marginally outlasts his skipper, as it happens, with Crawley departing in the seventh over, adjudged lbw to Martin Bicknell when appearing to be well forward and possibly outside the line of the off stump, to set the visitors off on the wrong foot at 5 for 1. Chapple then edges to Mark Butcher at second slip seven balls later to become the first victim of a devastating Tudor two-in-two, which rocks Lancashire back on their heels at 7 for 3. Crucially, Tudor's second scalp is Ganguly, who plays back to his first ball and pushes the ball to square leg but treads on his stumps in so doing - cue major Surrey celebrations both on and off the field.

The visitors are suddenly struggling desperately, though the dangerous Flintoff is still there and Neil Fairbrother, after a nervy start against Tudor, drills the big Surrey paceman for three boundaries through the point area to keep the scoreboard ticking over. Although the Lancashire left-hander wins these minor battles with Tudor he loses the war in the next over when two air shots outside his off stump are followed by a fatal nick, low to Butcher at second slip. This dismissal leaves the red rose county in terrible trouble at 33-4 and their position then deteriorates further two balls later when Graham Lloyd's indeterminate dab provides Jon Batty with a catch behind the wicket and Tudor with his fourth wicket of the innings. Surrey are absolutely cock-a-hoop, with half the Lancashire side gone for just thirty-three runs and their own total now assuming gargantuan proportions.

Everyone wonders how Flintoff will react to this situation. Will he still feel able to play his natural game and launch a counter-attack or will he try to hang around? Although he picks up two boundaries off Bicknell and, in partnership with Joe Scuderi, sees off both opening bowlers after excellent ten-over spells, he certainly appears to be reining himself back at this stage.

The replacements for Bicknell and Tudor, whose first burst has earned him the impressive figures of 10-6-28-4, are Saqlain Mushtaq, at the pavilion end, and Ben Hollioake, at the Vauxhall end, and the feeling that we might be in for some interesting cricket proves correct. Having lofted Saqlain's second delivery back over the bowler's head for a one-bounce four and then driven him to the extra cover fence in his second over, Flintoff goes one step better in the Pakistani off-spinner's third over by driving him high over wide long-on for six. The gauntlet has been thrown down and Saqlain is happy to take up the challenge, though he almost doesn't get a chance to gain his revenge as Hollioake induces a top-edged cut from his former England Under-19 team-mate in the next over, only to see Brown, at first slip, fail to hang on to a very sharp overhead chance.

Any fears that this might prove to be a costly miss are soon dispelled by Saqlain, though, as Flintoff falls to a catch at short leg from a quicker ball, delivered from round the wicket. As with Fairbrother before him, the Lancastrian has lost the war after an early taste of success in battle and, as a result, the scoreboard reads 85-6.

Scuderi, displaying a liking for the cut and steer to third man, subsequently shepherds his team through to the interval without further loss but they have sustained some potentially mortal wounds at the hands of Alex Tudor during a dominant first session for Surrey.

A marvellous morning's play then ends with a memorable moment for Ian Ward when he is presented with a very well-deserved county cap by Adam Hollioake as the home team leaves the field.

Lunch:- Lancashire 94-6 (Scuderi 25*, Hegg 1*) from 29 overs

Lancashire sink deeper into the mire in the second over after lunch when Scuderi goes for his favourite cut shot against Saqlain and top-edges to Batty, with the total advanced by just a Tudor no-ball in the session's opening over. Scuderi is out for twenty-five and Lancashire are 96-7.

The visitors' last hopes of attaining respectability, through Warren Hegg and Chris Schofield, are then dashed after just seventeen deliveries as Tudor gets back into the act with his fifth wicket of the innings. His victim is the young leg-spinner, who skies an ugly pull stroke to Saqlain at mid-off, having raised the Lancashire hundred with an edge to third man from the previous delivery.

A couple of cuts from Hegg excepted, the visitors have nothing more to offer before Tudor terminates the innings with ruthless efficiency, having the left-handed Keedy taken at third slip from a fine delivery and then bowling the former England wicketkeeper as he aims to leg with a wild and desperate slog. Lancashire have been bowled out in just 39.1 overs for a meagre 120 and Tudor has returned career-best figures of 7 for 48 during an outstanding spell of bowling to give his team a huge first innings lead of 190 runs. Surrey are consequently in a position from which defeat looks impossible, so they can already rest assured that they will extend their advantage over Lancashire in the Championship by, at the very least, three points at the conclusion of this match. Victory would stretch their lead by a massive fifteen points, however, so there is an awful lot to play for in the 158 overs that remain in the match.

During the break between innings Adam Hollioake springs a bit of a surprise - he decides against enforcing the follow-on, so Surrey will bat again. With the threat of rain always a possibility during this largely damp summer it's an interesting move, especially since the bowlers, with the possible exception of Tudor, have hardly been overworked in dismissing Lancashire so cheaply. It does give the reigning champions the opportunity to put the match completely beyond the reach of their title challengers, though, and it will also add insult to the injury that the red rose county will be feeling after their batting debacle.

If the move is indeed designed to demoralise the visitors then it works a treat as the Surrey openers get away to a very positive start against a dispirited-looking fielding side. Michael Smethurst certainly gets his comeuppance for returning 6-63 in the first innings as both openers rip into him during the sixth and seventh overs of his opening spell - after Ward hooks and drives boundaries to take Surrey through to a rapid fifty, Butcher follows up with four superb fours - cover drive, pull, pull, straight drive - in the following over.

With the home side racing along at five-an-over, Crawley clearly needs to act in order to slow Surrey's progress towards a declaration, so he introduces Schofield at the pavilion end to form an all-spin attack with Keedy, who has been wheeling away at the Vauxhall end since the ninth over of the innings. This not only has the desired effect of slowing the scoring but it also brings the wicket of Ward, who gets a thin legside edge to Warren Hegg from a leg-break in Schofield's second over with the score at seventy-four. Surrey are already far enough ahead for the loss of wickets to be largely inconsequential, however, and they continue to press on steadily as Butcher reaches a very good fifty, albeit with a rather fortunate inside edge past his leg stump off Keedy, from 55 balls in nine minutes over the hour.

As tea approaches, the left-handed opener advances on Keedy to drive him straight for the four that takes his side's total into three figures before Nadeem Shahid increases the tempo again, picking off four boundaries with a variety of cuts, sweeps and drives to take the Surrey lead beyond three-hundred.

Tea:- Surrey 117-1 (Butcher 67*, Shahid 22*) from 30 overs

Apart from a cover-drive for four by Shahid off Keedy, progress is initially slow after tea, partly due to the predictably negative line bowled by the Lancashire left-arm spinner and the accompanying defensive fields set by John Crawley. While Keedy bowls over the wicket into the rough with a 5-4 legside field, Joe Scuderi, who has taken over from Schofield at the pavilion end since tea, also plays his part by conceding just nine runs in the first four overs of his new spell.

Shahid eventually breaks free against Keedy, however, finding the rope at wide long-on and then cover, despite the fact that five men are now patrolling the boundary, and Butcher joins the party shortly afterwards with a brace of threes as the lead extends towards 350. In order to have a decent bowl at the opposition tonight, the run rate needs to be increased further, though, and Shahid does his best to achieve this by driving Scuderi to the extra cover fence on his way to a fine fifty, compiled from 83 balls during 76 minutes at the crease. This stroke brings an end to the medium-pacer's spell as Crawley reverts to Schofield, but the leg-spinner is no more capable of restraining the batsmen, Shahid reverse-sweeping him for three as the hundred partnership comes up at around four runs per over.

Having reached sixty-two, however, the former Essex batsman's attractive innings comes to an end a few overs later when he makes ground down the wicket to Keedy and drives a catch to cover, and Butcher then joins his team-mate back in the pavilion one over later. With his score on ninety-five, following a sweep for four in the over of Shahid's dismissal, the left-handed opener's slog-sweep at Schofield results in a skier towards mid-off which the bowler races back to catch. Although he has slowed quite considerably during the second half of his innings, Butcher's effort has been worthy of a hundred and he leaves the field to a generous ovation.

With the lead past 380, an immediate declaration seems certain but it's not forthcoming and Surrey press on further, with Adam Hollioake and Ali Brown having licence to thrill. They do this in style, too, as the members in the pavilion are sent scurrying for cover by three huge sixes in successive overs from Schofield. Hollioake is the first to strike, landing the ball just short of the committee room on the first-floor balcony, then Brown follows up with a truly massive blow which sends the ball soaring almost onto the top level of the pavilion - certainly one of the biggest hits ever seen at the ground - before settling for another drive which merely crashes against the top of the sightscreen, just below balcony level! This seems a fitting way for the innings to end with a signal from Adam Hollioake, who is back in the pavilion after advancing and missing a drive at Keedy in the previous over. With the scoreboard reading 227-4 at the declaration, Lancashire are left facing a theoretical target of 418 to win from a minimum of 104 overs, eight today and ninety-six, weather permitting, on the final day tomorrow.

Undeterred by Chapple's first innings failure, the visitors open with the 26-year-old pace bowler again and this time he does a good job, surviving with his captain until the close of play as Bicknell and Tudor, for once, stray too wide of off stump too often in a disappointing last eight overs. Surrey will now need to take all ten wickets tomorrow, which would appear to be quite a tough task.

Close:- Lancashire 19-0 (Crawley 10*, Chapple 7*) from 8 overs

VIEW FROM THE DRESSING ROOM - NADEEM SHAHID

I thought Lancashire made a big tactical mistake in this match by promoting Glen Chapple to open the batting against our quality of new-ball bowling - would you agree?
NS - Yes, it's hard enough for any tail-ender to face the new ball, let alone when it's in the hands of guys like Bickers and Tudes. I can only assume that they were hoping to protect Saurav Ganguly, who was the key to their batting.

What was your opinion of Alex Tudor's bowling during the Lancashire first innings?
NS - I thought Tudes bowled well in every game I played in, so this performance came as no surprise to me. He is an enormous talent and he bowled with great intelligence in this game.

VIEW FROM THE DRESSING ROOM - ALEX TUDOR

When Lancashire batted they opened with Glen Chapple. I felt it was a big mistake to pit a tail-ender against you and Bickers with the new ball - what was your view?
AT - Although Glen Chapple can bat, it did seem a strange decision and I think it asked too much of him. I think they were trying to keep people like Ganguly back until the ball was a bit softer but it didn't work and it just gave us more confidence.

You almost always seem to bowl well against Lancashire and this was no exception - is there any reason why you think this might be?
AT - I think it goes back to 1998 when I was hit for the world record number of runs in an over by Andrew Flintoff. I bowled tremendously well in the first innings there and got five wickets, then he came out and hit me to all parts of Old Trafford in the second innings. So I always remember that and really get myself up for when we play Lancashire. I tend to bowl pretty well to left-handers, too, and they've got quite a few of those so that probably comes into it as well.

You must have been very proud of your performance in the first innings when you recorded your career-best figures of 7 for 48.
AT - The funny thing was that I'd been out injured with a side strain and it was still very sore when this game came around so I wasn't sure if I should play or not. I think I know my body better these days, though, so I'm better at knowing which niggles I can play through and which ones I can't. Everyone realised it was a big game and wanted me to play so Keith Medlycott and Adam and the physio, John Gloster, gave me the confidence I needed to declare myself fit. And I think, in a way, this performance changed me as a bowler. Because I couldn't bowl at my fastest I cut down my pace a bit and concentrated on line and length and I proved that I can still do a very good job even when I'm not at top pace.

Fourth Day - Saturday 5th August

Surrey 310 and 227-4 declared; Lancashire 120 and 145

Surrey beat Lancashire by 272 runs
Surrey 18pts, Lancashire 3

Although he had played well the previous evening, Glen Chapple doesn't last long on day four as an attempted pull at the fourth ball of the fourth over, bowled by Alex Tudor, results in a skied mishit to Ben Hollioake at fourth slip. Chapple goes for seven, Lancashire are 23 for 1, and I think it's fair to describe the visitors' experiment as a failure.

Buoyed by this early wicket, Surrey then capture the very important scalp of Andrew Flintoff in Tudor's very eventful next over. Having been driven to the rope at cover and then cut for another boundary off a no-ball, the big paceman delivers a wide before following up with a high-bouncing delivery outside off stump which Flintoff slices fast and at head height to Ben Holioake in the gully. The Surrey all-rounder takes the catch with great aplomb, the county champions celebrate Tudor's ninth wicket of the match and a disappointed Flintoff departs for the pavilion at 37 for 2.

This dismissal brings together the two batsmen most likely to produce a long innings, John Crawley and Saurav Ganguly, and, while Martin Bicknell takes a rest ahead of a change of ends, Saqlain Mushtaq is brought into the attack at the pavilion end. Early in the day though it is, there is a feeling that this could be a crucial stage of the game and, as is so often the case in that situation, Saqlain delivers the goods for his team. After a quiet start, the off-spinner draws Crawley forward with the first ball of his third over and sees Adam Hollioake take a very sharp catch off bat and pad at silly point. As the Surrey team celebrates a vital breakthrough it emerges that this is Saqlain's two-hundredth first-class wicket for the county in only his thirty-fifth game, a stunning strike rate of almost six wickets per match.

At 45-3, Lancashire are now in desperate trouble and the home side's task of bowling the visitors out in the day suddenly looks that much easier. Another wicket or two before lunch would certainly make Surrey red-hot favourites to sew up victory but their path is now blocked by the experienced Fairbrother. The former England left-hander looks far from certain against Saqlain, however, edging a couple of deliveries to third man and almost being bowled when missing a slog-sweep, while Ganguly, on the other hand, appears happy against the spin but ill-at-ease when facing Tudor and then Bicknell from the Vauxhall end.

Eventually, as lunch approaches, Adam Hollioake pairs his spinners and gets the result he requires when Ian Salisbury induces the Indian left-hander to play on to a leg-break in his second over. It's another big wicket in the context of an important match and it leaves the visitors facing an uphill struggle to avoid defeat in the final two sessions.

Lunch:- Lancashire 93-4 (Fairbrother 22*, Lloyd 0*) from 35 overs

It takes just eleven deliveries after the interval for Surrey to take their next step on the road to victory as Graham Lloyd falls to a catch at silly point by Adam Hollioake off Saqlain, thereby adding a second innings contribution of just one to his first innings duck.

Although Fairbrother brings up the visitors' hundred in the following over with two boundaries off Salisbury, Lancashire now appear to be fighting a losing battle. The new batsman, Joe Scuderi, again shows a propensity for the cut, getting off the mark with an inside edge past his leg stump in trying the shot against Saqlain, before finding the cover fence twice against Salisbury. Fairbrother meanwhile continues to look uneasy when faced by Saqlain, twice edging just short of slip before finally middling a sweep to the backward square leg boundary. Ironically, after his struggles with the off-spinner, it turns out to be the leg-spin of Salisbury that brings about his downfall as an attempted sweep results in a gloved dolly catch to Ali Brown at leg slip with the batsman just five runs short of a half-century.

With plenty of time remaining and only four wickets left to fall, Lancashire must now realise that the game is up, and any doubts that the tide is flowing unstoppably in Surrey's direction are removed three balls later. Having popped his first delivery from Salisbury in the air past short leg, Warren Hegg leathers his second ball to the cover boundary and then sweeps violently at the next delivery, a legside full-toss. The ball screams off the bat at pace and appears to be heading for the fence at backward square leg until Mark Butcher, halfway back to the boundary, flings himself low to his right to pluck it out of thin air with his right hand. It's an amazing catch and, while the crowd applauds a sensational piece of cricket and the Surrey players rush over to the jubilant fielder to offer their congratulations, a disbelieving Hegg drags himself back to the dressing room.

It looks to be just a matter of time now before Surrey extend their lead in the Championship with a crushing victory - and so it proves. After four overs of resigned resistance, Chris Schofield snicks a Saqlain off-break to Butcher at second slip, then, three overs later, Salisbury tidies up the tail with two wickets in an over - Scuderi drives at a leg-break and edges to Jon Batty, while Michael Smethurst skies a drive to Martin Bicknell at a deepish mid-off. At 2.54pm exactly, it's game, set and match to Surrey. Ian Salisbury ends with five wickets in the innings, Alex Tudor has nine in the match, our Nat West Trophy defeat has been swiftly avenged, and Lancashire's unbeaten Championship record is a thing of the past.

Surrey 310 and 227-4dec; Lancashire 120 and 145
Surrey won by 272 runs. Surrey 18pts, Lancashire 3

SURREY v LANCASHIRE at THE OVAL. Played from 2nd - 5th August

Surrey won the toss   Umpires:- R. Palmer & J.F. Steele

SURREY - First Innings   **LANCASHIRE bowling**

Fall of wkt	Batsman	How Out	Score	Balls	4s	6s		O	M	R	W
2- 11	M.A. Butcher	c Fairbrother b Smethurst	4	33	0	0	Chapple	32	8	78	1
1- 10	I.J. Ward	c Flintoff b Smethurst	6	30	0	0	Smethurst	29	12	63	6
3- 12	Nadeem Shahid	lbw b Smethurst	1	9	0	0	Scuderi	21	5	65	2
6- 185	A.J. Hollioake *	c Hegg b Scuderi	80	170	11	1	Keedy	13	3	38	0
4- 108	A.D. Brown	c Flintoff b Smethurst	54	81	11	0	Flintoff	4.5	1	14	1
5- 164	B.C. Hollioake	lbw b Scuderi	24	58	2	0	Schofield	11	2	35	0
7- 217	J.N. Batty +	b Chapple	12	56	0	0					
8- 237	M.P. Bicknell	c Flintoff b Smethurst	28	90	2	0					
9- 294	I.D.K. Salisbury	lbw b Smethurst	35	74	4	0					
10- 310	A.J. Tudor	b Flintoff	35	54	7	0					
	Saqlain Mushtaq	Not Out	4	11	1	0					
	Extras (1b, 16lb, 8w, 2nb)		27								
	TOTAL	(110.5 overs)	310								

LANCASHIRE- First Innings   **SURREY bowling**

Fall of wkt	Batsman	How Out	Score	Balls	4s	6s		O	M	R	W
2- 7	G. Chapple	c Butcher b Tudor	4	29	0	0	Bicknell	10	3	20	1
1- 5	J.P. Crawley *	lbw b Bicknell	1	15	0	0	Tudor	15.1	6	48	7
6- 85	A. Flintoff	c Shahid b Saqlain	36	55	6	1	Saqlain	10	4	28	2
3- 7	S.C. Ganguly	hit wicket b Tudor	0	1	0	0	B.C. Hollioake	4	0	17	0
4- 33	N.H. Fairbrother	c Butcher b Tudor	15	36	3	0					
5- 33	G.D. Lloyd	c Batty b Tudor	0	2	0	0					
7- 96	J.C. Scuderi	c Batty b Saqlain	25	36	4	0					
10- 120	W.K. Hegg +	b Tudor	12	41	0	0					
8- 103	C.P. Schofield	c Saqlain b Tudor	4	9	1	0					
9- 119	G. Keedy	c B.C. Hollioake b Tudor	2	15	0	0					
	M.P. Smethurst	Not Out	0	1	0	0					
	Extras (3b, 4lb, 4w, 10nb)		21								
	TOTAL	(39.1 overs)	120								

SURREY - Second Innings

Fall of wkt	Batsman		How Out	Score	Balls	4s	6s
3- 191	M.A. Butcher		c & b Schofield	95	134	11	0
1- 74	I.J. Ward	c Hegg	b Schofield	20	50	3	0
2- 183	Nadeem Shahid	c sub	b Keedy	62	98	10	0
4- 219	A.J. Hollioake *	st Hegg	b Keedy	18	15	1	1
	A.D. Brown		Not Out	19	12	0	2
	B.C. Hollioake		Not Out	2	3	0	0
	Extras (9lb, 2nb)			11			
	TOTAL		(51.5 overs)	227 - 4 dec			

LANCASHIRE bowling

	O	M	R	W
Chapple	4	0	13	0
Smethurst	7	2	39	0
Keedy	22	2	79	2
Schofield	12.5	1	65	2
Scuderi	6	0	22	0

LANCASHIRE - Second Innings

Fall of wkt	Batsman		How Out	Score	Balls	4s	6s
1- 23	G. Chapple	c B.C. Hollioake	b Tudor	7	35	1	0
3- 45	J.P. Crawley *	c A.J. Hollioake	b Saqlain	21	54	1	0
2- 37	A. Flintoff	c B.C. Hollioake	b Tudor	10	9	2	0
4- 89	S.C. Ganguly		b Salisbury	27	61	3	0
6- 132	N.H. Fairbrother	c Brown	b Salisbury	47	85	7	0
5- 94	G.D. Lloyd	c A.J. Hollioake	b Saqlain	1	14	0	0
9- 145	J.C. Scuderi	c Batty	b Salisbury	21	51	4	0
7- 136	W.K. Hegg +	c Butcher	b Salisbury	4	3	1	0
8- 137	C.P. Schofield	c Butcher	b Saqlain	1	13	0	0
	G. Keedy		Not Out	0	8	0	0
10- 145	M.P. Smethurst	c Bicknell	b Salisbury	0	5	0	0
	Extras (2w, 4nb)			6			
	TOTAL		(56 overs)	145			

SURREY bowling

	O	M	R	W
Bicknell	11	4	12	0
Tudor	11	2	42	2
Saqlain	20	8	45	3
Salisbury	14	4	46	5

VIEW FROM THE DRESSING ROOM - ALEX TUDOR

After you made a couple of early breakthroughs you were able to sit back and watch our spinners finish the job off. I guess it must be a big help to you, from a fitness point of view, that we have two quality spinners to take some of the workload off you and Bickers?

AT - Yes, that's very true. In the first innings we usually have to work hard - that's our job - but in the second innings life is made a lot easier by having two world-class spinners. We know that we can run in hard for no more than perhaps twelve overs, hopefully make some breakthroughs, and then let Saqi and Sals come on to work their way through the middle- and lower-order to win the match, which is what happens nine times out of ten.

VIEW FROM THE DRESSING ROOM - NADEEM SHAHID

We had now recorded six wins on the trot and led the table by eleven points, so I guess we must have felt that the title was well within our grasp?

NS - Although we were very pleased with this win, I can honestly say that nobody was counting any chickens. We all know how quickly things can change and we still had crucial games to come against the top teams. But we were quietly confident.

KEITH MEDLYCOTT'S ASSESSMENT

Over a four-week period we had gathered huge momentum by beating Leicestershire twice, Yorkshire and Lancashire. The way the games were panning out, we now knew that if we could get eight days of good weather for the home games against Derbyshire and Durham and continue to play well - we were still going to be giving those sides due respect - then everything would be in our control.

Other Division One Matches

Surrey's comprehensive victory over Lancashire extended their lead over the red rose county to a very useful nineteen points, while Yorkshire now trailed by eleven, following a unimpressive bowling display at Taunton which had left them with ten points from a draw. Leicestershire's hopes of getting back into the frame were dented by a battling display from Kent which narrowly denied them the win that they badly needed and appeared to deserve.

August 2-5
Derby:- **Derbyshire drew with Hampshire.** Derbyshire 310 (Dowman 110, Lacey 55 not out, Mullally 9-93) and 293-9 (Sutton 79, Di Venuto 78 not out, Mullally 5-95); Hampshire 394 (Kenway 136, Mascarenhas 100, Smith 50). **Derbyshire 10pts, Hampshire 11**

Canterbury:- **Kent drew with Leicestershire.** Leicestershire 375 (Habib 78, Wells 72, Kumble 56); Kent 201 and 187 (Key 53, Kumble 6-44). **Kent 8pts, Leicestershire 11**

Taunton:- **Somerset drew with Yorkshire.** Somerset 359 (Rose 124, Trego 62) and 368-3 (Bowler 139 not out, Parsons 108 not out); Yorkshire 327 (Fisher 68, McGrath 56). **Somerset 11pts, Yorkshire 10**

COUNTY CHAMPIONSHIP DIVISION ONE AT 5TH AUGUST

Pos	Prev		P	Pts	W	D	L	Bat	Bowl	Last	Three	Res
1	1	Surrey	12	154	7	3	2	29	29	W18	W17	W16
2	2	Yorkshire	12	143	5	5	2	27	36	D10	D11	W20
3	3	Lancashire	12	135	5	6	1	21	30	L3	D9	W20
4	4	Somerset	12	112	2	7	3	29	31	D11	D9	L3
5	5	Leicestershire	11	111	3	5	3	27	28	D11	L6	W16
6	6	Kent	11	101	3	6	2	11	30	D8	D9	W17
7	7	Durham	11	86	2	3	6	18	32	D9	L6	L3
8	8	Derbyshire	12	80*	1	7	4	15	33	D10	D9	L3
9	9	Hampshire	11	74	1	4	6	13	33	D11	L6	D7
* Deducted 8pts for sub-standard pitch												

13 Homing In On Glory

The Championship victory over previously unbeaten Lancashire had been extremely impressive in that it had been achieved in approximately two-and-a-half days of actual playing time, with the opposition's twenty wickets being snapped up in just ninety-five overs. It had probably also forced Bobby Simpson, the Lancashire coach, into something of a rethink. A couple of weeks before the game at The Oval, he had gone on record as saying that he strongly believed his team could win the title because he had seen all the other first division sides, bar Surrey, and none of them had scared him. I should imagine that the power and ruthlessness of the county champions' display in the match that had been billed as a top-of-the-table showdown would certainly have given him a few nightmares to be getting on with!

Surrey's run of six successive wins in the Championship had merely confirmed them as the most potent team in the competition and had been fuelled by an extraordinary sequence of outstanding individual performances. Against Somerset it was Graham Thorpe (115), Jon Batty (100 not out) and Ian Salisbury (8-60, and 12-91 in the match); at Southampton the stars had been Saqlain Mushtaq (6-51, and 10-135 in the match) and Mark Butcher (116 not out); at Oakham we'd had Ali Brown's incredible 295 not out and 5-35 from Saqlain; in the Yorkshire game it had again been Brown (140 not out) and Saqlain (6-63 and 5-41, giving 11-104 in the match); at Guildford, Martin Bicknell's astonishing 7-72 and 9-47, for a match tally of 16-119, had been backed up by Ian Ward's 107; and, finally, against Lancashire, Alex Tudor had added his name to the roll of honour with 7-48, alongside Salisbury's 5-46. Totting it all up, I found that the six victories had yielded six centuries by five different players and nine instances of five wickets in an innings by four different players, leaving me wondering whether this string of individual performances within a fantastic run of team results had ever been equalled before or would ever be equalled in the future. How much longer could this stunning sequence be maintained?

Looking at the bigger picture, the club's position in the Championship race was now looking very promising. Since neither of our roses rivals could finish the season with more than nine victories and we were already up to seven, it looked safe to assume that two more wins would pretty much seal back-to-back titles for us. The remaining fixtures were of a wildly contrasting nature, though, since two tough-looking away trips to play our title rivals were very nicely balanced by home games against relegation-threatened Durham and Derbyshire. They might have beaten us on their own grounds but those two counties were surely very unlikely to pose us too many problems at The Oval. Weather permitting, our home matches therefore looked likely to provide us with the two wins we needed and, so long as we didn't get trounced at Scarborough and Old Trafford, then we would surely be home and dry, barring miracles.

Before we resumed our Championship quest with the home game against Derbyshire we had an opportunity to all but seal our promotion from the NCL Division Two and maybe take a giant leap towards winning the league title, too, with two matches in the space of four days against rival teams. The second of these matches had added significance since it was to be the first Surrey first team fixture played at Whitgift School in South Croydon.

OLD RIVALS FACE CRUCIAL CLASH AT LORD'S

The clash between the Surrey Lions and the Middlesex Crusaders in NCL Division Two was eagerly anticipated and a very important match for both sides. While Surrey were keen to clinch promotion as soon as possible, in order to concentrate their efforts on the Championship, Middlesex, enduring a pretty poor season all round, badly needed a victory to move themselves back into the top three places in the league. Currently lying in fourth position, having won their previous two matches, they were just two points behind the Warwickshire Bears and four adrift of the Nottinghamshire Outlaws. Their need was even greater than ours.

NCL DIVISION TWO - MATCH ELEVEN

MIDDLESEX CRUSADERS versus SURREY LIONS
at Lord's on Sunday 6th August

Surrey Lions (170-5) beat Middlesex Crusaders (167-8) by five wickets

Another superbly efficient performance by the Surrey Lions at the home of cricket saw them record an easy five-wicket win over their London-based rivals to move within eight points of securing promotion with five games to play.

Little went right for the home side after they won the toss and elected to bat, with Andrew Strauss falling lbw to a Bicknell inswinger from the final ball of the first over and Justin Langer rendered almost completely strokeless by some magnificent bowling from the Surrey opening pair. While Mark Ramprakash settled in well to play some elegant strokes through the covers and square leg, his Australian skipper failed to find his timing before departing to a juggling slip catch for a miserable 29-ball eight in the twelfth over.

The Middlesex middle-order was then blown away with the minimum of fuss by the usual tight mid-innings spells from Saqlain Mushtaq and Jason Ratcliffe as the Crusaders slumped to a desperate 83-5 after 24 overs. To all intents and purposes, Ramprakash was fighting a lone battle as he went on to complete a classy half-century from 86 balls shortly after Ratcliffe finished an excellent spell of bowling with figures of 9-1-21-1. The former Middlesex captain eventually departed in the thirty-seventh over with the score at 118, when Ben Hollioake knocked back his off stump, and the Crusaders only managed to get as far as 167 thanks to some bold late hitting from Simon Cook, whose run-a-ball twenty-eight contained a swept six off Saqlain and three fours.

Although a target of 168 didn't appear likely to seriously test the in-form Lions, both openers had early problems against Angus Fraser before falling in consecutive overs with the score at thirty-two and the run rate barely above two-and-a-half an over.

Fortunately for the league leaders, Nadeem Shahid and Ali Brown were not intimidated by the situation, quickly raising the tempo of the innings with a partnership of forty-five in just eight overs before Brown gave a simple catch to midwicket off Cook with the run rate now exceeding requirements.

While Shahid kept the scoreboard ticking over nicely, the new batsman, Adam Hollioake, soon assumed Brown's mantle and effectively ended the game as a contest when taking thirteen runs from Ben Hutton's first over and eight from his second. It would, in fact, have been twelve from the second but for umpire Hampshire's chest getting in the way of a fierce straight drive destined for the boundary!

The fifty partnership for the fourth wicket arrived in just 62 balls and the loss of the Surrey skipper, after an innings of forty-seven at better than a run a ball, was nothing more than an inconvenience as the Lions cruised towards victory. With the finishing line drawing ever nearer, Shahid ensured that he reached a well-deserved fifty from 79 balls by driving and pulling Paul Weekes for two fours in the thirty-ninth over, then Ratcliffe sealed the win with an off-driven boundary.

As a result of this comfortable victory Surrey were now four points closer to glory, while Middlesex's promotion hopes had taken a dive and their dismal Sunday League/National Cricket League run against their rivals from across the river had now extended to eleven years without a win. Since their last triumph in 1989 there had been nine Surrey victories and one tie.

Surrey Lions (170-5) beat Middlesex Crusaders (167-8) by five wickets

Surrey Lions 4pts

MIDDLESEX CRUSADERS v SURREY LIONS at LORD'S. Played on 6th August
Middlesex Crusaders won the toss   Umpires:- J.H. Hampshire & G. Sharp

MIDDLESEX CRUSADERS   **SURREY LIONS bowling**

Fall of wkt	Batsman		How Out	Score	Balls	4s	6s		O	M	R	W
1- 1	A.J. Strauss		lbw b Bicknell	0	6	0	0	Bicknell	9	0	24	1
2- 35	J.L. Langer *	c Brown	b Tudor	8	29	1	0	Tudor	7	2	24	1
6- 118	M.R. Ramprakash		b B.C. Hollioake	53	98	4	0	Saqlain	9	1	45	2
3- 65	P.N. Weekes		b Saqlain	16	26	1	0	Ratcliffe	9	1	21	1
4- 67	R.M.S. Weston	st Batty	b Saqlain	0	8	0	0	B.C. Hollioake	7	0	32	2
5- 83	D. Alleyne +		lbw b Ratcliffe	2	11	0	0	A.J. Hollioake	4	0	14	1
7- 156	B.L. Hutton	c Brown	b A.J. Hollioake	29	59	3	0					
	S.J. Cook		Not Out	28	28	3	1					
8- 163	R.L. Johnson		b B.C. Hollioake	4	3	1	0					
	A.W. Laraman		Not Out	3	2	0	0					
	A.R.C. Fraser	did not bat										
	Extras (7lb, 17w)			24								
	TOTAL		(45 overs)	167 - 8								

SURREY LIONS   **MIDDLESEX bowling**

Fall of wkt	Batsman		How Out	Score	Balls	4s	6s		O	M	R	W
2- 32	M.A. Butcher		run out	17	44	2	0	Fraser	9	1	27	0
1- 32	I.J. Ward		b Laraman	10	30	1	0	Laraman	9	1	34	1
	Nadeem Shahid		Not Out	50	81	6	0	Cook	7	0	31	1
3- 77	A.D. Brown	c Langer	b Cook	23	22	2	0	Johnson	6.1	1	23	0
4- 152	A.J. Hollioake *	st Alleyne	b Weekes	47	43	7	0	Weekes	6	1	25	2
5- 158	B.C. Hollioake	c Strauss	b Weekes	2	8	0	0	Hutton	2	0	22	0
	J.D. Ratcliffe		Not Out	4	7	1	0					
	J.N. Batty +	did not bat										
	M.P. Bicknell	did not bat										
	A.J. Tudor	did not bat										
	Saqlain Mushtaq	did not bat										
	Extras (8lb, 9w)			17								
	TOTAL		(39.1 overs)	170 - 5								

Other NCL Division Two Matches

The Surrey Lions now led the table by a massive twelve points and looked almost certain to be playing Division One NCL cricket in 2001. Meanwhile, Glamorgan Dragons added to Middlesex Crusaders' gloom by leapfrogging them into fourth place, courtesy of a narrow victory over the Durham Dynamos.

August 6
Derby:- **Hampshire Hawks beat Derbyshire Scorpions by 36 runs.** Hampshire 233 in 45 overs (Kendall 73 not out, Smith 61 not out, Kenway 53); Derbyshire 197 in 42.4 overs. **Hampshire Hawks 4pts**

Cardiff:- **Glamorgan Dragons beat Durham Dynamos by three wickets.** Durham 202-5 (Katich 70, Collingwood 66); Glamorgan 205-7 in 44.5 overs (Dale 73 not out). **Glamorgan Dragons 4pts**

NCL DIVISION TWO AT 6TH AUGUST

Pos	Prev		P	Pts	W	T	L	N/R	Last	Three	Res
1	1	Surrey Lions	11	40	9	0	0	2	W	W	W
2	2	Nottinghamshire Outlaws	10	28	7	0	3	0	L	L	W
3	3	Warwickshire Bears	10	26	6	1	3	0	W	L	W
4	5	Glamorgan Dragons	10	24	5	2	3	0	W	L	T
5	4	Middlesex Crusaders	11	24	5	1	4	1	L	W	W
6	6	Essex Eagles	10	18	4	0	5	1	L	W	W
7	7	Durham Dynamos	11	12	3	0	8	0	L	W	L
=	8	Hampshire Hawks	11	12	3	0	8	0	W	W	L
9	9	Derbyshire Scorpions	10	4	1	0	9	0	L	L	L

VITAL ENCOUNTER MARKS WHITGIFT'S DEBUT

Whitgift School could hardly have wished for a better fixture for its inaugural Surrey first team match since the game featured some of the biggest names in English domestic cricket, playing in a top-of-the-table clash between two of the country's biggest county clubs. As if this wasn't enough, the home team was fast closing in on promotion. All we needed now was a glorious summer's afternoon, a good crowd and a Surrey win!

NCL DIVISION TWO - MATCH TWELVE

SURREY LIONS versus WARWICKSHIRE BEARS
at Whitgift School, Croydon on Wednesday 9th August

Surrey Lions (211-9) beat Warwickshire Bears (108) by 103 runs

Surrey marked their debut at the very attractive Whitgift School ground with a crushing 103-run win over third-placed Warwickshire Bears to move ever closer to seemingly inevitable promotion and potential title glory.

After deciding to bat upon winning the toss, the Lions got away to a rather sticky start, with Ian Ward departing early and the score reaching only 26-1 after twelve overs. Although Surrey seemed to have problems at this point, the Bears had already suffered a serious setback of their own, however, with the loss of Ed Giddins, who had pulled up with an injury in his third over and limped off the field, never to return.

Despite the fact that the pitch was looking just a little tricky for batting, Nadeem Shahid gradually pulled the Lions round as a strangely out-of-sorts Alec Stewart struggled to find any fluency before lifting Ashley Giles to long-off in the nineteenth over with the total advanced to fifty-six.

This brought Graham Thorpe to the crease and he rapidly transformed the match with a truly outstanding innings. Although he soon lost Shahid, undone by a sharp piece of fielding by Dominic Ostler, the England left-hander looked to be on a different plane from everybody else, finding gaps in the field at will and then expanding his repertoire by driving both Giles and Neil Smith for huge straight sixes. Consequently, the Surrey score scorched from 100 to 150 in 47 deliveries and the Thorpe fifty arrived in just 49 balls.

Driven on by Adam Hollioake's good supporting knock of 21 from 19 balls, the Lions looked set for a substantial score when they reached 170-4 in the thirty-seventh over, but the loss of

Thorpe for an excellent 57-ball sixty-two, just minutes after his captain's departure, put a spanner in the Lions' works and a clatter of wickets to Allan Donald left Surrey slightly short of the mark that they had looked likely to attain.

Within ten overs of the Bears starting their reply, that late Lions collapse looked completely inconsequential, however, as four wickets fell for twenty-four runs, two to Alex Tudor, one to Martin Bicknell and the fourth to a run out, following an excellent pick-up and throw by Adam Hollioake.

When Michael Powell, for seven, and Trevor Penney, after a brave thirty-five, then became victims of Saqlain Mushtaq, and Neil Smith followed to a catch off Jason Ratcliffe the game was all but over inside twenty-one overs, with Warwickshire a miserable 73-7. Ashley Giles added a touch of respectability to the total, in partnership with Keith Piper, but the end came suddenly when the Lions' captain claimed the wickets of both men with successive balls, Giles to Shahid's third good catch of the innings and Piper clean bowled. With Giddins unable to bat, the Surrey Lions had clinched their 103-run victory with an incredible fifteen overs to spare and they marched on unbeaten at the top of the table with promotion now virtually assured.

After a thoroughly enjoyable afternoon, blessed by warm sunshine and a very good attendance, Whitgift School looked certain to figure in Surrey's 2001 fixture list.

Surrey Lions (211-9) beat Warwickshire Bears (108) by 103 runs

Surrey Lions 4pts

SURREY LIONS v WARWICKSHIRE BEARS at WHITGIFT SCHOOL, CROYDON. Played on 9th August
Surrey Lions won the toss   Umpires:- M.R. Benson & G.I. Burgess

SURREY LIONS   **WARWICKSHIRE bowling**

Fall of wkt	Batsman	How Out		Score	Balls	4s	6s		O	M	R	W
1- 13	I.J. Ward	st Piper	b Powell	8	20	0	0	Brown	9	3	23	0
2- 56	A.J. Stewart +	c Ostler	b Giles	19	54	2	1	Giddins	2.4	0	5	0
3- 82	Nadeem Shahid	run out		32	57	3	0	Powell	6.2	0	44	2
6- 180	G.P. Thorpe	c Giles	b Smith	62	57	3	2	Donald	9	1	40	3
4- 127	A.D. Brown	c Singh	b Powell	16	21	2	0	Giles	9	0	41	1
5- 170	A.J. Hollioake *	c Singh	b Smith	21	19	1	0	Smith	9	0	50	2
7- 182	J.D. Ratcliffe	c Smith	b Donald	2	5	0	0					
8- 193	A.J. Tudor	c Brown	b Donald	7	14	0	0					
9- 206	M.P. Bicknell	c Smith	b Donald	10	9	1	0					
	I.D.K. Salisbury	Not Out		8	11	1	0					
	Saqlain Mushtaq	Not Out		2	3	0	0					
	Extras (4b, 4lb, 16w)			24								
	TOTAL		(45 overs)	211-9								

WARWICKSHIRE BEARS   **SURREY LIONS bowling**

Fall of wkt	Batsman	How Out		Score	Balls	4s	6s		O	M	R	W
1- 2	N.V. Knight	c Thorpe	b Bicknell	1	5	0	0	Bicknell	7	0	23	1
3- 20	A. Singh	c Salisbury	b Tudor	5	21	0	0	Tudor	7	1	23	2
2- 13	D.P. Ostler	run out		5	12	0	0	Ratcliffe	6	0	25	1
6- 68	T.L. Penney	c Salisbury	b Saqlain	35	39	6	0	Saqlain	7	1	19	2
4- 24	D.R. Brown	c Hollioake	b Tudor	3	8	0	0	Salisbury	2	0	7	0
5- 56	M.J. Powell	c Shahid	b Saqlain	7	22	1	0	Hollioake	1	0	7	2
8- 108	A.F. Giles	c Shahid	b Hollioake	28	38	4	0					
7- 73	N.M.K. Smith *	c Shahid	b Ratcliffe	0	3	0	0					
9- 108	K.J. Piper +		b Hollioake	10	33	0	0					
	A.A. Donald	Not Out		0	0	0	0					
	E.S.H. Giddins	absent injured										
	Extras (4lb, 8w, 2nb)			14								
	TOTAL		(30 overs)	108								

NCL DIVISION TWO AT 9TH AUGUST

Pos	Prev		P	Pts	W	T	L	N/R	Last	Three	Res
1	1	Surrey Lions	12	44	10	0	0	2	W	W	W
2	2	Nottinghamshire Outlaws	10	28	7	0	3	0	L	L	W
3	3	Warwickshire Bears	11	26	6	1	4	0	L	W	L
4	4	Glamorgan Dragons	10	24	5	2	3	0	W	L	T
5	5	Middlesex Crusaders	11	24	5	1	4	1	L	W	W
6	6	Essex Eagles	10	18	4	0	5	1	L	W	W
7	7	Durham Dynamos	11	12	3	0	8	0	L	W	L
=	7	Hampshire Hawks	11	12	3	0	8	0	W	W	L
9	9	Derbyshire Scorpions	10	4	1	0	9	0	L	L	L

THE FLAME STILL FLICKERS FOR THE FOXES

While the top three sides in the Championship took a week's break to play NCL matches, Leicestershire kept their outside hopes of getting back into the Championship race alive with a hard-fought victory over Hampshire at Grace Road. Things were starting to look pretty bleak at the bottom for Derbyshire and Hampshire, though.

August 8-11
Southampton:- **Leicestershire beat Hampshire by 61 runs.** Leicestershire 266 (Habib 61, Dakin 60, Sutcliffe 53, Mullally 5-84) and 240; Hampshire 228 (Aymes 71) and 217 (A.C. Morris 60, White 50). **Leicestershire 17pts, Hampshire 4**

August 9-12
Chester-le-Street:- **Durham drew with Kent.** Kent 170 (Brown 5-59) and 354-7dec (Smith 175); Durham 223 (Speak 89 not out, Saggers 7-79) and 157-3 (Lewis 59 not out). **Durham 8pts, Kent 7**

COUNTY CHAMPIONSHIP DIVISION ONE AT 12TH AUGUST

Pos	Prev		P	Pts	W	D	L	Bat	Bowl	Last	Three	Res
1	1	Surrey	12	154	7	3	2	29	29	W18	W17	W16
2	2	Yorkshire	12	143	5	5	2	27	36	D10	D11	W20
3	3	Lancashire	12	135	5	6	1	21	30	L3	D9	W20
4	5	Leicestershire	12	128	4	5	3	29	31	W17	D11	L6
5	4	Somerset	12	112	2	7	3	29	31	D11	D9	L3
6	6	Kent	12	108	3	7	2	11	33	D7	D8	D9
7	7	Durham	12	94	2	4	6	19	35	D8	D9	L6
8	8	Derbyshire	12	80*	1	7	4	15	33	D10	D9	L3
9	9	Hampshire	12	78	1	4	7	14	36	L4	D11	L6

* Deducted 8pts for sub-standard pitch

PROMOTION IS ASSURED... WITH A MONTH TO GO!

When Middlesex Crusaders beat Warwickshire Bears by fifteen runs under the lights at Edgbaston on Wednesday 16th August, the Surrey Lions' promotion to NCL Division One was confirmed with a whole month of the season still to play. It was slightly disappointing that we weren't actually playing, let alone winning, a match when promotion was clinched but that was out of our hands and we were grateful for our London rivals' efforts on our behalf! It was a good victory for the Crusaders, who had been unfortunate not to beat another of the leading sides, the Nottinghamshire Outlaws, during the round of matches played on Sunday 13th and Monday 14th August. The game at Trent Bridge saw Middlesex on their way to a huge and surely unassailable total when rain had arrived to gift the Outlaws two points that they scarcely deserved.

August 13
Derby:- **Derbyshire Scorpions v Essex Eagles - No Result.** Essex 204-8 (Napier 78); Derbyshire 14-1 in 4 overs. **Derbyshire Scorpions 2pts, Essex Eagles 2**

Trent Bridge:- **Nottinghamshire Outlaws v Middlesex Crusaders - No Result.** Middlesex 241-3 in 37 overs (Ramprakash 61 not out, Alleyne 58). **Nottinghamshire Outlaws 2pts, Middlesex Crusaders 2**

August 14
Chester-le-Street:- **Warwickshire Bears beat Durham Dynamos by seven wickets.** Durham 202-7 (Collingwood 73 not out); Warwickshire 203-3 in 42.3 overs (Knight 75). **Warwickshire Bears 4pts**

Southampton:- **Glamorgan Dragons beat Hampshire Hawks by 5 runs.** Glamorgan 263-5 (Elliott 68, Newell 64, James 50 not out); Hampshire 258-9 (Kendall 85 not out, Thomas 4-42). **Glamorgan Dragons 4pts**

August 16
Edgbaston:- **Middlesex Crusaders beat Warwickshire Bears by 15 runs.** Middlesex 201-9 (Langer 93); Warwickshire 186 in 44 overs (Hutton 4-32). **Middlesex Crusaders 4pts**

NCL DIVISION TWO AT 16TH AUGUST

Pos	Prev		P	Pts	W	T	L	N/R	Last	Three	Res
1	1	Surrey Lions	12	44	10	0	0	2	W	W	W
2	2	Nottinghamshire Outlaws	11	30	7	0	3	1	N/R	L	L
3	3	Warwickshire Bears	13	30	7	1	5	0	L	W	L
4	5	Middlesex Crusaders	13	30	6	1	4	2	W	N/R	L
5	4	Glamorgan Dragons	11	28	6	2	3	0	W	W	L
6	6	Essex Eagles	11	20	4	0	5	2	N/R	L	W
7	7	Durham Dynamos	12	12	3	0	9	0	L	L	W
=	7	Hampshire Hawks	12	12	3	0	9	0	L	W	W
9	9	Derbyshire Scorpions	11	6	1	0	9	1	N/R	L	L

IT'LL BE DRY FOR DERBYSHIRE!

After the problems we had experienced at Derby earlier in the season, one thing was for certain as Derbyshire travelled to The Oval - they would be playing on a dry wicket! Looking back, perhaps we actually owed our visitors a debt of gratitude, since the events at the County Ground in early June had led to the phenomenal run that had taken us to the top of the County Championship table. They could clearly expect no favours from us here, however, as they battled to stave off almost certain relegation. With just the one four-day win and a sole NCL victory to their credit they *were* the weakest link... and if they lost this match then it looked like 'goodbye'!

COUNTY CHAMPIONSHIP - MATCH THIRTEEN

SURREY versus DERBYSHIRE
at The Oval

First Day - Wednesday 16th August

Derbyshire 118; Surrey 161-2

The Teams And The Toss - *Following his disappointing run in County Championship cricket, Ben Hollioake is dropped by Surrey and replaced by Gary Butcher, whose fine form with both bat and ball in the second eleven - including 132 not out, 71 not out and six wickets in his last game - has finally earned him another first-team opportunity. The side is otherwise unchanged from that which routed Lancashire in the previous match. Derbyshire, who choose to field two spinners in Simon Lacey (off-breaks) and Liam Wharton (orthodox left-arm) are at full strength but for the absence of Dominic Cork (with England) and wicketkeeper Karl Krikken (broken thumb). Stand-in skipper, Tim Munton, wins the toss for the visitors and decides to bat first.*

Having been limited to just a couple of one-day fixtures in the past two weeks, Martin Bicknell and Alex Tudor look a little ring-rusty during the opening overs, though Derbyshire, opening with Steve Stubbings and, surprisingly, Simon Lacey, fail to take full advantage. The Lacey experiment doesn't last long, in any case, as the off-spinner slips while turning for a second run to square leg in the sixth over and, after treatment on the pitch, is eventually stretchered off with what looks to be a knee problem.

This departure through injury is then quickly followed by the loss of a wicket when Bicknell pins the left-handed Stubbings on the crease with an inswinger and wins what looks like a straightforward lbw verdict with the score on twenty-four. This dismissal underlines the fact that Surrey's senior seam bowler now has his line properly adjusted, and his new-ball partner is soon offering the best possible proof that he has done likewise by knocking back Michael Di Venuto's middle stump with a fine inswinging yorker in the twelfth over. Tudor has thereby taken revenge for some of the rough treatment handed out to him by the Australian left-hander at Derby and the visitors are in a spot of bother at 30 for 2.

While Bicknell is causing Rob Bailey no end of problems and beating him consistently on both sides of the bat, Surrey's big fast bowler is getting better with every over and he has two confident appeals for lbw against Matthew Dowman turned down before he completes an initial nine-over burst at the Vauxhall end. Bicknell's equally impressive first stint ends simultaneously, heralding a double bowling change which sees the introduction of Gary Butcher and the skipper himself.

Despite these changes, runs prove no easier to come by for the Derbyshire pair, with Dowman, nowhere near as impressive as he had been at Derby, squeezing a Butcher yorker to the third man fence to raise the visitors' fifty and then edging Hollioake over the slips for another rather fortunate boundary. With Butcher getting the ball to swing and looking consistently dangerous, a wicket seems likely to come Surrey's way at any moment and, sure enough, it does, in the medium-pacer's fifth over, when Bailey plays across his front pad and falls leg-before for a painstaking nine, scored from seventy balls. At this point the visitors are 59-3 and they are very nearly 63-4 in Butcher's next over when the new batsman, Luke Sutton, edges a routine catch to third slip but survives when the Surrey captain surprisingly grasses the chance.

It's been a testing first session for Derbyshire and, since Saqlain has only bowled a couple of overs thus far and Ian Salisbury has yet to be utilised, they know that things are likely to get tougher still this afternoon.

Lunch:- Derbyshire 69-3 (Dowman 23*, Sutton 5*) from 31 overs

Martin Bicknell and Alex Tudor are back into the attack again immediately after lunch and Dowman at last produces a couple of well-timed strokes before lapsing back into his less impressive form with an edge over the slips off Bicknell. His luck can't last indefinitely, however, and, having almost presented Tudor with a catch at mid-off two balls previously, he finally falls to the persevering Bicknell when he clips a head-high catch to Nadeem Shahid at midwicket. With Dowman gone for thirty-six and the visitors now 85-4, Surrey look to be well on top.

This impression is merely confirmed by the events of the next two overs. Matthew Cassar, having immediately looked all at sea against Tudor, survives two loud lbw appeals from the big paceman before Luke Sutton further frustrates Bicknell with two outside edges in the same over. The first of these snicks flies to the third man boundary and the second to third slip, where the normally reliable Surrey skipper spills another regulation catch, allowing Sutton to add an escape on fifteen to his earlier reprieve on three.

While Bicknell continues to tear his hair out, Saqlain is reintroduced in place of Tudor at the Vauxhall end and, quite fittingly, Derbyshire's hundred comes up with an edged stroke to third man for three runs by Sutton.

The contest that the Surrey faithful have been waiting for - Saqlain versus Cassar - finally materialises in the Pakistani spin wizard's second over. To no-one's great surprise, the duel doesn't last long, however, with a completely bemused Cassar trapped on the crease and adjudged lbw after just a couple of balls. While Saqlain celebrates reaching fifty first-class wickets for the season in only his ninth match, Simon Lacey returns to the crease with a runner by his side and his team in dire straits at 106-5.

Lacey has only been back in the middle for eight deliveries when Derbyshire lose their sixth wicket, without addition to the total, as Luke Sutton drives at Bicknell and this time sees the resulting edge snapped up at second slip by Mark Butcher. It's looking like men against boys at this moment in time, though Lacey and Aldred do manage to cling on for four almost scoreless overs after the fall of the sixth wicket to see off Bicknell after a superb ten-over spell.

While Saqlain switches to the pavilion end, Bicknell's replacement, Gary Butcher, takes up the attack at the Vauxhall end... with stunning results.

Butcher's opening deliveries of his new spell bring an edged two and a sliced drive to the backward point boundary from Paul Aldred before the sixth flies off the outside edge to Martin Bicknell at third slip. Although Bicknell grabs at the ball and it escapes his grasp, fortunate is smiling on Surrey since Mark Butcher is on hand at second slip to complete the catch and give his younger brother a second wicket in the innings. With an unimpressive-looking tail to come, it's clear that Derbyshire are unlikely to progress too much further from their current 116-7. But no-one is quite prepared for the high drama that follows.

After Lacey adds two to the total with another edged stroke in Saqlain's next over, it's Gary Butcher versus Tim Munton. No contest! The visiting skipper pushes limply at his first ball, an outswinger, and the ball unerringly finds Bicknell at third slip again. This time there's no mistake, no need for a helping hand from Butcher senior, and Surrey's former Glamorgan all-rounder is on a hat-trick.

Surely it couldn't happen, could it? It would be too much of a *Boy's Own* cliché, wouldn't it? All is about to be revealed. The new batsman, Kevin Dean, presents a slight problem in that he is left-handed, so a change of line is required by Butcher for this most important delivery. The tension builds as he runs in from the Vauxhall end and bowls. The line is good, Dean flashes at the ball and, quite incredibly, it flies like an arrow off the edge to that man Bicknell, again at third slip. The Surrey swing king catches the ball cleanly just below waist height and Gary Butcher has taken a hat-trick on his return to the first team! Bicknell hurls the ball skywards and the celebrations begin for the first County Championship hat-trick taken by a Surrey bowler at The Oval since the late great Sylvester Clarke achieved the feat against Nottinghamshire in 1980. No wonder this moment feels so special for all Surrey folk. Butcher receives a well-deserved ovation and it dawns on us that we have almost witnessed what would surely have been a unique hat-trick, with all three victims taken at third slip. How bizarre would that have been if Bicknell had hung on to the first catch rather than donating it to the elder Butcher brother?

The excitement eventually subsides a little and everyone settles down as the last Derbyshire batsman, Liam Wharton, makes his way to the crease. If he bats below Dean, we reason, he can't be that good, can he? But surely Gary Butcher can't... He can! The very next ball smacks into Wharton's pads in front of all three stumps and umpire Julian responds in the affirmative to Surrey's confident and impassioned appeal. It's four-in-four! Amazing! Derbyshire are all out for just 118 and Gary Butcher has achieved one of the rarest feats in the first-class game to finish with 5 for 18. And this after almost four months in the wilderness of second eleven cricket.

The once-forgotten man will now always be remembered for today's achievement and he leads his team off the field with everyone in the ground on their feet and applauding. Butcher waves to the crowd as he goes and it's really emotional stuff to see the man who has stuck at it in the second team finally getting his chance and coming away with a truly magnificent reward.

In the excitement and emotion of the moment it's been easy to miss the fact that Surrey have, in a few short minutes, moved from a very strong position into a match-winning position... and also that tea will now be taken!

Tea:- Between Innings

During the interval the record books have been out. They reveal that Gary Butcher's four-in-four is only the thirty-second recorded instance of the feat being achieved in first-class cricket, the last being by Kevan James of Hampshire against the Indian touring side of 1996. The trick hadn't been turned in the County Championship since 1972, when Surrey's very own Pat Pocock had gone on to register five wickets in six balls, six in nine and seven in eleven against Sussex at Eastbourne. That was the measure of Butcher's achievement.

Without wishing to take anything away from his magnificent effort, I had felt that Derbyshire were actually quite lucky to reach 118, having appeared to be totally outplayed throughout the first two sessions. Not one batsman had looked remotely comfortable at the crease, with edges and miscues abounding. I'd therefore consulted my detailed notes of the innings and discovered that no fewer than forty-one runs - over a third of the visitors' total - had resulted from edged shots and false strokes. Enough said, I think.

The Surrey openers now have to build on the bowlers' good work and they start well against Tim Munton and the left-armer, Kevin Dean, running some great singles and punishing the occasional bad delivery with a firm stroke to the boundary. Although Dean twice manages to find Mark Butcher's outside edge, he rather sprays the ball around in his first spell and wastes the new ball, while Munton looks a mere shadow of the bowler who had caused so many problems on the damp wicket at Derby. As a result, Surrey race up to fifty in the eleventh over when Ian Ward clips the Derbyshire skipper to the square leg boundary and then follows up with a leg-glance worth four more runs.

Batting suddenly looks a far easier proposition and, consequently, Munton is forced into a double bowling change which brings Paul Aldred and Liam Wharton into the attack. It's the first sighting of young Wharton for most people and he makes a favourable early impression while Aldred starts well by forcing Ward into one edge which drops just short of second slip and another which flies over the top of the close-catching cordon. The scoreboard operators are still kept busy, however, especially during an uncharacteristically loose fifth over by Aldred when Ward clips through square leg for two and midwicket for three, before Butcher cuts and edges a brace of boundaries. There's no escaping the fact that Surrey have simply looked different class to their opponents in the game thus far and, when Ward brings up the home team's hundred in the same over that Butcher completes a well-played half-century from 91 balls in 104 minutes, the 1999 county champions are already within touching distance of Derbyshire's feeble total.

Munton takes the arrival of Surrey's hundred as a cue to make another double bowling change, returning to the fray himself in company with Matthew Cassar. This merely accelerates the run-flow, however, as Munton regularly overpitches and is driven straight and through the covers, while Cassar bowls both sides of the wicket and with variable length, allowing both batsmen to score all around the ground. As a result, Surrey take the lead at 6pm, shortly before Ward completes a top-class fifty, seventeen minutes after his opening partner but having received one fewer delivery.

Unfortunately for Surrey, the opening partnership is then cut off in its prime at 137 when Ward is beaten by a full-length inswinger from Cassar and adjudged lbw for an excellent fifty-seven. It's been a marvellously positive effort by the opening pair and it has shown up Derbyshire's earlier effort on what is clearly a good pitch. The new batsman, Nadeem Shahid, simply confirms the quality of the wicket by immediately pulling Cassar to the backward square leg boundary.

With Surrey in full control and passing the 150 mark as the day draws towards its close, Munton, clearly never a man to do things by halves, makes another double change of bowling, reintroducing Dean and Aldred. This time his move does eventually yield fruit, with Aldred tempting Butcher into a hook which results only in a miscue to Stubbings at deep backward square leg. Although the elder brother will be disappointed to have fallen twenty-two runs short of a century, it has certainly been quite a day for the Butchers as Mark leaves the field to warm applause. He is replaced in the middle by the regular Surrey nightwatchman, Ian Salisbury, who plays through to the close with Shahid, repelling a much-improved second spell by Dean and another good effort from Aldred, who has been the pick of the visitors' bowlers on a dire day for Derbyshire.

Close:- Surrey 161-2 (Shahid 13*, Salisbury 4*) from 49 overs

VIEW FROM THE DRESSING ROOM - GARY BUTCHER

This is clearly a very strong Surrey squad and a tough team to break into. When you are playing in the second eleven, how hard is it to balance the desire for first team cricket against the benefits of being part of a successful, trophy-winning set-up?
GB - If you want to be called a Championship winner then there's only one place to be playing your cricket and that's in the first team, so it can be very frustrating if you are not getting the chance to play there. My ambition was always to be in the first team and to be a part of what the club was achieving, so I was pleased when I finally I got my chance.

Some pundits wish to abolish second eleven county cricket. If you hadn't been getting regular second team cricket do you think you could have come back into the first team and made such an immediate impact?
GB - From a personal point of view, I believe I could have done, because I've played quite a lot of first-class cricket before and have had success with both bat and ball - so I know that I can produce the goods if I'm given the opportunity. But we couldn't do away with second eleven cricket, though, because our club cricket is still not strong enough. Although it's getting better, the pitches tend to be pretty average and I think we're a long way short of being able to take people out of the Surrey Championship and put them straight into first-class cricket. And the second eleven is valuable for the younger players, too, because it gives them the opportunity to play in four-day cricket, where they can learn how to play long innings and how to bowl on good flat wickets

Had you almost given up hope of getting a first team opportunity?
GB - No, I'd not given up hope but sometimes there were some very long and frustrating days in the second team. I was just desperate to be given an opportunity and luckily it came along.

It must have been especially exciting to come into the team as it was homing in on another Championship triumph?
GB - Yes, it made it a bit more special although, if anything, it put a little bit more pressure on me to perform because the team was playing so well. But I looked at it as a challenge - if you are going to play in this Surrey side then it's always going to be tough.

To take four wickets in four balls must have been beyond your wildest dreams, though?!
GB - Although it was very nice and something I'll remember for a long time, it was a bit freakish really - the ball was swinging about a lot and I just managed to get it in the right places. What I'd achieved didn't really sink in until I got off the field and then discovered that four-in-four hadn't been done for such a long time and only ever by thirty-two people. Suddenly I had people ringing me up, asking me for my thoughts and wanting me to talk them through it!

I thought the most impressive thing about the hat-trick was that you had to switch your line for the left-handed Kevin Dean, the third victim. I guess that made things more difficult for you.
GB - If anything, I was actually pleased to see a left-hander come in, especially as we were well into the tail - given the amount the ball was swinging, I knew that if I got the ball in anything like the right place I would have a good chance of getting him bowled or lbw. I wasn't expecting to get him caught at third slip, though!

You must have been quite touched by the very warm and generous applause you received as you left the field?
GB - Yes, it was a really special moment because there were quite a lot of people in the ground that day, especially in the pavilion and the surrounding areas. I'll certainly always remember walking off with the team behind me and everyone applauding.

VIEW FROM THE DRESSING ROOM - MARK BUTCHER

You must have been very pleased to see your brother finally being given a chance and then taking it with a headline-grabbing performance.
MB - Yes, he'd been a bit down because he felt his form in the second team had justified him being given a chance in the firsts. But suddenly it all came right for him - Ben hadn't had a great season and then Gary had a very good game against Leicestershire in the second team and was

given an opportunity. His bowling performance was extraordinary and the last thing Derbyshire would have expected when playing at The Oval against Saqlain and Salisbury was for G.P. Butcher to take five for nothing!

Absolutely right. It was hugely ironic that nine of their first innings wickets fell to the seamers because when we were up at Derby their supporters were saying that we would prepare a dry surface for our spinners in the return match at The Oval.
MB - We get that kind of comment everywhere now - they all believe that we prepare dustbowls for Solly and Saqi. The truth of the matter is that they can spin the ball on anything and the only time during the season that I can remember us playing on a big turner at The Oval, against Lancashire in the Nat West game, we came unstuck because it meant that *their* spinners were able to turn the ball as well. We've always said that we want to play on good pitches because our pair can still spin it on that kind of surface.

You and Wardy then got us away to a great start in reply. I thought that partnership almost sealed the game for us - fair comment?
MB - Yes, but it was very disappointing that we didn't go on to get full batting points the next day. We always felt that we would win the game from that position but we realised that we'd chucked some points down the drain by perhaps not being as professional as we might have been. Kevin Dean bowled well but he picked up several of his wickets with catches at midwicket and in the covers, so I think it was one of the few occasions all season when we didn't drill home our advantage.

Second Day - Thursday 17th August

Derbyshire 118 and 97; Surrey 260

Surrey beat Derbyshire by an innings and 45 runs
Surrey 17pts, Derbyshire 3

The opening over of day two brings mixed results, but overall triumph, for Tim Munton, as Nadeem Shahid's drive to the cover boundary is swiftly avenged with an lbw verdict from the final ball as the batsman only gets half-forward.
   Shahid's performance is then almost mirrored by Adam Hollioake when the Surrey captain follows up a cover-driven four off Aldred by offering a catching chance to Munton at second slip in the same bowler's next over. It's a fine delivery, bouncing and leaving the bat, that induces the edge from Hollioake but the Derbyshire captain's attempt to pull in the overhead chance at 170-3 is not of the same quality.
   Fortunately, the Surrey skipper doesn't let this escape affect him and before long he's glancing and square-driving the unlucky Aldred for the second and third boundaries of his innings. While the nightwatchman, Ian Salisbury, continues to hold his own, Hollioake is looking in dominant form, twice crashing Munton to the rope at cover and then bringing up a forty-minute half-century stand by lofting Aldred to the Vauxhall end boundary. The home team's captain has scored thirty-nine of the runs in the partnership but he adds only three more to his score before a change of bowling at the pavilion end brings about his downfall, Kevin Dean forcing him into flicking a catch to Di Venuto at short midwicket with a late inswinger of full length. It's a disappointing end to an extremely entertaining and purposeful 34-ball innings but it has put Surrey very much in charge at 219-4, with full batting points looking a definite possibility.
   The major threat to Surrey reaching their four-hundred target appears to be Dean, who looks much more threatening this morning and is swinging the ball quite prodigiously and, at times,

very late. One such delivery eventually unseats Salisbury, who pays the ultimate price for having the temerity to drive and hook the left-armer for boundaries by having his off stump knocked back as he attempts another drive. The members in the pavilion show their appreciation of the nightwatchman's fine effort as he makes his way back to the pavilion with the scoreboard reading 238 for 5, and the new batsman, Gary Butcher, gets an equally impressive ovation as he walks out to the middle, following yesterday's history-making heroics.

Shortly after Butcher joins Ali Brown at the crease, Matt Cassar is introduced into the attack in place of Aldred and Brown greets the new bowler with a couple of blasts to the boundary. Life is considerably more difficult against Dean, however, and Surrey have only just passed 250, courtesy of Butcher's lofted square drive, when the left-arm seamer produces a stunning burst of wickets to dismantle the home side's lower-order.

Brown goes first, clipping to midwicket, where Stubbings holds a good overhead catch, then, three balls later, Butcher forces a short delivery straight into the hands of Aldred at point. At 256-7, it looks like the number of batting points that Surrey might be capable of achieving now needs to be revised downwards, and that view is confirmed fourteen balls later when the destruction of Jon Batty's stumps by a terrific inswinging yorker reduces the hosts to 257-8.

Unfortunately for Surrey, there's no stopping the slide now and they don't even get close to a third point as Martin Bicknell, shuffling across his stumps, goes lbw to the returning Munton in the next over and then Saqlain Mushtaq falls in the same manner to his first ball, another deadly yorker-length inswinger from Dean.

Incredibly, 219 for 3 has become 260 all out, and the last five wickets have fallen for just five runs as Dean has, through a combination of great deliveries and questionable strokes, transformed his overnight analysis of 0 for 35 into 6 for 51, with a spell of 6 for 16 in 9.3 overs today. This highly commendable innings-wrecking effort seems very unlikely to have changed the course of the game but it has deprived Surrey of three precious batting points and who knows how important those could be come the end of the season. There will be plenty of time to reflect on this during the lunch interval.

Lunch:- Between Innings

Trailing by 142 runs on first innings, Derbyshire clearly face a huge task if they are to have any hope of getting back into the match and prevent Surrey from storming to a seventh successive County Championship victory.

They start well enough, though, with Luke Sutton, taking the injured Simon Lacey's place as stand-in opener, looking reasonably secure as Steve Stubbings mixes some attractive drives through the covers and mid-on with occasional streaky edges to the third man boundary off the luckless Alex Tudor.

After five largely frustrating overs, Tudor gives way to Gary Butcher at the Vauxhall end and, shortly afterwards, Martin Bicknell is replaced by Saqlain at the pavilion end, with the Derbyshire fifty having arrived in the previous over.

It's been a good effort by the visitors' makeshift opening pair to reach this milestone and, though the scoring rate slows against the first-change bowlers, they appear to be playing with a greater degree of confidence than in the first innings until Ian Salisbury enters the action in place of Butcher, who has been unable to reproduce his first-innings magic in an opening burst of four overs.

The Surrey leg-spinner certainly makes a dramatic impact on proceedings in his first over, having Stubbings taken at short leg with his fifth delivery and then producing an action replay with his sixth to send Michael Di Venuto packing in identical fashion for a golden duck. It's 68-2 and Surrey supporters are already getting the feeling that things could really happen now the spinners are operating in tandem. The speed of events takes everyone by surprise, however.

Although Rob Bailey prevents a second Surrey hat-trick in the match by keeping out the first delivery of Salisbury's next over, Saqlain soon has him edging a "wrong 'un" to slip, where Ali Brown performs an extended juggling act before hanging on to a catch which reduces Derbyshire to 69-3.

With the visitors' three best batsmen now back in the pavilion, Surrey are already well on their way to victory and the strong possibility of a two-day victory becomes a mere formality when Saqlain rips out the middle-order with three wickets in his next over. Sutton goes to the second delivery, brilliantly caught low down at silly point by the Surrey skipper, and Matt Cassar follows two balls later when he fails to make contact with an ugly slog and is comprehensively bowled. I doubt that Cassar has had time to remove his pads, let alone contemplate a desperate record of five dismissals at the hands of the Pakistani off-spinner in eight Championship innings, when his replacement, Simon Lacey, is joining him back in the 'hutch'. Like his team-mate before him, Lacey's innings has lasted just two balls, though his mode of dismissal, caught by Shahid at short leg is at least less embarrassing.

Saqlain has now picked up four wickets in his last seven balls at no cost and, in all, six wickets have fallen for just two runs as we have witnessed a very uneven confrontation between top-class spin bowling and what can only be described as club-standard batting. This is typified by the next dismissal, just three overs later, when Paul Aldred dances down the track to Salisbury, misses with a village green cowshot and is stumped by a distance. While it's fair to say that Derbyshire are already well beyond the point of no return, there really is no excuse for the visitors' apparent lack of professional pride in surrendering so meekly. Having scored four runs during his brief stay at the wicket, Aldred is actually fourth-top scorer in an innings which now stands at a pathetic 75-7 and the match now looks unlikely to reach the tea interval.

Predictably enough, the end comes fairly quickly, with Derbyshire's final three wickets falling in the space of twenty-three deliveries. Tim Munton, after picking up a couple of boundaries, eventually gets a leading edge back to Saqlain with the score advanced to ninety, following the second-highest stand of the innings with Matt Dowman, then the ninth wicket falls in the Surrey off-spinner's next over when Kevin Dean is undone by a 'deadly dart' which traps him lbw on the crease. Saqlain now has six wickets and he completes a stunning final return of 7 for 11, and the match, when Dowman plays back to the third ball of his following over and becomes another leg-before victim.

It's 4.20pm and a truly remarkable afternoon's cricket has seen the match completed in just five sessions. Without wishing to take any credit away from a tremendous Surrey bowling performance in this game, it has been obvious to everyone that Derbyshire have simply not been up to the task and their boasts at Derby in early June that they would easily avoid relegation have been made to look as foolhardy as I had thought them to be at the time. On the other side of the coin, Surrey, so humiliated on that day, are now looking increasingly likely to become the first county to win successive Championship titles since Warwickshire in 1994 and 1995.

Derbyshire 118 and 97; Surrey 260
Surrey won by an innings and 45 runs. Surrey 17pts, Derbyshire 3

SURREY v DERBYSHIRE at THE OVAL. Played from 16th - 17th August

Derbyshire won the toss   Umpires:- R. Julian & B. Leadbeater

DERBYSHIRE - First Innings   SURREY bowling

Fall of wkt	Batsman		How Out	Score	Balls	4s	6s		O	M	R	W
1- 24	S.D. Stubbings		lbw b Bicknell	11	21	1	0	Bicknell	19	7	36	3
	S.J. Lacey		Not Out	7	35	0	0	Tudor	15	4	34	1
2- 30	M.J. Di Venuto		b Tudor	10	15	0	0	Hollioake	5	2	10	0
3- 59	R.J. Bailey		lbw b G.P. Butcher	9	70	0	0	G.P. Butcher	7.3	3	18	5
4- 85	M.P. Dowman	c Shahid	b Bicknell	36	79	5	0	Saqlain	7	2	12	1
6- 106	L.D. Sutton +	c M.A. Butcher	b Bicknell	26	64	3	0					
5- 106	M.E. Cassar		lbw b Saqlain	1	14	0	0					
7- 116	P. Aldred	c M.A. Butcher	b G.P. Butcher	6	21	1	0					
8- 118	T.A. Munton *	c Bicknell	b G.P. Butcher	0	1	0	0					
9- 118	K.J. Dean	c Bicknell	b G.P. Butcher	0	1	0	0					
10- 118	L.J. Wharton		lbw b G.P. Butcher	0	1	0	0					
	Extras (4b, 4lb, 2w, 2nb)			12								
	TOTAL		(53.3 overs)	118								

SURREY - First Innings   DERBYSHIRE bowling

Fall of wkt	Batsman		How Out	Score	Balls	4s	6s		O	M	R	W
2- 152	M.A. Butcher	c Stubbings	b Aldred	78	142	12	0	Munton	20	3	69	2
1- 137	I.J. Ward		lbw b Cassar	57	103	5	0	Dean	19.3	5	51	6
3- 165	Nadeem Shahid		lbw b Munton	17	41	3	0	Aldred	21	8	68	1
5- 238	I.D.K. Salisbury		b Dean	24	71	3	0	Wharton	8	1	13	0
4- 219	A.J. Hollioake *	c Di Venuto	b Dean	42	34	6	0	Cassar	11	2	44	1
6- 255	A.D. Brown	c Stubbings	b Dean	15	36	3	0					
7- 256	G.P. Butcher	c Aldred	b Dean	7	25	1	0					
8- 257	J.N. Batty +		b Dean	0	12	0	0					
9- 259	M.P. Bicknell		lbw b Munton	3	10	0	0					
	A.J. Tudor		Not Out	0	2	0	0					
10- 260	Saqlain Mushtaq		lbw b Dean	0	1	0	0					
	Extras (4b, 11lb, 2w)			17								
	TOTAL		(79.3 overs)	260								

DERBYSHIRE - Second Innings   SURREY bowling

Fall of wkt	Batsman		How Out	Score	Balls	4s	6s		O	M	R	W
1- 68	S.D. Stubbings	c Shahid	b Salisbury	41	64	6	0	Bicknell	7	2	16	0
4- 70	L.D. Sutton +	c Hollioake	b Saqlain	23	65	2	0	Tudor	5	1	27	0
2- 68	M.J. Di Venuto	c Shahid	b Salisbury	0	1	0	0	G.P. Butcher	4	0	13	0
3- 69	R.J. Bailey	c Brown	b Saqlain	0	10	0	0	Saqlain	9.3	5	11	7
10- 97	M.P. Dowman	c Batty	b Saqlain	9	24	1	0	Salisbury	8	1	25	3
5- 70	M.E. Cassar		b Saqlain	0	2	0	0					
6- 70	S.J. Lacey	c Shahid	b Saqlain	0	2	0	0					
7- 75	P. Aldred	st Batty	b Salisbury	4	7	1	0					
8- 90	T.A. Munton *		c & b Saqlain	13	17	2	0					
9- 94	K.J. Dean		lbw b Saqlain	0	7	0	0					
	L.J. Wharton		Not Out	0	2	0	0					
	Extras (1b, 4lb, 2w)			7								
	TOTAL		(33.3 overs)	97								

SCOREBOOK EXTRACT - GARY BUTCHER'S 4 WICKETS IN 4 BALLS
(Reproduced by kind permission of Surrey C.C.C. Scoring by Keith Booth)

SCOREBOOK EXTRACT - DERBYSHIRE'S SECOND INNINGS COLLAPSE
(Reproduced by kind permission of Surrey C.C.C. Scoring by Keith Booth)

VIEW FROM THE DRESSING ROOM - GARY BUTCHER

Kevin Dean really swung the ball a lot - and late - as our innings rather fell away. I guess you don't very often encounter that sort of quality in second team cricket.
GB - That's true but, having played quite a lot of first-class cricket, it wasn't a shock to me - you know the bowling's going to be good. Although he bowled okay and swung the ball around, I think it must be said that we batted quite poorly against him - there were some pretty ordinary shots there.

When you bowled your first ball in the second innings were you thinking about the possibility of five-in-five?!
GB - It had crossed my mind before I got the ball in my hand but when my turn came to bowl I was just concentrating on getting the ball into play, really. As it happened, the batsman got a sneaky inside-edge, otherwise I think he would have been plumb lbw. So it wasn't to be.

Solly and Saqi really routed them in their second innings. What is it that makes them so special?
GB - It's mainly the fact that they can both spin the ball both ways and because they don't give you many bad balls to hit. It means that batsmen are usually just playing for survival against them, which is dangerous when there are fielders all around the bat. I remember when I played against them on a turning wicket at Swansea in 1998 that I was always wondering where my next run was coming from.

The next game was against Yorkshire at Scarborough - did we feel that the Championship would almost be ours if we avoided defeat?
GB - We were quietly confident but knew we would be in for a very tough game up there, especially with their strong seam attack. But if we played well then we knew that we wouldn't lose and then we had to feel confident of beating Durham at home, which would mean that we'd be in business.

KEITH MEDLYCOTT'S ASSESSMENT

This very important win put us in great shape for what was going to be a tough trip to Scarborough. We now knew that we would stay in control of our destiny if we could avoid defeat against Yorkshire.

Other Division One Matches

While Surrey were beating Derbyshire at The Oval, Yorkshire and Leicestershire were cancelling one another out in a rain-affected match at Grace Road, and Lancashire were recording a convincing win over Kent. Leicestershire were now out of the title race and Surrey's lead over their roses rivals had increased to significant proportions - eighteen points over Yorkshire and twenty over Lancashire. This represented an advantage of one whole game with only three matches to play.

August 16-19
Leicester:- **Leicestershire drew with Yorkshire.** Leicestershire 351 (Maddy 66, Habib 59, Burns 58, Silverwood 4-60); Yorkshire 340 (Lehmann 115, Hamilton 66). **Leicestershire 11 pts, Yorkshire 10**

Taunton:- **Somerset drew with Durham.** Durham 378 (Speak 78, Collingwood 74); Somerset 362 (Rose 102). **Somerset 11pts, Durham 10**

August 17-19
Old Trafford:- **Lancashire beat Kent by 154 runs.** Lancashire 236 (Saggers 4-54) and 198 (Schofield 70 not out); Kent 155 (Martin 5-42) and 125. **Lancashire 16pts, Kent 3**

\multicolumn{10}{c}{COUNTY CHAMPIONSHIP DIVISION ONE AT 19TH AUGUST}

Pos	Prev		P	Pts	W	D	L	Bat	Bowl	Last Three		Res
1	1	Surrey	13	171	8	3	2	31	32	W17	W18	W17
2	2	Yorkshire	13	153	5	6	2	30	39	D10	D10	D11
3	3	Lancashire	13	151	6	6	1	22	33	W16	L3	D9
4	4	Leicestershire	13	139	4	6	3	33	34	D11	W17	D11
5	5	Somerset	13	123	2	8	3	33	34	D11	D11	D9
6	6	Kent	13	111	3	7	3	11	36	L3	D7	D8
7	7	Durham	13	104	2	5	6	23	37	D10	D8	D9
8	8	Derbyshire	13	83*	1	7	5	15	36	L3	D10	D9
9	9	Hampshire	12	78	1	4	7	14	36	L4	D11	L6

* Deducted 8pts for sub-standard pitch

NCL TITLE JUST OUT OF REACH

After the comprehensive drubbing of Derbyshire in the Championship, no-one was prepared to bet against Surrey repeating their success in the NCL match on the Sunday. The league title was tantalisingly out of reach, however, even if the Lions were to beat the Scorpions, since Nottinghamshire Outlaws and Glamorgan Dragons, the only teams mathematically capable of catching the league leaders, were about to meet at Colwyn Bay. Whatever happened in that match - Outlaws win, Dragons win, no-result or tie - one or other of the two sides would still, theoretically at least, be able to overhaul Surrey. This was all assuming that the Lions won, however, against the side with just one NCL Division Two victory to their name all season.

NCL DIVISION TWO - MATCH THIRTEEN

SURREY LIONS versus DERBYSHIRE SCORPIONS
at The Oval on Sunday 20th August

Surrey Lions (176-4) beat Derbyshire Scorpions (175-9) by six wickets

In many ways this contest mirrored the game at Derby earlier in the season as it ultimately resulted in a Lions win which was rather more comfortably achieved than the cold statistics might suggest. Although only one over remained when Adam Hollioake pulled Rob Bailey to midwicket for two to seal Surrey's win, there had been little doubt about which way the game was going once the Lions' skipper and Jason Ratcliffe had stabilised the innings from a low point of 83-4 in the twenty-fifth over.

An admittedly less-than-inspiring match had started in interesting fashion with the unexpected sight of Saqlain Mushtaq opening the bowling with Martin Bicknell, no doubt to give Matt Cassar, opening the batting for Derbyshire, a few nightmares. This experiment was abandoned after just two overs and, ironically, Cassar then promptly chipped the first ball he received from the new bowler, Alex Tudor, to mid-on!

Making light of this early loss of a wicket, Michael Di Venuto and Rob Bailey gave the innings a base with a stand of thirty-five in seven overs before Martin Bicknell had the Australian left-hander caught behind. The capture of this key Scorpions' wicket turned out to be Bicknell's last act, however, as he left the field shortly afterwards, apparently feeling discomfort from his back again.

With Tudor resting after six overs at the Vauxhall end, Adam Hollioake now turned to his trusty mid-innings pairing of Jason Ratcliffe and Saqlain Mushtaq, but, while the off-spinner picked up two wickets as Derbyshire slipped from the relative heights of 82-2 to 105-5, Ratcliffe was a little below-par and gave way to Ian Salisbury in the twenty-seventh over. This proved to be a good move for Surrey, since the leg-spinner made an early strike, removing James Pyemont in his second over to reduce Derbyshire to 118-6, a point from which a challenging total was never going to be likely.

Although Bailey battled on to score forty-three and Paul Aldred struck a few lusty blows in his 33-ball innings of twenty-five, another clatter of wickets between the thirty-fourth and the thirty-ninth overs saw the score decline from 143-6 to 155-9, leaving the last pair at the crease with almost seven overs of the innings remaining to be bowled. Acceleration was therefore impossible and a return of just twenty runs from Dean and Wharton, though creditable, left the Lions with what looked to be a below-par target.

The unfortunate dismissal of Mark Butcher, run out when Dean deflected Ward's drive onto the non-striker's stumps in the fourth over of the home side's reply, gave the Scorpions an early boost, but all looked to be plain sailing for the Lions as Ward and Nadeem Shahid settled in and took the score to 65-1 in the nineteenth over. Loose shots by both batsmen - Shahid advancing on the left-arm spin of Wharton and missing an attempted drive over extra cover and Ward edging a drive at a very wide delivery - then pegged Surrey back to 79-3 and the loss of Ali Brown, playing across the line of a straight ball from the accurate Aldred, suddenly precipitated a minor crisis.

Luckily for Surrey, the experienced Adam Hollioake and Jason Ratcliffe were unfazed by the situation and, by the simple expedient of working the ball around the field for singles, a target of ninety-three runs from twenty-one overs when they first came together was reduced gradually to fifty-two from nine. With six wickets still in hand, the odds favoured the Lions at this point and the Scorpions' fate was then pretty much sealed by a twelve-run third over from the hapless Cassar, during which both batsmen found the boundary. Although Munton, and then Dean, returned to the fray to support the occasional off-spin of Bailey, the damage had been done and any lingering hopes the visitors harboured of snatching a win were laid to rest when Ratcliffe drove Dean for a handsome six over long-on from the first ball of the forty-third over.

Surrey Lions (176-4) beat Derbyshire Scorpions (175-9) by six wickets

Surrey Lions 4pts

SURREY LIONS v DERBYSHIRE SCORPIONS at THE OVAL. Played on 20th August
Derbyshire Scorpions won the toss   Umpires:- R. Julian & B. Leadbeater

DERBYSHIRE SCORPIONS   **SURREY LIONS** bowling

Fall of wkt	Batsman	How Out		Score	Balls	4s	6s		O	M	R	W
1- 16	M.E. Cassar	c Salisbury	b Tudor	9	17	1	0	Bicknell	7	0	21	1
2- 51	M.J. Di Venuto	c Batty	b Bicknell	30	44	4	0	Saqlain	9	1	34	2
7- 143	R.J. Bailey		b Hollioake	43	76	4	0	Tudor	6	1	29	1
3- 89	M.P. Dowman	c Brown	b Saqlain	24	26	3	0	Ratcliffe	7	0	34	0
4- 91	S.D. Stubbings	run out		0	0	0	0	Salisbury	9	0	32	3
5- 105	L.D. Sutton +		b Saqlain	3	11	0	0	Hollioake	7	1	20	1
6- 118	J.P. Pyemont	c Shahid	b Salisbury	10	13	2	0					
9- 155	P. Aldred	c Ward	b Salisbury	25	33	2	1					
8- 154	T.A. Munton *		c & b Salisbury	1	6	0	0					
	K.J. Dean	Not Out		8	19	0	0					
	L.J. Wharton	Not Out		7	25	0	0					
	Extras (5lb, 10w)			15								
	TOTAL	(45 overs)		175- 9								

SURREY LIONS   **DERBYSHIRE** bowling

Fall of wkt	Batsman	How Out		Score	Balls	4s	6s		O	M	R	W
1- 11	M.A. Butcher	run out		2	14	0	0	Munton	9	1	29	0
3- 79	I.J. Ward	c Sutton	b Aldred	34	71	2	0	Dean	8	1	31	0
2- 66	Nadeem Shahid	st Sutton	b Wharton	23	45	2	0	Aldred	9	0	26	2
4- 83	A.D. Brown		b Aldred	8	10	1	0	Wharton	9	0	36	1
	A.J. Hollioake *	Not Out		48	67	2	0	Cassar	3	0	20	0
	J.D. Ratcliffe	Not Out		42	57	3	1	Bailey	6	0	29	0
	J.N. Batty +	did not bat										
	M.P. Bicknell	did not bat										
	A.J. Tudor	did not bat										
	I.D.K. Salisbury	did not bat										
	Saqlain Mushtaq	did not bat										
	Extras (3b, 2lb, 14w)			19								
	TOTAL	(44 overs)		176- 4								

Other NCL Division Two Matches

The Nottinghamshire Outlaws' drubbing of the Glamorgan Dragons made the picture crystal clear in the race for the Division Two title. The Surrey Lions needed four more points to be absolutely certain of winning the league - or for the Outlaws to lose one of their remaining four fixtures. Since Surrey were playing the Essex Eagles in a floodlit encounter at Colchester on the following Wednesday it was now in their own hands to win the title on the field of play.

August 20
Colchester:- **Hampshire Hawks beat Essex Eagles by six wickets.** Essex 184-8 (Mullally 4-30); Hampshire 188-4 in 36.3 overs (Smith 62, Kenway 56). **Hampshire Hawks 4pts**

Colwyn Bay:- **Nottinghamshire Outlaws beat Glamorgan Dragons by eight wickets (Duckworth-Lewis method).** Glamorgan 104 in 26 overs (Reiffel 3-8); Nottinghamshire 131-2 in 21.3 overs (Bicknell 59 not out). **Nottinghamshire Outlaws 4 pts**

NCL DIVISION TWO AT 20TH AUGUST

Pos	Prev		P	Pts	W	T	L	N/R	Last	Three	Res
1	1	Surrey Lions	13	48	11	0	0	2	W	W	W
2	2	Nottinghamshire Outlaws	12	34	8	0	3	1	W	N/R	L
3	3	Warwickshire Bears	13	30	7	1	5	0	L	W	L
4	4	Middlesex Crusaders	13	30	6	1	4	2	W	N/R	L
5	5	Glamorgan Dragons	12	28	6	2	4	0	L	W	W
6	6	Essex Eagles	12	20	4	0	6	2	L	N/R	L
7	7	Hampshire Hawks	13	16	4	0	9	0	W	L	W
8	7	Durham Dynamos	12	12	3	0	9	0	L	L	W
9	9	Derbyshire Scorpions	12	6	1	0	10	1	L	N/R	L

14 Decisive Days And Dastardly Deeds

It was now crunch time, since two titles were within Surrey's grasp. If current form could be maintained then no-one had any doubts that both trophies would be secured, but crucial matches lay ahead in the Championship, most notably the clash with Yorkshire at Scarborough.

The NCL Division Two title looked as good as won, however, since nobody could see any possibility of Surrey crumbling to defeat in their final three games while Nottinghamshire Outlaws won all of their last four. The opportunity to sew things up was just around the corner, in any case, as the Lions visited Castle Park in Colchester to take on the Essex Eagles. The trophy would be there, ready and waiting, should we clinch the all-important victory against an Eagles team whose promotion hopes had all but died.

NCL DIVISION TWO - MATCH FOURTEEN

ESSEX EAGLES versus SURREY LIONS
at Castle Park, Colchester on Wednesday 23rd August

Essex Eagles (206-8) beat Surrey Lions (183) by 23 runs

The Surrey Lions lost their chance to secure the NCL Division Two title at Castle Park when they went down to their first defeat of the season, by twenty-three runs, at the hands of a Stuart Law-inspired Essex Eagles. They would now have to wait eleven days until their next match, coincidentally away to second-placed Nottinghamshire Outlaws, or rely on their Trent Bridge rivals slipping up against Middlesex Crusaders on Bank Holiday Monday.

The game at Colchester had started promisingly, with Martin Bicknell and Alex Tudor keeping Law and Nasser Hussain down to just nine runs in the first five overs, before the England captain suddenly reeled off three successive boundaries against Tudor, with a pull and two straight drives. From that moment onwards everything changed - although, quite bizarrely, Hussain lost his way completely and was never the same again, Stuart Law suddenly started to run riot, and Surrey were under the cosh for almost thirty overs.

After the Essex fifty had rattled up inside ten overs, Law completed a stunning 45-ball half-century four overs later with the total at seventy-seven, forcing Adam Hollioake to replace Bicknell and the out-of-sorts Tudor with Saqlain Mushtaq and Jason Ratcliffe. Despite the best efforts of this pair, the home openers continued to prosper and when Ian Salisbury's opening over yielded eleven runs the Eagles were flying high at 128-0 after twenty-five overs. A final total well in excess of 250 was now looking likely but once the Surrey skipper joined forces with his leg-spinner the picture again changed dramatically.

Although Hussain reached fifty in 86 deliveries, shortly ahead of Essex passing 150 in the thirtieth over, he was now struggling badly, frequently miscuing his shots and scoring almost exclusively in the third man region, so it came as no surprise when he skied an ugly slog at Hollioake almost vertically to Alec Stewart with the total standing at 161. At last, a break!

Crucially for Surrey, the dynamic Law then followed his skipper back to the pavilion in the following over, his outstanding knock of ninety-two from 94 balls ended by a Salisbury leg-break which induced a miscued drive to short third man, and the Lions suddenly had an outside chance of getting back into the game.

No-one could have anticipated a sudden clatter of six wickets for thirty-three runs in the space of twelve overs, though! While nothing should be taken away from Hollioake or Salisbury, who both bowled with skill and intelligence to outwit many of their victims, it was amazing to see how easy the Eagles made it for them, as a succession of batsmen threw their wickets away with wanton strokes into the waiting hands of fielders. Both bowlers ended up with four wickets as the Essex innings faded away to 206-8.

Despite losing Alec Stewart with the score at twenty-eight, the Lions looked to be roaring to title glory when they reached 58-1 in the thirteenth over of their reply, but the loss of Ali Brown and Nadeem Shahid in the space of six deliveries to the economical pairing of Ronnie Irani and the impressive rookie paceman, Andrew McGarry, resulted in a serious loss of momentum. Although the left-handed combination of Thorpe and Ward kept the score ticking over with some daredevil running between the wickets, neither man was able to find the boundary and Thorpe's frustration eventually told, with a top-edged sweep off Grayson finding the safe hands of Tim Mason at short fine leg.

At 98-4, the Surrey target was now 109 runs from twenty-one overs, a reasonable task on a good batting track but not so easy on this pitch, which had given assistance to all bowlers, particularly the spinners, throughout. A forthright innings from Adam Hollioake seemed likely to turn the game in the Lions' favour, however, as a fifty partnership in eleven overs took the score through to 149-4 with almost ten overs remaining.

Bafflingly, with the title now beckoning, Ward appeared to lose patience against Danny Law and the visitors then proceeded to emulate their hosts, with a succession of woeful strokes reducing them to a hopeless 164-9. Martin Bicknell and Saqlain Mushtaq tried hard to retrieve the situation, but the damage had been done and the Eagles deservedly ended the Lions' thirteen-game unbeaten run when Saqlain holed out off Ashley Cowan with nine balls remaining.

Essex Eagles (206-8) beat Surrey Lions (183) by 23 runs

Essex Eagles 4pts

ESSEX EAGLES v SURREY LIONS at COLCHESTER. Played on 23rd August
Essex Eagles won the toss Umpires:- J.H. Hampshire & D.R. Shepherd

ESSEX EAGLES

Fall of wkt	Batsman	How Out	Score	Balls	4s	6s	SURREY LIONS bowling	O	M	R	W
1- 161	N. Hussain	c Stewart	b Hollioake	57	102	4	0	Bicknell	7	0	27	0
2- 164	S.G. Law	c Hollioake	b Salisbury	92	94	11	1	Tudor	6	0	44	0
3- 168	G.R. Napier	c Bicknell	b Salisbury	2	8	0	0	Saqlain	9	1	34	0
4- 180	R.C. Irani *	c Bicknell	b Hollioake	8	18	0	0	Ratcliffe	5	0	22	0
5- 180	S.D. Peters	c Brown	b Salisbury	7	10	1	0	Salisbury	9	2	32	4
6- 180	A.P. Grayson	c Stewart	b Salisbury	0	2	0	0	Hollioake	9	0	38	4
	J.S. Foster +		Not Out	11	15	0	0					
7- 187	D.R. Law	c Thorpe	b Hollioake	2	11	0	0					
8- 197	A.P. Cowan	c Shahid	b Hollioake	3	5	0	0					
	T.J. Mason		Not Out	8	7	1	0					
	A.C. McGarry	did not bat										
	Extras (5b, 4lb, 3w, 4nb)			16								
	TOTAL		(45 overs)	206-8								

SURREY LIONS

Fall of wkt	Batsman	How Out	Score	Balls	4s	6s	ESSEX EAGLES bowling	O	M	R	W
3- 58	A.D. Brown		b McGarry	27	38	3	0	Cowan	8.3	0	38	2
1- 28	A.J. Stewart +	c D.R. Law	b Cowan	13	19	2	0	D.R. Law	8	1	45	3
2- 58	Nadeem Shahid	c Foster	b Irani	14	23	2	0	Irani	8	1	23	1
4- 95	G.P. Thorpe	c Mason	b Grayson	19	37	0	0	McGarry	8	2	20	2
5- 149	I.J. Ward		b D.R. Law	25	64	0	0	Mason	6	0	29	0
6- 154	A.J. Hollioake *	c Napier	b D.R. Law	36	41	4	0	Grayson	5	0	19	1
7- 161	J.D. Ratcliffe	c Cowan	b McGarry	9	8	1	0					
8- 164	A.J. Tudor	c Irani	b D.R. Law	3	6	0	0					
	M.P. Bicknell		Not Out	15	9	2	0					
9- 164	I.D.K. Salisbury		run out	0	4	0	0					
10- 183	Saqlain Mushtaq	c D.R. Law	b Cowan	4	13	0	0					
	Extras (9lb, 7w, 2nb)			18								
	TOTAL		(43.3 overs)	183								

CL DIVISION TWO AT 23RD AUGUST

Pos	Prev		P	Pts	W	T	L	N/R	Last	Three	Res
1	1	Surrey Lions	14	48	11	0	1	2	L	W	W
2	2	Nottinghamshire Outlaws	12	34	8	0	3	1	W	N/R	L
3	3	Warwickshire Bears	13	30	7	1	5	0	L	W	L
4	4	Middlesex Crusaders	13	30	6	1	4	2	W	N/R	L
5	5	Glamorgan Dragons	12	28	6	2	4	0	L	W	W
6	6	Essex Eagles	13	24	5	0	6	2	W	L	N/R
7	7	Hampshire Hawks	13	16	4	0	9	0	W	L	W
8	8	Durham Dynamos	12	12	3	0	9	0	L	L	W
9	9	Derbyshire Scorpions	12	6	1	0	10	1	L	N/R	L

LANCASHIRE FAIL TO JOIN SURREY AT THE SUMMIT

While Surrey were missing out on the chance to claim the NCL Division Two crown at Colchester, another round of Championship matches was taking place and, after four hard days, Lancashire eventually failed in their bid to draw level with the reigning champions at the top of the table, being held to a draw by Leicestershire on a very good pitch at Grace Road. Things were looking increasingly good for Surrey.

August 22-25
Derby:- **Derbyshire beat Durham by 232 runs.** Derbyshire 167 (Bailey 54) and 476-7dec (Cork 200 not out, Dowman 140); Durham 144 and 267 (Katich 70, Collingwood 66). **Derbyshire 15pts, Durham 3**

Canterbury:- **Kent beat Hampshire by 15 runs.** Kent 323 (Nixon 134 not out, Mullally 5-90) and 146 (Warne 6-34); Hampshire 156 (Prittipaul 52, Saggers 5-47) and 298 (Kendall 72, McCague 5-52). **Kent 18pts, Hampshire 3**

Leicester:- **Leicestershire drew with Lancashire.** Leicestershire 372 (DeFreitas 97, Habib 93, Dakin 50) and 408-6 (DeFreitas 123 not out, Habib 73, Sutcliffe 52); Lancashire 574-5dec (Crawley 139, Fairbrother 100, Ganguly 87, Hegg 65 not out, Flintoff 55). **Leicestershire 9pts, Lancashire 12**

COUNTY CHAMPIONSHIP DIVISION ONE AT 25TH AUGUST

Pos	Prev		P	Pts	W	D	L	Bat	Bowl	Last	Three	Res
1	1	Surrey	13	171	8	3	2	31	32	W17	W18	W17
2	3	Lancashire	14	163	6	7	1	27	36	D12	W16	L3
3	2	Yorkshire	13	153	5	6	2	30	39	D10	D10	D11
4	4	Leicestershire	14	148	4	7	3	37	35	D9	D11	W17
5	6	Kent	14	129	4	7	3	14	39	W18	L3	D7
6	5	Somerset	13	123	2	8	3	33	34	D11	D11	D9
7	7	Durham	14	107	2	5	7	23	40	L3	D10	D8
8	8	Derbyshire	14	98*	2	7	5	15	39	W15	L3	D10
9	9	Hampshire	13	81	1	4	8	14	39	L3	L4	D11
* Deducted 8pts for sub-standard pitch												

THE LIONS' NCL TITLE IS CLINCHED ON SURREY SOIL...
BY MIDDLESEX!

Who would have believed it - the NCL Division Two title being clinched for the Lions on Surrey soil by Middlesex! It sounds strange but that's what happened on Bank Holiday Monday as the Crusaders, playing a first team match at Richmond for the first time, comfortably defeated the Nottinghamshire Outlaws in a game reduced by rain to twenty-one overs per side. It was hugely ironic that our north London rivals, of all people, had now confirmed both our promotion and our league title by winning games while we were not in action, but I'm sure no-one really minded. We would be playing in the top division next year and now we had a trophy to boot! It was one down, one to go as Surrey prepared for the all-important Championship game at Scarborough.

August 27
Derby:- **Glamorgan Dragons beat Derbyshire Scorpions by one wicket.** Derbyshire 211 in 45 overs (Bailey 64); Glamorgan 212-9 in 44.5 overs (James 56, Powell 53). **Glamorgan Dragons 4pts**

Chester-le-Street:- **Essex Eagles beat Durham Dynamos by one wicket (Duckworth-Lewis method).** Durham 188-8 in 43 overs (Katich 63, Collingwood 50); Essex 167-9 in 32.1 overs (Jefferson 50, Killeen 4-32). **Essex Eagles 4pts**

August 28
Richmond:- **Middlesex Crusaders beat Nottinghamshire Outlaws by 23 runs.** Middlesex 148-3 in 21 overs (Ramprakash 53 not out); Nottinghamshire 125-7 in 21 overs. **Middlesex Crusaders 4pts**

August 29
Chester-le-Street:- **Hampshire Hawks beat Durham Dynamos by seven wickets.** Durham 161-8; Hampshire 165-3 in 39.1 overs (Smith 88 not out). **Hampshire Hawks 4pts**

NCL DIVISION TWO AT 29TH AUGUST

Pos	Prev		P	Pts	W	T	L	N/R	Last	Three	Res
1	1	Surrey Lions	14	48	11	0	1	2	L	W	W
2	2	Nottinghamshire Outlaws	13	34	8	0	4	1	L	W	N/R
3	4	Middlesex Crusaders	14	34	7	1	4	2	W	W	N/R
4	5	Glamorgan Dragons	13	32	7	2	4	0	W	L	W
5	3	Warwickshire Bears	13	30	7	1	5	0	L	W	L
6	6	Essex Eagles	14	28	6	0	6	2	W	W	L
7	7	Hampshire Hawks	14	20	5	0	9	0	W	W	L
8	8	Durham Dynamos	14	12	3	0	11	0	L	L	L
9	9	Derbyshire Scorpions	13	6	1	0	11	1	L	L	N/R

SURREY IN CHARGE AS SCARBOROUGH TEST LOOMS

Lancashire's inability to win at Grace Road had seriously dented their chances of a first outright County Championship triumph since 1934 and it appeared to leave Yorkshire as the principal contenders for Surrey's crown. Keith Medlycott's team still seemed to be very much in pole position, however, since the white rose county really needed to beat the leaders at Scarborough if they were to keep alive hopes of recording their first success in the premier county competition for thirty-two years. A defeat would end Yorkshire's challenge instantly, while a draw would surely leave them with too much ground to make up over the last two matches. The key factor, as everyone knew, was Surrey's penultimate game at home to Durham, since it had 'home-banker' written all over it, given fair weather.

That was in the future, though, and we first had to concentrate all our efforts and energies on the battle at North Marine Road, Scarborough. A fair number of Surrey supporters were going to be at the ground for this crucial game and everyone was looking forward to some good cricket, though we had pre-match misgivings about the type of pitch that might be served up for the contest. In the past, the Scarborough C.C. ground had been noted for its magnificent square and pitches but, in more recent times, Yorkshire had been known to 'spice up' the wicket in order to make life easier for their battery of seam bowlers. After the humiliation David Byas' team had suffered at the hands of Saqlain and Salisbury at The Oval it was obvious that we were going to find grass left on the pitch for our visit. We just had to hope that they wouldn't go too far and produce a wicket that was overly sporty for such an important clash.

COUNTY CHAMPIONSHIP - MATCH FOURTEEN

YORKSHIRE versus SURREY
at Scarborough

First Day - Wednesday 30th August

Surrey 330-8

The Teams And The Toss - *There's bad news for Surrey ahead of this critical clash, with Martin Bicknell's back injury ruling him out of the match. Ben Hollioake gets the nod to replace him and he will take the new ball alongside Alex Tudor, while Surrey resist any temptation to omit Ian Salisbury, who is celebrating a well-deserved call-up for England's winter tours to Pakistan and Sri Lanka. In the absence of the injured Ryan Sidebottom, Yorkshire give a debut to 20-year-old seamer, Greg Lambert, who makes up a four-man front-line seam attack with Chris Silverwood, Matthew Hoggard and Gavin Hamilton. There is no specialist spinner in their side and Simon Guy retains his place behind the stumps ahead of the recently-axed Richard Blakey. The pitch is every bit as green as had been anticipated, so it is entirely predictable that David Byas, making his comeback appearance after a spell on the sidelines with a knee injury, should invite Surrey to bat when Adam Hollioake calls incorrectly at the toss.*

The most important match of the season gets under way in overcast conditions in front of a very good-sized crowd with Chris Silverwood and Matthew Hoggard firing the opening salvos for Yorkshire. In such seamer-friendly conditions it is flabbergasting to see that David Byas has posted only two slip fieldsmen for both bowlers and that Hoggard has three single-savers on the legside in addition to the obligatory long leg. It is, therefore, inevitable that the day's first four, in the seventh over, comes when Ian Ward edges the ball at catchable height through the vacant third slip area.

The Surrey opener then follows up with a much more convincing boundary, clipped through midwicket off Hoggard in the following over, as the Yorkshire bowling proves rather erratic in terms of line, length and overall quality. Silverwood does find a good ball for Ward in his sixth over, however, and the ball flies, at comfortable height, straight to Gavin Hamilton at third slip, the position having been belatedly filled by Byas after Ward's earlier edge. Unfortunately for Silverwood and the home side, Hamilton is unable to take the routine chance, perhaps explaining why Byas hadn't bothered positioning anyone there before!

Since Hamilton has, by now, replaced Hoggard at the pavilion end, he has a chance to make amends and he does so by dismissing Mark Butcher in his next over. The former England opener has made a quiet start and his score has only reached eight when he nicks a good delivery to Simon Guy behind the stumps. Surrey are now 29-1.

A change of batsman, Shahid for Butcher, is followed immediately by a change of bowler, as young Lambert steps up to take over from Silverwood at the Trafalgar Square end of the ground. His first ball in first-class cricket is clipped to square leg for three runs by Ward but, thereafter, he settles down, two wides apart, to complete three reasonable overs. Hamilton is meanwhile proving to be the most threatening bowler on view to date, beating the bat on a number of occasions without adding to the wicket he had picked up in his second over. Surrey are grateful then for a poor fourth over from Lambert, who is driven through the covers by Shahid and through wide mid-on by Ward, as Surrey pass fifty. Both of these strokes, though apparently well timed, earn only three runs since the outfield is as luxuriantly-grassed as the pitch and also a little damp after overnight rain.

Lambert's looseness sees him replaced by Hoggard for the twenty-first over of the morning but the England paceman is far from impressive in his second spell, conceding two cuts for four and a pair of drives for three to Shahid during a three-over burst which costs sixteen runs. Although Ward has, in the meantime, glanced and driven boundaries of his own off Hamilton, he also has another slightly fortunate moment when he edges to third man for four.

With this very valuable stand now past fifty, the Yorkshire skipper puts his faith in Gary Fellows and Chris Silverwood for the final half-hour before lunch. Yorkshire are in desperate need of another breakthrough but Fellows starts poorly against Shahid and the former Essex batsman takes full advantage by crashing two lovely drives through the off-side to take his score up to twenty-nine. Alas, his innings goes no further as Fellows nips the fourth ball of his second over back into the batsman's pads to win an lbw verdict from umpire Harris. A score of 93-2 at this point still represents a very good effort by Surrey, however, and their skipper takes them past the hundred mark with driven and hooked boundaries from Silverwood in the following over.

As lunch arrives shortly afterwards we are able to reflect on a fine morning for the visitors. Having lost the toss, there were fears amongst the Surrey fans that the team could potentially find themselves in real trouble, with five or six wickets down by lunch, but this grim scenario hasn't materialised thanks to a combination of excellent batting and some rather wayward bowling. Hamilton apart, the Yorkshire seamers have bowled too short and too wide, and, as a result, the batsmen have not been made to play at enough deliveries. The dropped catch which gave Ward a second life appears to have been the most significant moment of the session and this missed opportunity has been compounded by a rather uninspiring, and at times shoddy, ground fielding effort. Round one very much to Surrey.

Lunch:- Surrey 106-2 (Ward 39*, A.J. Hollioake 11*) from 32 overs

With the weather much improved, Surrey start brightly after lunch as both Hollioake and Ward find the boundary, against Silverwood and Fellows respectively, and the left-handed Surrey opener then completes an excellent half-century, from 113 balls in 151 minutes, during the fifth over of the afternoon.

In a repetition of tactics used during the morning session, Byas switches his bowlers rapidly, introducing Hamilton for Fellows and Hoggard for Silverwood, in an apparent attempt to unsettle the batsmen and keep all his pacemen fresh. Hoggard's return gets away to a poor start, however, when Ward drives his first ball to the cover boundary, while Hamilton is more accurate, conceding nothing in front of the wicket. It's Hoggard who eventually makes the break for Yorkshire, though, as Ward pops the ball up towards mid-on when a delivery appears to 'stop' on him - Simon Widdup runs in and takes a good low catch with the score at 147 to end the third-wicket partnership shortly after it has passed fifty.

With Hollioake raising the 150, courtesy of a glance to the fine leg boundary in Hoggard's next over, Surrey are still looking in very good shape at this stage, but things are about to change with Yorkshire's capture of two wickets in the space of four overs.

Having replaced Hamilton at the pavilion end, Lambert is the first bowler to strike, claiming his maiden first-class wicket when he gets a lifting ball to flick Ali Brown's glove on the way through to wicketkeeper Simon Guy as the batsman tries to shoulder arms. Brown is out for two and Surrey are 158-4. Then, in the eighth over of a much improved third spell of the day, Hoggard tempts Hollioake to drive at a delivery wide of off stump and sees the resulting outside edge again swallowed up by Guy, this time low to his right.

Yorkshire must now sense a chance to get back into the game with their visitors having declined to 168-5 but, fortunately for Surrey, Gary Butcher is looking to be in good form as he reels off three elegant drives to finally see off Hoggard after an eleven-over stint from the Trafalgar Square end. The man who Butcher has recently replaced in the Surrey team, Ben Hollioake, again fails to make a mark, however, as an under-edged cut at the second ball of a new spell from Fellows provides Guy with his fourth catch of the innings.

A score of 185-6 then becomes 197-7 just five overs later when the white rose comeback continues with the capture of Butcher's wicket by Hamilton. Having looked in very little trouble at all during his time at the crease, the fall of the younger Butcher brother, caught low down at cover from a slightly uppish drive, comes as something of a surprise and gives the many Yorkshire supporters in the ground further hope.

The safe haven of the tea break is just five overs away at this point and, much to the relief of the Surrey faithful, Jon Batty and Ian Salisbury see their side through without further loss. While the home team has won the session, the visitors will be happy that they have already got runs on the board, especially since there have been signs of uneven bounce in the pitch during the afternoon.

Tea:- Surrey 208-7 (Batty 11*, Salisbury 0*) from 72 overs

The period of play immediately after tea looks to be vital, with Yorkshire needing to dispose of the Surrey tail quickly if they are to complete their comeback. It is surprising, therefore, that David Byas chooses to pair Chris Silverwood with, first, the medium pace of Fellows and then the inexperienced Lambert for the opening overs of the session. Although Lambert is driven for two boundaries in his first over by Jon Batty, before tightening his line and length, it's Silverwood who turns out to be the weakest link for the home side, however, as he bangs the ball in too short and is cut repeatedly in a woefully misdirected five-over spell.

After ten overs of the final session, with the total having advanced by thirty-two runs, the Yorkshire skipper is rightly becoming a worried man and, consequently, he makes a double bowling change by recalling Matthew Hoggard at the Trafalgar Square end and pairing him with Darren Lehmann.

The Australian's occasional left-arm spin looks unlikely to cause any problems, initially, as Batty's square-cut boundary completes an extremely important fifty partnership for the eighth wicket, but in his second over Lehmann sees Salisbury, on ten, missed at slip by Byas as a delivery turns sufficiently to take the edge of a defensive bat. One run accrues from the fumbled opportunity, allowing Batty, the dominant partner in the stand thus far, to rub salt into Yorkshire's wound by sweeping the next ball to the rope at fine leg. Having endured a lean time with the bat since his maiden century against Somerset, it's terrific for Surrey fans to see 'JB' coming good at such a vital time and closing in on a half-century.

It is, therefore, most disappointing to see him fall just short of the mark when he fails to clear mid-off with a drive from a Lehmann full-toss six overs later. The Surrey 'keeper can feel justifiably proud of his innings of forty-seven, though, since it has been largely responsible for taking the champions from a somewhat perilous 197-7 to a position at 275-8 where they can potentially control the game.

After fairly sedate beginnings, Salisbury has steadily moved up through the gears and he continues to increase the tempo following his partner's demise, with a fine pull to the square leg boundary seeing Hoggard out of the attack and heralding the return of Hamilton, the undoubted pick of the bowlers to date. With Alex Tudor making a composed start, the Surrey score continues to build towards three-hundred and it becomes increasingly clear that Yorkshire will pay a heavy price for not including a specialist spinner in their side when Lehmann produces a truly awful ninth over - it costs eleven runs and contains every kind of rank delivery imaginable, including a bouncer which Tudor hooks for four. Yorkshire heads drop visibly and the visitors' third batting point duly arrives in Hamilton's next over, which turns out to be another untidy affair.

With the day drawing to a close and the new ball soon due, Byas now turns back to his opening pair, but it's too little, too late, since his side is already in some disarray. The first over of Hoggard's return, the final one with the old ball, sees a Salisbury single turned into a five by four overthrows, then Tudor manages to run two from the next delivery when his top-edged hook falls into space at square leg. This leaves Hoggard fuming and Byas seething and when Tudor square drives the next ball beautifully for four you get the feeling that someone is set to explode!

To add to Yorkshire's frustrations, Silverwood's first over with the new ball doesn't turn out to be any better, as Salisbury clips his first ball to the midwicket boundary and then follows up with a cut for two, a deliberate upper-cut over the diminutive Simon Guy for a four that completes a nine-over fifty stand, and a leg-glance for a single.

With the batsmen content to play out the last three overs quietly, this just about concludes the entertainment for the day after an amazing final session which has seen Surrey add 122 runs for the loss of just one wicket. Despite being put in on a well-grassed pitch that has offered extravagant movement off the seam and occasional uneven bounce, the reigning champions have dominated the day with a marvellous team effort. Although only one man has reached fifty, there have been no fewer than six contributions of between twenty-three and forty-seven and four partnerships of fifty-plus. The top-order ensured that the potential disaster of 150 all out was never a possibility and then the lower-order responded in style after the stumble to 197-7.

The bigger picture is just as promising, too, since Surrey are now virtually assured of a minimum of six points from the game, even if they were to somehow lose, and a minimum of ten points should the game end in a draw. Yorkshire's chances of closing the gap at the top of the table are already looking slim, therefore, and they really have to find some way of winning the match from the current position. Are they good enough to do that? I think not.

Two other factors add to the home side's problems. The weather forecast is quite poor for later in the week, should they manage somehow to get themselves into a winning position, and, more importantly, the pitch is under severe scrutiny. Having already carried out a close examination of the surface before the start of play, the Pitch Liaison Officer, Mike Denness, is again out in the middle with the groundsman as the last few members of a very impressive first-day crowd of some six thousand filter from the ground.

Close:- Surrey 330-8 (Salisbury 47*, Tudor 23*) from 104 overs

VIEW FROM THE DRESSING ROOM - MARTIN BICKNELL

You must have been very disappointed to miss out on this game, on the greenest of wickets.
MB - Yes, I'd been having a few problems in the game before this one with some back spasms that I thought would sort themselves out with a bit of a break. So I then played in a John Paul Getty game on the Bank Holiday Monday, the day before we were due to leave for Scarborough, to test it out. I bowled a spell and then found that I couldn't come back later so I knew I was struggling. Then, when I woke up the next morning, I found that I could hardly move, so I had to go and have my back scanned and obviously had no chance of travelling to Scarborough. Fortunately, it was nothing too serious as it turned out.

VIEW FROM THE DRESSING ROOM - ADAM HOLLIOAKE

What was our initial view of the Scarborough pitch?
AH - Unlike at Derby, we knew exactly what this pitch was going to play like as soon as we saw it. The most disappointing thing, though, was that we knew what the wicket was going to be like before we even got to the ground and, in fact, I'd go so far as to say that there was definite intent to produce a poor pitch here. When the Pitch Liaison Officer saw it before play started he could see it was bad so I suggested to him that maybe he could ask the groundsman to take all the grass off it - then we would have a good pitch, no problems, no-one getting docked points and hopefully a good game with the best team winning. We were quite happy for that to happen but it didn't, unfortunately, so we were left with this ludicrous situation where we had a showpiece match, which should have been the highlight of the season, where the pitch took all the headlines - and that, obviously, is not good for the game.

I would imagine that we must have been concerned to lose the toss and be put in?
AH - When the coin came down as it did, I didn't even bother to wait to hear what he said, I just turned around and walked off and signalled to the dressing room that we were batting. And the guys responded brilliantly, no-one showed disappointment because we knew the job we had to do. Having been fortunate enough to win the toss, I think they showed why they didn't win the competition by the way they bowled at us - they just bowled short and tried to hit us... and at the end of the day we got 356, which was beyond our wildest dreams. They bowled very poorly and we played unbelievably well.

VIEW FROM THE DRESSING ROOM - IAN WARD

What were your initial thoughts when you saw the pitch that had been prepared for the match?
IW - My first thought was that it was a pity Bickers wasn't playing because on that track he'd have had the game won for us in less than two days. It was obvious that they were intent on trying to blast us out with their seamers, which was a bit of a gamble because we've got good seamers ourselves. And then I thought it was a great shame that county cricket had been dragged down to this level. This isn't the way forward for English cricket - we should be developing our cricketers on the best possible pitches, not what we were presented with here. It was particularly disappointing that the practice wicket, just a few strips down the square, was probably the best track I've batted on for about three years, whereas the pitch being used for the match looked like it had been used a couple of weeks before and then had nothing done to it, bar the addition of a few white lines and two sets of stumps.

Given the state of the pitch and the fact that we had been put in, did you feel that your most important innings of the season, to date, was ahead of you as you went out to bat?
IW - No, I wasn't looking at it like that, I was thinking solely about what I had to do, which was to get through the first hour and see off the opening attack of Silverwood and Hoggard - which is a hard enough task on a good pitch, let alone this one. Fortunately, we had a bit of luck, I was dropped early on and they bowled too short, simple as that.

I thought it was a brilliant effort by the top order to get us safely through the new ball and to lunch with only two wickets down. I guess you must have felt very pleased as you went off for lunch?
IW - Yes, definitely, it was a fair effort and I would say that we had the upper hand for that period. The number of runs we scored was almost irrelevant - on that pitch, against that attack, we just wanted to get through losing as few wickets as possible. So we were mildly content at lunch to have lost just two wickets - but we knew that the next period was going to be just as difficult, so we had to keep going.

I thought that Jon Batty and Ian Salisbury also batted particularly well after we had suffered a mid-innings wobble. Fair comment?
IW - Yes, absolutely, the top order ground them down and then we once again showed our strength in depth with the bat to capitalise on their tiredness and their mistakes as the day wore on. Every run over two-hundred was just another nail in their coffin and stuffed the decision to play the game on such a poor wicket back down their throats. I think the people within the Yorkshire club who put this thing in progress really need to take a good hard look at themselves.

VIEW FROM THE DRESSING ROOM - JON BATTY

What was our initial view of the Scarborough pitch?
JB - Having played at Scarborough a few years ago, I felt the pitch was much greener than was "normal" - but that is what I had expected, bearing in mind that they don't have world-class spinners, as we do.

At 197-7 we were struggling a little. Was your innings of forty-seven in some ways a better effort, because of its importance, than your century against Somerset?
JB - It was particularly sweet for me because I had been working on a technical aspect of my game for a large part of the season and this was the first match in which I felt it all came together. But I was very disappointed to have thrown my wicket away as I did.

Second Day - Thursday 31st August

Surrey 356 and 53-2; Yorkshire 158

I suppose it is inevitable that the Scarborough pitch dominates the county cricket headlines in the newspapers this morning, though it is at least nice to see a couple of pictures showing how full the ground was on the first day. One of these black-and-white photos, of Adam Hollioake leaving the field after his dismissal, with a packed terrace behind him, could quite easily have been mistaken for a 1950's shot, but for the crash helmet in his hand and the manufacturers' logos on his bat. The size of the attendance will probably have been the only thing to have cheered Yorkshire C.C.C. on day one, however.

As everyone prepares for the second day's action, there is another potential cloud on the white rose county's horizon, however. The pitch this morning definitely looks a lighter shade of green and though I, like many others, had assumed that this was as a result of it becoming drier overnight, there are rumours of something more sinister having taken place - it is being said that a mower has been run over the pitch to take quite a lot of grass off the surface. Surely Yorkshire wouldn't have stooped to that level, would they? This rumour gains further credence, however, with the appearance on the ground of Richard Arnold, a Surrey supporter whose guest house bathroom overlooks the ground. His first, completely unprompted, comment is that he had seen the groundsman mowing what he thought was the match pitch at about 8.45am. Knowing it to be against the laws of the game, he had assumed that he must be mistaken and that the mower must have been at work on a different strip, but now we are all having serious doubts about what has been going on. If it is indeed true that a significant amount of grass has been removed from the pitch in mid-match then someone has clearly breached not only the laws of cricket but also the spirit of the game. It will be interesting to see whether anything comes of this.

Back out in the middle, Yorkshire make a good start to day two when Alex Tudor is trapped leg-before by a fine yorker-length delivery from Hoggard in the second over of the morning and, with Surrey now 333-9, the home fans are clearly hoping that Yorkshire will be able to finish the innings off before the Championship leaders gain another all-important batting point. Their hopes soon recede, however, as Ian Salisbury completes a tremendous half-century from, 101 balls in 151 minutes, in the next over from Silverwood and then looks on as Saqlain blasts the former England paceman for two fours, one through backward square leg and the other through backward point. Salisbury follows up by lifting Hoggard over cover for another boundary, and then a single from a no-ball in the following over finally brings up 350 for Surrey. Although the innings ends two overs later when Saqlain's outside edge off Silverwood is well picked up in front of first slip by a diving Guy, the visitors appear to have already amassed an insurmountable total, especially since the pitch has played one or two tricks this morning, with a couple of attempted bouncers just not getting up as expected.

As Yorkshire start out on their pursuit of Surrey's 356, the visiting supporters are hoping for a couple of wickets before lunch. No-one expects these two wickets to come from the first two balls of the innings, however! It's almost fantasy cricket as Alex Tudor's opening delivery nips back to trap Simon Widdup stone-dead lbw on the crease and then his second takes the edge of Anthony McGrath's tentative defensive bat on the way through to Jon Batty. Who could have believed this - Alex Tudor is on a hat-trick after his first two deliveries!

It's certainly very good news for Surrey to have got the dangerous Lehmann to the crease against the new ball, even though he allows the hat-trick delivery to pass by comfortably outside his off stump and then gets off the mark with an on-driven two. As opening overs go, Tudor's couldn't have been much better and, to give another good-sized Yorkshire crowd their due credit, the big paceman gets a fine ovation as he takes up his fielding position at long leg at the end of the over. After all the skullduggery that appears to have taken place at Scarborough to date, it's very refreshing and heartening to witness such a sporting reaction from the fans.

After his new-ball partner's opening over, Ben Hollioake certainly has something to compete with as he takes up the attack for the second over from the pavilion end. Although he can't possibly emulate Tudor's two-wicket feat, he does manage to pick up one, however, when he produces a stunning inswinging yorker to uproot the left-handed Vic Craven's leg stump. It's 4 for 3 and Surrey are in seventh heaven, while Yorkshire and their fans are in a state of shock.

The hosts are very fortunate, too, that their score doesn't become 4 for 4 in the following over, when Tudor's front-foot transgression spares Lehmann after the batsman's wild swish results in an edge to Batty. I guess that kind of score would have been too much to hope for in any case and, since the only possible way is up for Yorkshire from this desperate situation, it's almost inevitable that a period of recovery follows.

Inevitably, the fightback is led by Lehmann, while David Byas contents himself with a supporting role. In the hope of finding the batsman's edge again, Tudor continues to slant the ball across Lehmann, but he pays a heavy price in doing so, as any slight errors in width or length are heavily punished by the Australian left-hander. Meanwhile, at the other end, the Yorkshire skipper rarely looks comfortable, even though he does eventually produce a classical off-drive for four off Tudor and then takes the fourth-wicket stand through to fifty in the twelfth over by clipping Hollioake to the midwicket boundary.

As Yorkshire's position continues to improve, Tudor takes a well-earned break after eight overs, with Gary Butcher's introduction allowing Ben Hollioake to switch to the Trafalgar Square end. There's clearly something about the end of the ground that has a home-from-home sound for the Surrey lads, since the former England all-rounder picks up the fourth wicket of the innings in only his second over from that end. Byas is his victim, taken at short leg off bat and pad, after a valuable but far from convincing 57-ball stay at the wicket. The Yorkshire skipper's team is back in the mire again at 73-4 as he departs, and all their hopes are, as per usual, resting with Lehmann, who completes a typically forthright half-century from 58 balls in 89 minutes in the following over when he glances, drives and steers Gary Butcher for a total of nine runs.

Surrey are clearly delighted with their efforts as lunch arrives one over later and the teams make way for the brass band that entertains the crowd during the intervals at Scarborough. From a Yorkshire point of view, it seems highly appropriate that they immediately burst into a rendition of 'The Theme From Mission Impossible'!

Lunch:- Yorkshire 84-4 (Lehmann 51*, Fellows 1*) from 21 overs

Yorkshire are quickly out of the blocks after lunch and their total races into three figures inside two overs as Fellows and Lehmann flay Tudor and Ben Hollioake for three off-side boundaries. The Surrey new-ball pair soon regains control, however, as Lehmann snicks Hollioake streakily to third man and Tudor makes another breakthrough for his side by inducing an edge from Fellows which Batty takes behind the stumps. Yorkshire are now 112-5 and the only thing that prevents the visitors from making further progress in the next twenty minutes is a shower of rain which drives the umpires and players temporarily from the field.

As if to prove his point, it takes no more than an over for Surrey to plunge their hosts deeper into the chasm of despair after the resumption, with the key batsman, Darren Lehmann, the man to depart. It's a bonus for the visitors that the Australian is run out by his partner, Gavin Hamilton, who pushes the ball into the covers, calls his team-mate for a single and then sends him back too late to beat Ian Ward's sensible throw to the bowler, Ben Hollioake, who has made his way back to the non-striker's stumps. Lehmann departs the scene with anger etched all over his face and it's a fair bet that no-one asks him for his autograph as he leaves the field.

Everyone appreciates the significance of this wicket and it knocks all the remaining stuffing out of Yorkshire. From 123-6 at the point of Lehmann's dismissal, they slump further to 130-8 as Simon Guy and Chris Silverwood depart in successive overs from Tudor and Hollioake. Although he only lasts eleven balls, Guy looks utterly out of his depth as Tudor either raps his pads or beats him outside the off stump with every ball of his thirteenth over before nailing him lbw with the first ball of his fourteenth, then Silverwood falls to the opening ball of the next over when Hollioake gratefully accepts a low return catch poked tamely back at him by the batsman. Tudor now leads Hollioake by four wickets to three and Yorkshire appear to be sinking fast.

As it happens, the boat stays afloat a little longer than anticipated as Hoggard shows a little more tenacity and ability with the bat than expected and Hamilton produces one or two nice strokes. Yorkshire even make it through to 150 as both batsmen drive Tudor for three, before the big fast bowler leaves the field in apparent physical discomfort, possibly cramp, at the conclusion of his seventeenth over. Tudor's well-being will now be a major factor in the equation when Adam Hollioake makes his decision as to whether or not he will enforce the follow-on. Although this matter generates a lot of debate amongst the Surrey faithful, there's no doubt which side is in total control of the match.

Tudor's departure has, of course, forced a bowling change, with Saqlain Mushtaq being introduced at the pavilion end. As he is setting his field, a Yorkshire fan somewhere behind me bawls out "You'll not get any wickets on *this* track, lad".

The gentleman concerned is reminded of this comment when, seven balls later, the Surrey off-spinner has two wickets to his name at no cost! His second delivery, floated up into the blockhole, completely confounds and bowls a bemused Hamilton, while the first ball of his second over brings further success when the last man, Lambert, provides Adam Hollioake with a bat-pad catch at silly point.

As our Yorkshire friend devours a huge slice of humble pie, the players head off for tea with the home team all out for 158, some 198 runs adrift of Surrey's first innings total. The reigning champions' performance in the field has been exemplary, with Tudor (4-75) and Hollioake (3-67) both excellent, all possible catching chances taken and Batty in good form throughout behind the wicket.

With three bowling points now secured to add the four points picked up for batting, and a minimum of four draw points surely to come, another huge step has been taken towards the retention of the title.

Tea:- Between Innings

During the afternoon, radio reports have stated that meetings are to be held this evening to decide whether or not Yorkshire will be deducted points for the pitch they have produced for this match - the decision will then be announced either tonight or tomorrow morning.

One thing that has already been ascertained, however, is that Surrey will bat again, with Adam Hollioake's hand probably forced by the potential injury or cramp suffered by Alex Tudor and the fact that Ben Hollioake has bowled nineteen overs already today.

It is hard to imagine that Yorkshire will be that enthusiastic about fielding again, in any case, and a couple of scruffy opening overs, featuring two overthrows and a wide, suggest that the home side might well be suffering a hangover from their dismal batting effort. They are temporarily lifted, however, when Chris Silverwood removes Ian Ward with the first ball of the third over, the batsman flirting outside his off stump and edging to wicketkeeper Guy without a run to his name and the total on five.

This wicket prompts a period of sensible circumspection by Mark Butcher and Nadeem Shahid as Silverwood produces his best spell of the match, though Butcher eventually breaks free with a square-cut boundary off Hoggard, and Shahid immediately takes on Hamilton with lofted drives over cover and midwicket when the Scottish all-rounder is introduced at the pavilion end.

It all seems to be going well for the visitors as the total advances to thirty-two, but Hamilton has a score to settle with Shahid and duly takes revenge for those early boundaries in his fourth over when the Surrey number three shoulders arms and loses his off stump.

The wicket-taker is surprisingly given only one more over before the debutant Lambert joins forces with Hoggard in the attack. Although the latter is very unlucky not to claim the wicket of Adam Hollioake with the score on thirty-seven, when Craven drops a straightforward catch at mid-off, the Surrey batsmen have relatively few problems in reaching fifty before bad light brings an early close at 6.10pm with an incredible twenty-two overs remaining to be bowled.

Close:- Surrey 53-2 (M.A. Butcher 30*, A.J. Hollioake 5*) from 26 overs

VIEW FROM THE DRESSING ROOM - ADAM HOLLIOAKE

Was your decision not to enforce the follow-on largely determined by Alex Tudor's cramp and the fact that Ben had already bowled nineteen overs in the day?
AH - Pretty much so, yes. At that time we felt that we still had plenty of time to win the game if we batted again - we weren't to know that we were going to get hardly any play for the next two days. Additionally, I felt that their only possible chance of winning the game was if I made them follow on and then opened the bowling with myself and Gary (Butcher)!

Third Day - Friday 1st September

Surrey 356 and 89-3; Yorkshire 158

The decision has been made - Yorkshire are to be deducted eight points for producing a pitch rated as "poor". The official ECB statement, released the previous night, read as follows:-
"A pitch panel, comprising Mike Denness and Alan Fordham, met today to discuss the pitch currently in use in the PPP Healthcare County Championship match between Yorkshire and Surrey. The pitch has been ruled as poor and the penalty of an eight-point deduction has been imposed on Yorkshire. The panel have to decide two factors on the evidence heard and what they physically see using their cricket experience. The first is what rating to give the pitch. The second is whether there are sufficient extenuating circumstances which would negate the imposing of a points penalty. The pitch meets two of the criteria for a poor pitch in that there has been undue seam movement and uneven bounce at any time in the match. It has therefore been rated poor."

Clearly, and quite rightly, this decision had not been taken lightly - but I was convinced that it was the right one for cricket in this country. In my view, we simply have to stamp out this practice of preparing poor quality pitches if we are to produce top quality cricketers. Is it any surprise, for example, that Yorkshire struggle to bring through good young batsmen and spinners when they play most of their home games on wickets that are no good to anyone but seam bowlers? One of my Yorkshire friends has told me that Darren Lehmann has warned the county that they won't produce any top-class young batsmen until they provide good quality pitches - yet it seems that the powers-that-be think they know better. More fool them.

The main consequence of the points deduction, of course, is that Yorkshire's already fragile title hopes have been shattered. Although this is fantastic news for Surrey, I do still feel a degree of sympathy for their many loyal supporters, who can have no real influence over things like pitch policy. They deserve better.

As do all the spectators at the ground on the third morning of the match. After very heavy and prolonged overnight rain - I went out with some of my fellow Surrey supporters and got soaked to the skin, so I know how bad it was! - the players and spectators are greeted by a lovely sunny morning... but no cricket. Although the outfield is understandably very wet and a prompt start would, therefore, have been impossible, it appears that we are going to have to wait a very considerable time before we see any play, owing to the fact that a lot of water has penetrated under the covers that protect the bowlers' run-up at the pavilion end of the ground. I call them covers but, quite frankly, they look little better than heavy-duty plastic bin-liners, so I'm not the slightest bit surprised that they have failed to do an adequate job when confronted by last night's downpour. It's sad to report that spectators had not been warned about the possibility of the lengthy delay before paying their money at the turnstiles and, quite incredibly, once in the ground they are still allowed to tramp all over the outfield for some considerable time before an announcement is made to ask them to leave the pitch. To further add to everyone's irritation, the ground staff stand about doing absolutely nothing, even though it is clear where the offending area is in the bowler's take-off area.

The umpires appear for an official first inspection at 10.50am and are joined by David Byas. Much discussion follows, with the Yorkshire captain's gestures and body language clearly suggesting that he doesn't want to play. Even from the distance of the boundary, it's patently obvious that there is conflict between Byas and Messrs Dudleston and Harris, maybe as a result of the umpires expressing concern about the pitch on day one. The umpires eventually ask the groundsman to fork the very wet area which is causing all the problems, prompting the question as to why he had not used his experience and initiative to do this earlier, and, with Byas having departed the scene, Adam Hollioake and Keith Medlycott make their way out to the middle to assess the situation and express their views.

With little else to do, the Surrey supporters on the ground chat with the locals and we are left dumbfounded by the stream of gossip that emanates from our Yorkshire counterparts - Darren Lehmann has, allegedly, been fined £3000 for damage he did to the dressing room after his run out dismissal yesterday; Chris Silverwood is joining Surrey; Paul Franks is leaving Nottinghamshire for Yorkshire; Matthew Wood is moving from Yorkshire to Worcestershire; and the covers on the bowlers' run-ups were ripped by vandals during the night. No-one has any idea if any of these stories are true but the one tale that *nobody* believes is that some people from the hospitality areas are responsible for today's problems, since they emptied bottles of wine over the troublesome run-up late last night. It's all pretty bizarre stuff, especially the thought of Yorkshiremen wasting good wine by 'watering' the run-ups, but I suppose when people have nothing better to do then they are likely to make up any old stories for a laugh!

The inadequate covering for the run-ups is no laughing matter, however. The Yorkshire club must have top-class covers at Headingley, so why didn't they transport them here for this match? I put this question to my Yorkshire friend and he tells me that it's a matter of 'local pride' as Scarborough Cricket Club would have felt their own covering was good enough. Quite frankly, I'm amazed by this reply. This is professional cricket we are talking about. It's the most important match of the season, with a large crowd guaranteed - around 4,500 for the second day after the first day's 6,000 - yet 'local pride' has been allowed to come into the equation. With a responsibility to the game, the players and the spectators, Yorkshire should surely have insisted on transporting their covers from Headingley - and to hell with the feelings of Scarborough C.C. and the relatively minor cost of the operation. The whole situation is almost incredible, in the truest sense of the word, and the Yorkshire club's apparent disregard for their members and the paying public, most of whom have been extremely pleasant and friendly towards the visiting supporters, is truly shocking.

Thankfully, as the ground dries out, we are at least treated to the sight of the ever-popular Saqlain playing cricket on the outfield with some of the children - this man's enthusiasm knows no bounds! - before the game is hijacked by Dickie Bird, who inevitably insists on a head-to-head confrontation with the Surrey off-spinner. Everyone seems to enjoy the contest, however, and it does, at least, put smiles back on a few faces.

Finally, after all the chat and the frustration, we get some action. The umpires decide on a 3.30pm start and the Yorkshire players drag themselves out onto the pitch, most of them making it very obvious that they don't want to play. I find their attitude appalling. Not only are they demonstrating contempt for the spectators, the vast majority of them home fans after all, but they are displaying a most negative response to the situation their team now faces. Following their points deduction, it is now absolutely certain that in order to maintain any outside chance of overhauling Surrey in the title race they simply *must* find a way to win the current match. Of course it is a 1,000 to 1 shot, given their current predicament, but they sure as hell aren't going to be able to win the match if they are sitting in the dressing room. If their captain and their coach had shown a more positive attitude and a less sulky nature then maybe play could even have started a little earlier... but that's Yorkshire's problem.

Unfortunately, by the time play starts, there are nasty grey clouds building up in the distance and our time looks limited. Chris Silverwood does manage to have Adam Hollioake caught at deep backward square leg, not for the first time this season, when he hooks at a bouncer, but the only noteworthy performance, otherwise, is the positive batting of Mark Butcher, who contributes three well-executed boundaries in advancing Surrey's lead to 287 before tea arrives after a spell of play lasting just eleven overs.

Sadly, the sky is now slate grey and a thunderstorm breaks during the tea interval to bring an end to one of Yorkshire County Cricket Club's least glorious days. Everyone who has been at the ground will remember today for a very long time - but, unfortunately, for all the *wrong* reasons.

Tea and Close:- Surrey 89-3 (M.A. Butcher 49*, Brown 4*) from 34 overs

VIEW FROM THE DRESSING ROOM - ADAM HOLLIOAKE

Very wet conditions virtually wiped out the third day's play. I thought their covers for the run-ups looked rather inadequate - was that how you saw it?
AH - Yes, it was just one area around where the bowlers were going to be taking off that stopped us getting out in the middle to play. It was very disappointing and very amateurish, really. I think it summed up our whole time in Scarborough, to be honest.

Fourth Day - Saturday 2nd September

Surrey 356 and 89-3 declared; Yorkshire 158 and 68-0

Match Drawn - Surrey 11pts, Yorkshire 7

Heavy overnight rain again leads to a much-delayed start, giving everyone plenty of time to take in the latest Scarborough gossip - it alleges that both Martyn Moxon and David Byas have been reported to the ECB for verbal abuse of the umpires - and to read the morning papers. It is revealed in the match report that the Yorkshire players had refused to take lunch with the Surrey players yesterday and, since this appears to be fact rather than rumour, one can only agree with the correspondent from *The Times*, who describes it as "a show of petulance that was unbecoming of professional sportsmen."

With the game now certainly ruined as a contest, a 3pm inspection results in the announcement of a 4pm start, prompting a Surrey declaration to set Yorkshire a purely theoretical target of 288 to win from a minimum of thirty-two overs.

Avoiding the calamitous start of their first innings, the home openers, Widdup and Craven, see off initial bursts of six and four overs respectively from Tudor and Ben Hollioake before being confronted by spin. It's a pretty pointless exercise for everyone concerned, really, and the Yorkshire batsmen come through their test with surprisingly few alarms to confirm the rain-wrecked draw and Surrey's ever-tightening grip on the Championship trophy.

Surrey 356 and 89-3 declared; Yorkshire 158 and 68-0
Match Drawn. Surrey 11pts, Yorkshire 7

YORKSHIRE v SURREY at SCARBOROUGH. Played from 30th August - 2nd September
Yorkshire won the toss   Umpires:- B. Dudleston & J.H. Harris

SURREY - First Innings   YORKSHIRE bowling

Fall of wkt	Batsman	How Out		Score	Balls	4s	6s		O	M	R	W
1- 29	M.A. Butcher	c Guy	b Hamilton	8	33	0	0	Silverwood	23.3	6	76	1
3- 147	I.J. Ward	c Widdup	b Hoggard	59	145	8	0	Hoggard	30	1	100	3
2- 93	Nadeem Shahid		lbw b Fellows	29	52	4	0	Hamilton	20	6	53	2
5- 168	A.J. Hollioake *	c Guy	b Hoggard	37	78	6	0	Lambert	14	2	36	1
4- 158	A.D. Brown	c Guy	b Lambert	2	12	0	0	Fellows	14	5	27	2
7- 197	G.P. Butcher	c Lehmann	b Hamilton	27	53	4	0	Lehmann	9	0	34	1
6- 185	B.C. Hollioake	c Guy	b Fellows	4	22	0	0					
8- 275	J.N. Batty +	c Hamilton	b Lehmann	47	100	6	0					
	I.D.K. Salisbury		Not Out	57	111	4	0					
9- 333	A.J. Tudor		lbw b Hoggard	24	43	2	0					
10- 356	Saqlain Mushtaq	c Guy	b Silverwood	12	21	2	0					
	Extras (15b, 15lb, 6w, 14nb)			50								
	TOTAL		(110.3 overs)	356								

YORKSHIRE - First Innings   SURREY bowling

Fall of wkt	Batsman	How Out		Score	Balls	4s	6s		O	M	R	W
1- 0	S. Widdup		lbw b Tudor	0	1	0	0	Tudor	17	1	75	4
3- 4	V.J. Craven		b B.C. Hollioake	2	4	0	0	B.C. Hollioake	19	1	67	3
2- 0	A. McGrath	c Batty	b Tudor	0	1	0	0	G.P. Butcher	4	1	13	0
6- 123	D.S. Lehmann		run out	66	74	7	0	Saqlain	1.1	1	0	2
4- 73	D. Byas *	c Shahid	b B.C. Hollioake	19	57	3	0					
5- 112	G.M. Fellows	c Batty	b Tudor	16	23	3	0					
9- 156	G.M. Hamilton		b Saqlain	23	49	2	0					
7- 125	S.M. Guy +		lbw b Tudor	0	11	0	0					
8- 130	C.E.W. Silverwood		c & b B.C. Hollioake	3	6	0	0					
	M.J. Hoggard		Not Out	10	21	0	0					
10- 158	G.A. Lambert	c A.J. Hollioake	b Saqlain	1	6	0	0					
	Extras (3lb, 2w, 13nb)			18								
	TOTAL		(41.1 overs)	158								

SURREY - Second Innings   YORKSHIRE bowling

Fall of wkt	Batsman	How Out		Score	Balls	4s	6s		O	M	R	W
	M.A. Butcher		Not Out	49	128	5	0	Silverwood	13	2	24	2
1- 5	I.J. Ward	c Guy	b Silverwood	0	4	0	0	Hoggard	15	2	36	0
2- 32	Nadeem Shahid		b Hamilton	13	30	2	0	Hamilton	5	1	11	1
3- 67	A.J. Hollioake *	c Craven	b Silverwood	13	44	0	0	Lambert	4	0	10	0
	A.D. Brown		Not Out	4	16	0	0					
	Extras (6b, 2lb, 2w)			10								
	TOTAL		(37 overs)	89 - 3 dec								

YORKSHIRE - Second Innings   SURREY bowling

Fall of wkt	Batsman	How Out	Score	Balls	4s	6s		O	M	R	W
	S. Widdup	Not Out	38	87	5	0	Tudor	6	1	13	0
	V.J. Craven	Not Out	17	66	2	0	B.C. Hollioake	4	0	15	0
							Saqlain	8	1	18	0
	Extras (7lb, 6nb)		13				Salisbury	6	2	13	0
	TOTAL	(25 overs)	68 - 0				Brown	1	0	2	0

233

VIEW FROM THE DRESSING ROOM - ADAM HOLLIOAKE

There was a rumour going around the ground that a mower was run over the pitch before the start of the <u>second</u> day's play. Was there any truth in that, as far as you are aware?
AH - Yes, that's true - and I feel very strongly about what happened on that second morning. I haven't said anything about it before because I didn't want it to take anything away from the fact that we won the Championship and because, at the end of the day, we went up there and did a great job. Before the game started we said in the dressing room that we knew it was a bad pitch but that it wasn't going to change between the start and the end of the game, so we just had to get out there and win on it - if we want to be called the best side in the country then we have to win in all conditions. The most important thing about this game, though, was that it showed me how far we had come since Derby - we were now mentally strong enough to deal with the situation. We were able to put the pitch to the back of our minds, accept the challenge it presented, play with all the odds against us and hold our heads up high. And I was so proud of the team at Scarborough - the way everyone held themselves both on and off the field. It was certainly my proudest time as Surrey captain, so far, because no-one complained and no-one moaned about anything, despite the fact that we were, generally speaking, treated like dirt up there.

One example being when the Yorkshire players refused to take lunch with us?
AH - Yes, I'm not sure why that was, because, to be fair, a lot of their players are actually very nice guys, but I think it would be reasonable to say that the people who run their team are less than......

Honourable?
AH - ...less than honourable... less than intelligent, I think it's fair to say!

Some Yorkshire members told me that the Yorkshire club thinks the wicket at Scarborough is too good and produces boring draws unless grass is left on it to help the bowlers. What is your view of that?
AH - As far as I'm concerned, players, captains and chief executives aren't paid to make decisions about the type of pitch that the groundsman produces. As players, we are paid to go and play the game of cricket and the man who is paid to produce the pitch should be allowed to prepare the best possible wicket. I think it's very arrogant of people within the Yorkshire club to make those decisions because it means they are questioning the decisions of the person who is paid to do the job. The most frustrating thing was that we could see that they can produce a great pitch there, because the net wicket that we practised on was a fantastic surface. The pitch we played the match on was quite clearly the greenest and the worst on the square and the dressing room attendant, who was a club player there, told us that even the pitches they play club matches on don't start that green.

As a group of supporters, we felt that Yorkshire had been prepared to do anything, within the laws or not, to gain an advantage over us and it left a very bad taste in the mouth. Was that maybe how the players felt, too?
AH - Yes, I think that was the feeling we had, too, though it should be noted that we never really said anything while we were up there, we just tried to go out there with smiles on our faces. The biggest tragedy was that the game that should have been the showpiece of the whole Championship season was marred by a minority of one or two people who just wanted to vent their frustrations at Yorkshire's shortcomings in the four-day form of the game.

VIEW FROM THE DRESSING ROOM - JON BATTY

Having drawn this match, did we now feel that the Championship title was almost in the bag?
JB - I don't remember feeling that it was in the bag, but more that we were one step closer to the title. We were still aware that Lancashire were serious contenders but the draw had removed Yorkshire from the running.

KEITH MEDLYCOTT'S ASSESSMENT

The pitch at Scarborough was a major disappointment, especially when you compared it to the two other wickets that had been cut on the square, one of which was for a club game and the other for the National League match which followed our game. Both were far superior to the pitch they had prepared for a four-day match and we were very disappointed, as professional cricketers, to see what they had produced.

All in all, a lot of pretty unpleasant things went on at Scarborough but I'm proud to say that we took it all in our stride and I have to give the players the utmost credit for the way they handled themselves, both on and off the pitch. Although circumstances were far from perfect, we prepared well, we practised hard whenever the weather allowed, we didn't hide behind closed doors when flack was flying and I also hope that we entertained the crowd - we always made it very clear that we wanted to get out onto the field to play the game. The players certainly did everything that could have been expected of them and it showed how much we had learned from our problems at Derby. As a dressing room we had responded and improved - we made no excuses, no-one complained, no-one moaned or groaned when balls beat the bat - we simply hung on in there, we were strong and we batted bloody well in difficult conditions. And Yorkshire were now out of the race for the title.

Other Division One Matches

Yorkshire might have felt hard done by over what happened at Scarborough but it should be remembered that they'd been very lucky to escape a points deduction when they played Kent at Headingley in mid-June and it also had to be noted that their form in the second half of the season had been more akin to that of the relegation candidates than that of the title challengers. Surrey's advantage over Lancashire now stood at an imposing nineteen points with two games to play and it also appeared to be much to the champions' advantage that their next opponents, Durham, had been all but assured of relegation after losing to fellow strugglers Hampshire in this round of matches.

August 31-September 3
Chester-le-Street:- **Hampshire beat Durham by six wickets.** Durham 320-9dec (Lewis 70, Katich 60, Speight 55, Daley 50) and 39-1dec; Hampshire 69-0dec and 292-4 (Kendall 119 not out, Laney 52). **Hampshire 15pts, Durham 3**

September 1-4
Taunton:- **Somerset drew with Leicestershire.** Somerset 411-7dec (Blackwell 109, Cox 58) and 90-2; Leicestershire 470 (Maddy 102, Wells 98, Habib 72, Smith 69, Burns 57). **Somerset 12pts, Leicestershire 11**

COUNTY CHAMPIONSHIP DIVISION ONE AT 4TH SEPTEMBER

Pos	Prev		P	Pts	W	D	L	Bat	Bowl	Last Three Res		
1	1	Surrey	14	182	8	4	2	35	35	D11	W17	W18
2	2	Lancashire	14	163	6	7	1	27	36	D12	W16	L3
3	4	Leicestershire	15	159	4	8	3	42	37	D11	D9	D11
4	3	Yorkshire	14	152*	5	7	2	30	42	D-1	D10	D10
5	6	Somerset	14	135	2	9	3	38	37	D12	D11	D11
6	5	Kent	14	129	4	7	3	14	39	W18	L3	D7
7	7	Durham	15	110	2	5	8	26	40	L3	L3	D10
8	8	Derbyshire	14	98*	2	7	5	15	39	W15	L3	D10
9	9	Hampshire	14	96	2	4	8	14	42	W15	L3	L4

* Deducted 8pts for sub-standard pitch

OUTLAWS LIE IN WAIT TO AMBUSH THE CHAMPIONS

After four tense and, in some ways, rather unpleasant days in Scarborough, everyone now had to head off to Trent Bridge for the Lions' penultimate NCL fixture. It was really a game that everybody - bar my Surrey-supporting friends in Newark! - could have done without. With the Division Two title now safely secured and a potentially decisive Championship match to come against Durham next week, it was, understandably, hard to see the Surrey Lions fielding a full-strength side or even being one-hundred percent committed for the fixture. We had to be careful, however, because there were still a number of teams in the promotion shake-up who had every right to expect a full-on effort from Surrey against the second-placed Outlaws, who were doubtless keen to avenge their humiliation at Guildford as well as strengthen their promotion claims.

NCL DIVISION TWO - MATCH FIFTEEN

NOTTINGHAMSHIRE OUTLAWS versus SURREY LIONS
at Trent Bridge on Sunday 3rd September

Nottinghamshire Outlaws (288-4) beat Surrey Lions (225-3) by 63 runs

As expected, the Lions fielded a much-changed side for the match at Trent Bridge and to no-one's great surprise they went down to defeat by sixty-three runs in one of the higher-scoring games of the season.

As well as giving first-team competitive debuts to Philip Sampson and Tim Murtagh, two other second eleven regulars, Gareth Batty and Carl Greenidge, were given another opportunity to step up a level. Unfortunately for this quartet they quickly discovered that their chance had come on a superb Trent Bridge pitch, surrounded by a lightning fast outfield. Consequently, most of the bowlers suffered and the Lions' fielders spent the whole of the Outlaws innings chasing balls unavailingly to the boundary as Darren Bicknell and Jason Gallian piled up a record-breaking Nottinghamshire opening stand of 196 in 33 overs. After a fine knock of 84 from just 80 balls, Gallian finally became one of three victims for Ali Brown during a good spell of off-spin bowling, while the former Surrey opener went on to complete an excellent century from 137 balls in 130 minutes before being run out. The innings was then given further late impetus by Chris Read, who plundered two sixes and two fours when Tim Murtagh was called up to bowl the final over from the Radcliffe Road end. It was an unfortunate way for the England Under-19 seamer to finish, since he had impressed greatly while conceding just fifteen runs and beating the bat on numerous occasions during his first six overs of the innings.

A Surrey victory was always a long shot, but it quickly faded out of sight as some high quality new-ball bowling from Reiffel and Harris kept the scoring rate below three for the first thirteen overs of the innings and Ali Brown laboured uncharacteristically for twenty-six balls before edging behind for just five. Although Nadeem Shahid played very well and provided some entertainment in recording a 98-ball century, Ian Ward and Gary Butcher needed to maintain a similar tempo to give the Lions any degree of hope. Since they were unable to do this, the game quickly petered out in very tedious style, with a substantial Outlaws victory never in any doubt.

Nottinghamshire Outlaws (288-4) beat Surrey Lions (225-3) by 63 runs

Nottinghamshire Outlaws 4pts

NOTTINGHAMSHIRE OUTLAWS v SURREY LIONS at TRENT BRIDGE. Played on 3rd September
Nottinghamshire Outlaws won the toss   Umpires:- D.J. Constant & R.A. White

NOTTINGHAMSHIRE OUTLAWS / **SURREY LIONS bowling**

Fall of wkt	Batsman	How Out	Score	Balls	4s	6s		O	M	R	W
4- 247	D.J. Bicknell	run out	115	147	14	0	Greenidge	3	0	25	0
1- 196	J.E.R. Gallian *	c & b Brown	84	80	12	0	Murtagh	8	1	52	0
2- 208	J.E. Morris	c Greenidge b Brown	9	9	0	1	Sampson	5	0	43	0
3- 222	P. Johnson	c Ratcliffe b Brown	8	8	0	0	Ratcliffe	9	0	46	0
	U. Afzaal	Not Out	22	17	2	0	Butcher	4	0	28	0
	C.M.W. Read +	Not Out	26	10	2	2	G.J. Batty	9	0	48	0
	P.J. Franks	did not bat					Brown	7	0	39	3
	P.R. Reiffel	did not bat									
	D.S. Lucas	did not bat									
	A.J. Harris	did not bat									
	R.D. Stemp	did not bat									
	Extras (3b, 4lb, 15w, 2nb)		24								
	TOTAL	(45 overs)	288 - 4								

SURREY LIONS / **NOTTS OUTLAWS bowling**

Fall of wkt	Batsman	How Out	Score	Balls	4s	6s		O	M	R	W
2- 99	I.J. Ward	c Read b Franks	46	74	4	0	Reiffel	7	1	16	1
1- 14	A.D. Brown	c Read b Reiffel	5	26	0	0	Harris	9	0	42	0
	Nadeem Shahid	Not Out	109	108	11	0	Lucas	9	0	60	0
3- 138	G.P. Butcher	run out	14	30	1	0	Franks	9	0	42	1
	G.J. Batty	Not Out	26	34	1	0	Stemp	9	0	45	0
	A.J. Hollioake *	did not bat					Afzaal	1	0	4	0
	J.D. Ratcliffe	did not bat					Bicknell	1	0	2	0
	J.N. Batty +	did not bat									
	T.J. Murtagh	did not bat									
	P.J. Sampson	did not bat									
	C.G. Greenidge	did not bat									
	Extras (4b, 6lb, 11w, 4nb)		25								
	TOTAL	(45 overs)	225 - 3								

Other NCL Division Two Matches

The Outlaws' victory over the Lions greatly enhanced their promotion prospects and maintained their second place in the table, while Warwickshire beat Derbyshire by 44 runs to move up to third. With two rounds of matches to play, the Middlesex Crusaders and the Glamorgan Dragons also remained in contention for promotion.

September 3
Southend:- **Essex Eagles beat Glamorgan Dragons by 4 runs.** Essex 289-5 (Peters 73 not out, Jefferson 65, Napier 52); Glamorgan 285 (James 88 not out, Newell 78, Maynard 61, Cowan 4-44). **Essex Eagles 4pts**

Edgbaston:- **Warwickshire Bears beat Derbyshire Scorpions by 44 runs.** Warwickshire 233-8; Derbyshire 189 in 43 overs (Di Venuto 84, Dagnall 4-34). **Warwickshire Bears 4pts**

NCL DIVISION TWO AT 3RD SEPTEMBER

Pos	Prev		P	Pts	W	T	L	N/R	Last	Three	Res
1	1	Surrey Lions	15	48	11	0	2	2	L	L	W
2	2	Nottinghamshire Outlaws	14	38	9	0	4	1	W	L	W
3	5	Warwickshire Bears	14	34	8	1	5	0	W	L	W
4	3	Middlesex Crusaders	14	34	7	1	4	2	W	W	N/R
5	4	Glamorgan Dragons	14	32	7	2	5	0	L	W	L
6	6	Essex Eagles	15	32	7	0	6	2	W	W	W
7	7	Hampshire Hawks	14	20	5	0	9	0	W	W	L
8	8	Durham Dynamos	14	12	3	0	11	0	L	L	L
9	9	Derbyshire Scorpions	14	6	1	0	12	1	L	L	L

15 So Near Yet So Far

Surrey were now closing in fast on their second trophy of the season and, more importantly, on back-to-back County Championship triumphs. With a nineteen-point lead going into the penultimate round of matches we were still not certain to clinch the title even if we recorded a maximum twenty-point win against Durham, however, since Lancashire would have to drop points at home to Somerset for our final match at Old Trafford to become an irrelevance. To make matters worse for everyone at The Oval, Lancashire were starting their fixture on the Friday, two days after ours, owing to the fact that they were playing Somerset in a floodlit NCL Division One game on the Wednesday evening. There was a strong possibility, therefore, that we might, as in the NCL, become champions whilst not playing. Everyone was wishing that we had a couple more bonus points to our credit going into the Durham match.

All of this supposed that we would actually beat Durham, of course, though even the most pessimistic of Surrey fans would have felt confident about us despatching an all-but-relegated side with a very clear weakness where spin was concerned. Such was the mediocrity of Durham's spin attack, that they had considered the possibility of tempting John Emburey out of retirement to play in the match at The Oval, had they been in with a chance of staying up. The fact that the north-eastern county had, quite sensibly, accepted their inevitable relegation was underlined by the abandonment of this idea.

Whatever happened over the course of the next four days, one thing was for certain - this match couldn't possibly generate anything like the amount of scandal, rumour, intrigue and controversy that we had encountered at Scarborough! Perhaps the match at North Marine Road was best summed up by Robert Mills of *The Yorkshire Post* on the Monday after the game. Although I wasn't able to agree with absolutely everything in a reasonably well-balanced article, it would certainly be hard to argue that his headline wasn't spot-on - **Yorkshire And Scarborough Not Up To Task.**

COUNTY CHAMPIONSHIP - MATCH FIFTEEN

SURREY versus DURHAM
at The Oval

First Day - Wednesday 6th September

Surrey 243-0

The Teams And The Toss - *Although the summer's international matches have now been completed, Alec Stewart and Graham Thorpe are not permitted to return to the Surrey line-up. The champions-elect therefore make just one change from Scarborough, with Martin Bicknell sufficiently recovered from his back strain to replace Ben Hollioake. Durham are close to full strength, though their line-up shows three changes in personnel from the side that triumphed so convincingly at the Riverside at the start of the season, with Michael Gough, Andrew Pratt and Nicky Phillips in for Nick Speak, Nicky Peng and Melvyn Betts. Since that match in May, Speak had been deposed as captain and replaced by Jon Lewis, Pratt had taken the wicketkeeping gauntlets from Martin Speight and the promising young Peng had, sadly, been dropped after a miserable run of form in the first team since his stunning debut. On a grey and overcast morning, Adam Hollioake elects to bat when he wins the toss.*

Although play starts on time, the morning's action is badly disrupted by two rain breaks and the umpires eventually decide to take an early lunch at 12.55pm. During the two brief passages of play that prove possible, Steve Harmison succeeds in finding the edge of both openers' bats, though his direction proves rather variable as he also concedes six runs in wides.

Lunch:- Surrey 26-0 (M.A. Butcher 9*, Ward 9*) from 5.5 overs

Poor Harmison's radar is no better adjusted after the interval, as his first three overs contain another wide, two leg byes, four byes and a batch of six more wides. Since Simon Brown has meanwhile been contributing two maiden overs, the last twenty runs scored, including six before lunch, have all been extras originating from the bowling of Harmison. It's a quite bizarre sequence and when another set of four byes whistles past Pratt in the lanky paceman's next over the Surrey fifty arrives with no fewer than twenty-seven of the runs having come in extras! With the ball swinging around quite considerably at this stage, Brown manages to get the ball past the bat on a number of occasions to emphasise the fact that Harmison's opening burst, though undoubtedly quick, represents a terrible waste of the new ball.

It comes as no surprise then that the scoring rate drops considerably when the steady Neil Killeen replaces Harmison at the Vauxhall end, with runs, for a while, coming largely through well-taken singles.

The tempo eventually picks up again, however, when Collingwood replaces Brown, after a good spell of 10-5-15-0 from the former England left-armer, and when Killeen is punished twice in an over by Ward for straying onto leg stump. Both batsmen are now looking well set and, following a square-cut boundary by Butcher in Nicky Phillips' opening over, Ward takes Surrey through to three figures with a pair of cover drives, for two and then three runs, in the twenty-ninth over of the innings, delivered by Collingwood. Owing to the major contribution made by extras, Butcher has just thirty-six, and Ward a mere thirty, of the first hundred runs scored. Surrey clearly couldn't have wished for a better start to the game that they hope might see them clinching the title and Jon Lewis has all the problems, with his soon-to-be-relegated side struggling again.

In an attempt to make a breakthrough before lunch, the beleaguered Durham skipper brings Harmison back for a second spell, this time from the pavilion end. Although the young fast bowler seems less prone to spraying the ball around wildly following this change of ends, he still presents the batsmen with too many legside run-scoring opportunities, and Ward takes advantage by gratefully driving and clipping the ball repeatedly through midwicket and square leg. Butcher meanwhile bides his time against the off-spin of Phillips, waiting patiently for the short ball outside off stump and then hammering it to the cover or backward point boundary. With one such stroke he reaches his fifty from his 108th delivery after 134 minutes at the crease and Ward follows him to the milestone on the stroke of tea, five overs later. Although his half-century is reached in less impressive style, with an edge between the 'keeper and slip from an off-break by the newly-introduced Michael Gough, Ward's 132-ball, 148-minute effort is no less valuable in the quest for victory and the title.

Tea:- Surrey 142-0 (M.A. Butcher 53*, Ward 51*) from 43 overs

That annihilation of Surrey at Chester-le-Street in early May must seem a million miles away for Durham as they resume after tea with the champions-elect in a powerful position after just forty-three overs of play in the match. Reasonably enough, Jon Lewis elects to pair Nicky Phillips and Simon Brown for the opening overs of the final session, but the off-spinner is easily milked for singles while the left-arm swing bowler proves incapable of reproducing the impressive form he showed earlier in the day, drifting far too often onto the batsmen's pads and paying the price. Ward, in particular, takes full toll of Brown's wayward line, clipping him to the midwicket boundary three times in three overs, leaving the Durham captain with yet another headache.

Although Lewis does eventually regain a measure of control by replacing Brown with Killeen at the Vauxhall end, the initial breakthrough of the innings still proves elusive as the score gradually rises towards and beyond two-hundred. Phillips meanwhile continues to wheel away from the pavilion end without ever looking very threatening as the Surrey openers move into the nineties in consecutive overs with a sudden, but brief, burst of scoring. Singles then become the order of the day again for a while before Harmison returns for a final three-over blast at the Vauxhall end. In the big paceman's opening over, Durham come close to a wicket for the first time since Ward's edge off Phillips before tea but only through a close-shave run out attempt - Ward pushes into the covers and Jimmy Daley hits the striker's stumps with Butcher, on ninety-three, only just squeaking home. Had there been a third umpire in operation then it's possible that Durham's quest for a wicket might have been at an end.

Having survived this scare, Butcher moves to ninety-nine with an all-run four from an extra-cover drive off Harmison before both men complete well-deserved centuries from consecutive deliveries in the next over from Phillips. Butcher gets there first, from 215 balls in 262 minutes, when he pushes a single to midwicket, then Ward cuts the next delivery through the covers for four to complete his third ton of the season from 232 balls. Although both batsmen enjoy their moments of celebration, they are clearly not finished yet as Butcher plays out the last over from Harmison to ensure that the pair will be back tomorrow, with the record Surrey partnership against Durham just two runs away.

Close:- Surrey 243-0 (M.A. Butcher 100*, Ward 103*) from 76 overs

VIEW FROM THE DRESSING ROOM - IAN SALISBURY

I suppose we had something to prove to Durham in this match, following our early season annihilation up at the Riverside?

IS - The defeat up there had proved to us how hard it was going to be to retain the title and also emphasised something that we had said to ourselves at the start of the season - that we were the county champions from September to April but, once the new season came around, then we were just one of nine teams who would be trying to win the title. They beat us soundly in that game and the result left them near the top of the table and us near the bottom, but we always knew that things would be very different by the time this return match came around.

Second Day - Thursday 7th September

Surrey 453-4 declared; Durham 165-6

The opening two overs of the second day closely mirror those of day one as a Brown maiden is followed by an over costing twelve runs from Harmison. Mark Butcher ensures that he and Ian Ward have a share in the record for the highest partnership for Surrey against Durham with a push backward of square leg for two, before smashing the previous mark in style with a deliberate upper-cut over the third man boundary for six. To celebrate the fact that this stroke has also brought up the Surrey 250 and a second batting point, Butcher then cuts the next delivery backward of square for four.

At this very early stage it looks like Harmison might be in for another day he will want to forget but, to be fair, he settles down well after this loose start and produces his best spell of the match. Simon Brown is, meanwhile, still occasionally beating the outside edge with his outswinger and it's quite a surprise when he is withdrawn, in favour of Nicky Phillips, after just four overs. Jon Lewis' thinking is probably based around the fact that he has a new ball due in fifteen overs' time and that appears to be confirmed when Harmison is replaced shortly afterwards by Collingwood, as opposed to Killeen. Unfortunately for the Durham skipper, the newly-introduced medium-pacer looks unlikely to keep things tight until that new ball becomes available as Ward instantly clips him for successive boundaries, one each side of the square leg umpire. It's pretty depressing stuff for the rookie captain and things don't improve for him when Butcher edges Phillips at catchable height between 'keeper and slip, much as Ward had done to reach fifty on day one. The major difference here is that Butcher is already on 127 and the score is a mammoth 290-0!

Two overs further down the line, Surrey reach three-hundred and move another point closer to the retention of their title as Phillips completes his twenty-ninth wicketless over. Since the potential salvation of the new ball is now only a handful of overs away, the Durham off-spinner finds himself briefly paired with Simon Katich, who bowls a couple of overs of left-arm unorthodox spin from the Vauxhall end. It seems like a worthwhile experiment by the visiting skipper, but there is still no sign of a wicket as Butcher greets the Australian's entrance with a late cut to the boundary in an over, costing eight, which also sees Surrey's senior opening batsman through to his 150 from 285 balls after 342 minutes at the crease.

The next milestone, reached in the following over from Phillips, is an even more impressive one, as Butcher and Ward erase Brian Lara and Keith Piper from the record books by surpassing the Warwickshire pair's stand of 322 to register the highest-ever partnership for any wicket against Durham. The previous record was set, in 1994, on the occasion of Lara's world record 501 not out, when some of the later bowling was of a decidedly friendly nature.

Just as on that occasion, Durham are clearly in need of some inspiration, so it's just as well for them that the new ball is now available. It's no great surprise that Lewis decides against entrusting the new 'cherry' to Harmison, giving Brown first use from the pavilion end and opting for Killeen at the Vauxhall end. As so often happens when the harder ball comes when two batsmen are already set, the run rate initially surges upwards, with both batsmen notching two boundaries as the score rushes past 350 and the penultimate batting point is safely gathered in.

With everyone now beginning to wonder how much further this opening stand can extend, it comes to an unfortunate end at 359 in the 107th over when Brown claims and gains an lbw decision against Ward. From my position, right behind the bowler's arm on the pavilion balcony, it appears that umpire Lloyds must be feeling sorry for the visiting team's bowlers since the ball looks to be both too high and going down the legside. Although one might have a little sympathy for the fielding side in situations such as this one, it's disappointing that a stand which had already reached seventh on the list of Surrey's all-time highest partnerships has been denied the opportunity of climbing still higher by a pretty feeble lbw verdict. As Ward leaves the field to a wonderful ovation, he at least has the sizeable consolation of 144 runs to his name, and he knows that his contribution to this match has already gone a long way towards ensuring victory and another County Championship success for his team.

Since a very positive-looking Nadeem Shahid announces his arrival at the crease by finding the boundary rope with two lovely drives, and the likes of Ali Brown and Adam Hollioake are still to come, Durham must actually wonder about the wisdom of making this breakthrough, though they do almost pick up their second wicket in three overs when Jimmy Daley makes a valiant attempt to hang on to a very difficult one-handed diving catch at cover offered by Butcher off Simon Brown. It barely counts as a chance, to be fair, and, with the batsman on 172 and the score at 368-1 at the time, it hardly looks likely to change the course of the match.

Lunch:- Surrey 381-1 (M.A. Butcher 174*, Shahid 17*) from 113 overs

Jon Lewis opts to start with Harmison and Phillips after lunch and his tall speedster continues to improve by producing his best spell of the innings, finding the edge of Butcher's bat with successive deliveries in the second over of the session. You have to feel sorry for the 21-year-old paceman, though, because the first nick flies through the vacant slip area and is misfielded on the boundary for four and then the second goes to the rope at fine leg via the inside edge - two good balls, two edges, eight runs! A less impressive delivery, short and wide of off stump, in his next over brings Surrey's all-important final batting point at four-hundred when Shahid flashes the ball to the fence at backward point, then an assault on Phillips in the following over completes the fifty partnership for the second wicket. It also sees Butcher through to 191, the highest individual score by a Surrey batsman against Durham, in the over before his dismissal. Harmison is the man with something to celebrate as he defeats Butcher's drive and hits the top of the batsman's stumps to end a quite magnificent innings with the total at 413.

It's all too late for Durham, of course, but they do manage to pick up another two wickets in the next six overs as Surrey press on towards a declaration. The first of these comes when Phillips claims a very belated first scalp of the innings, courtesy of Shahid's drive to wide mid-on with the score advanced to 421, then, three overs later, Adam Hollioake, having swept Phillips for six in a run-a-ball innings of twenty, provides Harmison with a second wicket by top-edging a hook to fine leg.

There's now only time for a couple of good strokes by Gary Butcher and Ali Brown before the Surrey skipper calls his batsmen in with the score at 453-4 to leave Durham a potentially awkward seventeen overs' batting before tea. Hollioake's declaration also confirms Durham's expected relegation, since the men from the Riverside had needed a full twenty points from the match to maintain even a mathematical chance of avoiding the drop. Surrey, needing the maximum possible return from the game themselves, of course, are well on their way with the full five batting points secured, but they now face the task of taking twenty Durham wickets in seven-and-a-half sessions of play. This will be made all the more difficult if the unsettled weather that has been forecast materialises over the next two days.

The champions-elect are, therefore, keen to capture two or three wickets before tea as Durham start their pursuit of 304 to avoid the follow-on with openers Lewis and Gough facing up to Bicknell and Tudor.

Gough is the more aggressive of the Durham pair in the early stages, though his runs come from a mixture of nicely struck on-drives and edgy steers to third man past a heavily-populated slip cordon. Lewis, meanwhile, adopts a very passive role and pays the penalty in the seventh over when a big inswinger from Bicknell homes in successfully on his off stump as he shoulders arms. It's the early breakthrough that Surrey wanted so badly and it leaves Durham at 22-1 with their skipper on his way back to the pavilion with just a single to his name.

Lewis' replacement at the crease is Simon Katich, and the young Australian makes a good start, striking both opening bowlers for a boundary through mid-off before clipping Ian Salisbury to midwicket for another four to raise the Durham fifty when Adam Hollioake introduces his spinners for the last four overs of the session.

Tea:- Durham 55-1 (Gough 24*, Katich 20*) from 17 overs

Saqlain and Salisbury resume after tea and, within five overs, spin has struck its opening blow of the innings when Michael Gough is trapped on the crease and comprehensively beaten by Saqlain's 'bullet' ball. The former England Under-19 captain is adjudged lbw for twenty-eight and Durham are 66 for 2.

Although the pitch is giving assistance to the spinners - witness Salisbury's spitting googly which strikes Jon Batty a nasty blow above the eye - Katich plays with great assurance, using his feet well to drive both spin twins to the cover boundary and then on-driving Saqlain for the sixth elegant four of his innings. Regrettably for Durham, Paul Collingwood is nothing like as strong a player of slow bowling and he has only been at the wicket for five overs when Salisbury dismisses him for four with the total advanced to eighty-nine. The wicket owes more to an excellent effort in the field than anything else, however, as the batsman's tame chip towards mid-on is magnificently held by Alex Tudor, who runs in, plunges forward and grabs the ball right-handed just inches from the turf. This special effort by such a tall man puts another bonus point in the kitty and leaves Surrey in a very strong position.

Although his flow of boundaries has now dried up, Katich remains a serious threat and, by sweeping and driving a succession of singles, he ensures that the spinners are unable to dictate to him as he makes his way to a very good half-century from 75 balls in 95 minutes. In the meantime, Jimmy Daley, another of the Durham middle-order men with a poor reputation against spin, appears to have settled in quite well, taking his side past a hundred with a cover-driven boundary off Salisbury and then clipping the leg-spinner through midwicket for three. The Sunderland-born right-hander's innings is nipped in the bud at fourteen, however, by another inspired piece of Surrey fielding - with Salisbury again the bowler to profit - as his full-blooded square cut is brilliantly hauled in by the diving Ian Ward at cover.

Salisbury now has two wickets to his name and it almost becomes three with his very next delivery as his former Sussex team-mate, Martin Speight, edges a fine leg-break past the right hand of second slip. The erstwhile Durham wicketkeeper fails to take full advantage of this stroke of luck, however, progressing only by a couple of swept boundaries, at the expense of Saqlain, before Salisbury snares him six overs later. The sweep which had proved so profitable against the off-spinner turns out to be his undoing against the leg-spinner as the ball lobs up short on the off-side, possibly via his glove, and Adam Hollioake runs forward from his position at second slip to pouch the catch. With Speight gone for twelve and Durham 137-5, things are looking very good for the reigning champions.

They will not be able to rest easily until they have disposed of Katich, however, and, though they seem to have contained the Australian reasonably well, he continues to play the Surrey spinners as well as anyone in recent times and clearly has the potential to play a long innings - if he gets support from the other end.

Surprisingly, as we enter the last four overs of the day's play, the Durham batsmen, rather than playing for stumps, seem to up the tempo, with Katich glancing and driving Saqlain for a pair of twos and Pratt tickling a Salisbury delivery to fine leg for three. Far from being a problem for Surrey, this late burst of activity actually brings unexpected success for the home county, since Katich, on seventy-seven, suddenly charges at Salisbury, misses his intended slog-sweep and is comfortably stumped by Batty with the score at 162. It's an amazing way for an outstandingly well-controlled innings to end - not that anyone with Surrey leanings is complaining!

As the players leave the field fourteen balls later, with Salisbury having taken 4-62 to compensate for the fact that Saqlain (1-65) has had a rare off-day, everyone appreciates that this late bonus wicket has left Durham struggling desperately at 165-6 and has given the champions every chance of wrapping up victory, and maybe even the Championship, tomorrow.

Close:- Durham 165-6 (Pratt 15*, Phillips 0*) from 49 overs

MARK BUTCHER/IAN WARD RECORD PARTNERSHIP STATS CHART

Over	Milestone	P'SHIP STATS Balls	P'SHIP STATS Mins	BUTCHER STATS Balls	BUTCHER STATS Mins	BUTCHER STATS 6	BUTCHER STATS 4	WARD STATS Balls	WARD STATS Mins	WARD STATS 6	WARD STATS 4
12	50 partnership	69	43								
29	100 partnership	174	107								
38	BUTCHER 50	>	>	108	134	-	7				
43	WARD 50	>	>	>	>	>	>	132	148	-	4
44	150 partnership	264	154								
63	200 partnership	375	221								
75	BUTCHER 100	>	>	215	262	-	12				
75	WARD 100	>	>	>	>	>	>	232	263	-	9
78	250 partnership	467	274								
93	300 partnership	557	326								
98	BUTCHER 150	>	>	285	342	1	17				
104	350 partnership	624	366								
107	359 partnership	637	375								
107	WARD 144	>	>	>	>	>	>	329	375	-	13

THE TEN HIGHEST SURREY PARTNERSHIPS OF ALL TIME

Runs	Wkt	Batsmen	Opposition	Venue	Year
448	4th	R.Abel (193) & T.W.Hayward (273)	Yorkshire	The Oval	1899
428	1st	J.B.Hobbs (261) & A.Sandham (183)	Oxford Univ	The Oval	1926
413	3rd	D.J.Bicknell (186) & D.M.Ward (263)	Kent	Canterbury	1990
379	1st	R.Abel (173) & W.Brockwell (225)	Hampshire	The Oval	1897
371	2nd	J.B.Hobbs (205) & E.G.Hayes (276)	Hampshire	The Oval	1909
364	1st	R.Abel (193) & D.L.A.Jephson (213)	Derbyshire	The Oval	1900
359	1st	M.A.BUTCHER (191) & I.J.WARD (144)	DURHAM	THE OVAL	2000
353	3rd	A.Ducat (271) & E.G.Hayes (153)	Hampshire	Southampton	1919
352	1st	T.W.Hayward (204*) & J.B.Hobbs (159)	Warwickshire	The Oval	1909
344	2nd	A.Sandham (239) & R.J.Gregory (154)	Glamorgan	The Oval	1937

VIEW FROM THE DRESSING ROOM - IAN WARD

Your opening stand with Mark Butcher was the seventh highest partnership for any Surrey wicket ever and I thought it should have extended further. Did you think the umpire might have been feeling sorry for the long-suffering Durham bowlers when he adjudged you lbw?!

IW - Well, Jeremy Lloyds thought the ball was going to hit the stumps... I disagreed... but, there you go, you can't win 'em all! It was disappointing, but if you'd said at the start of the game that we were going to put on 359 then we would have taken that and been very content!

I thought Simon Katich looked a very good player and played our spinners as well as almost anyone had all season. What was your view?
IW - Yes, he's a very good player - I've played against him a couple of times in Australia and seen him play in a few Shield games for Western Australia at the WACA and he shapes up very well. He's suffered with a chronic fatigue illness over the past couple of years but he seems to be fully recovered now and looks a real star for the future. Unfortunately for England, he's yet another Australian who will have learned a lot from the finishing school of county cricket.

VIEW FROM THE DRESSING ROOM - MARK BUTCHER

That was some partnership that you and Wardy put together!
MB - The wicket up at Chester-le-Street at the start of the season was probably as bad as any we played on all year, in terms of the amazing amount of movement that the seamers were able to get out of it, so it was nice here to be batting on what was an absolute belter. And we played them off the park, much as they had done to us up there.

I didn't feel that the pair of you got the credit you deserved in the press, where they seemed to concentrate on the quality of the Durham bowling. I didn't think the bowling was half as bad as they made out, actually - what was your view?
MB - I think the realisation was that the bowling wouldn't do you any harm if you didn't take liberties with it. We could have tried to batter people out of the attack or played flashy strokes but we just kept it simple, really - I think we just did a very professional job on what was a very good wicket.

VIEW FROM THE DRESSING ROOM - IAN SALISBURY

That was a terrific opening partnership by Ian Ward and Mark Butcher - do you think they have got stronger as a pair this season?
IS - Being an opening batsman is one of the hardest jobs in cricket, because things can be very unpredictable when you are facing that new ball every time - if you make one mistake then you can be out of the game for the rest of the day. In some ways they both had a difficult season, but they are certainly getting stronger as a pair in the way they work together - their running and their understanding is brilliant, they both practise very hard, they are both very good professionals and they are both very determined to do well. This partnership was reward for all their hard work.

Simon Katich looked very good during his innings of 77 - how highly did you rate him?
IS - I'd rather talk about good young English players, of course, but he was very well organised and looked really impressive. Having played at Durham all year, where the pitches aren't so easy, I think his eyes lit up when he saw this really good track at The Oval and he batted very well indeed until he played an absolutely awful shot towards the end of the day... thankfully!

Third Day - Friday 8th September

Surrey 453-4 declared; Durham 241 and 10-0

Incessant drizzle, starting just before play is about to commence, brings worry and frustration throughout the morning. It's a grim and gloomy day in London, though conditions are clearly better up in Manchester, where Lancashire's match starts on time, with Somerset batting. We would have preferred Lancashire to be batting, since we need our red rose rivals to drop points if we are to clinch the title here at The Oval by beating Durham - and they are clearly far more likely to drop batting points than bowling points.

As the light rain continues to fall, Surrey's hopes of recording a three-day victory vanish and we are left hoping that we can at least get some play in today, since it would be asking a lot to have to capture fourteen wickets tomorrow. Suddenly our prospects of retaining the Championship aren't looking quite so bright.

Eventually, much to everyone's relief, the rain stops and the umpires declare that play will start at 3pm, with a minimum of forty-three overs to be bowled.

When the players then finally emerge onto the field, it's clear that Adam Hollioake's hand is going to be forced by indifferent light, so he opens with his spin twins, Salisbury from the pavilion end and Saqlain from the Vauxhall end. With a damp outfield ensuring that the ball can't be kept completely dry, it's clearly not an ideal situation and the task of the overnight pair, Andrew Pratt and Nicky Phillips, is consequently made considerably easier. Although there are still moments of anxiety for both players, Pratt progresses with some pleasant drives through mid-off and extra cover, while Phillips plays second fiddle, scoring just seven runs in the thirteen surprisingly wicketless overs that the spinners manage to deliver before tea. The Durham batsmen have done a great job for their side in this short session and Surrey's slight concerns at this stage are magnified significantly by the news from Old Trafford that Somerset have been bowled out for just 132.

Tea:- Durham 194-6 (Pratt 34*, Phillips 7*) from 62 overs

Durham flash past the two-hundred mark in the first over after the break as Phillips forces Salisbury to the cover boundary and then smashes a legside full-toss through midwicket for a second four. He then appears to offer a comfortable catching chance to Adam Hollioake at silly point in the next over from Saqlain, before Salisbury eases Surrey's nerves by finally breaking the troublesome seventh-wicket partnership at forty-three, with Pratt the man to go, thanks to some quick thinking by Jon Batty. The batsman advances on Salisbury, stuns a yorker-length delivery into the ground and, as the ball trickles backwards, the Surrey wicket-keeper grabs it and removes the bails with the batsman still out of his crease. This dismissal gives Salisbury his third five-wicket analysis of the season and, though there has been an element of luck about the way the wicket has come about, the bowler deserves praise for getting the ball into the blockhole and the 'keeper earns full credit for being alert to the possibilities.

Although this breakthrough has suddenly brightened a frustrating day, the light out in the middle is still a major worry for Adam Hollioake and, while Saqlain and Salisbury continue to wheel away, the number of lights aglow on the scoreboard increases from three to four to five. Clearly the Surrey skipper will have to stick with his spinners now, though there must be moments when he wishes he could unleash his opening bowlers as nine overs pass without any further success for the spinners. With Saqlain back to something approaching his best today, it's bad luck rather than bad bowling that stops the spin twins from rattling through the Durham tail, as any number of deliveries fizz past both the inside and outside edges of the bat.

Finally, with Surrey nerves perhaps starting to show, a change of angle from Salisbury brings the vital break for the home side. Coming around the wicket to Killeen, he traps the visitors' number nine plumb in front of the stumps with an excellent quicker googly and gives his team renewed hope of finishing the Durham first innings tonight. This looks increasingly important, too, since reports are coming in of Lancashire having reached seventy without loss in their reply to Somerset's dismal total at Old Trafford.

Fortunately for Surrey, the tail subsides fairly quickly after Killeen's departure, with the last two wickets falling in eight overs at a cost of sixteen runs. Phillips' brave and lengthy vigil ends with a bat-pad catch to Nadeem Shahid at short leg off Saqlain with the total at 237, then, following a lofted on-drive for four, Harmison becomes Salisbury's seventh victim of the innings when he misses a sweep at a low full-toss and is adjudged lbw.

Having been the man principally responsible for Durham's dismissal for a score some 212 runs in arrears of Surrey's 453, Salisbury leads his team from the field with figures of 7-105 to his name and a hearty ovation ringing in his ears.

With nine overs left for play, Salisbury and his team-mates are back out in the middle just ten minutes later for the start of Durham's follow-on innings. Since the light is still dreadful, Adam Hollioake has only one option... to hand the new ball to his spinners. The first two overs yield a boundary apiece to the openers, as Lewis clips Saqlain through midwicket and Gough forces Salisbury to the rope at extra cover but, thereafter, it's little more than a battle for survival until the umpires decide, with just over three overs remaining, that the light is too bad even for spinners to be bowling.

Although it's extremely disappointing that barely forty overs have been possible today, the time out in the middle has been well spent in finishing off the Durham first innings. Taking ten wickets tomorrow won't be straightforward but it'll be a great deal easier than getting fourteen would have been! The biggest worry for day four might be the weather, however, since the forecast is again poor.

Nor is the news from Old Trafford particularly encouraging... Lancashire are in total control of their match, closing at 142-3, with Mike Atherton 54 not out. So much could depend on what happens in both games tomorrow.

Close:- Durham 10-0 (Lewis 4*, Gough 5*) from 5.4 overs

VIEW FROM THE DRESSING ROOM - IAN SALISBURY

We didn't get much play on day three, due to rain, but we did at least finish off their first innings. That seemed to be very important at the time. Would you go along with that?

IS - Definitely, it was quite a worrying day. We were a bit edgy anyway, because, as often happens in sport, when you get close to winning something you actually get more nervous. We didn't want to have to go to Old Trafford needing to win, so we obviously wanted to wrap this game up quickly, but the rain meant that we couldn't start until mid-afternoon. Then, when we got out onto the field, there was rain in the air, we didn't know how many overs we were going to be able to play for and, because the light was too bad for the seamers to bowl, Saqi and I had to bowl in conditions - cold and wet - that were totally unsuitable for us. Normally, you would expect us to wrap up the innings very quickly but, given the situation, and with the whole side feeling a bit on edge because of all the bad weather that was around, I think we were very happy just to get those last four wickets before the close. That was a massive boost to us because getting fourteen wickets on the last day with rain around would have been a big ask.

Fourth Day - Saturday 9th September

Surrey 453-4 declared; Durham 241 and 144

Surrey beat Durham by an innings and 68 runs
Surrey 20pts, Durham 2

It's another grey and gloomy morning as play commences on day four but Surrey make the brightest of starts by picking up wickets with the fifth and sixth balls of the day.

After Ian Salisbury completes last night's unfinished over, Alex Tudor steams in from the Vauxhall end to trap Jon Lewis lbw on the crease with his third delivery and then have the dangerous Simon Katich excellently held by a flying Jon Batty when the Australian gets a big outside edge to the very next ball. These two fine deliveries give Surrey a perfect start, with the instant dismissal of the opposition's best batsman representing a huge bonus.

It's particularly unfortunate then that, in the time it takes for Tudor to complete his excellent first over and for Martin Bicknell to deliver a maiden, the light deteriorates quite markedly. Consequently, Adam Hollioake is again forced to turn to spin in order to prevent the umpires from taking the players off the pitch.

While the fact that the opening bowlers are unable to use the new ball is something of a setback and the threat of rain gives further cause for concern, there is at least good news from Manchester, where Lancashire have lost two early wickets, including Atherton, in slipping to 160-5. This score is conveyed to those of us sitting in front of the committee room by the Club President, John Major, who is keeping tabs on the state of affairs at Old Trafford via Ceefax. It really is very good news for Surrey, too. If the weather allows us enough playing time to win this game today, then it's looking likely that the Championship will be ours by the end of the match, since Lancashire appear certain to drop batting points from their current position.

Meanwhile, out in the middle, the light gradually improves and Surrey move another step closer to victory when the unfortunate Collingwood is run out when backing up, as Ian Salisbury deflects a forcing stroke from Michael Gough onto the non-striker's stumps. It's a very cruel way to go, but the Durham batsman is out for four and the visitors are now 30-3.

Since the dark clouds are now lifting and the light has become acceptable to the umpires, the Surrey skipper immediately recalls his opening bowlers. Alex Tudor therefore resumes with his figures standing at 1-0-6-2 and, during an impressive spell from the Vauxhall end, he adds to his wicket collection when Gough, perhaps deceived by a slower ball, drives a catch to Salisbury at extra cover with the total only advanced as far as forty-three.

Things are looking good for the champions-elect and their position is further strengthened just one ball later, thanks to some great thinking from both Adam Hollioake and Ian Salisbury. Despite the fact that Bicknell has only bowled three overs in his spell, the Surrey captain recalls his leg-spinner at the pavilion end, presumably to exploit Jimmy Daley's vulnerability against spin, and Salisbury instantly vindicates Hollioake's decision by sending down a googly first-up to the unsuspecting batsman - trapped on the crease and clearly expecting a leg-break, Daley is comprehensively bowled as the ball spins back from outside his off stump. For the second time in the session, Surrey have captured two wickets with consecutive balls and, as a result, Durham slump to a dismal 43-5.

Faced by a fairly hopeless position, Martin Speight attempts to play his natural game, bringing up the visitors' fifty with a clip wide of mid-on for three off Salisbury and steering Tudor to the fence at third man. Meanwhile, at the other end, Andrew Pratt, who had appeared pretty competent when facing the spinners in the first innings, now looks rather out of his depth when up against a fired-up Tudor. Besides edging the big fast bowler twice to the third man boundary for four, the Durham wicketkeeper survives a couple of catching chances, the first a very sharp one to Shahid at short leg and the second a regulation edge which somehow evades Mark Butcher at second slip and flies off to the fence for four more runs. He then adds insult to injury when he finally locates the middle of his bat to clip the Surrey paceman to the midwicket boundary in the final over of the session.

It has been a great morning for the Tudor-inspired home side but a little of the gloss is taken off by a hugely disappointing lunch score from Old Trafford. Warren Hegg and the previously out-of-form Graham Lloyd have succeeded in pulling their side round to an improbable 310-5 by the break, Lloyd's contribution being a quick-fire 126. Hopes of Somerset dismissing the opposition for under four-hundred are fast receding.

Lunch:- Durham 84-5 (Speight 18*, Pratt 19*) from 33 overs

Ian Salisbury and Martin Bicknell are Adam Hollioake's choice of bowlers at the start of the potentially decisive afternoon session and, though the leg-spinner starts with a full-toss which Speight despatches to the backward square leg boundary, runs soon prove very hard to come by. Although Pratt brings up the fifty partnership for the sixth wicket with a tickle to fine leg for two off Salisbury, the left-handed Durham wicketkeeper is beaten countless times outside his off stump by Bicknell and it's entirely predictable that the 'stroke' with which he takes his team past 100 three overs later is an uncontrolled edge to the third man boundary.

While the Durham duo continues to frustrate the Surrey bowlers here at The Oval, the news from Old Trafford is mixed. It appears that Lancashire are closing in on their fourth batting point, despite the loss of Graham Lloyd almost immediately after lunch with the score at 312. We need those last four wickets to fall quickly.

We also require five more Durham wickets here and, in an effort to achieve this, Adam Hollioake replaces Ian Salisbury with Saqlain Mushtaq at the pavilion end. The change of bowler appears to make no difference to Pratt, however, as he immediately edges the off-spinner for three!

With all due respect to the visitors' stumper, it's incredible that he is still at the crease with thirty-one runs to his name, but, fortunately for Surrey, his innings goes no further. Before Bicknell finally gets his man in his tenth over, he has to endure frustration of a different kind as Speight thumps him over, and then through, extra cover, for four and three runs respectively, but I'm sure that Surrey's senior paceman feels it's a fair deal when he removes Pratt with the final ball of the over. The mode of dismissal is pretty much as expected, with an edge in the direction of third man brilliantly intercepted and held by Nadeem Shahid at fifth slip. This breakthrough brings sighs of relief all round and increased belief that victory will soon be ours, leaving the Championship trophy in our hands, or at least within touching distance. Since Lancashire have, by now, passed 350 and they still have four wickets in hand, it looks like it will only be the latter, sadly.

First, we must complete the job in hand, however, and while Speight remains defiant, seeing off Bicknell with a pull to the square leg fence and a clip through midwicket for two, Saqlain causes immediate consternation for Nicky Phillips. Now back in tandem with his 'twin', the Surrey off-spinner soon puts Phillips out of his misery with a well-pitched "wrong 'un" that the opposition off-spinner nicks to Jon Batty, then he watches his leg-spinning partner take the champions-elect to within an ace of victory in a double-wicket maiden over. Salisbury's first victim is his former Sussex colleague, who edges a leg-break to the Surrey skipper at second slip after a well-played knock of forty-eight, and he follows up, three balls later, by bowling Stephen Harmison behind his legs to chalk up his fiftieth first-class wicket of the season.

The business is almost done now with Durham at 133-9 and victory is clinched four overs later when Killeen, having swept Salisbury for two boundaries in the leg-spinner's previous over, attempts the shot again but succeeds only in looping a simple catch to Batty behind the stumps. I'm not sure what the ball has come off but Killeen walks anyway, so it doesn't matter one iota - we've won the match and, with it, almost certainly, the Championship!

As a disappointingly small crowd rises to acclaim the team's achievement, the players form into a celebratory huddle out on the square, before leaving the field to a standing ovation. With eleven wickets in the game, Ian Salisbury is the hero of the hour, though it's entirely typical that all four front-line bowlers have been excellent throughout the match, and the whole team acknowledges the cheers that rain down on them as they make their way back into the dressing room. We *might* have just retained the title, but, frustratingly, we don't actually know for sure.

It's a strange scenario. Should we be celebrating or not? As supporters gradually gather on the outfield in front of the Bedser Stand, news is coming through that Lancashire have lost their seventh wicket at 379 but it looks like Somerset's bowlers are still going to fail to dismiss their hosts for under four-hundred. In the meantime, the players, led by Alex Tudor and Ian Salisbury, make their way down onto the outfield to shake hands with the fans and accept their congratulations. It does seem that everyone has decided that we *are* the 2000 County Champions, though no-one feels quite able to celebrate properly. Like many other people, I find the situation extremely frustrating, especially since the trophy is here and Tim Lamb of the ECB is on hand to present it.

Just to raise my hopes slightly, Ceefax suddenly records an eighth wicket for Somerset with the Lancashire total on 396. My eyes are now glued to the television screen which I can see through one of the committee room windows. Come on, Somerset, you can do it! No... they can't. Warren Hegg hits an unknown bowler for a boundary to complete Lancashire's amazing recovery from 160-5 to a full hand of batting points. How disappointing.

They still need to win their game, of course, but it looks highly likely and it won't, of course, happen until tomorrow, at best, when our moment at The Oval will have long since passed. Additionally, it has also been reported that Lancashire could face a points deduction for producing a slightly damp pitch, but the verdict again won't be known until later today or tomorrow. That would be no way to clinch a title anyway.

It's unfortunate that this potentially magical moment has been spoiled by the current scenario, but I remind myself that, while the Championship title might not be officially ours today, it certainly will be sometime next week at Old Trafford. There is no way that Lancashire will be able to win the match by twenty points to nil - it's hardly ever happened in the recent history of the competition and it would require Lancashire to make 400-2, bowl us out for under two-hundred and then win the match. That sort of thing doesn't happen to a poor side, let alone this Surrey team. And even if we did somehow get ourselves into a hole, Adam Hollioake could declare with eight wickets down to deny Lancashire a bowling point.

So, as the celebrations continue in a fairly restrained kind of way, I look ahead to Manchester next week. I will be fortunate enough to be there at the moment when the winning of the title is officially confirmed and there will be a sprinkling of other Surrey fans there, too, but it's quite sad that most of those here at The Oval today won't be present to share the moment.

Once all the players and fans have dispersed, I retire to The Beehive with a group of the club's travelling supporters to celebrate our victory. Although today's clinching of the title has been about as far removed as imaginable from the style of victory and the scenes at The Oval last September, the important thing is that Surrey have again come out on top and the 1999 champions are now also, all bar mathematically, the champions of 2000.

Surrey 453-4 declared; Durham 241 and 144
Surrey won by an innings and 68 runs. Surrey 20pts, Durham 2

SURREY v DURHAM at THE OVAL. Played from 6th - 9th September

Surrey won the toss   Umpires:- J.W. Lloyds & N.A. Mallender

SURREY - First Innings								**DURHAM bowling**			
Fall of wkt	Batsman		How Out	Score	Balls	4s	6s	O	M	R	W
2- 413	M.A. Butcher		b Harmison	191	344	23	1	Brown	26	7	77	1
1- 359	I.J. Ward		lbw b Brown	144	329	13	0	Harmison	26	6	105	2
3- 421	Nadeem Shahid	c Collingwood	b Phillips	33	54	4	0	Killeen	19	4	60	0
4- 437	A.J. Hollioake *	c Brown	b Harmison	20	20	2	1	Collingwood	14	2	53	0
	A.D. Brown		Not Out	5	15	1	0	Phillips	39.5	7	110	1
	G.P. Butcher		Not Out	10	11	1	0	Gough	2	0	9	0
	J.N. Batty +	did not bat						Katich	2	0	9	0
	M.P. Bicknell	did not bat									
	A.J. Tudor	did not bat									
	I.D.K. Salisbury	did not bat									
	Saqlain Mushtaq	did not bat									
	Extras (11b, 19lb, 20w)			50							
	TOTAL		(128.5 overs)	453 - 4 dec							

DURHAM - First Innings

Fall of wkt	Batsman		How Out	Score	Balls	4s	6s
1- 22	J.J.B. Lewis *		b Bicknell	1	17	0	0
2- 66	M.A. Gough		lbw b Saqlain	28	68	3	0
6- 162	S.M. Katich	st Batty	b Salisbury	77	119	8	0
3- 89	P.D. Collingwood	c Tudor	b Salisbury	4	16	1	0
4- 113	J.A. Daley	c Ward	b Salisbury	14	25	1	0
5- 137	M.P. Speight	c Hollioake	b Salisbury	12	18	2	0
7- 205	A. Pratt +	st Batty	b Salisbury	36	76	3	0
9- 237	N.C. Phillips	c Shahid	b Saqlain	29	98	4	0
8- 225	N. Killeen		lbw b Salisbury	8	31	1	0
10- 241	S.J. Harmison		lbw b Salisbury	9	26	2	0
	S.J.E. Brown		Not Out	0	7	0	0
	Extras (6b, 5lb, 12nb)			23			
	TOTAL		(82.3 overs)	241			

SURREY bowling

	O	M	R	W
Bicknell	7	3	20	1
Tudor	6	1	14	0
Saqlain	35	8	91	2
Salisbury	34.3	8	105	7

DURHAM - Second Innings

Fall of wkt	Batsman		How Out	Score	Balls	4s	6s
1- 16	J.J.B. Lewis *		lbw b Tudor	8	21	2	0
4- 43	M.A. Gough	c Salisbury	b Tudor	20	71	3	0
2- 16	S.M. Katich	c Batty	b Tudor	0	1	0	0
3- 30	P.D. Collingwood		run out	4	19	0	0
5- 43	J.A. Daley		b Salisbury	2	18	0	0
8- 133	M.P. Speight	c Hollioake	b Salisbury	48	86	6	0
6- 120	A. Pratt +	c Shahid	b Bicknell	31	73	5	0
7- 129	N.C. Phillips	c Batty	b Saqlain	1	12	0	0
10- 144	N. Killeen	c Batty	b Salisbury	14	22	3	0
9- 133	S.J. Harmison		b Salisbury	0	3	0	0
	S.J.E. Brown		Not Out	0	5	0	0
	Extras (3b, 5lb, 8nb)			16			
	TOTAL		(54.3 overs)	144			

SURREY bowling

	O	M	R	W
Saqlain	12	3	23	1
Salisbury	20.3	8	49	4
Tudor	11	2	41	3
Bicknell	11	5	23	1

VIEW FROM THE DRESSING ROOM - IAN SALISBURY

Although you ended up with eleven wickets in the match, you somehow still managed to receive criticism from the reporters at the match for bowling too many loose balls. Do you find it easier to disregard this kind of unjust criticism these days?

IS - I try to, but it's still a bit upsetting. If someone had read what the reporters said after the first innings then they would have thought that I'd taken 0-100 off twenty overs, instead of 7-105 at three runs an over. I don't suppose those reporters would have taken into consideration the fact that the ball was wet and how hard it was for a spinner to bowl that day, plus, having just been picked for England, they were possibly looking for an angle to give me some stick again. But I just try to laugh about it now and it's become a bit of a running joke in our changing room - the guys say to me 'I see from the papers that you bowled badly again yesterday'!

Do you think part of the problem is that these journalists simply don't understand the difficulties of leg-spin bowling?

IS - Quite probably - that's why, when I got picked for England, I tried to get across in interviews exactly what it's like to be a leg-spinner. It is probably the most difficult art in cricket, as a bowler, so you are always going to bowl more bad balls than other types of bowler. But they don't seem to understand - maybe they just don't love the game!

This win as good as clinched the Championship, didn't it?
IS - Yes, and I think we showed that with our celebrations, really. We were disappointed that we didn't mathematically win it at The Oval so that we could have received the trophy in front of all the fans - that's why we came down from the dressing room to show our appreciation to all those people who had watched us and supported us throughout the season.

Personally, I wasn't quite sure how much to celebrate - did the players have that problem, too?
IS - Definitely not! We knew we'd won it, so we didn't hold back, to be honest!

VIEW FROM THE DRESSING ROOM - IAN WARD

To all intents and purposes this win clinched the Championship, didn't it? Does anything in particular stick in your mind about the moments after we claimed the final wicket?
IW - To be honest, my mind went back to the game against Kent at Canterbury, when Tudes and I were chasing another batting point as the rain was coming down. I had a couple of balls at the end and if I'd only managed to get one of those balls through the covers for two or three runs then we would have won the Championship here by winning this match. So that was a bit disappointing - it would have been nice to have clinched the title for certain and not to have needed to get a point up at Old Trafford.

To what degree did the players feel able to celebrate?
IW - Some more than others felt the ability to celebrate and some more than others did it exceptionally well! Unfortunately, I wasn't one of them - I knew I was playing the next day so I had to restrain myself!

VIEW FROM THE DRESSING ROOM - MARK BUTCHER

Everyone must have been delighted for Ian Salisbury, who picked up another good haul of wickets in this game and thoroughly deserved his England recall.
MB - Yes, he had a magic year - he was always putting heavy spin on the ball and his control was immaculate for most of the season. The only really ordinary spell I can remember him bowling was when Darren Lehmann got after him at The Oval but otherwise he bowled magnificently from start to finish.

KEITH MEDLYCOTT'S ASSESSMENT

Lancashire played exceptionally well to win their match against Somerset with maximum points but our win here meant that it counted for nothing. I was particularly pleased to see the opening pair produce such a big partnership because that was an area where we had fallen short all season. We want to see a lot more stands of 200-plus as they really hurt the opposition and enable you to build imposing totals. Given good weather you can then go on and finish the job off, as we did here.

Other Division One Matches

Although Lancashire went on to complete a resounding victory over Somerset on day three of their match, one glance at the table told Surrey's players and supporters all they needed to know. Since their total number of wins could not be equalled by Lancashire, the men from Old Trafford faced the impossible task of beating Surrey by twenty points to nil in the final game of the season. It couldn't happen... and Surrey were, all but mathematically, the County Champions of 2000!

September 6-9
Southampton:- **Hampshire beat Derbyshire by an innings and 3 runs.** Hampshire 522 (Prittipaul 152, Kendall 143, Mascarenhas 62); Derbyshire 352 (Bailey 90, Sutton 77) and 167 (Bailey 53, Udal 5-58). **Hampshire 20pts, Derbyshire 6**

September 7-10
Canterbury:- **Yorkshire beat Kent by 32 runs.** Yorkshire 401 (McGrath 133, Lehmann 116) and 145 (Ealham 5-35); Kent 317 (Dravid 72) and 197 (McCague 72). **Yorkshire 20pts, Kent 6**

September 8-10
Old Trafford:- **Lancashire beat Somerset by an innings and 109 runs.** Somerset 132 (Chapple 4-34) and 222 (Bowler 75); Lancashire 463-9dec (Hegg 128, Lloyd 126, Atherton 57). **Lancashire 20pts, Somerset 3**

COUNTY CHAMPIONSHIP DIVISION ONE AT 10TH SEPTEMBER

Pos	Prev		P	Pts	W	D	L	Bat	Bowl	Last	Three	Res
1	1	Surrey	15	202	9	4	2	40	38	W20	D11	W17
2	2	Lancashire	15	183	7	7	1	32	39	W20	D12	W16
3	4	Yorkshire	15	172*	6	7	2	35	45	W20	D-1	D10
4	3	Leicestershire	15	159	4	8	3	42	37	D11	D9	D11
5	5	Somerset	15	138	2	9	4	38	40	L3	D12	D11
6	6	Kent	15	135	4	7	4	17	42	L6	W18	L3
7	9	Hampshire	15	116	3	4	8	19	45	W20	W15	L3
8	7	Durham	16	112	2	5	9	27	41	L2	L3	L3
9	8	Derbyshire	15	104*	2	7	6	19	41	L6	W15	L3

* Deducted 8pts for sub-standard pitch

NCL DIVISION TWO - MATCH SIXTEEN

SURREY LIONS versus DURHAM DYNAMOS
at The Oval on Sunday 10th September

Durham Dynamos (251-5) beat Surrey Lions (192) by 59 runs

Surrey's young Lions went down to another defeat in their final NCL match of the season, as Durham enjoyed their first-ever taste of limited-overs success over the men from The Oval.
Fielding an unchanged side from the previous week's match at Trent Bridge, Surrey were again committed to bowling first on a good pitch when Jon Lewis won the toss for the Dynamos and, apart from two early successes for Carl Greenidge, their largely inexperienced attack endured a pretty miserable afternoon. With the Lions' first-choice bowlers all injured or resting, Jimmy Daley and Paul Collingwood took their chance to rack up some rare runs against Surrey, compiling a record-breaking stand of 177 in 33 overs to ensure a formidable total for their team. But for an impressive mid-innings spell by Philip Sampson and an effective late effort by Adam Hollioake, the damage could have been far worse, as Collingwood scorched to 86 from 97 balls and Daley recorded the first-ever century by a Durham batsman against Surrey in the short-course limited-overs competition. His hundred arrived in the penultimate over after 129 balls at the crease and included eleven fours and one six.

In order to reach a target of 252 the Lions needed a consistent batting effort and they were given the ideal start by an outstanding opening partnership worth eighty-seven in twelve overs, during which Ali Brown raced to a half-century from just thirty-six balls. Unfortunately for Surrey, the medium-paced Ian Hunter then dismissed Brown, Ward and Shahid in the space of twelve deliveries and, as the fourth-wicket pair of Gary Butcher and Gareth Batty tried to stabilise the innings, all momentum was lost, leaving too much to be done in the later overs. Once the Dynamos were on top they refused to let go and Nicky Phillips and Paul Collingwood cleaned up the lower-order as the situation became increasingly desperate.

Durham Dynamos (251-5) beat Surrey Lions (192) by 59 runs

Durham Dynamos 4pts

SURREY LIONS v DURHAM DYNAMOS at THE OVAL. Played on 10th September
Durham Dynamos won the toss   Umpires:- J.W. Lloyds & N.A. Mallender

DURHAM DYNAMOS — **SURREY LIONS bowling**

Fall of wkt	Batsman	How Out	Score	Balls	4s	6s		O	M	R	W
5- 251	J.A. Daley	c Butcher b Hollioake	105	134	11	1	Greenidge	9	0	49	2
1- 23	M.P. Speight	c G.J. Batty b Greenidge	15	14	1	1	Murtagh	9	0	50	1
2- 31	S.M. Katich	c G.J. Batty b Greenidge	2	7	0	0	Ratcliffe	7	0	33	0
3- 208	P.D. Collingwood	b Murtagh	86	97	8	1	Sampson	7	0	24	0
4- 245	J.J.B. Lewis *	c Shahid b Hollioake	25	19	4	0	Butcher	4	0	28	0
	J. Wood	Not Out	0	1	0	0	G.J. Batty	2	0	16	0
	A. Pratt +	did not bat					Hollioake	7	0	39	2
	N.C. Phillips	did not bat									
	M.M. Betts	did not bat									
	I.D. Hunter	did not bat									
	N. Killeen	did not bat									
	Extras (1b, 11lb, 2w, 4nb)		18								
	TOTAL	(45 overs)	251- 5								

SURREY LIONS — **DURHAM DYNAMOS bowling**

Fall of wkt	Batsman	How Out	Score	Balls	4s	6s		O	M	R	W
2- 94	I.J. Ward	c Speight b Hunter	41	43	5	0	Killeen	7	0	43	1
1- 87	A.D. Brown	c Killeen b Hunter	51	38	7	1	Betts	4	0	26	0
3- 99	Nadeem Shahid	c Pratt b Hunter	6	8	1	0	Wood	8	1	31	0
6- 171	G.P. Butcher	b Killeen	37	61	3	1	Hunter	5	0	23	3
4- 137	G.J. Batty	b Phillips	20	30	2	0	Phillips	9	0	30	4
5- 153	A.J. Hollioake *	b Phillips	5	12	0	0	Collingwood	7.3	1	30	2
9- 184	J.D. Ratcliffe	c Phillips b Collingwood	12	24	0	0					
7- 180	J.N. Batty +	b Phillips	4	10	0	0					
8- 181	T.J. Murtagh	c & b Phillips	0	1	0	0					
10- 192	P.J. Sampson	c Lewis b Collingwood	4	9	0	0					
	C.G. Greenidge	Not Out	3	7	0	0					
	Extras (9lb)		9								
	TOTAL	(40.3 overs)	192								

Other NCL Division Two Matches

Nottinghamshire Outlaws confirmed their place in NCL Division One for the 2001 season after edging out Glamorgan Dragons by three runs at Trent Bridge, while Warwickshire Bears earned themselves the third promotion slot with a 37-run victory over Middlesex Crusaders at Lord's. Although Middlesex could still, potentially, equal the Bears' tally of thirty-eight points in the final round of matches, they would not be able to match Warwickshire's nine wins.

September 9
Lord's:- **Warwickshire Bears beat Middlesex Crusaders by 37 runs.** Warwickshire 172 in 42.5 overs (Singh 74); Middlesex 135 in 41 overs (Hutton 49). **Warwickshire Bears 4pts**

September 10
Southampton:- **Derbyshire Scorpions beat Hampshire Hawks by 4 runs.** Derbyshire 195-9 (Sutton 53 not out, Pyemont 50, Warne 4-23); Hampshire 191-9 (Kenway 90, Cassar 4-29). **Derbyshire Scorpions 4pts**

Trent Bridge:- **Nottinghamshire Outlaws beat Glamorgan Dragons by 3 runs.** Nottinghamshire 229-9 (Johnson 62, Afzaal 51); Glamorgan 226-9 (Maynard 88 not out). **Nottinghamshire Outlaws 4pts**

NCL DIVISION TWO AT 10TH SEPTEMBER

Pos	Prev		P	Pts	W	T	L	N/R	Last	Three	Res
1	1	Surrey Lions	16	48	11	0	3	2	L	L	L
2	2	Nottinghamshire Outlaws	15	42	10	0	4	1	W	W	L
3	3	Warwickshire Bears	15	38	9	1	5	0	W	W	L
4	4	Middlesex Crusaders	15	34	7	1	5	2	L	W	W
5	6	Essex Eagles	15	32	7	0	6	2	W	W	W
=	5	Glamorgan Dragons	15	32	7	2	6	0	L	L	W
7	7	Hampshire Hawks	15	20	5	0	10	0	L	W	W
8	8	Durham Dynamos	15	16	4	0	11	0	W	L	L
9	9	Derbyshire Scorpions	15	10	2	0	12	1	W	L	L

WELCOME TO WHITGIFT

(Marcus Hook)

(Reg Elliott)

(Reg Elliott)

Three views of the South Croydon ground as the Surrey Lions took on the Warwickshire Bears

POSTCARDS FROM SCARBOROUGH 1

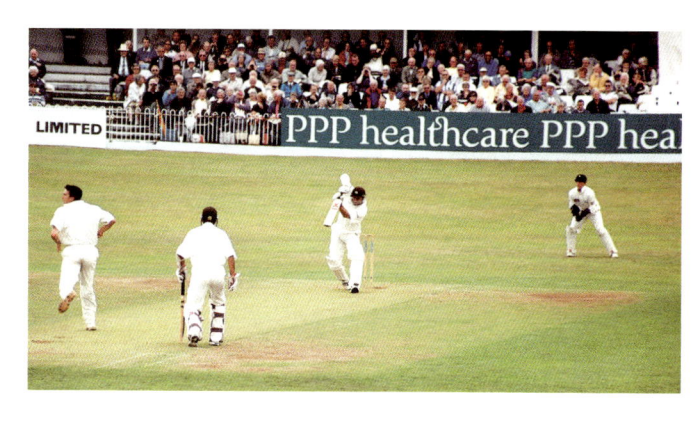

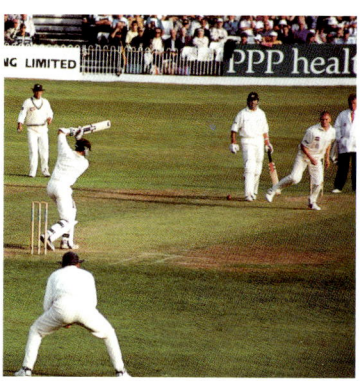

TOP - Ian Ward drives Gavin Hamilton straight down the ground on the first morning
MIDDLE - Jon Batty hands out similar treatment to Matthew Hoggard
BOTTOM - Alex Tudor has Anthony McGrath taken at the wicket from the second ball of Yorkshire's reply
All photos by Reg Elliott

POSTCARDS FROM SCARBOROUGH 2

TOP - The faces of Yorkshire fans in the background register shock as Ben Hollioake rips out Vic Craven's off stump to reduce Yorkshire to 4 for 3
BOTTOM - Hollioake strikes again as David Byas pops up a catch to Nadeem Shahid at short leg
Both photos by Reg Elliott

BUTCHER & WARD POST 359 TO SET UP VICTORY OVER DURHAM

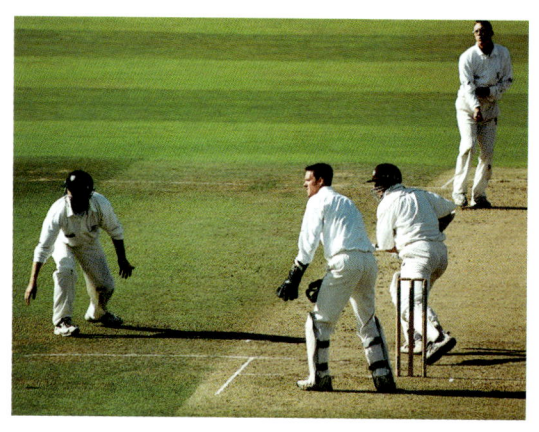

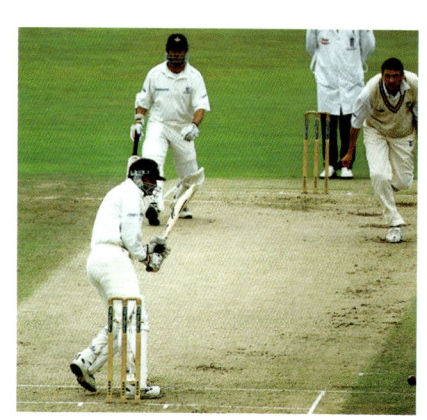

TOP - Mark Butcher drives through midwicket
MIDDLE - Ian Ward cuts Nicky Phillips backward of point
BOTTOM - Mark Butcher clips Steve Harmison through backward square leg
All photos by Marcus Hook

THE BOWLERS TAKE UP THE BATON

TOP - Jon Lewis is bowled by Martin Bicknell at the start of Durham's first innings
MIDDLE - Simon Katich is well caught first ball by an airborne Jon Batty early in the second innings
BOTTOM - Jimmy Daley is bamboozled and bowled by Ian Salisbury's googly as Surrey move closer to glory
All photos by Reg Elliott

SURREY'S DOUBLE BECKONS AS DURHAM CRUMBLE TO DEFEAT

(Reg Elliott)

(Richard Spiller)

(Reg Elliott)

TOP - Durham lose their eighth wicket as Speight falls to Adam Hollioake's catch off Salisbury
MIDDLE - Adam Hollioake applauds his team from the field with the title almost secured
BOTTOM - Saqlain Mushtaq, Jon Batty and Nadeem Shahid lead some low-key celebrations

THE TITLE CLINCHED AND CELEBRATED AT OLD TRAFFORD

(John Dawson - Cricket Images)

(Trevor Jones)

(Trevor Jones)

TOP - A jubilant Alex Tudor celebrates the title-clinching dismissal of Saurav Ganguly with Martin Bicknell
MIDDLE - The Surrey team savours their triumph in front of the pavilion shortly after receiving the trophy
BOTTOM - Adam Hollioake and Micky Stewart are all smiles in the gathering gloom

END-OF-SEASON AWARDS EVENING

TOP - The triumphant Surrey squad poses with the County Championship trophy
BOTTOM - Martin Bicknell collects the Player Of The Season award from chairman Michael Soper
Both photos by Phil Booker

16 Doubling Up With Delight

Manchester seemed a long way for everyone to travel for one point, but since it was the point that would rubber-stamp our Championship title I don't suppose anyone minded too much. Three wickets or two-hundred runs would be sufficient, though the thought of Surrey declaring when eight wickets down to deny Lancashire a point was apparently causing consternation at the ECB. Although I felt that we were unlikely to get ourselves into a position where we would need to consider taking such drastic action, it seemed a legitimate tactic to me. Ironically, one of the reasons why the title wasn't already in the bag was Somerset's tactical declaration when eight wickets down at Taunton in the first match of the season! It had happened in other matches during the season, too, so it seemed utterly stupid that people were now making a song and dance about it just because of the added significance of the point concerned. There was also talk of a match referee being appointed for this game, just in case any skullduggery went on. Unfortunately, the ECB was two weeks late with this idea... where was the match referee when we *really* needed one, at Scarborough?!

COUNTY CHAMPIONSHIP - MATCH SIXTEEN

LANCASHIRE versus SURREY
at Old Trafford

First Day - Wednesday 13th September

Lancashire 324; Surrey 28-2

The Teams And The Toss - For the final match of the season, Surrey field the same eleven that beat Durham, while Lancashire are without their captain, John Crawley, who is suffering from appendicitis. Although Andrew Flintoff, like Alec Stewart and Graham Thorpe, is rested by England, Mike Atherton is allowed to play in the match. Warren Hegg captains Lancashire and he elects to bat first on winning the toss.

Lancashire's decision to bat merely confirms what we all pretty much knew anyway - that the home side is fully aware that a twenty-nil points victory in this game is beyond the realms of possibility. If they'd felt that they had any chance of pulling it off then surely they would have taken on the easier part of the job, bowling Surrey out for under two-hundred, before attempting the Everest-climb of scoring 400 for 2!

To make that kind of score, whether batting first or second, would clearly require a huge effort from Mike Atherton, of course, but, as it happens, he scores just five before Martin Bicknell snares him with a delivery that appears to both cut back and keep low. As the ball thuds into his pads, Atherton knows his fate and he is walking long before umpire Julian's finger has reached the peak of its elevation. It's 10-1 and, strange though it seems to be saying it with only seventeen balls bowled in the match, the writing is on the wall!

The second-wicket pair of Mark Chilton and Saurav Ganguly certainly ride their luck in the early stages of their partnership, with both men edging deliveries to third man and Chilton surviving a confident appeal for a catch behind the wicket off Bicknell.

It's not just bad luck that prevents Surrey from sealing the Championship title in double-quick time, however, since both batsmen offer a catching chance which isn't taken. In the eleventh over, Chilton, on seventeen, is missed by Mark Butcher at second slip off Bicknell, then in the very next over from Tudor, it is Ganguly who is reprieved, when on nine, by Ian Salisbury at short extra cover. Both chances are low but acceptable and had they been taken then the title would have been sewn up inside the first hour's play. As it is, an edged four to third man off Bicknell by Chilton brings up the Lancashire fifty in the fifteenth over and then Tudor suffers even worse luck in the following over when Ganguly picks up two streaky boundaries, one with an edge and another achieved involuntarily when he tries to withdraw his bat from a ball outside off stump. That said, there are a couple of elegant drives mixed in with the moments of good fortune, one such stroke coming from Ganguly in Gary Butcher's opening over after replacing Tudor at the Stretford end.

The feeling that it isn't going to be Surrey's morning is underlined again, however, when Saqlain takes over from Bicknell at the Warwick Road end. In the Pakistani off-spinner's second over, Ganguly comes charging down the pitch, misses with a wild slog and is bowled, only to be saved by the umpire's call of 'no-ball'.

Thereafter, the batsmen appear to settle down and they look to be gaining the upper hand as they pick off a boundary apiece and push the score up to ninety-nine. With lunch only minutes away, disaster strikes, however, as Chilton is run out following a horrendous breakdown in communications with his partner. Having pushed the ball into the covers, Chilton sets off for a single, apparently oblivious to the fact that Ganguly hasn't moved. By the time he realises this, he has strayed too far to get back to the striker's end and Alex Tudor's direct-hit throw at the stumps seals his fate. Surrey are now just one wicket from the title but, hard though Saqlain and the newly-introduced Ian Salisbury try, they are unable to nail the trophy in the two overs that remain before the interval.

Lunch:- Lancashire 104-2 (Ganguly 46*, Fairbrother 0*) from 29 overs

Poor Alex Tudor. Having had no luck before lunch, his opening over after the break sees him suffer even greater misfortune as Neil Fairbrother first edges him just to the left of Ali Brown at first slip and then through the hands of Mark Butcher at second slip. Both chances are fairly straightforward and the fact that the ball ends up speeding away to the rope at third man on each occasion only makes matters worse. Are Surrey showing a few nerves as they strive for the Championship-clinching wicket?

Tudor is, initially, no more fortunate in his next over, either, as Ganguly steers another delivery from the tall fast bowler to the third man boundary to reach a 98-ball half-century and then slices the ball over backward point for another four. It is beginning to look as if Tudor might have done better to stay in bed this morning until his luck suddenly changes when Ganguly again flashes wildly outside the off stump. The ball inevitably takes the edge and flies at great speed to the left of third slip, but this time the big Surrey paceman is fully rewarded for his effort as Adam Hollioake flings himself to his left to pull off a spectacular catch. That's it! At 1.36pm exactly, Surrey are duly confirmed as the 2000 County Champions and the on-field celebrations can commence. The players form into one of their familiar huddles and the twelfth man, Ben Hollioake, rushes out on to the field to join them. There have been some apparently nervy moments today before the team's goal has been attained but they have finally got there and it's fitting that Tudor has got the wicket after his outstanding bowling in the innings to date. Perhaps most importantly of all, he now has an Old Trafford memory which will forever eclipse his less-than-happy memory of the 1998 match on this ground.

The celebrations completed, it's back to business, though it is quite possible to imagine that the game might lose some of its intensity now. Initially, this doesn't appear to be the case, however, as Tudor rips out Graham Lloyd's middle stump with a fine yorker and sees Chris Schofield missed, on nought, ironically enough at third slip by Adam Hollioake, before Saqlain beats Fairbrother's defensive stroke with an absolute beauty that pitches on leg stump and hits off. It's 125-5 and the champions are looking to finish the season in style.

Although a minor recovery now follows, with Schofield forcing the ball twice to the cover boundary to raise the 150, Saqlain soon hits back with two strikes in four balls - Schofield falling in almost identical fashion to Fairbrother, except that this time the off stump is knocked clean out of the ground, and Chapple departing lbw when caught on the crease, having played down the wrong line - to reduce the home side to 154-7.

With very limited batting resources remaining, Lancashire appear to be really struggling but Warren Hegg looks in good form after his 128 in the previous game against Somerset and, with Gary Keedy as a passive partner, he propels his side towards and then beyond two-hundred. While Saqlain occupies the Warwick Road end throughout the session, Adam Hollioake rotates his other bowlers at the Stretford end, though neither Martin Bicknell nor Ian Salisbury prove able to prevent the stubborn eighth-wicket partnership from passing fifty.

Finally, the Surrey skipper brings himself into the attack and things really start to happen, with Hegg completing a valiant half-century from just 69 balls, Keedy recording a career-best score when he reaches thirty and the century stand clicking up in the penultimate over before tea. It's looking very much like the partnership will be resuming after the interval, too, as Keedy produces, arguably, the best stroke of his innings by driving Hollioake to the cover boundary, but the final ball of the session produces a belated breakthrough for Surrey as the Lancashire tail-ender drives again, but this time slices low to Nadeem Shahid in the gully.

Tea:- Lancashire 261-8 (Hegg 59*) from 72 overs

It's a new partnership but a familiar scenario after tea - Saqlain wheels away continuously at the Warwick Road end, Hegg continues to dominate the scoring for the home side and a tail-ender hangs on in a supporting role at the other end. The Lancashire wicketkeeper is playing a very impressive innings, scoring all around the wicket as he sees off a three-over blast from Alex Tudor and shepherds the total up towards three-hundred.

The once unlikely third batting point is eventually secured by his partner, Michael Smethurst, courtesy of an inside-edge off Adam Hollioake which cannons into the helmets behind Jon Batty to earn five runs, and, just to further frustrate the Surrey skipper, the Lancashire paceman then lofts the next delivery fractionally over cover's head for three more runs. Almost before we know it, Lancashire have registered another fifty partnership, though the pairing of Salisbury with his spin twin soon afterwards finally brings an end to Surrey's suffering. Smethurst is ninth out, with the score at 315, when he is blown away, lbw, by Saqlain's now familiar 'bullet' ball then, with Hegg edging ever closer to a well-deserved century, Peter Martin rather thoughtlessly sweeps Salisbury straight into the waiting hands of Ian Ward at deep backward square leg.

There's much sympathy for Hegg as he leaves the field to a fine ovation for a marvellous innings which has, for the second match running, transformed his team's fortunes. Having conceded their highest total of the season, and a score of over three-hundred for only the third time in the Championship campaign, Surrey's bowlers look decidedly weary as they head for their dressing room.

It's now down to the batsmen to see out the last eight overs of the day, but, unfortunately, the visitors get off to a poor start with the loss of two wickets in the first four overs. Mark Butcher, having survived a very loud lbw appeal from the first ball of the innings bowled by Martin, finds himself less fortunate when trapped on the back foot four balls later, then Nadeem Shahid falls to Chapple in almost identical fashion three overs afterwards, though on this occasion the ball appears to have shot through rather low. Luckily for the visitors, Ian Ward looks in superb touch right from ball one and, in company with his skipper, he sees the 2000 County Champions through to the close without further loss.

With the title now secured, the presentation of the trophy can take place in the gathering gloom. The official handover takes place up on the top level of the pavilion, amidst the now customary champagne-spraying, then, once Adam Hollioake has completed some interviews in the pavilion, he rushes out to join his team for further photographs on the outfield in near darkness. It has to be a pretty hurried session, however, since the team has a date at Old Trafford - that's the *football* ground as opposed to the *cricket* ground - as tonight the nation's cricket champions will be watching their footballing counterparts playing Anderlecht in the UEFA Champions League. While Manchester United will have to battle very hard if they are to win that title, there can surely be no disputing the fact that Surrey are the number one team in Europe when it comes to cricket!

Close:- Surrey 28-2 (Ward 18*, Hollioake 6*) from 8 overs

VIEW FROM THE DRESSING ROOM - GARY BUTCHER

I thought Tudes bowled really well, with no luck at all in Lancashire's first innings. Figures of 2 for 98 from nineteen overs most certainly didn't do him justice. Would you agree with that view?
GB - Yes, it's fair to say that it just wasn't T's day! He bowled superbly, with good pace and he kept going past the outside edge but just didn't have the luck - he should have ended up with six or seven wickets and we should have been going off the field with Lancashire all out for about 150. I felt very sorry for him because he tried really hard. Most of those ninety-eight runs he conceded went to third man, too.

It was unusual to see an opposition tail add so many runs against us. Was that largely because the bowlers were tired after a long hard season?
GB - Credit to Warren Hegg, he played very well, but I think that once the title was clinched we just wanted to get off the pitch, put our feet up and enjoy the celebrations!

VIEW FROM THE DRESSING ROOM - ADAM HOLLIOAKE

If we had been forced into a tight corner, would you have declared our first innings with eight wickets down to seal the Championship title?
AH - No, we decided before the game started that we weren't going to do that - we felt that if we weren't good enough to win it properly then we'd rather not win it at all. So many sides had tried to pull stunts against us during the season that we decided we'd feel better with ourselves if we won the title without having to resort to things like that. I think it's important that you hold the moral high ground wherever possible and that you try to win the right way. A lot of people might not like us, for whatever reasons, but at least I'd like to think that we played fair throughout the whole year.

When we clinched the title with your fine slip catch the team went into an extended huddle. Are you at liberty to tell me what was said in that huddle or is it something that you wish to keep private?
AH - I don't think anything hugely intelligent or revealing was said! We might have expressed relief that we had at last held a catch because we had already missed enough chances as it was, but I think it was more about being together - pulling tightly together into that huddle just represented the way that we had been so tight as a unit all season. And I guess it was also just a way for us, the eleven players, to enjoy that special moment for ourselves, with no-one else around.

VIEW FROM THE DRESSING ROOM - MARTIN BICKNELL

Having missed out in 1999 when you were injured for the decisive match against Nottinghamshire, you must have been thrilled to actually be on the pitch this year when the title was clinched?
MB - Yes, it was fantastic. After my back problems, I was just desperate to get back out on the park for the last two matches. I'd been very much fifty-fifty for the Durham game but I knew I could get through my first spell and then, the way the Oval pitches are normally, I guessed that I wouldn't need to come back for another bowl. I knew that I had to be there, though, and it was just a case of getting through those last two games.

It was tense stuff as we attempted to pick up that final point. Did last-minute nerves account for the catches we put down in the first session?
MB - No, I think we were just dreadful! I think we had mentally switched off because we knew we were going to win the title and we weren't as intense or focused as we should have been. People were just sitting back and waiting for it to happen, to be honest, and it ended up being one of those days in the field where nothing goes right.

It must have been a great feeling when Adam picked up the crucial catch to secure the title. Can you remember what went through your mind at that time?
MB - It was more a feeling of relief than anything else. Once we'd beaten Durham, which became a tense game because of all the rain that was around, we'd done some celebrating on that Saturday night and so that felt like the moment when we'd won the Championship, really. The Lancashire game was just about dotting the i's and crossing the t's, to be honest, so it was just a relief to secure the inevitable final point.

It was surprising to see an opposition tail scoring so many runs against us. I assume it can be explained by the bowlers being tired and 'demob happy' after a long season?!
MB - Yes, I think we were definitely mentally switched off by that stage, after putting so much into a long hard season. There was nothing else to play for and, while we didn't want to lose the game, obviously, I think we were all keen to get through to the end of the game and get it all over and done with.

Second Day - Thursday 14th September

Lancashire 324; Surrey 297-9

The start of the second day's play is delayed by an hour, following overnight rain and morning drizzle. While the outfield is drying, some of the Surrey players are on the outfield playing football, perhaps inspired by watching Manchester United's 5-1 victory over Anderlecht last night.

By 11.30am they are back in cricket mode, though, with Ian Ward and Adam HolY resuming the Surrey innings. Peter Martin and Glen Chapple open proceedings for Lancashire, and the Surrey skipper starts as he means to go on, cutting and driving a boundary in each of the first two overs and totally dominating the action. While Ward plays his normal steady game, surviving a routine catching chance to Ganguly at third slip along the way, Hollioake treats Martin with utter contempt, thrashing him out of the attack during a two-over assault which sees him finding the boundary rope on no fewer than four occasions, and raising both the Surrey fifty and the half-century partnership in the process.

Michael Smethurst, Martin's replacement, initially fares no better, as the visiting skipper, his power and timing absolutely awesome, drives successive fours through mid-off and extra cover to move his score on to forty-five and his boundary count up to nine. Sadly for Surrey, and for the crowd, this wonderfully entertaining knock is terminated in Smethurst's second over when Hollioake frustratingly fails to build on a great start once again, his stumps rearranged in attempting a drive that would have taken him through to a 39-ball half-century. As it is, he falls one run short of the mark, though the spectators are quick to show their appreciation for a quite sublime cameo.

Hollioake's replacement at the crease, Ali Brown, looks like he might be aiming for a fast fifty, too, as he gets away to a flying, though not so convincing, start. Successive boundaries off Chapple, the first edged over the slips, take him up to eleven in no time before he loses his batting partner to an edged drive in the former England 'A' paceman's next over. With Ward gone for twenty-eight, Surrey are now struggling a little at 95-4.

The score then almost becomes 103-5 in the penultimate over before lunch when Gary Butcher, on four at the time, almost becomes a third Chapple victim as he edges low to Graham Lloyd at first slip but escapes as the ball goes to ground. Although the guilty fielder is doubtless disappointed to have missed this catch, he clearly doesn't let it affect him as he makes no mistake when he gets a chance to atone for his error in the final over of the session. Chris Schofield, brought on for the obligatory over of spin before lunch, lures Brown into a drive which ends in Lloyd's hands at cover, having seen two of his first three deliveries smashed to the boundary.

It's been a hugely entertaining session of cricket - eighteen overs, eighty-three runs, three wickets - but Surrey are now in a spot of bother.

Lunch:- Surrey 111-5 (G.P. Butcher 4*) from 26 overs

Glen Chapple and Michael Smethurst are the men entrusted with forcing home Lancashire's advantage after the break, but they find Gary Butcher and Jon Batty to be doughty opponents. While Butcher is prepared to bide his time and pick up the occasional single, the boundaries come largely from the bat of Batty, with three cuts finding the rope backward of point in one four-over passage of play.

Having drawn a blank after half-a-dozen overs apiece, Chapple and Smethurst are then replaced in a double change which sees the reintroduction of Martin and Schofield. The Surrey sixth-wicket pair's sensible, measured rebuild of the innings continues against the new bowlers, with Batty putting his favourite sweep shot into operation against the leg-spinner to take the total past 150.

It has only got as far as 161, though, when Schofield strikes back, having the Surrey 'keeper taken at slip by Lloyd when a well-pitched leg-break takes the edge of a defensive bat. Besides setting the visitors back on their heels again, this sixth wicket of the innings is an important one for Lancashire, since it assures them of the runners-up spot in the County Championship for a third successive year. It's a fine achievement by the red rose county but everyone at The Oval will be quite happy to see them continue in the role of bridesmaids!

As Ian Salisbury now joins Butcher at the wicket, the home captain opts for an all-spin attack, with Gary Keedy getting his first bowl of the innings. This move has the effect of slowing the scoring rate, initially, until Butcher advances on Keedy to drive him straight for four and then cuts him square for another boundary which takes the total up to 175 and therefore snuffs out any possibility of Surrey having to follow on. This is just as well, since Salisbury departs almost immediately, taken behind the wicket by Hegg after getting an outside edge to a drive at a Schofield leg-break. Nor does Alex Tudor last long, edging Keedy between Hegg and first slip for four, before falling lbw when trying to pull a short delivery from Schofield - Surrey are back in trouble at 193-8.

Fortunately for the double champions, Butcher is playing a splendid innings, using his feet well to both spinners and driving them through, over or wide of mid-on to record a 109-ball half-century after 134 minutes at the crease. Martin Bicknell supports sensibly to ensure that tea is reached without further loss.

Tea:- Surrey 212-8 (G.P. Butcher 60*, Bicknell 3*) from 64 overs

The roles are reversed after the break, with Bicknell scoring the bulk of the runs during a very quiet opening spell against the spinners. Although only one boundary comes in the first forty-five minutes, when Bicknell late-cuts Keedy, something of a stalemate seems to be developing, so Warren Hegg recalls Chapple in place of his left-arm spinner at the Stretford end. This proves to be a good move, since the new bowler terminates another threatening Surrey stand at exactly fifty in his fourth over when Butcher hooks the ball straight down Smethurst's throat at long leg. Although he has rather lost his way after tea, adding only six runs to his score in fourteen overs, it's been a very mature and impressive innings from the 25-year-old all-rounder and there can be no doubt that he has fully justified his elevation from the second eleven.

From here on in, it's fun all the way as sun - yes, sun - stops play on two occasions and Saqlain batters the bowlers all around the park. The problem with the Old Trafford square is that it is the wrong way round - during the closing weeks of the season the sun starts to set behind the bowler's arm and reflects light up off the playing surface, dazzling the batsmen.

It can't be any more dazzling than Saqlain's strokeplay, however, as the Pakistani spinner takes a liking to Chapple's bowling, crashing him through extra cover for four and then smashing him straight for six in successive overs. Keedy is then driven over mid-off for another boundary before Smethurst, Chapple's replacement at the Stretford end, is lofted over mid-on and cracked through extra cover for boundaries which complete a 76-ball fifty partnership in the final over of the day.

The lower-order has, once again, come to Surrey's rescue and left the game nicely poised at the halfway point.

Close:- Surrey 297-9 (Bicknell 46*, Saqlain 33*) from 91 overs

VIEW FROM THE DRESSING ROOM - GARY BUTCHER

You must have been delighted with your innings of sixty-six as we were looking rather shaky at 111-5. Would you say that this was a better knock than your seventy at Edgbaston during the 1999 season?
GB - Yes, I'd say so, because at Edgbaston we already had a lot of runs on the board when I came in. I was pleased, personally, to get some runs in the first team to follow my five wickets against Derbyshire and I think this innings would have pleased most of our lads, too, because no-one was keen to have to come out and field again at the end of a long hard season!

Third Day - Friday 15th September

Lancashire 324; Surrey 297-9 (No play - rain)

There's never any possibility of play on day three as constant, occasionally heavy, rain leaves the ground saturated and necessitates a lunchtime abandonment. What had looked likely to be a very interesting four-day match will now almost certainly end in stalemate.

Fourth Day - Saturday 16th September

Lancashire 324 and 304-9 declared; Surrey 359

Match Drawn - Surrey 11pts, Lancashire 10

Surrey's final day of the season gets off to a prompt start, with Graham Lloyd behind the stumps in place of Warren Hegg, who had received a nasty crack on the foot while keeping wicket on the second day.

It looks unlikely that today's play will produce any fireworks, but there's always a chance of some entertainment while Saqlain is at the crease and he doesn't disappoint, top-edging a hook at Smethurst for four in the second over of the morning. During the next over, from Chris Schofield, Martin Bicknell reaches a very well-played fifty from 119 balls in the same number of minutes when his square cut crosses the boundary rope at backward point.

Much to Lancashire's frustration, the visitors eventually move into the lead when Bicknell takes consecutive boundaries off Schofield and the last-wicket pair registers a century partnership, from just 141 balls, two overs later. By now, with Keedy having joined his fellow spinner in the attack, each batsman is within touching distance of a milestone - Saqlain is chasing another Surrey half-century, while Bicknell is on the verge of completing five-hundred County Championship runs in a season for the first time. For a split second, as Saqi edges Schofield between the stand-in 'keeper and first slip, it looks like both men may be denied their glory, but the ball races away to the rope to complete the Pakistani spin king's fifty from 76 balls in 96 minutes and then, later in the same over, Bicknell late cuts for two to achieve his goal, too. As we later discover, this makes the Surrey swing maestro the only man in the 2000 Championship season to complete the double of five-hundred runs and fifty wickets.

Finally, with Surrey's lead up to thirty-five, the first ball of a new spell from Smethurst brings the visitors' innings to an end, a full-length delivery extracting Saqlain's off stump in clinical style with the last-wicket stand worth a very creditable 116.

Lancashire now have around an hour to bat before lunch and, after a couple of boundaries from Atherton, they lose both openers to successive deliveries, Chilton feathering the final ball of Bicknell's third over to Batty, who picks up a fine low catch, and Atherton - not for the first time in the 2000 season - losing his off stump to Tudor from the first delivery of the next over. At 17-2, Lancashire look as if they could be in some danger, but the feeling that the atmosphere out in the middle is pretty relaxed is underlined when Neil Fairbrother arrives at the crease to be greeted by four Surrey fielders standing shoulder-to-shoulder in the area of second and third slip!

As it happens, they should perhaps have been standing in the gully/backward point region, since that is where most of the shots go as the left-handed combination of Ganguly and Fairbrother rattles up a fifty partnership in just thirty-five balls, with Tudor bearing the brunt of the assault and disappearing for seven boundaries, not all off the middle of the bat, in three overs.

It looks to be a sign of things to come when the final five overs of the session are delivered by that legendary off-spin duo, Mark Butcher and Ali Brown!

Lunch:- Lancashire 85-2 (Ganguly 40*, Fairbrother 24*) from 15 overs

With Saqlain Mushtaq and Martin Bicknell not reappearing after the interval, their places being taken by Ben Hollioake and the first team physio, John Gloster, the bowling remains in the hands of the new Surrey spin twins. It's no reflection on their bowling, of course, but I decide, for the first time all season, to abandon my note-taking except for significant events! And there turns out to be quite a few of those!

The Lancashire hundred comes up with a slog-sweep for six off Mark Butcher by Ganguly, who then completes a 57-ball, 56-minute half-century in the next over from the same bowler. Quite incredibly, Butcher then rattles through the Lancashire middle-order, taking five wickets in the space of eleven overs from the Warwick Road end. The catalogue of dismissals is as follows:-

Saurav Ganguly - drives a catch to wide, deep mid-on - out for 65, Lancashire 125 for 3
Graham Lloyd - drags a drive to wide mid-on - out for 1, to complete a 2000 County Championship sequence against Surrey of 0,1,1,1 - Lancashire 127 for 4
Chris Schofield - bowled when missing a wild slog to leg - out for 9, Lancashire 147 for 5
Glen Chapple - top-edges a cut to a juggling Alex Tudor at slip, via Jon Batty - out for 5, Lancashire 159 for 6
Gary Keedy - lbw, hitting across line of ball turning from leg stump - out for 1, Lancashire 161 for 7

The jubilant Butcher therefore has career-best figures and his first-ever five-wicket haul in first-class cricket. This swag-bag of wickets almost swells to six, too, but Ian Ward grasses an overhead catch at deep mid-on, offered by Smethurst with the score at 189-7.
While Butcher has been running through the home side's batting, Ali Brown has been desperately seeking his maiden first-class wicket and his unofficial record as the worst bowler, statistically anyway, in first-class cricket is looking safe, with his career record now nought for something like three-hundred! As a result of Brown's continuing barren spell, we are 'treated' to a display of Adam Hollioake's wrist spin in the final forty-five minutes before tea.

Tea:- Lancashire 224-7 (Fairbrother 73*, Smethurst 36*) from 63 overs

Career-firsts and career-bests are two-a-penny during the final session, which starts with Nadeem Shahid running in from beyond the boundary rope to deliver the first ball at medium pace. Mike Smethurst is the first to a landmark, recording a maiden first-class fifty from 59 balls in fifty-one minutes, before offering Ali Brown two caught-and-bowled chances, both of which are spurned. It is beginning to look like Brown doesn't want a first-class wicket, but then maybe he just wants a higher-profile batsman for his first scalp? If this is the case, then he gets his wish when he traps Neil Fairbrother on the crease with a quicker ball and wins an lbw verdict, with the Lancashire left-hander just ten runs short of becoming only the second man to score a Championship century against Surrey in 2000. Although Browny has broken his duck, he now has an average of 328.00! Ouch!
One maiden first-class wicket is then closely followed by a second, when Jon Batty has Smethurst taken by Bicknell at mid-off to produce a scorecard entry which looks very much back to front. In years to come will people really believe that it was caught Bicknell, bowled Batty?!
The season then ends with further off-spin offerings from Messrs Ward and Bicknell and a few lusty hits from a hobbling Hegg. It's been a very light-hearted finale, but the bottom line is that Surrey have ended up heading the 2000 County Championship table by twenty clear points... and you can't argue with that!

Lancashire 324 and 304-9 declared; Surrey 359
Match Drawn. Surrey 11pts, Lancashire 10

LANCASHIRE v SURREY at OLD TRAFFORD. Played from 13th - 16th September
Lancashire won the toss   Umpires:- R. Julian & G. Sharp

LANCASHIRE - First Innings

Fall of wkt	Batsman		How Out	Score	Balls	4s	6s	SURREY bowling	O	M	R	W
1- 10	M.A. Atherton		lbw b Bicknell	5	15	0	0	Bicknell	14	2	49	1
2- 99	M.J. Chilton		run out	30	68	6	0	Tudor	19	2	98	2
3- 121	S.C. Ganguly	c Hollioake	b Tudor	54	101	8	0	G.P. Butcher	4	0	11	0
5- 125	N.H. Fairbrother		b Saqlain	10	27	2	0	Saqlain	34	8	81	4
4- 123	G.D. Lloyd		b Tudor	1	5	0	0	Salisbury	10.5	1	38	1
6- 154	C.P. Schofield		b Saqlain	24	41	3	0	Hollioake	6	0	21	1
	W.K. Hegg *+		Not Out	93	130	10	0					
7- 154	G. Chapple		lbw b Saqlain	0	3	0	0					
8- 261	G. Keedy	c Shahid	b Hollioake	34	96	6	0					
9- 315	M.P. Smethurst		lbw b Saqlain	17	39	3	0					
10- 324	P.J. Martin	c Ward	b Salisbury	4	12	1	0					
	Extras (19b, 7lb, 6w, 20nb)			52								
	TOTAL		(87.5 overs)	324								

SURREY - First Innings

Fall of wkt	Batsman		How Out	Score	Balls	4s	6s	LANCASHIRE bowling	O	M	R	W
1- 2	M.A. Butcher		lbw b Martin	0	4	0	0	Martin	12	1	51	1
4- 95	I.J. Ward	c Hegg	b Chapple	28	62	2	0	Chapple	26	4	79	3
2- 13	Nadeem Shahid		lbw b Chapple	2	9	0	0	Smethurst	17.1	4	53	2
3- 79	A.J. Hollioake *		b Smethurst	49	39	9	0	Schofield	30	5	94	4
5- 111	A.D. Brown	c Lloyd	b Schofield	23	31	4	0	Keedy	21	4	60	0
9- 243	G.P. Butcher	c Smethurst	b Chapple	66	157	10	0					
6- 161	J.N. Batty +	c Lloyd	b Schofield	24	60	4	0					
7- 179	I.D.K. Salisbury	c Hegg	b Schofield	3	24	0	0					
8- 193	A.J. Tudor		lbw b Schofield	5	13	1	0					
	M.P. Bicknell		Not Out	79	159	8	0					
10- 359	Saqlain Mushtaq		b Smethurst	54	79	6	1					
	Extras (8b, 14lb, 4w)			26								
	TOTAL		(106.1 overs)	359								

LANCASHIRE - Second Innings

Fall of wkt	Batsman		How Out	Score	Balls	4s	6s	SURREY bowling	O	M	R	W
2- 17	M.A. Atherton		b Tudor	11	13	2	0	Bicknell	6	1	22	1
1- 17	M.J. Chilton	c Batty	b Bicknell	5	18	1	0	Tudor	5	1	41	1
3- 125	S.C. Ganguly	c Salisbury	b M.A. Butcher	65	72	11	1	M.A. Butcher	27	7	86	5
8- 274	N.H. Fairbrother		lbw b Brown	90	200	13	0	Brown	24	9	56	1
4- 127	G.D. Lloyd	c Brown	b M.A. Butcher	1	10	0	0	Hollioake	9	1	31	0
5- 147	C.P. Schofield		b M.A. Butcher	9	17	2	0	Shahid	1	0	6	0
6- 159	G. Chapple	c Tudor	b M.A. Butcher	5	22	0	0	Batty	6	0	21	1
7- 161	G. Keedy		lbw b M.A. Butcher	1	13	0	0	Ward	5	2	10	0
9- 274	M.P. Smethurst	c Bicknell	b Batty	66	86	11	2	G.P. Butcher	2	0	10	0
	P.J. Martin		Not Out	5	26	1	0					
	W.K. Hegg *+		Not Out	21	35	4	0					
	Extras (18b, 3lb, 4nb)			25								
	TOTAL		(85 overs)	304 - 9 dec								

VIEW FROM THE DRESSING ROOM - MARTIN BICKNELL

Were you aware while you were batting that you were closing in on five-hundred Championship runs for the season?

MB - I was fully aware of it, actually, although I didn't think I'd be able to get there! I knew I needed seventy-nine but that was just a distant hope when I went out to bat on the second evening. With my back still being sore, I hadn't been that fussed about batting at all, initially, but once I got past fifty I realised that I had a good chance and I didn't want to miss it because it's such a milestone. It rounded off the season perfectly for me to end up with sixty wickets and five-hundred runs.

VIEW FROM THE DRESSING ROOM - ADAM HOLLIOAKE

Mark Butcher's occasional off-spin at one point appeared to put us in with a chance of winning the match. Were you ever tempted to bring back the front-line bowlers to have a stab at bowling Lancashire out and chasing a total?

AH - Not really. Once we'd won the Championship all the intensity went out of the game and all the injuries that people had been carrying throughout the year raised their heads - Solly had been struggling with a painful elbow for the last month of the season, for example, and couldn't have bowled, Saqlain had his bad knee and Bickers had been having back problems. Once the adrenaline stops pumping it's much harder to play through these injuries, so we just decided to enjoy ourselves and play it out as a draw.

KEITH MEDLYCOTT'S ASSESSMENT

This did have the potential to be a good game of cricket but with the players tired after a long season, the title decided and Saqi unable to take the field because of illness it did rather peter out. Some people felt we could have pushed harder to win the game but you have to realise that once you have achieved your goal you want to enjoy the moment and the adrenaline which has helped you play on through niggles and injuries stops flowing and you start to feel the pain!

After clinching the title on the first day we'd all gone over the road to watch Manchester United play a European Champions League match which was a great experience for us - there we were, the champions watching the champions! When we turned up for play the next morning it was raining so some of us had a game of football on the outfield and I'm sad to report that Tudes, who was pretending to be Ryan Giggs, won the penalty shoot-out competition!

Other Division One Matches

Having outscored Lancashire by eleven points to ten at Old Trafford, Surrey extended their final winning margin to a nice round twenty points, which suggested we were a whole game better than our closest rivals - that seemed about right, especially since we had recorded two more wins than both Yorkshire and Lancashire. The whole table appeared to give a pretty fair reflection of the teams' abilities, actually, with Derbyshire, Durham and Hampshire clearly the three worst teams over the course of the season and the top four having a very predictable look about it. I'd over-rated Hampshire and under-rated the roses counties in my pre-season predictions, but then I'd got the most important thing right - Surrey to end as champions!

September 13-16
Derby:- **Derbyshire drew with Somerset.** Somerset 311-9 (Bowler 117 not out, Dean 4-47). **Derbyshire 7pts, Somerset 7**

Southampton:- **Yorkshire beat Hampshire by 72 runs.** Yorkshire 205 (Warne 5-92) and 265 (Lehmann 92, Hamilton 61); Hampshire 213 (Kendall 73, Warne 65, Middlebrook 6-82) and 185 (Kenway 58). **Yorkshire 16pts, Hampshire 4** *(Hampshire subsequently deducted 8pts for substandard pitch)*

Leicester:- **Leicestershire drew with Kent.** Kent 228-8 (Dravid 77, Stelling 5-49). **Leicestershire 6pts, Kent 5**

Pos	Prev		P	Pts	W	D	L	Bat	Bowl	Last	Three	Res
1	1	Surrey	16	213	9	5	2	44	41	D11	W20	D11
2	2	Lancashire	16	193	7	8	1	35	42	D10	W20	D12
3	3	Yorkshire	16	188*	7	7	2	36	48	W16	W20	D-1
4	4	Leicestershire	16	165	4	9	3	42	39	D6	D11	D9
5	5	Somerset	16	145	2	10	4	41	40	D7	L3	D12
6	6	Kent	16	140	4	8	4	18	42	D5	L6	W18
7	7	Hampshire	16	112*	3	4	9	20	48	L-4	W20	W15
8	8	Durham	16	112	2	5	9	27	41	L2	L3	L3
9	9	Derbyshire	16	111*	2	8	6	19	44	D7	L6	W15

COUNTY CHAMPIONSHIP DIVISION ONE - FINAL TABLE

* Deducted 8pts for sub-standard pitch

BEARS AND OUTLAWS END ON A HIGH

Both Nottinghamshire Outlaws and Warwickshire Bears won their final match of the season to take closer order behind the triumphant Surrey Lions at the top of the table. Anyone glancing at the final table in years to come will think that it was a close-run thing for the Division Two title... which, as we of course know, it wasn't!

September 17

Derby:- **Durham Dynamos beat Derbyshire Dynamos by 1 run.** Durham 229-7 (Daley 54, Collingwood 52); Derbyshire 228-8 (Cassar 126, Killeen 6-31). **Durham Dynamos 4pts**

Chelmsford:- **Warwickshire Bears beat Essex Eagles by six wickets.** Essex 152 in 41.2 overs (Grayson 64); Warwickshire 153-4 in 35.1 overs (Smith 75 not out). **Warwickshire Bears 4pts**

Cardiff:- **Middlesex Crusaders beat Glamorgan Dragons by six wickets.** Glamorgan 191-9 in 42 overs (Powell 86, Laraman 6-42); Middlesex 193-4 in 42 overs (Langer 76 not out). **Middlesex Crusaders 4pts**

Southampton:- **Nottinghamshire Outlaws beat Hampshire Hawks by 3 runs.** Nottinghamshire 234-8 (Afzaal 95 not out); Hampshire 231-8 (Kendall 63, Prittipaul 61). **Nottinghamshire Outlaws 4pts**

NCL DIVISION TWO - FINAL TABLE

Pos	Prev		P	Pts	W	T	L	N/R	NRR	Last	Three	Res
1	1	Surrey Lions	16	48	11	0	3	2	11.93	L	L	L
2	2	Nottinghamshire Outlaws	16	46	11	0	4	1	-2.18	W	W	W
3	3	Warwickshire Bears	16	42	10	1	5	0	7.10	W	W	W
4	4	Middlesex Crusaders	16	38	8	1	5	2	-0.26	W	L	W
5	5	Essex Eagles	16	32	7	0	7	2	0.36	L	W	W
6	5	Glamorgan Dragons	16	32	7	2	7	0	-2.19	L	L	L
7	8	Durham Dynamos	16	20	5	0	11	0	0.32	W	W	L
8	7	Hampshire Hawks	16	20	5	0	11	0	-5.78	L	L	W
9	9	Derbyshire Scorpions	16	10	2	0	13	1	-9.00	L	W	L

17 Leading Questions, Leading Answers

Here is a selection of leading questions put to the players at the end of the season, along with some of the most interesting answers.

> *Did the introduction of two divisions, with promotion and relegation, sharpen up the competition in the Championship?*

ALISTAIR BROWN - Certainly. It's a must, it's got to be the way forward, and I'd like to see more movement towards the first division, with it becoming like the Premiership in football. I'd like to see the cream rising to the top to give a really strong and competitive first division, with only the best sides playing there.

IAN WARD - It definitely added spice and an extra dimension to the cricket. There were no joke games and everyone always had something to play for.

> *I guess it was also a better system for the fact that you played every other team both home and away?*

IAN WARD - Yes, it's better because you play all the bigger sides, like Lancashire, Yorkshire and Leicestershire, twice which can only make for stronger, more competitive cricket. Eventually, the cream will rise to the top and county cricket will be in good shape.

> *As reigning champions did we feel any greater pressure of expectation at the start of the season? Did everyone want to beat us that much more because we were the champions?*

ALISTAIR BROWN - Everyone's always out to beat Surrey, in any case, but even more so as champions. Personally, I didn't feel any greater pressure but I felt greater expectation purely because I *expected* us to win the Championship - had we not done so then I would have been very disappointed indeed.

> *How does the 2000 Championship success compare with the 1999 triumph?*

ADAM HOLLIOAKE - I think the best way to sum it up is to say that in 1999 we **thought** we had the side to win it, so the emotion when we won it was one of elation, whereas in 2000 the principal feeling was one of relief because we had *expected* to win the title.

MARK BUTCHER - It's hard to balance it out because in 1999 we had to use more players because we had more international call-ups and we remained unbeaten, whereas this year the standard was tougher with two divisions and we had to come from quite a long way behind, so I think both wins were equally satisfying.

> *What was your most treasured memory of the season from a personal point of view?*

ALISTAIR BROWN - Apart, obviously, from the 295 at Oakham, the highlight would have to be dismissing Neil Fairbrother at Old Trafford to finally get Martin Bicknell off my back about me not having a first-class wicket to my name! He won't be able to rib me about it anymore when we go out to dinner... though I can still mention the fact that he hasn't got a first-class century!

MARK BUTCHER - I think the best moment for me was the catch that I took to dismiss Warren Hegg in the very important match against Lancashire at The Oval - he swept hard, I made a speculative dive for the ball and it stuck in the webbing between my thumb and forefinger. We were playing some magic cricket at that stage of the season and I think the way that half-chance stuck in my hand nicely summed up the way things were going for us at the time.

> **And what was your most treasured memory of the campaign from a _team_ perspective?**

IAN WARD - It would have to be Bickers' consistency of performance throughout the year. It was obviously highlighted at Guildford, but he really is the absolute business as far as I'm concerned and I can hold nobody in higher regard than I do Martin Bicknell - a great bloke who deserves all the success that comes his way. His performances throughout the season just epitomised everything about Surrey, really.

MARK BUTCHER - Probably the way we beat Durham at The Oval with all the rain around and worries about whether we would be able to get enough play to bowl them out - I thought we played fantastically well in that game. If you put that together with the way we played at Scarborough then I think you've got the two best team performances of the year.

ADAM HOLLIOAKE - I'd say it was the final session on day two at Guildford, when we took those six wickets, followed closely by the win at Headingley in the Benson And Hedges Cup quarter-final.

MARTIN BICKNELL - Nothing can compare with the feeling of winning matches and winning trophies. Although it was nice to do so well at Guildford, I'm now at the stage of my career where my personal ambitions, in terms of things like playing for England, come second to my ambitions for team. I think that's pretty much the same for everyone as they get older.

> **Would it be fair to say that on a good pitch we are a notch above every other side in the Championship at the moment?**

ADAM HOLLIOAKE - I'm not sure I'd say a notch above, but I think we have greater belief than other sides when we get on a good wicket. We feel that we are very hard to beat on that type of pitch and, because we play such aggressive cricket, we feel that, over the course of four days, the opposition will have at least one really bad session against us, be it with the bat or the ball.

MARK BUTCHER - Definitely. Sides are aware of what we are capable of doing to them if the pitch is good and flat, and it's a great compliment to us when we turn up at an away ground to find a green or damp pitch.

IAN SALISBURY - Probably, yes. We've got great balance in our side between flair and steadiness and a very well-balanced bowling attack. We usually win at The Oval, where the pitches have been voted the best of the season, and we generally win away from home when the wicket is good, too, so that must say something. We have a lot of excellent players because they have grown up playing on good-quality pitches and I think that if the other counties produced the best possible wickets then they would be more likely to produce players to compete with us.

> *Looking on from the outside, whether you are performing out in the middle or playing football or Frisbee, it appears that everyone is having a great deal of fun and the team spirit seems to have gone up a level even from the heights of 1999. Is that a fair comment?*

MARTIN BICKNELL - We sometimes look at other sides doing their drills and whatever, and it looks so tedious that we just have to laugh, really. They are trying hard to do all the right things but they are missing the basic point that you have got to enjoy what you do. We always start the day with a game of football or some other game to get everyone running around and having a laugh and into a competitive frame of mind, and that kind of thing gives everyone such a lift compared to the boring sprints and run-throughs that we see other sides doing.

ALISTAIR BROWN - Medders is very good in that regard and I think Johnny Gloster, our physio, is something of an unsung hero - he's like a member of the team, he gets involved in everything and he's very good for us. I just don't think there's a missing link - we all get on very well in one another's company, we enjoy great banter and there's no backstabbing - it's just a perfect team, with everyone gelling particularly well together.

IAN SALISBURY - I think we are growing together as human beings and mates as well as team-mates - we're very close as a side and we have great respect for one another both as cricketers and as friends.

> *Every time I see a pre-match practice session, I am impressed by how hard everyone seems to work at their game. Would it be true to say that we now have an unsurpassed culture of excellence within the club?*

ALISTAIR BROWN - I think the principal difference between now and, say, five or six years ago, is that everything we now do is based on quality rather than quantity. For example, we used to do lots of fielding work in the old days - we'd run here, we'd run there and we'd do lots of catches... but it was all mind-numbingly boring stuff - nowadays everything is short, sharp and very focused and, because a lot of what we do is team-orientated, competitive stuff, it's so much more enjoyable.

IAN WARD - We certainly have a very strong work ethic, both as individuals and as a team, and the guys who lead us, Medders and Smokey, have both got their fingers on the pulse and can read what the players need at any given time. And the beauty of the side we have got together at the moment is that everyone appreciates that success doesn't come without a lot of hard work.

ADAM HOLLIOAKE - Absolutely, mediocrity is just not accepted. For example, in the old days someone might go for a diving catch and drop it and everyone would say 'good effort' - nowadays we pretty much *expect* that sort of catch to be held. We just don't stand for mediocrity... unless it's the last game of the season at Old Trafford with the Championship title already won!

IAN SALISBURY - We are always trying to better ourselves. The more we win then the more other sides will want to beat us, so we will have to keep working harder and keep improving. We have an appraisal, chaired by the captain, after each and every game where we discuss all the things we did well and all the things that we didn't do so well and can improve on. If you didn't have a very open and honest changing room, like we have, then you wouldn't be able to do that.

MARTIN BICKNELL - I think so, yes. Everyone has so much personal pride in their performance and we have guys who work exceptionally hard at their game, Ian Ward being the classic example - he'll rarely have a day off during the season.

JON BATTY - I would agree that we do have a huge desire within the club to better ourselves, both as individuals and as a team. Every player in the squad works exceptionally hard on their game, not just during the season but in the off season as well, when most of the hard work is done. This effort extends from the senior players right down to the most junior players.

> *I thought we looked a much fitter team than most of our opponents throughout the season. Is that an area we have worked hard on?*

ADAM HOLLIOAKE - We are getting fitter every year and we train very hard through the winter. We have fitness assessments at the start of every season and over the last two years we have improved by an average of ten percent each year - and I dare say we'll be another ten percent fitter this season. It's amazing, really - the average weight of our players has gone up by about a stone, yet the body fat has come down by about five percent and everyone does better in our speed and endurance tests. When I first joined Surrey I think we had quite a few blokes on the staff who were an embarrassment as professional sportsmen but when I look around our side now there's no-one who can't take a diving catch or pull off a run out, because our level of fitness has gone up so much.

> *Was it frustrating, in some ways, to miss out on a lot of Surrey's success due to your position as an England-contracted player?*

ALEC STEWART - 'Frustrating' probably isn't the word - it's just a case of accepting that this is going to be the norm from now on. England is now the most important thing for everyone in first-class cricket, so you just have to change your thought patterns slightly - whereas it used to be, say, Darren Gough of Yorkshire and England, it's now Darren Gough of England and Yorkshire.

> *What do you think was the principal reason for the turnaround in out National League form in 2000?*

IAN WARD - In 1998 and 1999 I think there was a feeling that the National League just got in the way of our quest for the Championship - we were so hungry for that first Championship success in twenty-eight years that Sunday would come along and we'd almost want to get the match out of the way so that we could concentrate our minds on the next four-day game. With that millstone no longer around our necks, we were able to focus more attention on the National League in 2000.

ADAM HOLLIOAKE - Over the years, I think that once we've got behind in the one-day league we've found it hard to motivate ourselves, and I think that partly stems from the fact that the Sunday League has been thought of in Surrey circles as something of a joke competition, with our tradition very much being based on Championship cricket. For the last two or three seasons the players had got sick of people talking about how poor we had been in the National League rather than how well we had done in the Championship, so we were determined to change that attitude and really go out hard to win our first four or five games. We felt that the natural habit we then fell into would last us through the rest of the season and so it proved, which was very pleasing.

What do you see as our aims for 2001?

ALEX TUDOR - The Championship is always the main competition and it would be a tremendous feat to win it three times in a row - that would be awesome. I'd also like to play in a Lord's cup final for the first time.

IAN WARD - Our aim at the start of the season will be to win all four trophies - we certainly won't be picking and choosing between the competitions. Obviously, we've won a few trophies over the past few seasons but we've still not got close to achieving what Warwickshire did in the mid-1990s when they won three competitions. So we'll be aiming to emulate that and until it's proved that we can't win all four then that's what we'll be going for.

MARTIN BICKNELL - Our priority will always be the Championship. That's the way the guys are - we like to be judged mainly on our first-class record - but the one-day trophies are a welcome distraction and we'll be trying as hard as anybody. Nobody would enjoy a Lord's final more than me because there's nothing better than playing in front of 30,000 people, so I'll be busting a gut to get there, don't you worry!

JON BATTY - I believe that the aim should be to win all four competitions. That might sound unlikely but you must try to win every game you play and if you achieve that then the larger goal will be achieved, too. With the squad we have got there is no reason why this aim should be unrealistic. Obviously it would be a huge ask, but we must set ourselves high standards and not settle for mediocrity.

IAN SALISBURY - My main wish for 2001 would be for everyone to stay fit and not get injured, because if that happens then everything else can look after itself. But if we can maintain or improve on our current standards then we won't be far away in all four competitions.

18 Looking Back, Looking Forward

As in 1999, Surrey were worthy county champions and their performances and statistics made it very hard for anyone to argue that they had not been the best team in the competition. Early season wobbles apart, they had been the dominant county in the division, with closer analysis of the matches involving the leading sides proving quite revealing. Taking the results of the fixtures between Surrey, Lancashire, Yorkshire and Leicestershire in isolation, the eventual champions scored four wins and two draws, whereas Lancashire achieved home victories over both Yorkshire and Leicestershire plus three draws and a defeat. Neither the white rose county nor the Foxes managed to record a win against their leading rivals, with Yorkshire recording a four-two draws-to-defeats split, against Leicestershire's three-three. The table below shows all the results of the final top four in the Championship.

	Surrey		Lancs		Yorks		Leics		Som't		Kent		Hants		Durham		Derby	
	H	A	H	A	H	A	H	A	H	A	H	A	H	A	H	A	H	A
Surrey	-	-	W	d	W	d	W	W	W	d	d	d	W	W	W	l	W	l
Lancs	d	l	-	-	W	d	W	d	W	d	W	d	W	d	W	W	d	d
Yorks	d	l	d	l	-	-	d	d	W	d	W	W	W	W	d	W	W	d
Leics	l	l	d	l	d	d	-	-	W	d	d	d	W	W	d	W	d

Since the teams along the top are listed in the order in which they finished in the league, wins become less significant as you move from left to right across the table - though you do, of course, need to beat the weaker sides if you want to win championships!

This table also shows quite clearly that home advantage is significant, with only seven of the victories by the top four having come away from home as against twenty on home soil. It's particularly interesting to see that Somerset drew against all of the leading sides at Taunton, yet lost to all four counties on their travels, and that Lancashire were able to record home victories over Yorkshire, Leicestershire, Somerset, Kent and Hampshire while managing only to draw when playing away to those same counties.

With home advantage so important, there are still some people who would suggest that Surrey's success must be based around them tailoring their pitches to suit their spin twins, Saqlain and Salisbury. They are wrong - and there are two reasons why this myth should now be laid to rest, once and for all.

The first of these is that the pitches at The Oval were rated as the best in the country in 2000, scoring consistently high marks from the umpires to earn Paul Brind the coveted Groundsman Of The Year award. Congratulations to Paul and his staff for their efforts, and also to Bill Clutterbuck and his team at Guildford, since the Woodbridge Road pitch came second in the outgrounds league. Some excellent research by Richard Spiller of *The Surrey Advertiser* has subsequently revealed that this was only the second time since the Groundsman award was introduced over twenty years ago that the county adjudged to have played their home games on the best wickets has also emerged as winners of the Championship. Paul Brind's accolade therefore underlined the fact that Surrey were prepared to take on the opposition on a true and fair surface which gave everyone an equal chance to shine - and that certainly hasn't been true of all the Championship-winning teams of the past twenty-odd years! The other Groundsman-Championship double, incidentally, was achieved in 1982 by Middlesex, who, of course, had no say in the type of wickets prepared for them at Lord's.

The second reason for dismissing the spin-friendly pitches theory is the record of opposition spinners at The Oval in Surrey's two Championship-winning seasons. In 1999, the visiting slow bowlers managed to bag twenty-six Championship victims at a hefty cost of 36.95 runs apiece - and these figures included Muttiah Muralitharan's haul of 10-154 for Lancashire - while opposition tweakers in 2000 secured just twenty scalps at 43.35 each, including a contribution of 7-112 from Shane Warne. These statistics graphically illustrate the fact that it is only *quality* spin bowlers who succeed at The Oval. If the pitches really were dustbowls that turned square from day one, then the average county spinner would also enjoy success, which, as the above figures illustrate, is most certainly not the case.

No, Surrey's success is down to the more obvious things, like a group of well-led quality players under the guidance of a young and impressive manager. This is a powerful combination and it isn't to be found anywhere else in county cricket at the moment. Some teams may have one, or maybe two, of the components - good captains looked to be especially thin on the ground last season - but only Surrey have the full set. Nor must we overlook the fact that the second eleven, under the skilled guidance of Alan Butcher, produces players who are capable of stepping into the first team and performing with distinction. All in all, it's a potent brew.

The 2000 Championship success was in some ways an even better team effort than the 1999 triumph with most of the players making very significant contributions at some time or another. It is probably best, therefore, not to pick out a series of individuals, though it should perhaps be said that Martin Bicknell was, again, a worthy winner of the two Player Of The Season awards in my eyes. Neither would it be unreasonable to wonder how many wickets Saqlain would take if he ever got to play a *complete* season with Surrey!

With or without the Pakistani off-spinner, the team played some breathtaking cricket during the campaign, especially during the run of seven successive Championship victories, and I yearned for the chance to see this Surrey side, in this form, pitted against the world's Test sides, since I honestly believed that they would be capable of beating some of them. Surrey versus Zimbabwe? It would be a Surrey win, no sweat! We'll never know for sure about that, of course, but I certainly find it hard to imagine that there is a better team playing in any nation's domestic cricket at the current time. If only it were possible to pit the champions of each of the Test-playing nations against one another for a series of matches!

It wasn't only Championship success that Surrey enjoyed in 2000, though, since we also had the very pleasant bonus of picking up some limited-overs silverware, with the much-improved performances in the National League Division Two seeing us to the title in style with matches to spare. Although it has to be said that there were some desperately poor teams in the second division - I, for one, believe that the split into two leagues is already showing - you can do no more than go out and beat the opposition that is on the park. This was done with ruthless efficiency as the team showed much-improved form with the bat and appeared to operate to a better, and more settled, game plan when in the field. For example, the mid-innings bowling partnership of Jason Ratcliffe and Saqlain Mushtaq, though it might, initially, have seemed like an unlikely pairing, rarely failed to produce the goods. With the fielding also showing a marked improvement throughout an impressive National League season, the only slight concern I still had was the batting order and the small matter of whether or not Ali Brown should open the innings in limited-overs matches. Statistics from recent seasons suggest that the use of Brown at the top of the order fails much more often than it succeeds these days and I would prefer to see the tactic used only on flat tracks or when chasing a large total batting second. While flexibility seems desirable, it does, however, fly in the face of the belief that a consistent game plan, as demonstrated by the currently very successful Gloucestershire side, is vital for success in one-day cricket. I'm sure this question of where Ali Brown should bat causes as much debate in the dressing room as it does amongst the club's supporters! One thing is for certain, though - all components of the Surrey Lions' game will need to be on song for the sterner encounters that lie ahead in NCL Division One if we are to become as good a side in one-day cricket as we are in the four-day game.

The 2001 season will certainly present us with some exciting challenges, not least of which is the opportunity to become the first county for thirty-three years to win three consecutive County Championship titles, the feat having last been achieved by Yorkshire when they claimed the crown in 1966, 1967 and 1968. There might still be a long way to go to emulate the seven Championships achieved by the Surrey side of the 1950s, but three in a row would undoubtedly be special since a hat-trick of titles has only ever been achieved on eight occasions in the competition's 110-year history - five times by Yorkshire, twice by Surrey and once by Lancashire. With this goal to aim for, there should be no danger of complacency creeping into the team's performance.

The team will also be stronger in 2001, following the signings of two quality performers during the winter. Mark Ramprakash and Ed Giddins look to be the right players for the right areas of the team, strengthening the top-order batting and the seam attack, the only two real areas of concern over the past two seasons.

Ramprakash's natural habitat is number three in the order, a position which has been a slight problem area for a while now, and his presence behind Mark Butcher and Ian Ward should ensure that opposition opening bowlers find it much harder to penetrate through to the middle-order, even in favourable bowling conditions. I must say that the confirmation of the signing of 'Ramps' left me sporting a permanent grin for the rest of the day - not only because I felt it made further success for Surrey more likely, but also because he is such an elegant and attractive batsman to watch. He has certainly played some outstanding innings *against* Surrey over the years, but, for obvious reasons, I'd never been able to appreciate and enjoy them as much as I should have done - I now hope to put matters right as he plays that kind of innings *for* us!

Although I would have to be honest and admit that the capture of Ed Giddins didn't excite me as much as the recruitment of Ramprakash, I regard it as a more important signing, since it gives us added depth in an area where we have possessed only limited quality over the course of the last two or three seasons. We have, on occasions, been rather exposed on seamer-friendly pitches and our perceived Achilles heel might even have encouraged lesser teams to prepare 'sporty' wickets deliberately when we visited them. With the ability to field a trio of the quality of Bicknell, Tudor and Giddins, it seems unlikely that any counties will now be tempted to try this! It also gives the captain and coach improved cover should Alex Tudor be awarded an England contract, as well as the option to 'rotate' our seamers for those matches when the presence in our side of two spinners necessitates the selection of only two pacemen. Perhaps most importantly, it should mean that we will be less likely to have to field an opening bowler who is not fully fit, as we had to with Bicknell and Tudor on a few occasions in 1999 and 2000.

The recruitment of these recent England cricketers will, no doubt, create further anti-Surrey feelings, largely fuelled by jealousy. This is sad and regrettable but we will still be able to field more 'home-grown' players than the vast majority of the other counties and it should also be remembered that these are the first major signings we have made since Ian Salisbury's move from Sussex at the end of the 1996 season - so we have hardly been major players in the 'transfer market'. What is undeniable, however, is that we have added players of class and quality to our squad, thereby sticking to Keith Medlycott's belief that the club should only bring in players who are better than those you already possess - clearly the case with Giddins and Ramprakash. Since these signings, comparisons have also been made between Surrey and Manchester United, and in some ways they are justified, because, like them, we have built, and are continuing to develop, a very successful side around a nucleus of home-developed youngsters. I feel sure that Surrey, like our football counterparts, will continue their tradition of developing youngsters, especially since the Manager fully appreciates that younger players must constantly be integrated into the team to avoid the dangerous situation where a whole side grows old together. I believe that his use of a number of second eleven rookies in the final National Cricket League matches of the season - a decision for which he received unjust criticism - demonstrated his commitment to the younger element, although those concerned will doubtless appreciate that they have now got to be very good if they truly want to play for Surrey. If players like Murtagh, Greenidge, Sampson, Bishop, Amin, Carberry and Porter, to name but a handful, prove good enough then they will be given opportunities, I'm sure. At least these young guys should enjoy an easier transition to first team county cricket through coming into a successful team, rather than a struggling one.

So, whatever the supporters of other counties or some of those bitter media men might have to say, let us thoroughly enjoy the club's current success and not let anyone spoil it for us. Things have improved greatly for Surrey since the bleak mid-90s and if everyone continues to pull together then the future should remain very bright.

As far as goals for 2001 are concerned, I know that most of the players feel that a clean sweep of the trophies, though extremely tough to achieve, is far from impossible. While I expect the National League Division One to be very even and competitive, as it was in 2000, making it hard to predict, I would hope that the two knockout cups might, at the very least, produce Surrey's first appearance in a Lord's final since 1997. A tough fourth round draw in the Trophy has sent us to Headingley, however, so we will face an early test there. The County Championship, therefore, continues to look like the competition most likely to bring success, especially since the first division appears to be a lot stronger for the addition of Northamptonshire, Essex and Glamorgan and the loss of Derbyshire, Durham and Hampshire. I regard this as being to Surrey's advantage since I believe that wins will be harder to achieve for all but the very best teams. Surrey are the one side capable of beating any opposition, though an ageing but Murali-inspired Lancashire might have the ability to do likewise. Sides like Yorkshire and Leicestershire, whose victories in 2000 came largely at the expense of teams who finished in the bottom half of the table, might well find the going much tougher in a stronger first division.

Since I started this book with a prediction that Surrey would win the County Championship of 2000, I therefore see no reason why I shouldn't end it by stating that I think they will win it again in 2001!

19 Appendix - Averages And Statistics

COUNTY CHAMPIONSHIP AVERAGES 2000

Batting	M	I	NO	Runs	HS	Ave	100	50	Ct	St
A.D. Brown	16	23	5	935	295*	51.94	2	4	16	-
M.A. Butcher	16	25	4	891	191	42.43	2	3	13	-
I.J. Ward	16	25	3	894	158*	40.64	3	3	4	-
G.P. Butcher	4	4	1	110	66	36.67	-	1	-	-
Nadeem Shahid	9	12	0	434	80	36.17	-	3	13	-
M.P. Bicknell	15	18	2	500	79*	31.25	-	4	5	-
A.J. Hollioake	16	23	0	689	80	29.96	-	3	27	-
A.J. Tudor	14	16	6	283	64*	28.30	-	1	5	-
A.J. Stewart	3	4	0	108	42	27.00	-	-	7	-
I.D.K. Salisbury	16	19	6	313	57*	24.07	-	2	6	-
G.P. Thorpe	8	12	0	280	115	23.33	1	1	6	-
J.N. Batty	13	16	2	276	100*	19.71	1	-	29	7
Saqlain Mushtaq	12	14	2	217	66	18.08	-	2	8	-
B.C. Hollioake	10	14	1	14	29	10.92	-	-	8	-
J.D. Ratcliffe	2	4	0	28	26	7.00	-	-	2	-
I.E. Bishop	2	3	0	14	12	4.67	-	-	-	-
Also Batted:-										
C.G. Greenidge	3	2	0	9	6		-	-	-	-
R.M. Amin	1	1	0	3	3		-	-	1	-

Bowling	O	M	R	W	Ave	Best	RPO	10wm	5wi
Saqlain Mushtaq	451.2	127	1016	66	15.39	7-11	2.25	2	6
M.P. Bicknell	413.2	115	1052	60	17.53	9-47	2.54	1	3
I.D.K. Salisbury	380.3	101	984	52	18.92	8-60	2.58	2	3
A.J. Tudor	304.3	71	1071	47	22.79	7-48	3.51	-	3
B.C. Hollioake	117.5	25	407	11	37.00	4-41	3.45	-	-
Also Bowled:-									
A.J. Hollioake	42.2	12	119	3		1-8		-	-
C.G. Greenidge	35.0	13	106	1		1-35		-	-
I.E. Bishop	29.0	8	98	2		1-24		-	-
A.D. Brown	28.0	9	70	1		1-56		-	-
M.A. Butcher	27.0	7	86	5		5-86		1	-
G.P. Butcher	21.3	4	85	5		5-18		1	-
R.M. Amin	21.0	4	67	0				-	-
J.D. Ratcliffe	9.5	2	46	1		1-21		-	-
J.N. Batty	6.0	0	21	1		1-21		-	-
I.J. Ward	5.0	2	10	0				-	-
Nadeem Shahid	1.0	0	6	0				-	-

INDIVIDUAL CENTURIES

For (9)

	Batsman	Opposition	Venue
295*	A.D. Brown	Leicestershire (1st inns)	Oakham School
191	M.A. Butcher	Durham (1st)	The Oval
158*	I.J. Ward	Kent (1st)	Canterbury
144	I.J. Ward	Durham (1st)	The Oval
140*	A.D. Brown	Yorkshire (2nd)	The Oval
116	M.A. Butcher	Hampshire (2nd)	Southampton
115	G.P. Thorpe	Somerset (1st)	The Oval
107	I.J. Ward	Leicestershire (1st)	Guildford
100*	J.N. Batty	Somerset (1st)	The Oval

Against (1)

	Batsman	For	Venue
102	B.F. Smith	Leicestershire (1st inns)	Guildford

INDIVIDUAL FIVE WICKETS

For (17)

	Bowler	Opposition	Venue
9-47	M.P. Bicknell	Leicestershire (2nd inns)	Guildford
8-60	I.D.K. Salisbury	Somerset (2nd)	The Oval
7-11	Saqlain Mushtaq	Derbyshire (2nd)	The Oval
7-48	A.J. Tudor	Lancashire (1st)	The Oval
7-72	M.P. Bicknell	Leicestershire (1st)	Guildford
7-105	I.D.K. Salisbury	Durham (1st)	The Oval
6-47	Saqlain Mushtaq	Somerset (1st)	The Oval
6-51	Saqlain Mushtaq	Hampshire (1st)	Southampton
6-63	Saqlain Mushtaq	Yorkshire (1st)	The Oval
5-18	G.P. Butcher	Derbyshire (1st)	The Oval
5-35	Saqlain Mushtaq	Leicestershire (2nd)	Oakham School
5-41	Saqlain Mushtaq	Yorkshire (2nd)	The Oval
5-46	I.D.K. Salisbury	Lancashire (2nd)	The Oval
5-57	A.J. Tudor	Hampshire (2nd)	The Oval
5-64	A.J. Tudor	Derbyshire (1st)	Derby
5-85	M.P. Bicknell	Durham (1st)	Chester-le-Street
5-86	M.A. Butcher	Lancashire (2nd)	Old Trafford

Against (9)

	Bowler	For	Venue
7-34	T.A. Munton	Derbyshire (1st inns)	Derby
6-51	K.J. Dean	Derbyshire (1st)	The Oval
6-63	M.P. Smethurst	Lancashire (1st)	The Oval
6-75	A.D. Mullally	Hampshire (1st)	Southampton
6-87	J. Ormond	Leicestershire (1st)	Guildford
5-31	S.K. Warne	Hampshire (2nd)	The Oval
5-40	R.J. Sidebottom	Yorkshire (1st)	The Oval
5-41	P.S. Jones	Somerset (1st)	Taunton
5-90	S.K. Warne	Hampshire (2nd)	Southampton

HIGHEST PARTNERSHIPS - FOR AND AGAINST

1st	359	M.A. Butcher (191)	Ward (144)	Durham (1st)	The Oval
2nd	190	M.A. Butcher (82)	Thorpe (115)	Somerset (1st)	The Oval
3rd	74	Ward (158*)	B.C. Hollioake (29)	Kent (1st)	Canterbury
4th	109	A.J. Hollioake (47)	Brown (71)	Hampshire (1st)	Southampton
5th	144	Shahid (80)	Brown (140*)	Yorkshire (2nd)	The Oval
6th	57	Ward (107)	Brown (34)	Leicestershire (1st)	Guildford
7th	60	Batty (100*)	Bicknell (34)	Somerset (1st)	The Oval
8th	141	Brown (295*)	Tudor (22)	Leicestershire (1st)	Oakham Sch
9th	64*	Ward (158*)	Tudor (33*)	Kent (1st)	Canterbury
10th	141	Brown (295*)	Saqlain Mushtaq (66)	Leicestershire (1st)	Oakham Sch

1st	73	J. Cox (34)	M.E.Trescothick (45)	Somerset (1st)	The Oval
2nd	89	M.J. Chilton (30)	S.C. Ganguly (54)	Lancashire (1st)	Old Trafford
3rd	108	S.C Ganguly (65)	N.H. Fairbrother (90)	Lancashire (2nd)	Old Trafford
4th	128	M.E.Trescothick (85)	M.Burns (81)	Somerset (1st)	Taunton
5th	102	R. Dravid (71)	M.A. Ealham (83)	Kent (2nd)	The Oval
6th	77	M.P. Speight (48)	A. Pratt (31)	Durham (2nd)	The Oval
7th	87	M.P. Dowman (69)	D.G. Cork (44*)	Derysbire (1st)	Derby
8th	113	N.H. Fairbrother (90)	M.P. Smethurst (66)	Lancashire (2nd)	Old Trafford
9th	54	W.K. Hegg (93*)	M.P. Smethurst (17)	Lancashire (1st)	Old Trafford
10th	90	A.D.Mascarenhas (59)	S.R.G. Francis (30*)	Hampshire (2nd)	The Oval

COUNTY CHAMPIONSHIP DIVISION TWO - FINAL TABLE

Pos	County	P	Pts	W	D	L	Bat	Bowl
1	Northamptonshire	16	188	7	5	4	39	45
2	Essex	16	165	5	9	2	28	41
3	Glamorgan	16	160	5	8	3	27	41
4	Gloucestershire	16	158	6	6	4	20	42
5	Worcestershire	16	151	5	6	5	25	42
6	Warwickshire	16	150	2	11	3	47	35
7	Nottinghamshire	16	148	2	10	4	41	43
8	Middlesex	16	138	2	8	6	36	46
9	Sussex	16	134	3	7	6	31	39

NATIONAL CRICKET LEAGUE DIVISION ONE - FINAL TABLE

Pos	County	P	Pts	W	T	L	N/R	NRR
1	Gloucestershire Gladiators	16	38	9	0	6	1	1.26
2	Yorkshire Phoenix	16	36	9	0	7	0	5.97
3	Northamptonshire Steelbacks	16	36	9	0	7	0	-3.99
4	Leicestershire Foxes	16	34	7	2	6	1	-0.46
5	Kent Spitfires	16	32	7	0	7	2	6.18
6	Somerset Sabres	16	30	7	0	8	1	-0.60
7	Worcestershire Royals	16	28	6	0	8	2	-4.24
8	Lancashire Lightning	16	28	6	1	8	1	-6.83
9	Sussex Sharks	16	26	5	1	8	2	0.35

MODE OF DISMISSAL TABLES

BATSMEN - HOW DISMISSED

Name	Bowled	LBW	Ct W/k	Ct Other	Ct & B	St'ped	Run Out	TOTAL
Amin	0	0	0	0	0	0	1	1
Batty	3	3	0	8	0	0	0	14
Bicknell	4	4	3	3	1	0	1	16
Bishop	2	0	0	1	0	0	0	3
Brown	2	3	4	8	0	1	0	18
Butcher, G.P.	0	0	0	3	0	0	0	3
Butcher, M.A.	3	4	5	7	1	0	1	21
Greenidge	1	1	0	0	0	0	0	2
Hollioake, A.J.	3	2	7	9	0	2	0	23
Hollioake, B.C.	0	4	2	7	0	0	0	13
Ratcliffe	3	0	1	0	0	0	0	4
Salisbury	2	4	2	5	0	0	0	13
Saqlain	3	3	2	4	0	0	0	12
Shahid	3	5	1	3	0	0	0	12
Stewart	1	1	1	0	1	0	0	4
Thorpe	2	5	3	2	0	0	0	12
Tudor	4	3	0	3	0	0	0	10
Ward	0	4	7	10	0	0	1	22
TOTALS	36	46	38	73	3	3	4	203

BOWLERS - HOW WICKETS TAKEN

Name	Bowled	LBW	Ct W/k	Ct Close	Ct Out	Ct &B	Stumped	Hit wkt	TOTAL
Batty	0	0	0	0	1	0	0	0	1
Bicknell	9	13	13	19	5	1	0	0	60
Bishop	1	1	0	0	0	0	0	0	2
Brown	0	1	0	0	0	0	0	0	1
Butcher, G.P.	0	2	0	3	0	0	0	0	5
Butcher, M.A.	1	1	0	2	1	0	0	0	5
Greenidge	0	1	0	0	0	0	0	0	1
Hollioake, A.J.	1	0	1	1	0	0	0	0	3
Hollioake, B.C.	2	2	4	2	0	1	0	0	11
Ratcliffe	0	1	0	0	0	0	0	0	1
Saqlain	8	20	4	23	4	5	2	0	66
Salisbury	9	11	3	14	10	0	5	0	52
Tudor	7	6	11	16	5	1	0	1	47
TOTALS	38	59	36	80	26	8	7	1	255

NCL DIVISION TWO AVERAGES 2000

Batting	M	I	NO	Runs	HS	Ave	R/100b	100	50	C/S
G.P. Thorpe	8	8	3	344	126*	68.80	78.18	1	2	7
Nadeem Shahid	7	7	2	239	109*	47.80	71.98	1	1	6
A.J. Stewart	5	5	1	164	72*	41.00	56.74	-	1	3/1
A.J. Hollioake	14	13	4	346	111	38.44	84.59	1	-	7
I.J. Ward	14	13	1	429	90*	35.75	62.35	-	3	3
A.D. Brown	14	14	0	330	51	23.57	82.29	-	1	6
J.D. Ratcliffe	13	9	4	107	42*	21.40	70.86	-	-	5
B.C. Hollioake	8	5	0	93	42	18.60	63.69	-	-	3
Saqlain Mushtaq	9	4	3	15	7*	15.00	39.47	-	-	2
M.A. Butcher	10	10	0	138	47	13.80	50.73	-	-	2
M.P. Bicknell	11	4	1	37	15*	12.33	102.77	-	-	3
I.D.K. Salisbury	6	4	1	23	13	7.66	52.27	-	-	6
J.N. Batty	9	3	0	18	8	6.00	50.00	-	-	5/1
A.J. Tudor	10	6	2	22	7	5.50	57.89	-	-	1

Also Batted:-										
C.G. Greenidge	6	1	1	3	3*		42.85	-	-	3
I.E. Bishop	2	0	0	0	0	-		-	-	-
G.P. Butcher	2	2	0	51	37		56.04	-	-	1
G.J. Batty	2	2	1	46	26*		71.87	-	-	2
P.J. Sampson	2	1	0	4	4		44.44	-	-	-
T.J. Murtagh	2	1	0	0	0	0.00		-	-	-

Bowling	O	M	R	W	Ave	Best	RPO	4wi
A.J. Hollioake	59.4	1	263	23	11.43	5-29	4.40	2
I.D.K. Salisbury	36.4	2	141	11	12.81	4-32	3.84	1
Saqlain Mushtaq	77.0	10	260	18	14.44	3-12	3.37	-
M.P. Bicknell	87.0	11	241	15	16.06	3-14	2.77	-
B.C. Hollioake	47.4	0	181	11	16.45	4-42	3.79	1
A.J. Tudor	68.0	9	281	14	20.07	4-26	4.13	1
J.D. Ratcliffe	89.0	3	354	10	35.40	3-39	3.97	-

Also Bowled:-								
C.G. Greenidge	34.2	1	185	4		2-43	5.38	-
T.J. Murtagh	17.0	1	102	1		1-50	6.00	-
I.E. Bishop	12.0	1	48	1		1-22	4.00	-
P.J. Sampson	12.0	0	67	0	-		5.58	-
A.D. Brown	11.0	0	57	4		3-39	5.18	-
G.J. Batty	11.0	0	64	0	-		5.82	-
G.P. Butcher	8.0	0	56	0	-		7.00	-

LIMITED-OVERS AVERAGES 2000

Batting	M	I	NO	Runs	HS	Ave	R/100b	100	50	C/S
A.J. Stewart	12	12	4	513	97*	64.12	61.88	-	4	8/1
G.P. Thorpe	14	13	4	482	126*	53.55	75.20	1	3	8
Nadeem Shahid	7	7	2	239	109*	47.80	71.77	1	1	6
I.J. Ward	21	17	1	497	90*	31.06	58.81	-	3	4
A.J. Hollioake	21	18	5	403	111	31.00	81.25	1	-	8
J.D. Ratcliffe	20	13	6	165	42*	23.57	80.88	-	-	5
M.A. Butcher	16	16	3	296	87*	22.76	52.48	-	1	5
A.D. Brown	21	21	0	427	59	20.33	80.71	-	2	11
B.C. Hollioake	13	9	0	142	44	15.77	63.39	-	-	6
M.P. Bicknell	17	5	1	62	25	15.50	119.23	-	-	4
Saqlain Mushtaq	12	4	3	15	7*	15.00	39.47	-	-	3
I.D.K. Salisbury	11	6	3	44	21*	14.66	65.67	-	-	7
A.J. Tudor	16	8	3	32	10*	6.40	57.14	-	-	3
J.N. Batty	9	3	0	18	8	6.00	50.00	-	-	5/1

Also Batted:-										
C.G. Greenidge	9	1	1	3	3*		42.85	-	-	3
I.E. Bishop	4	0	0	0	0		-	-	-	1
G.P. Butcher	2	2	0	51	37		56.04	-	-	1
G.J. Batty	2	2	1	46	26*		71.87	-	-	2
P.J. Sampson	2	1	0	4	4		44.44	-	-	-
T.J. Murtagh	2	1	0	0	0		0.00	-	-	-

Bowling	O	M	R	W	Ave	Best	RPO	4wi
A.J. Hollioake	90.4	2	411	32	12.84	5-29	4.53	3
M.P. Bicknell	139.0	21	373	23	16.21	3-14	2.68	-
Saqlain Mushtaq	104.0	11	356	21	16.95	3-12	3.42	-
A.J. Tudor	118.0	16	490	25	19.60	4-26	4.15	1
I.D.K. Salisbury	74.4	3	276	12	23.00	4-32	3.69	1
B.C. Hollioake	73.5	0	335	13	25.76	4-42	4.53	1
J.D. Ratcliffe	123.5	7	494	17	29.05	3-15	3.98	-

Also Bowled:-								
C.G. Greenidge	52.2	1	294	4		2-43	5.62	-
I.E. Bishop	23.0	4	92	3		2-22	4.00	-
T.J. Murtagh	17.0	1	102	1		1-50	6.00	-
A.D. Brown	12.0	0	66	4		3-39	5.50	-
P.J. Sampson	12.0	0	67	0		-	5.58	-
G.J. Batty	11.0	0	64	0		-	5.82	-
G.P. Butcher	8.0	0	56	0		-	7.00	-

Acknowledgements

As was the case with **'The Dream Fulfilled'**, I couldn't have done it all on my own! Many people with Surrey at heart have assisted me, in ways both large and small, with the production of this book. Although every contribution is very much appreciated, I would like to register special thanks to the people below, who have all supplied things that I couldn't produce myself:-

Keith Medlycott and the players, who provided all of us with some special memories and another County Championship triumph. If you keep winning it then I'll keep writing it, guys! Extra special thanks to those who freely subjected themselves to my end-of-season cross-examination. I hope my books will provide you with a tangible reminder of your success in years to come when you have hung up your bats.

All the photographers, but most notably Reg Elliott, whose excellent action shots deserve an even wider audience than my books are able to provide.

The compilers of statistics and run charts, who always seem to be willing and able to supply me with the information I need.

PHOTOGRAPHS
Reg Elliott
Marcus Hook
Richard Spiller
Peter Frost
Phil Booker
Steve Porter of The Surrey Advertiser
Terry Habgood of The Surrey Advertiser
John Dawson - Cricket Images
John Banfield
Michael Cunnew
Tony Eva - Sports Pictures

STATISTICAL AND SCOREBOOK INPUT
Richard Arnold
Keith Booth
Mark Newson

RUN CHARTS
Keith Seward

OTHER
John Major
Michael Soper
Elliott Hurst, my special envoy to Barbados!
Sue Leach, my postal proof-reader!
All the staff at Surrey County Cricket Club who I have contact with throughout the year

Sponsor-Subscribers

'Doubling Up With Delight' would not have been possible without the financial support of Surrey County Cricket Club, my principal sponsors, or the following sponsor-subscribers. I dedicate this book to all of you, with grateful thanks.

Les Allen	**Marcus Hook**	**Tony Packwood**
Derek Annetts	**Roger Hudson**	**Wayne Pearce**
Sarah Atkins	**Trevor Humphreys**	**John Per**
John Banfield	**Elliott Hurst**	**Keith Porter**
Andrew Bartlett	**Alan B. Jones**	**Alison Prater**
Derek Beard	**Alan and Joyce Jones**	**David Rankin**
Lester Brown	**Chris Keene**	**Vijay Rathor**
Ron Cronin	**Barry Kitcherside**	**David Sawyer**
Michael Culham	**Jonathan Kravet**	**David Seymour**
Tony Dey	**Dominic Lang**	**Alec Sidebotham**
Vic Dodds	**Tim Lee**	**Brian Simmons**
Paul Edwards	**Charles Lehec**	**Gordon Smith**
Reg Elliott	**Stephen Lilley**	**Richard Spiller**
Keith Evemy	**Don McKay**	**Chris Stoneman**
Evelyn Fowler	**Steve Mills**	**John Taverner**
Andrew Gasson	**Peter Molyneux**	**Iain Taylor**
Brian Gee	**Paul Monaghan**	**Peter Thomson**
Doug Ginn	**David Murray**	**Richard Thorp**
John Hall	**James Murray**	**Jane Wiltshire**
Edward Handley	**Jim Murray**	**Peter Withey**
Mark Hilton	**L.J.A. Murrell**	**Steve Wooding**

If you would be keen to become a sponsor-subscriber for any future books about Surrey County Cricket Club that might be produced by Trevor Jones then please write to the author at **P.O. Box 882, Sutton, Surrey, SM2 5AW** or email him at tj@sportingdeclarations.co.uk

Surrey C.C.C. Supporters' Club

Should you wish to become a member of the Surrey C.C.C. Supporters' Club please write to:- Chris Keene, 164 Tubbenden Lane, Orpington, Kent BR6 9PT. Membership rates for 2001 are:- Full Members £5, Junior and Senior Members £3 (Junior members - under 18 on 01/01/2001; Senior members - over 60 on 01/01/2001)

Other Books By Trevor Jones

The following books by Trevor Jones about Surrey County Cricket Club are still available and may be purchased directly from the publisher at the discounted prices detailed below.

Order from **Sporting Declarations Books**, P.O. Box 882, SUTTON, SM2 5AW.
Cheques/postal orders payable to *Sporting Declarations Books,* please.

Pursuing The Dream - My Season With Surrey C.C.C.

The ultimately-doomed Championship challenge of 1998 forms the central plank of Trevor Jones' first book, a fan's diary of a season following his team around the country. The author's personal day-by-day account of the summer balances sharp observations and opinions on both the county and international game with tales of the lighter moments of his season with Surrey. Received impressive critical acclaim, including a three-ball review in Wisden Cricket Monthly.

Published April 1999
256 pages

Hardback edition   0 9535307 0 1   Price - £9.95 + £1.50 UK p&p
Softback edition   0 9535307 1 X   Price - £6.95 + £1.00 UK p&p

The Dream Fulfilled - Surrey's 1999 County Championship Triumph

Almost certainly the most detailed account of a Championship-winning season ever written, *'The Dream Fulfilled'* records Surrey's 1999 campaign and contains all the features that are to be found in *'Doubling Up With Delight'* plus 'Man Of The Day' and 'Man Of The Match' verdicts, press quotes and views from the other counties. Highly acclaimed everywhere it was reviewed, this book will be treasured by Surrey fans for years to come.

Published April 2000
376 pages, including 24 pages of full-colour photographs

Hardback only   0 9535307 2 8   Price - £14.99 + £2.00 UK p&p

Further information can be found at **www.sportingdeclarations.co.uk**

Comments can be directed to the author at **tj@sportingdeclarations.co.uk**